ATLAS
OF
SNAKES
OF THE
WORLD

JOHN COBORN

To Mum and Dad
with thanks

Distributed in the UNITED STATES by T.F.H. Publications, Inc., One T.F.H. Plaza, Neptune City, NJ 07753; in CANADA to the Pet Trade by H & L Pet Supplies Inc., 27 Kingston Crescent, Kitchener, Ontario N2B 2T6; Rolf C. Hagen Ltd., 3225 Sartelon Street, Montreal 382 Quebec; in CANADA to the Book Trade by Macmillan of Canada (A Division of Canada Publishing Corporation), 164 Commander Boulevard, Agincourt, Ontario M1S 3C7; in ENGLAND by T.F.H. Publications, PO Box 15, Waterlooville PO7 6BQ; in AUSTRALIA AND THE SOUTH PACIFIC by T.F.H. (Australia) Pty. Ltd., Box 149, Brookvale 2100 N.S.W., Australia; in NEW ZEALAND by Ross Haines & Son, Ltd., 82 D Elizabeth Knox Place, Panmure, Auckland, New Zealand; in the PHILIPPINES by Bio-Research, 5 Lippay Street, San Lorenzo Village, Makati, Rizal; in SOUTH AFRICA by Multipet Pty. Ltd., P.O. Box 35347, Northway, 4065, South Africa. Published by T.F.H. Publications, Inc. Manufactured in the United States of America by T.F.H. Publications, Inc.

THE ATLAS OF
SNAKES
OF THE WORLD

JOHN COBORN

A juvenile Coachwhip, *Masticophis flagellum*. Photo: B. Kahl.

CONTENTS

CONTENTS

CONTENTS

Elaphe guttata "rosacea," the Lower Florida Keys variant of the Corn Snake. Photo: R. D. Bartlett.

Introduction

As far as I am aware, there is no book available that covers every modern genus of the suborder Serpentes from a husbandry angle. I remember the frustration this caused me years ago when I first became a reptile-house keeper in a British zoological garden. At that time I regularly received shipments of reptiles from many parts of the world as we built up our collection. Although the major part of these shipments consisted of the well-known and popular species, there was almost always the odd unknown species that posed problems with its husbandry as well as its identification. Of course, we could eventually put a name on the specimen, often by simply referring to a regional field guide. At the time there were a few comprehensive guides available for places like Europe, North America, and South Africa, but if your shipment came from Southeast Asia, Brazil, or West Africa, for example, then you had a problem. The specimen would then have to be taken to a museum with a resident herpetologist for identification.

Having identified the species, however, our problems were far from resolved. Field guides and museums may give you extremely comprehensive information on the identification of specimens, but they rarely give guidance on the captive husbandry of any particular species. Clues to its natural habitat also were sparse. You may have been informed of the general area of its collection, but notes on ecology were rarely given. On looking through some of the older field guides and museum catalogues you might find such informative information for a particular species as: Europe—shores of the Mediterranean; N.W. Thailand; or approx. 35 km east of Mexico City! There is no indication of whether it was found on the beach, up a tree, in a lake, or under a stone, which at least would give slight clues to its habitat.

Modern reptile husbandry is necessarily based on a knowledge of the native habitat of each individual species combined with the collective published experiences of generations of herpetologists. Since my early days as a reptile-keeper, I have built up a considerable herpetological library in order to increase my prospects of identifying a particular species, finding out about its habitat, and discovering some of the finer points of its captive husbandry. To discover some of this information you often have to refer to several books and papers, a time-consuming task.

I have prepared this book in the hope that it will alleviate some of the difficulties experienced by amateur and professional herpetologists in finding particular information on snakes and their husbandry. I have tried to arrange the work in such a way that advice is immediately at the fingertips of anyone requiring this information urgently. This book is not intended to be a field guide to the snakes of the world, but should be used in conjunction with a good guide to the area from which the species or genus originates (if such exists). Part I is a general introductory husbandry section, but in part II I have endeavored to include examples from almost every living genus of snakes, with brief notes on their appearance, habits, habitats, and husbandry. This has posed a number of problems due to the often conflicting information found in the literature, and I have therefore chosen to drive a middle course through the information I have found, with the emphasis on current trends.

Finally, although I have drawn from a wealth of my own experiences in preparing this work, I do not profess to have kept or even seen more than a token number of the species mentioned, but I have freely used the literature in order to gain further information on particular species with which I have had little or no experience. My major reference has been Obst, Richter, and Jacob, *The Completely Illustrated Atlas of Amphibians and Reptiles* (TFH), perhaps one of the most comprehensive terrarium books ever produced. Where I have failed to find specific information, I have resorted to providing theoretical information based on the natural habitat of the species. In such cases I have indicated that further research is required.

John Coborn
Nerang, Queensland

Attitudes and misconceptions about snakes are changing for the better. Photo: S. C. and H. Miller.

Snakes and Man

Many successful (and some not quite so successful) books have been written about snakes, which is surprising when you consider that an estimated 99% of all people profess to not liking them. However, not liking them does not necessarily mean that they do not want to know more about them. Being naturally curious, the average human wants to know at least something about everything and quite often wants to know a little more about those things that frighten him or that he does not fully understand. Because snakes are imagined to come under the categories of evil, dangerous, slimy, devious, and unknown, people like to know more about them. This is why snake books are read by a lot of people, even by those who rarely, if ever, see a snake that is not safely behind glass in a zoo or reptile park.

ATTITUDES, MYTHS, AND LEGENDS

Despite this apparent quest for knowledge, I am continually amazed at the ignorance of the average person regarding snakes. On learning of my interest in snakes, many new acquaintances will proceed to tell me stories about their own experiences with the reptiles. These stories are probably based on fact but are usually laced with an incredible amount of dramatic garbage. In some cases the story may have been manufactured to improve the macho image of the teller, but in most cases I am convinced that the narrator fully believes every aspect of his exaggerations.

However, on occasion I have been in the company of people who have been unaware of the fact that I have more than a passing interest in snakes, and the subject of the reptiles has arisen for one reason or another. Inevitably, each member of the group will attempt to out-macho the next with his snakey reminiscences. On learning of my knowledge of the subject, however, the stories will quickly be modified to a milder form. One way of reducing the professed fearlessness of such a group is to produce a harmless snake in their midst!

Although only about 10% of the world's 2,700 or so snake species are venomous (and an even smaller percentage is dangerously venomous), the serpentine form has throughout history been a symbol of fear to the majority.

There is evidence to suggest that the fear and loathing of snakes is acquired rather than inherited. Young children who have yet to be indoctrinated will handle snakes with no qualms (a point that should be considered from the safety angle by the snake-keeper). Later, as these same children begin to understand the snakey conversations they hear, their whole attitude to serpents will change.

This arises from discussion with parents, relatives, and friends who are continually reminding each other that snakes are "creepy."

Having lectured on snakes and other animals to all age groups, I can illustrate these last points by saying that children up to the age of 6 or 7 make by far the best pupils! Can it be that the small percentage of venomous snakes that are potential killers have given all of the others a bad reputation? This certainly cannot be so in countries where there are no venomous snakes, but in no country has the reputation of snakes escaped the entrepreneurs who exploit snakes to make money. I suppose I should theoretically plead guilty to this point as the writer of this book. Snakes appear in fiction novels, in films, and on television. They are exhibited in the live state in wildlife parks and zoos and, in some countries, as fairground sensations and roadside attractions. In some countries, traveling snake exhibitors whose only claim to being herpetologists is that they have been bitten several times by highly venomous snakes make a living by sensationalizing the reptiles.

Indian Cobras (*Naja naja*) were once thought to be reincarnated spirits. Photo: R. T. Zappalorti.

Facing Page: Venomous snakes such as Wagler's Pit Viper have been held sacred by cults throughout the world. Photo: B. Kahl.

snake and utter a scream, upon which Tarzan will leap up and grab the docile, harmless snake by the neck and simulate a wrestling match, perhaps falling into the river to improve the spectacle. Eventually the evil snake will be overcome and be flung away. Tarzan and Jane clench in a victorious embrace, and the audience sighs with relief.

The present attitude to snakes by man is, however, not difficult to understand, and its origins must date back to the times of the earliest men. Although snakes are the most specialized members of the reptile class, they were around a long time before the first men appeared. Early man had many dangers to contend with. While he obviously could appreciate the dangers associated with large carnivorous animals such as bears, wolves, and tigers, the fact that a relatively small venomous snake could cause a dramatic and painful death would have appeared sinister and mysterious. It is therefore not surprising to learn that, over the centuries, certain snakes have become items of worship by many races and tribes at some time or another.

In parts of Africa, the Rock Python was worshipped by some cultures and the killing of one was regarded as a serious crime that resulted in capital punishment. This form of worship was exported to the Americas during the slave-trading era, and in Haiti today it still manifests itself in the practice of voodoo. In Central America the ancient Aztecs worshipped Quetzalcoatl, the plumed serpent, as the Master of Life. The Chinese imperial dragon is said to be a mixture of snake, lizard, and crocodile, while in Japan the god of thunder was portrayed as a serpent.

In the village of Cuccullo in Italy, snakes are collected by villagers and paraded through the streets as a tribute to St. Dominic of Folingo, a statue of whom is draped with the serpents (after the ceremony the mainly harmless snakes are released). In the USA, snakes have been used in worship by certain Christian sects since the turn of the century. Some of the most bizarre are those who handle rattlesnakes in the belief that their faith will protect them from envenomation. Unfortunately, the faith of some has not been of sufficient intensity!

In India, cobras were regarded as reincarnations of important people and were known as nagas (from which the generic name *Naja* is derived). The nagas (or the female naginis) were worshipped and feared by the villagers as they were capable of controlling the weather and could bring benefit or disaster alike. In Malaya, the well-known Snake Temple of Penang contains hundreds of venomous snakes (mainly Wagler's Pit Vipers) that are fed and cared for by the monks; the temple has become a popular tourist attraction.

The Australian Aborigines are not without their snake myths and legends. The giant rainbow serpent is associated with the creation of life. It lives in water holes that it prevents

Remember how often you have seen a snake illustrated in all its exaggerated, venom-dripping, open-mouthed, sharp-fanged glory on the cover of a detective or spy novel. Inside, the book may not even mention a snake, and if it does, then what is said is likely to consist of a load of unqualified trash! Have you ever observed your family or friends as they are watching a jungle movie on TV? Perhaps Tarzan and Jane are indulging in an amorous encounter in the African bush, unaware that a Boa Contrictor (from South America!) or a Reticulated Python (from Southeast Asia!) is creeping up on them. The suspense increases as the snake slowly slides, tongue flickering, nearer and nearer to them. The females (usually) in the audience will cling to each other, perhaps look away, and may make utterances of horror. The children will imitate them, and the mothers will draw them to their bosom and force them also to look away. Eventually Jane will spot the

from drying up, and the snake appears in many versions of traditional aboriginal art.

The mysterious nature of snakes has led them to appear in folklore for many generations. The first stories would have been passed on from one generation to. the next, picking up a new piece of embroidery each time the story was told. As far as is known, the first attempt at recording such stories with the pen was made by a Syrian monk in Alexandria who wrote the first *Physiologus*, a kind of popular zoological textbook.

The Amphisbaena of mythology bears little similarity to the living lizard-like reptiles now known as amphisbaenians. This *Amphisbaena fuliginosa* from South America is fairly typical of the group. Photo: R. S. Simmons.

The original manuscript has been lost, but there have been innumerable translations and retranslations into many languages, the most noteworthy ones being by Aristotle and Plinius the Elder, who doubtlessly added their own share to the improbabilities already recorded. When confronted with one of these beastiaries (as they were called in the Middle Ages), Martin Luther regarded it as the work of Satan, an opinion with which the modern herpetologist may heartily agree!

An account of the earliest English translation of the *Physiologus* was given by James Carlill (1922) in *Epic of the Beast*, published by G. Routledge and Sons and E. P. Dutton. The following excerpts refer to snakes:

"The Serpent: When it grows old, its eyes become dim. It then fasts for 40 days until its skin becomes withered. It then glides into a crevice and rubs off the old skin and thus becomes young again. When it goes to a stream to drink, it carries not its poison with him but leaves it behind in its hole. When it sees any naked person, it is at once afraid and turns away, but a clothed person it springs upon at once. When the hunter comes to the serpent to kill it, the serpent abandons its whole body to the death but guards only its head.

"The Adder or Asp: Has the appearance of an ordinary snake, but the male lives in the East and the female in the West and they both go to the South. And the female gnaws the head of the male and becomes with child; but the male dies. The children, when grown up, gnaw the head of their mother and she also dies. Every adder burns up the grass where it lies in its nest within a circle of three feet. Anything coming within the range of seven feet, either man or

beast, it surely dies. The adder can be enchanted by flattering words, so she stops her ears not to hear the hunter. If she hears his voice, she dies at once.

"The hunter stops his lungs, ears and nose with seven ells of rotted plants and seperates her tail from her ears. He then becomes her master and takes from her what he wishes."

These stories may seem extremely far-fetched, but if analysed, you can see that many of the points raised are based on fact and you can understand the many tales and legends that have arisen about snakes.

As they can move without legs, a remarkable feat by any standards, it is not surprising that even more remarkable stories have arisen. In Chinese art, the snake was supplied with legs and wings so that it became the dragon. The ancient Egyptians were troubled with winged snakes that, according to Herodotus, were dangerous creatures living in trees in Arabia and were forced down by the burning of styrax. They were then devoured by the ibises that consequently became sacred to the Egyptians. Even as late as 1557, a French poet wrote:

"Dangereuse est du serpente la nature, Qu'on voit voler pres le Mont Sinai.

"Qui ne seait de la voir esbahy, Si on a peur, voyant sa portraiture?"

("Dangerous is the nature of the snake, Which one can see flying around Mt. Sinai.

"Who would not be frightened by such a view, While even their picture makes your flesh creep?")

There are reports that in ancient China there were serpents that could entwine and kill an elephant, and youngsters of these snakes were often found in newly laid goose eggs. Another serpent god in Mexico, Tezcatlipoca, could swallow men whole. In Greek legend Hercules, as soon as he was born, had to fight off two serpents sent to swallow him. Serpents may have had one head, two heads, or many heads, as in the case of the Hydra or the Medusa. In Italy, the boa would pursue herds of cattle, cling to their udders, and destroy them. The Asp had a very bad name, even before it bit Cleopatra; evidently it always ran about with its mouth wide open, emitting steam, and it had a jewel embedded in its head. If anyone tried to charm it with a musical instrument, it would hold one ear to the ground and block the other with the tip of its tail! Sea serpents have been the scourge of sailors since time immemorial. As early as the Trojan War, Lycaon and his sons were devoured by sea serpents for punishment after he had warned the Trojans of the Wooden Horse. For centuries sea serpents have been seen and illustrated by generations of sailors.

A discussion of snake myths and legends can hardly omit mention of the Amphisbaena. This mythical creature had a head at both ends that it held onto each other and moved in the manner of a hoop. Apart from its novel method of locomotion its further attributes included eyes that shone like lamps and a complete

Trogonophis wiegmanni, an amphisbaenid from Eurasia, displays the regular circular rows of scales known as annulations or rings, an obvious distinguishing feature from the snakes. Photo: R. S. Simmons.

imperviousness to cold weather. Of course the creatures that now form the suborder Amphisbaenia in the order Squamata bear little relationship to the mythical reptile other than having the same name.

Even today, new myths about snakes are arising, particularly among country folk. A recent discussion I had with farmers in a local hostelry in Queensland revealed that the Carpet Python and the King Brown Snake had now hybridized (a genetic impossibility), producing a fierce venomous serpent 5 meters (16 ft) in length. Another interesting fact learned was that there are two kinds of Bandy-bandy, the Dull-eyed and the Bright-eyed, the former being completely harmless, while the latter is highly venomous (this story at least is based on fact). A further fact learned was that if you kept a Blue-tongued Skink under the house, one would never be troubled with snakes!

The USA is not without its modern serpentine myths. One of the most horrifying must be that of the Coachwhip, which pursues its victim at the speed of a horse and, on catching him, binds him to a tree trunk with its coils, then proceeds to whip him to death with its tail! Other less horrifying but no less fascinating myths include the fact that the Milksnake is frequently accused of stealing milk from the udders of cows—a crime that also is perpetrated by other species in other countries! In the Arbuckle Mountains of southern Oklahoma, the inhabitants believed that their land harbored the king of all rattlesnakes. He was as broad as the back of a dog and as long as two ponies, with a string of rattles the length of a man's arm. In his head was a great diamond, and studding his long sides were other diamonds so brilliant that they would dazzle the eyes of any man who gazed upon them in the light of the sun (after J. Frank Dobie, 1965).

There are many, many other myths, legends, and tall stories surrounding snakes. Only a few choice examples can be included in this book, but references to volumes containing such

delights will be found in the bibliography. However, the author would like to include two more gems to whet the appetites of those wishing to further investigate this peripheral aspect of serpentology.

Also taken from J. Frank Dobie's book is a tale that came from Georgia in 1927. Some workmen on a power line through a swamp aroused a rattlesnake, which on striking somehow hung his fangs in the tire of an automobile. The tire must have been very thin, for the fangs penetrated far enough to puncture the inner tube and could not be withdrawn. Presently it was noticed that as the tire went down the rattlesnake was blowing up. The air pressure was presumably transmitted through the hollow fangs of the reptile. Anyway, the reptile soon became so full of air that it exploded.

In his book *Snakes—Mainly South African* (1955), Walter Rose describes a method of protecting oneself from an attack by a python that he found in a missionary magazine published in Africa. Paraphrased by Clifford H. Pope in 1965, the author has further paraphrased it as follows: If attacked you should not run, as the python can move faster. Rather than try to escape, you should simply lie flat on

Coachwhips such as this *Masticophis flagellum piceus* from the southwestern U.S. have long been the source of myths and misguided folklore. Photo: R. Anderson.

A large Timber Rattlesnake, *Crotalus h. horridus*, is an impressive and very dangerous animal, so it is not surprising that numerous stories have developed around the species. Photo: R. Everhart.

your back with your legs extended and together and your arms held straight against your sides. Should the python examine you and try to force his head beneath you, you should remain calm and still, otherwise he may succeed, which will enable him to get around you for a squeeze. After a period of frustration, he will give up and attempt to swallow you from one end, most probably beginning with the foot. This will not hurt at first, so you must remain calm to avoid convincing him that you need a bit of a squeeze, a process that sooner or later becomes painful and unhealthy to your shape. When his jaws reach your knee, carefully take the knife from your pocket and slit the distended side of his jaw. There is no instruction on what one should do if he starts swallowing you at your head end, or if you do not happen to have a knife in your pocket!

In history, snakes have often had more practical uses. Hannibal, for example, arranged to have urns containing live venomous snakes thrown into the Pergamanian ships, an act that brought about his victory. There are several reports of Amerindians using rattlesnakes and other venomous species as aids to the invasion of neighboring tribes. Even God used snakes to punish the children of Israel. In the Book of Numbers we find: "And the Lord sent fiery serpents among the people, and they bit the people and much people of Israel died."

SNAKES IN MEDICINE

Snakes have long been attributed with medicinal powers. To primitive man, creatures that possessed such remarkable properties would necessarily contain some powerful cures and antidotes. Early medicine men were continually using parts and extracts of snakes as cures for all kinds of maladies. Even today, not only do medicine men in many primitive tribes still use snakes for their magical curing powers, they are also used by healers in more backward parts of civilized countries.

Among the first significant people to widely believe in the healing powers of snakes were the ancient Greeks. Owing to their ability to cast off their old skins and reappear sleeker and apparently healthier, snakes were regarded as symbols of reincarnation and healing. The Greek god of medicine, Aesculapius, was originally portrayed as a serpent but later, when he attained human form, he carried a staff entwined with one or two serpents. This staff is known as a caducius and has today become the symbol of many organizations connected with health, hygiene, and medicine. The European Aesculapian Snake, *Elaphe longissima*, is so named after its apparent association with Aesculapius. This docile and harmless species was widely believed by the Greeks and later the Romans as healthy to have around them and was encouraged to live in and around their homes.

Elaphe longissima, long noted for its docility, may be one of the few snakes ever introduced on purpose into new territory by an expanding civilization. Photo: B. Kahl.

The Romans are thought to have introduced these snakes to many parts of their empire, and this may account for modern relict populations of *E. longissima* in parts of central Europe.

The healing powers of snakes have been used in different ways by various peoples. In parts of Africa, natives may wear strings of snake bones around their necks, wrists, or waists to ward off evil spirits, to strengthen parts of the body, or, paradoxically, to protect against snakebite.

From medieval times to relatively recently, snakes have been used in Europe to treat all manner of ailments. The following story is taken from *Curiosities of Natural History* by Francis T. Buckland (1860) and is paraphrased by the present author:

Near the village of Saffia, about 8 miles from the city of Bracciano in Italy, there was a cavern called La Grotta del Serpi (Snake Cave), which was large enough to hold two men. The interior of the cave was perforated with many pipe-like holes after the fashion of a sieve, from which a great number of particolored snakes came forth at the beginning of spring each year; none of these snakes, it is said, were imbued with the power of poisoning. In this cave they were accustomed to exposing persons afflicted with elephantiasis, leprosy, paralysis, diseases of the joints, gout, etc. Presently, falling into a perspiration from the warmth of the subterranean exhalations, the patients were said to be divested of all vicious and virulent humors by the suction and licking of serpents casting off their skins, which twined themselves about the whole of the body of the sick man. After being applied for some time, this treatment would restore the patient to perfect health.

Later investigations by scientists led to the conclusion that the "curative powers" were not so much possessed by the serpents, but due to the hot vapors, possibly containing sulphur, for the cave is in a district abounding with hot volcanic springs and cracks from which issue all sorts of vapors, the results of volcanic action.

In Europe, vipers were endowed with the most amazing medicinal powers. In one of his sermons in 1712, the Rev. W. Derham stated: "That vipers have their great uses in physick is manifest from their bearing a great share in some of our best antidotes, such as Theriaca Andromachi and others; also in the cure of elephantiasis and other like stubborn maladies, for which I shall refer to the medical writers."

Theriaca, as mentioned above, is a pharmaceutical word for treacle or viscous potion. Theriaca was originally an antidote for venomous bites of many kinds but later became a major remedy for all manner of complaints. Essence of vipers mixed with herbs and sometimes containing pieces of viper flesh was widely used in Europe as a medicine. During the great plague of London in 1665, compound tincture of vipers was much used with success. During the Renaissance period, at the University of Bologna the professors had a heated debate on whether the inclusion of flesh

of gravid vipers in the Theriaca would reduce its potential. Around the same period it was believed that wine fortified by preserved vipers was a cure for leprosy. After taking such a medicine, one leper was said to have shed his skin in the manner of a serpent, reappearing with a complexion as smooth and sleek as a freshly shed snake.

In Southeast Asia many peoples believed, and some still do, in the healing powers of various serpents. In China, many people made a living as snake catchers, selling their wares to apothecaries who would make all kinds of snake products to sell as cures for various ailments. Parts of snakes (including the shed, dried, or pickled skin; the flesh, the fat, the head; the heart, the intestines, and the gall bladder; even the ground bones and the eyes) were—and, the author is reliably informed, still are—offered for the treatment of such maladies as headache, earache, toothache, convulsions, epilepsy, insanity, poor eyesight, common colds, malaria, arthritis, gout, rheumatism, and even impotence! In the Americas, snake fat and oil have long been regarded by various Indian tribes as a remedy for various complaints. European settlers in North America must have combined what was learned from the Indians with what they brought from the Old World. Rattlesnake oil was once sold throughout the USA as a home remedy for such ailments as sore throats, toothache, deafness, lumbago, and rheumatism. In Central and South America, snake oil is still used in poultices to cure such things as the common cold as well as various skin and joint conditions.

Recent uses of snakes by the medical profession have a more logical scientific basis than those of the past. The basis on which snakes were used in medicine was, as recently as the first quarter of the present century (and even more recently in some cases), composed of a mixture of fact and myth. It was only near the middle of the 19th century, when the real medical revolution began, that a more logical approach to the treatment of diseases and conditions began.

In advanced nations, snakes have now taken a back seat with regard to popular treatments.

Today several species of venomous snakes, such as this Malayan Moccasin, *Agkistrodon (Calloselasma) rhodostoma*, are cultivated as sources of important drugs. Photo: M. J. Cox.

This is not to say that snakes and other animals have not contributed immensely to our knowledge of life and evolution by studies of comparative anatomy and physiology. Comparatively recent studies on the venom of various poisonous snakes have led to the production of drugs useful in the treatment of such conditions as blood disorders and arterial and heart diseases. The clotting or anticoagulant power of some venoms has no doubt played an important part in the selection of these venoms. As an example, the venom of the Malayan Moccasin, *Agkistrodon rhodostoma*, has been used to produce a drug called Arvin. The venom of this snake contains an enzyme that rapidly removes fibrinogen from the blood, thus inhibiting the formation of blood clots. Arvin is a refined form of the venom and may be used as an anticoagulant in circulatory diseases. In order to produce quantities of venom for research and production of drugs, *A. rhodostoma* is now bred in relatively large numbers in laboratories.

Research into the venom has necessarily led to indirect research into the captive husbandry and breeding of certain species, a fact that is useful to both the research scientist and the casual snake-keeper. Research is also being conducted into the neurotoxic venoms (those possessed mainly by elapid snakes) in the hope that they may be of use in the treatment of nervous disorders.

Of course, the main reason for keeping venomous snakes in captivity (apart from showing to the public) is to have a ready supply of venom for use in the preparation of antivenin used as antidotes against snakebite.

SNAKE CHARMERS

The mysterious properties of snakes have, over the centuries, led them to being exploited by various witch doctors, magicians, and showmen as a means of making a living. The snake charmers of India are probably the best known examples in the trade. Cobras that spectacularly spread their hoods usually are used in these displays. The snakes are kept in wickerwork or raffia baskets. The charmer squats down in front of the basket, removes the lid, and the disturbed snake rears up in its customary threat display. If a snake should be stubborn and refuse to rear up, it will be encouraged to do so by a sharp tap on the basket or on the body. The charmer then proceeds to play music on a woodwind instrument that traditionally was made from gourds and bamboo tubes, but many modern charmers are not averse to using plastic trumpets or other such instruments if available! On hearing the music, the serpent is apparently mesmerized and fascinated, moving itself from side to side in rhythmic swaying movements. As no snake is capable of appreciating airborne sounds, it is not the music that is doing the mesmerizing. In fact, the serpent is not mesmerized at all, but is behaving in the way any cobra would when threatened. It rears the front third of its body

Everyone has seen film of Indian and other snake charmers, but it is hard to outgrow the thrill of seeing a large cobra rise and spread its hood seemingly in response to the music. Photo: R. T. Zappalorti.

and spreads its hood in order to impress any would-be aggressor. It is, in fact, a warning that more unpleasant things are likely to occur if the aggressor does not go away! When playing his music, the charmer holds his instrument toward the head of the snake and moves it from side to side. The snake follows these movements with its eyes and begins to sway in time with the moving of the pipe. That the music has nothing to do with the dancing of the snake has been demonstrated many times by producing a similar reaction using non-musical items such as sticks, umbrellas, and even bananas.

Perhaps lesser known but no less spectacular snake charming acts may be seen in other parts of Asia, North Africa, and the Middle East. In parts of Burma, girl charmers use King Cobras, *Ophiophagus hannah*, in an act that reaches its climax when the girl bends forward and kisses the snake on top of its head.

Many snake charmers are quite knowledgeable with regard to the care and habits of their snakes. However, in areas where replacement snakes are easy to obtain, charmers may be more mercenary with regard to their charges. The act of defanging a snake or sewing its mouth shut in order to reduce the danger of a bite can only reduce the reptile's life. Many authentic charmers keep their snakes in their original condition and, of course, run the risk of venomous bites—often with serious consequences.

The widespread Western Rattlesnake, *Crotalus viridis*, of Canada and the United States was widely used in snake oil curatives as well as native Indian religious ceremonies. Photo: S. Kochetov.

SNAKE SHOWMEN AND ANTIDOTE SELLERS

Snake showmen were at their most numerous in the latter half of the last century and the first half of the present century. Mainly of European descent, these showmen were a sort of logical extension of the traditional snake charmers encountered during the period of colonization. These people exploited for monetary gain the fear that the majority have for snakes. Snake exhibitions would be set up at any spot guaranteed to pull large crowds, such as at agricultural or trade shows. In the USA these showmen were a common sight at shows all over the country. Often they used rattlesnakes that had been severely mutilated by removing the fangs. Many of these showmen further supplemented their income by selling antidotes for snakebite. They would claim to have been saved several times by their own antidotes, which were often a concoction of the most bizarre (but usually inexpensive) ingredients. The recipe was usually kept strictly secret and often died with its inventor.

Modern medicine has found no evidence that any of these early snake antidotes were indeed effective. We now know that in perhaps 90% of all cases of venomous snakebite too little venom is injected to produce any serious or lasting consequences. This of course means that any quack remedy had a 90% chance of success (providing the remedy itself does not kill the patient!). Many remedies were very expensive but popular and made their inventors a lot of money.

In Australia, one of the most reputable antidotes was Underwood's Antidote for the Bite of Snakes and Other Venomous Reptiles. Invented by one Charles Underwood (said to have been an ex-convict), it was priced at 10 shillings per bottle of 4 drams (rather expensive in 1850). The antidote is said to have been a turbid fluid, brownish in color and with a thick sediment. The instructions for use were: Apply the liquid to the part bitten, by a quill or any other method, and one application is quite sufficient for a perfect cure. That the antidote was effective can be seen from the following newspaper extracts. The *Cornwell Chronicle* of 29th November 1859 reported: "Snake Antidote.... another extraordinary cure has been effected by Underwood, upon the servant of Mr. Jessop of Muddy Plains, who was severely bitten by a snake some days since. There can be scarcely a doubt as to the efficiency of the antidote, from the numerous respectable vouchers which he possesses. The public are, however, too prone to neglect these discoveries. We understand Underwood acquired it in the Brazils, and it is well known how skilful the Indians of South America are in the cure of the bites of venomous reptiles."

One of Underwood's many respectable vouchers was a letter published in the *Hobart Town Advertiser* and dated 20th January 1859: "Mr. Editor, - Seeing an advertisement referring to Underwood's antidote in your columns of this date, it has just jogged my memory,—and I think that it is rather neglecting on my part for not writing to you before about the matter,—if you could find space in your local to put it before the public.

"At Stoney Steps, about three weeks ago, one

of my quarrymen's wife was picking up some sticks and bark to light the fire with, by the side of a stump, when stooping, a Black Snake flew from the top of the stump and bit her in the thick part of the arm. Fortunately I had bought a bottle of Underwood's Antidote from Mr. Millhouse (Underwood's sole agent) some time previously, and left it in the hut in case of an accident. The men applied the antidote and the woman was soon well in a day or two after. My carter's dog was bitten in the foot, and it screamed fearfully, and I got two men to hold it until I ran to the hut for the Antidote; and in a very short time the dog was all right; and I should strongly recommend every person engaged in the bush to have this Antidote by them in case of an accident.

I am Sir, yours &c., John Gillon."

The twist in this story is that Underwood himself died in 1862 after being bitten on the finger by a Tiger Snake. Although he had applied his antidote, he fell half an hour later complaining of head pains. He was carried to his bed, where he seemed to have a fit, dying shortly afterward. On postmortem examination, the cause of death was given as snake poison.

There were, of course, many other snake showmen and sellers of antidotes and numerous stories to go with them. The above has been given as an example of the type of material one can research from the literature. In spite of the improbabilities of the showmens' cures, many of them have contributed indirectly to antivenin research in the quest to find a real antidote to venomous snakebites. Showmen were often bitten by venomous snakes, either accidentally or by allowing the snake to bite them. Many showmen believed that if they received enough mild bites, they would become immune to the bites of all snakes. Unfortunately, this was not always the case and many a showman has eventually succumbed to an exceptionally virulent injection of poison or by being bitten by a species to which he was not usually accustomed.

Some of the great snake men who survived many a snake bite include C. J. P. Ionides and Ram Chandra, both of whom have had their stories well documented. Ionides, the legendary Bwana Nyoka and former big game hunter, spent the latter part of his life as a snake catcher in East Africa, where he died in 1968. Many of the specimens he caught found their way to the reptile houses of zoos throughout the world. The story of Ionides's life makes fascinating reading and should not be omitted from the reading material of the budding serpentophile. Another fascinating life story is that of Ram Chandra, the Indian Cobra Boy, a snake showman in Australia who survived the bite of the Taipan in 1957. In 1975 Ram Chandra was awarded the British Empire Medal for his work in collecting Taipans and producing venom for the Commonwealth Serum Laboratories. He is still alive at the time of this writing and still makes occasional appearances with some of his snakes. Information on books about these men may be found in the bibliography.

ZOOS, SOCIETIES, AND THE PET TRADE

During the latter half of the 19th century, the advent of zoological collections open to the public aroused a wider interest in wildlife of all sorts. Zoos in major cities and towns gave urban residents the opportunity to see animals that they could hitherto only speculate upon. Snakes could be viewed through the glass windows of primitive terraria, most of which were little

Today's zoos are perhaps more important for their breeding programs than for their exhibits. Zoos have bred many spectacular and uncommon snakes, such as this orange juvenile *Corallus caninus*, the Emerald Tree Boa, that have later entered the hobby as affordable, adaptable pets. Photo: S. Kochetov.

more than aquarium tanks without water. Heating arrangements usually consisted of central heating of the whole reptile house, with a constant high temperature (except when the system failed) day in and day out, year in and year out. No regard was given to the thermoregulatory requirements of reptiles; indeed, little was known about it. Needless to say, early zoos were little more than consumers of wildlife of all sorts. If a reptile died in the reptile house, it was relatively easy to get another from the wild to replace it. Due to lack of knowledge of basic requirements, reptiles died of starvation and disease, and captive breeding was virtually unheard of. Even as recently as the 1950's, captive reproduction in reptiles was the exception rather than the rule and the most usual births were from females captured when already gravid.

It is only during the last three or four decades that major advances in our knowledge of the biological requirements of reptiles have led to successful captive breeding of many species through several generations. However, a great deal of further research is required before we can regard ourselves as thoroughly proficient in this field.

Many zoos today are leaders in the breeding of captive reptiles. Unfortunately, probably due to the advent of excellent wildlife films on television and the increased possibility of traveling to exotic locations, many zoos are finding it increasingly hard to make ends meet and have had to resort to various non-scientific gimmicks in order to keep the visitors flowing through the gates. One such gimmick is the snake sit-in, in which a person lives, eats, and sleeps within a cage full of venomous snakes for several weeks in order to break the world record.

The pet trade seldom is large enough or well enough organized to seriously affect populations of common snakes, but this is not true of the hide industry. Many Asian, African, and South American snakes of medium to large size, such as *Acrochordus granulatus*, a wart snake, have been killed in tremendous numbers to provide skins for wallets, boots, belts, and other such expensive novelties. Hide hunting in combination with habitat destruction could lead to the extinction of many once common species in just a few decades. Photo: Dr. S. Minton.

Snake Evolution, Classification, and General Biology

It is a well-known fact that snakes are reptiles, members of the class Reptilia. Within the Reptilia we find four orders: Testudines (turtles & tortoises); Crocodylia (crocodiles, alligators, and the gavial); Rhynchocephalia (the lizard-like Tuatara of New Zealand, comprising just one living species); and the Squamata (lizards, amphisbaenians, and snakes). Snakes form the suborder Serpentes within the order Squamata, which they share with two other suborders, the Lacertilia (lizards) and the Amphisbaenia (amphisbaenians). These classifications will be discussed in greater detail later in the chapter.

The Squamata is by far the greatest reptilian order, containing about 5,800 living species, including some 3,000 lizard species, about 130 amphisbaenian species, and approximately 2,700 snake species. It is almost impossible to give exact numbers of species in such great orders, due to the frequent reclassification by taxonomists as further research is conducted and as new species are discovered and others become extinct. As far as the discovery of new species goes there cannot now be many left, but some are still occasionally found, especially lizards. By comparison to the Squamata, the other orders of living reptilians are relatively sparse in species: Testudines, with about 220; Crocodylia, with 21; and Rhynchocephalia with a single species. In evolutionary terms, the snakes form the most advanced group of the Reptilia.

EVOLUTION

Our knowledge of snake evolution is sparse, but in order to begin to understand the position of these reptiles in zoological classification it is necessary to discuss their evolution in relation to both the other reptilian orders and other classes of vertebrates. Going back to the very dawn of life itself, it is widely accepted that life began in the water and that it consisted of single-celled organisms that gradually evolved into more complex animal and plant forms. By studying fossil remains of myriads of generations of extinct organisms, scientists have pieced together the process of evolution. To keep things simple, one can say that the first vertebrates

Lizards are the closest relatives of the snakes, and snakes probably evolved from a lizard vaguely similar to the living monitor lizards. Shown here are two of the larger pet lizards, the Common Tegu, *Tupinambis teguixin*, above, and the Savannah Monitor, *Varanus exanthematicus*, below. Photo: I. Francais.

(animals with backbones) were fishes: for millions of years numerous fish species were virtually the rulers of the seas. The first organisms to venture onto the land were plants, followed by invertebrates. It was not until the appearance of the crossopterygian or lobe-finned fishes during the Devonian period (about 380 million years ago) that a chance for vertebrates to conquer the land arose.

One genus of lobe-finned fishes is of particular importance. *Eusthenopteron* was on a direct line to the early amphibians. They had developed limb-like fins that enabled them to crawl over land from one water course to the next. In addition, we can assume that primitive lungs developed that enabled the fish to spend longer periods out of the water. It was some 35 million years later that the first actual amphibian evolved from these piscine ancestors. Amphibians are today represented by frogs, toads, salamanders, newts, and caecilians. One or more groups of early amphibians were ancestors of the reptiles.

The earliest amphibian known from the fossil record was *Ichthyostega* (which literally translated from the Latin means land-fish). *Ichthyostega* had retained many of the characteristics of its crossopterygian ancestors. It had a solidly constructed skull about 15 cm (6 in) in length of a pattern very comparable with the advanced crossopterygians, although it had lost some typical fish bones (those that covered the gill plates, for example). Of more importance were changes in the skull's proportions—the skull in front of the eyes had become greatly enlarged and the rear part considerably reduced as compared to the fishes. This meant that it had a relatively longer snout and much more efficient sense of smell that enabled it to detect the weaker atmospheric scent of its terrestrial prey. Although the tail had retained many of its fish characteristics, the fins had developed into four sturdy limbs, each possessing five digits, that were quite capable of

carrying the animal around on the land.

The Devonian was followed by the Carboniferous period, an epoch that was very favorable to the evolution of many amphibian species. Extensive swamps were commonplace over much of the earth; the atmosphere was almost permanently moist; and mud, decaying vegetation, and fallen trees provided a perfect environment. Many of the amphibians spent more and more time completely out of the water, where they benefited from the myriads of species of terrestrial invertebrate prey that hitherto had had no vertebrate predators to contend with.

Eventually, many amphibian species only returned to the water in order to spawn, laying soft-shelled eggs that hatched into gill-bearing, fish-like larvae. These developed into terrestrial forms only after a protracted aquatic youth, a trait that most of the modern amphibians have retained to this day.

The emergence of aquatic life onto the land can be considered as one of life's greatest achievements and somewhat comparable with man's arrival on the surface of the moon. There are several theories as to why the land was colonized by those particular creatures at that particular time. It has been suggested that it was paradoxically a quest for more water that caused the first crossopterygian fishes to move out of their river and lake environments in search of *lebensraum*. They may have been forced to seek out new bodies of water due to excessive drought or overcrowding and thus struggled to survive as they wondered over the land. All this, of course, took hundreds of millions of years, and the changes from aquatic to terrestrial life would have been very gradual. Eventually, every niche on the earth's surface capable of supporting life was colonized at one time or another; as one niche was destroyed, another was left to be colonized by something else. However, the habitats of the amphibians were somewhat limited. Although amphibians could

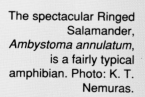

The spectacular Ringed Salamander, *Ambystoma annulatum*, is a fairly typical amphibian. Photo: K. T. Nemuras.

Varanus komodoensis, the Komodo Dragon, a monitor lizard and thus a cousin of today's snakes. There still are many uncertainties as to the real ancestors of snakes. Photo: J. Coborn.

live for long periods on the dry land, they had to remain near water or at least in humid areas, as in arid conditions fluid loss through the naked, porous skin was rapid and often fatal.

So, in order to further exploit the terrestrial environment, more important evolutionary adaptations were required, the most important being means of combating water loss. The answer was a protective cover to the skin, which eventually evolved into the typical reptilian scales. At the same time, the development of the first hard-shelled eggs took place. This meant that internal fertilization became necessary and that these particular animals were no longer amphibians, but had become primitive true reptiles that could live and reproduce on the land, even considerable distances away from open bodies of water. Moreover, the eggs could be more safely concealed from predators on the dry land; they could be buried in the ground or hidden away somewhere among dense vegetation. These eggs had large yolks containing enough nutrients to enable the embryos to develop somewhat further than the larval amphibians before they hatched, giving them a greater chance of survival. Of course, the embryos still had to go through the early stages of development but they were now enclosed in a sort of sac, called the amniotic membrane.

The embryo grew in the watery amniotic fluid contained in the inner membrane, receiving oxygen from the outside and disposing of carbon dioxide by means of another membrane, the allantois. A further membrane, called the chorion, surrounded the whole lot just inside the outer tough, protective shell.

The egglaying reptiles therefore had a tremendous advantage over the amphibians, which had to spend all their time near water and lay their eggs in it. The chances of many of these amphibian eggs and the larvae hatching from them eventually reaching maturity were sparse, as many fishes and all amphibians were carnivorous—the larger devouring the smaller and the smaller eating the eggs and larvae of the larger, as well as each other! The vertebrates thus began to colonize the dry land that had hitherto been the realm of plants and some invertebrates. The first reptiles continued to develop into varied forms, each development being a further improvement for a terrestrial

existence. Some developed their dry land hunting prowess, developing strong, muscular limbs that helped them pursue their prey speedily as well as escape from larger predators that were also developing. Others returned to the water to catch fish or amphibians in their strong jaws.

Toward the latter part of the Carboniferous period, the earth's climate began to change dramatically. Most of the typical swamps of the era dried up and many of the amphibians became extinct. This was an advantageous period for the animals that were already terrestrial and laid shelled eggs.

During the early Permian period (280-260 million years ago) herbivores had yet to develop and the reptiles had to feed on each other. Various adaptations for gripping, tearing, and chewing had to evolve in this tremendously competitive time as thousands of different species developed. Legs became longer and moved below the body rather than being at the sides, enabling animals to run faster and longer. Herbivores developed and many niches were taken up by these para-mammals, some of which are believed to have developed fur. At this time, in fact, the first true mammals appeared (mammals are furred and suckle their young).

The next periods, the Triassic and Jurassic, saw the rise of the dinosaurs and the extinction of the para-mammals. The giant reptiles were the dominant creatures on earth for the next 140 million years before they eventually died out toward the end of the Cretaceous period.

The ancestors of our modern snakes and lizards were also making their appearance during these periods, though fossil records of the early Squamata are somewhat sparse. The Lacertilia probably branched off from the primitive order Eosuchia during the Triassic period (240-200 million years ago), though the oldest direct ancestors of our modern lizards are known from fossils of the Upper Jurassic period (about 140 million years ago). Small lizards and snakes, particularly the latter, pose immense problems to paleontologists and, unlike the generally massive bones of the dinosaurs, are known only from scattered fragments of skulls and vertebrae. Piecing such fragments together is infinitely more difficult than the hardest of jig-saw puzzles, especially when most of the key pieces are missing. Much of our knowledge of the evolution of the Squamata remains, for the time being, necessarily sparse, but as research with modern equipment progresses we will doubtless soon be able to find more positive solutions to those problems that are only partially resolved.

It is generally accepted that snakes evolved from lizards, but any direct connection is yet to be discovered. The term "missing link" is especially significant when applied to snake phylogeny, as only a few fossil snake genera have been found and no species intermediate to lizards have been discovered. One fairly plausible theory is that snakes evolved from burrowing lizards that first lost their limbs, external ears, and, almost, their eyesight. During the burrowing period, the unique sense of prey detection, using the forked tongue and the Jacobson's organ and possibly the beginnings of heat reception pits in some species, began to develop. Eventually certain species again ventured onto the land surface, the lidless eyes redeveloped, but external ears and limbs were lost forever (though some of the more primitive snake families still possess

Elaphe guttata guttata (Linnaeus, 1766), the Corn Snake. This amelanistic, captive-bred specimen is a fine example of the species first described by Linnaeus in 1766 as *Coluber guttata*. Another subspecies, *E. g. emoryi* (Baird & Girard, 1853), the Great Plains Rat Snake, was described as a full species in 1853 but is now known to interbreed (intergrade) with the eastern Corn Snake where their ranges come into contact. Photo: Dr. W. E. Burgess.

vestigial pelvic girdles), being replaced by other sophisticated means of hearing and locomotion.

All this, of course, would have taken millions of years. Today we still have burrowing snakes, legless amphisbaenians that possess some characteristics of both lizards and snakes, and many legless lizards; what we do not have is a concrete link between the suborders. Snake evolution for the time being still remains a partial mystery.

CLASSIFICATIONS

It was only toward the latter part of the 18th century that a logical system of animal and plant classification began to be developed. During the period of European exploration of the continents and seas it became apparent that the number of animal and plant species being discovered was almost infinite. Zoological and botanical specimens were collected from all corners of the globe and brought back to the museums of European universities, where scientists had the task of examining them and trying to fit them

into a category. It soon became apparent that a system of classification was required that was not only logical but international. It was imperative that work of scientists in Paris or London, for example, could be communicated to those in Berlin or Oslo. For this reason, scientific literature usually was presented in classical Latin as this had been the universal language of learned scholars for generations.

It was the Swedish naturalist Karl von Linne (1707-1779) (generally known as Linnaeus, a Latinization of his name) who revolutionized our systems of classification by inventing his *binomial system of scientific nomenclature* and publishing it in his *Systema Naturae*. The science of naming and identifying species and putting them into a comparative classification is known as *taxonomy*, and Linnaeus can be regarded as the father of this science. The binomial system consisted of applying a double Latin name to every species. The pioneer system was of course primitive by today's standards, but it set a precedent for the following generations of taxonomists.

Many beginners to hobbies involving plants or animals are horrified at their first glimpse of scientific nomenclature and the prospect of learning it, but the serious hobbyist, whether he is a horticulturist, an aquarist, or an amateur herpetologist, is unlikely to get very far unless he knows at least the basics of the subject.

Natural classification is a hierarchial arrangement of animals or plants into different groups, based on differences and similarities among them. The bottom rank in this arrangement is the species, one of a group of organisms that are all essentially the same, at least with very little variation, and which interbreed to produce more individuals of a similar type. A number of species that are not essentially similar but have several characteristics in common are grouped into a genus (plural: genera). Genera are placed into families, families into orders, orders into classes, classes into phyla (plural of phylum), and so on. The number of similarities between members of a group becomes increasingly less at each step up the hierarchial ladder. For example, the genera of one family have fewer characters in common than do species of any genus. Additional categories such as subfamily and infraorder may be used.

Taxonomy, which is the study of the theory, procedure, and rules of classification of organisms, is a complex subject that has caused much argument and controversy among scientists for generations. There have been several schools of thought as to what constitutes a natural classification. Some maintain that phylogenetic relationships should be reflected in classification and assume that members of the same group, at whatever hierarchial level, should share a common ancestry. Taking our knowledge of snake evolution as an extreme example, it can be seen that such a classification is difficult to produce and must be based largely on theory. The procedure of evolution at different rates in different lineages adds a further difficulty to the system. Another theory is that classification should be based on similarities and differences of appearance (phenotype) and include observations on the anatomy, physiology, morphology, embryology, cytology, and biochemistry of living organisms. Modern classification is based on phylogeny as far as this is known, but in those groups where evolutionary information is sparse then it is supplemented with a degree of calculated guesswork.

The binomial system devised by Linnaeus is still used today but in a much improved form. Each new species discovered is given a two-part name (known as a binomial and made up of the generic name and the specific or trivial name) by the taxonomist who gives it its first scientific description (not necessarily the discoverer). Thus, in the species *Crotalus atrox* (Western Diamondback Rattlesnake), *Crotalus* is the generic name that is applied to all snakes in that genus (all 27 of them) and *atrox* is the specific name that is applied to a single species only. The name of the original author(s) and the year of description are written after the binomial. For example, *Crotalus atrox* Baird & Girard, 1853; *Crotalus adamanteus* Beauvais, 1799; *Crotalus durissus* Linnaeus, 1758. In cases where the species has been moved to a genus other than that in which it was described, the original author(s) of the original name is still retained, but in parentheses. For example, *Elaphe guttata* was originally described by Linnaeus as *Coluber guttatus*, thus its full name is given as *Elaphe guttata* (Linnaeus, 1766).

There are strict rules governing the naming and publishing of new animal species. These are governed by the International Commission of Zoological Nomenclature in their published *Code of Zoological Nomenclature*. An international committee sits at regular intervals to decide specific problems about names to be applied and to consider proposals for the changing of existing names and modifications of the *Code*.

The study of Latin names can be an interesting and informative sideline to the hobbyist, and it will certainly help to have a Latin dictionary. Taking *Crotalus atrox* as an example, we find that *Crotalus* is derived from *crotalum*, a rattle or castanet, while *atrox* means hideous, dreadful, atrocious, fierce, brutal, or unyielding; it is obvious why this name was applied to the Western Diamondback Rattlesnake. In some cases, the name of the discoverer or someone else the taxonomist wishes to honor will be Latinized and included in the trivial name (called a patronym), thus *Trimeresurus wagleri* (Boie, 1827) named in honor of Johann Georg Wagler (1800-1832), a German zoologist. Sometimes the name of the country to which the snake is native will be part of the binomial, thus *Acrantophis madagascariensis*. In a few cases the generic name may be based on a

personal or geographical name, for example *Boulengerina* (after George Albert Boulenger [1858-1937], Belgian-born herpetologist attached to the British Museum); and *Madagascarophis* (after the island on which it is found).

Sometimes species show relatively constant geographical variation in scale counts, color, or form. Such variations may not be sufficient to warrant separate specific classification, so they are classified as subspecies. In such cases a third name is added to the binomial, making it a trinomial. Subspecies will interbreed quite readily and indeed do so at the borders of their individual ranges, producing examples with characteristics from both groups; such individuals are known as intergrades. A good example of subspecific nomenclature is that applied to the North American Rat Snake, *Elaphe obsoleta*, of which many authorities recognize five to eight subspecies including the Black Rat Snake, *E. o. obsoleta*; the Yellow Rat Snake, *E. o. quadrivittata*; the Gray Rat Snake, *E. o. spiloides*; and the Texas Rat Snake, *E. o. lindheimeri*. The first subspecies described has its name (also that of the species) repeated in the trinomial (as in *E. o. obsoleta* above), while

The subspecies concept often is hard to grasp at first. The Black Rat Snake, *E. o. obsoleta* (above), does not look much like the Yellow Rat Snake, *E. o. quadrivittata* (below), but they share many features of structure and meristics (counts) as well as having similar juvenile patterns. Most importantly, they intergrade where their ranges overlap, and they thus are subspecies. Specimens from the zone of intergradation may resemble either subspecies or be intermediate in some features. Photos: Above: C. Banks; Below: R. Anderson.

The Gray Rat Snake, *Elaphe obsoleta spiloides*, retains as an adult the pattern typical of juveniles of all the subspecies of *obsoleta*, but it also intergrades with the subspecies that surround its range.
Photo: R. T. Zappalorti.

further subspecies receive a new subspecific name placed after the specific name. Subspecific names are written in the same way as specific ones, thus: *Elaphe obsoleta quadrivittata* (Holbrook, 1836).

In serious publications, generic, specific, and subspecific names are almost always written in italic script (or underlined when italic script is not available) to avoid confusion with common names or with the text in which they are cited. This is particularly useful when a biologist or other interested person is studying papers or books written in a foreign language or alphabet. A person who understands only English, for example, will be able to tell if a German, Japanese, or Russian text is about a particular genus or species as the names will appear in italicized Roman script, whatever characters are used in the bulk of the text. This will give the reader an idea as to whether it will be worthwhile having the text translated.

It will be noted that scientific names often are abbreviated. When a species is first mentioned in a text, the full scientific name (with or without its author) is usually given, but when the same name is repeated it is abbreviated. For example: *Leptotyphlops sundevalli* is abbreviated to *L. sundevalli*, while *Python molurus bivittatus* is abbreviated to *P. m. bivittatus*.

Having discussed classification and taxonomy briefly, as it is applied to the whole of the animal kingdom but using snakes for examples, the following table demonstrates the classification of three snake species within the suborder Serpentes.

TABLE 1

Sample Classification of Three Snake Species

KINGDOM	Animalia	All animals	
PHYLUM	Chordata	Animals with notochord	
SUBPHYLUM	Vertebrata (Craniata)	Vertebrates	
CLASS	Reptilia	All reptiles	
ORDER	Squamata	Lizards, amphisbaenians, and snakes	
SUBORDER	Serpentes	All snakes	
INFRAORDER	Scolecophidia	Henophidia	Caenophidia
FAMILY	Typhlopidae	Boidae	Colubridae
SUBFAMILY	—	Pythoninae	Colubrinae
GENUS	*Typhlops*	*Python*	*Elaphe*
SPECIES	*T. diardi*	*P. regius*	*E. guttata*

REPTILIAN BIOLOGY

Biology means the study of life, so when we talk about the biology of snakes this includes every scientific discipline pertaining to the suborder Serpentes. However, before delving into the particular biology of serpents, it is essential to know a little about the general biology of reptiles. All reptiles have certain anatomical and physiological similarities, though many of these may not at first seem apparent. A knowledge of these will enable the prospective snake-keeper to deal more adequately with the animals in his or her care. Reptiles were the first vertebrates to become fully terrestrial and independent of bodies of water to breed. This was accomplished though a combination of internal fertilization through copulation and the development of the first shelled egg. These together constitute one of the great evolutionary advances. Without it, the birds and the mammals, including ourselves, would never have appeared on the surface of the earth. Of course, the egg alone did not prepare the reptiles for terrestrial habitation, and indeed the egg was one of the later adaptations to occur. The whole animal gradually developed characteristics suited to its terrestrial existence and many of these characteristics have been passed on to today's living reptiles.

A reptile can be described as a tetrapod (meaning four-limbed—somewhat paradoxical when referring to snakes, but it is assumed that snakes evolved from four-limbed ancestors) having a skin composed of horny scales that in some groups are reinforced with bony osteoderms. The skin is relatively impermeable to water and reduces loss of body fluids through evaporation, in addition to reducing dilution of the body fluids by osmosis in wet conditions. The head usually is carried on a relatively long neck and, through articulation of the atlas vertebra with the condyle of the skull, is able to perform the useful function of moving the head up and down or from side to side. The relatively small brain is encased in a relatively solid bony skull and has a moderately developed cerebrum. A partial secondary palate, which in the higher vertebrates separates the nasal and oral cavities, occurs in most reptiles and is complete in the crocodilians.

The lower jaw is composed of three to six separate bones plus the quadrate, which allows articulation with the upper jaw. The teeth are located on the edges of the jaw bones and sometimes (especially in some snakes) on the palatal bones. The teeth may be of several different forms, depending on the position on the jaw: fused to the side of the jaw (pleurodont), fused to the summit of the jaw (acrodont), or contained in sockets (thecodont). In most species the teeth are replaced several times in succession (polyphyodont). All reptiles possess a tongue that is typically (though not always) highly mobile and considerably extensible (particularly in snakes).

The differentiation of the vertebral column into distinct regions, typical of the mammals, makes its appearance in the reptiles, although among the reptiles it is only the crocodilians that show five clear-cut regions. The limbs are laterally oriented in many species and typically end in five clawed digits. The limbs may be partially reduced or absent in some lizards and are invariably absent in snakes (though some primitive species still possess a vestigial pelvic girdle).

All reptiles respire by means of lungs and have a three-chambered (four-chambered in the crocodilians) heart. Like the amphibians and the fishes, reptiles are poikilothermic in that they do not automatically retain a constant normal body temperature (as do the homoiothermic birds and mammals) but rely on the environment to thermoregulate.

BIOLOGY OF SNAKES

The foregoing brief outline of reptilian biology serves as an introduction to the biology of snakes. The order Squamata includes the lizards and the amphisbaenians as well as the snakes and it will be necessary to refer to the former suborders while discussing the latter. The order Squamata contains highly specialized groups that have colonized almost every available habitat, with the exception of the polar regions. Species are found in tropical rain forests and arid deserts; in alpine meadows, coniferous forests, and temperate heathland; in salt and fresh water; some have even exploited the changes on the earth's surface brought about by man's agricultural and forestry activities. Within these climatic and topographical regions, they have further developed into arboreal, terrestrial, burrowing, and aquatic forms. It is little wonder that such a cosmopolitan group of animals has evolved an almost confusing diversity of form and habit.

Within subspecies there often are recognizable variants now considered too ill-defined to be worth bearing a scientific name. This grayish type of Yellow Rat Snake once was considered a subspecies, *williamsi*, but today it is thought to be a synonym of *Elaphe o. quadrivittata*. Photo: R. D. Bartlett.

Many lizards tend toward leglessness, and dozens of species are totally legless. The anguid glass lizard *Ophisaurus ventralis* (top) and the pygopodid *Delma australis* are both very snake-like at first glance—and even second glance—but they have external ear openings and eyelids, both features absent in all snakes (no exceptions). Not all legless lizards have both eyelids and ear openings, however. Photos: Top: R. S. Simmons; Bottom: C. Banks.

Only the fact that reptiles are poikilothermic has prevented them from colonizing latitudes and altitudes where the permafrost precludes hibernation below ground.

Lizard or Snake

There are numerous differences between typical lizards and typical snakes, but there are very few characteristics that provide a concrete distinction between members of the two suborders. Some lizards have evolved on a line parallel to that of the snakes and in the process have acquired certain snake-like characteristics (loss of limbs for example), while some snakes have retained certain obvious lizard characteristics (vestiges of hind limbs for example). The two groups are obviously very closely related, thus zoologists have classified them together in the same order.

If confronted with a legless, serpentine reptile, you can tell whether it is a snake or a lizard by examining the following points. First ascertain whether movable eyelids are present; if so the animal is definitely a lizard—most legless lizards possess movable eyelids but no snakes do. Next look for external ear openings; if present, the animal is definitely a lizard—no snakes have external ear openings. Further points to examine include the tongue, which is invariably notched in legless lizards, rather than forked as in snakes. The tail of legless lizards is often easily lost through autotomy whereas (with very few exceptions) snakes cannot voluntarily shed their tails.

Snake Anatomy, Physiology, and Behavior

The most outstanding and well-known feature of snakes is that they are limbless, although in some of the more primitive families a vestigial pelvic girdle is present and may be visible as an external pair of small, horn-sheathed claws or spurs placed near the cloaca. One obvious characteristic of snakes is the elongate, flexible body with little or no differentiation between head, neck, thorax, abdomen, and tail. The head and neck region is usually more or less distinct from the thoracic region in terms of diameter (the degree of distinction of the head from the body by the neck is a major guide to the identification of many genera or species). The trunk, comprising the largest (at least the most voluminous) portion of the animal, is roughly cylindrical in shape, though the geometry of cross-sections varies somewhat from species to species, depending on the habitat; this may be circular, vertically or horizontally ovoid, or triangular. The ventral surface is usually

flattened, and there is often a slight ridge along the flanks between the dorsal and ventral surfaces. Examination will determine that the snake's body ends and the tail starts at the vent (the external opening of the cloaca), the common orifice for excretory and reproductive functions. The tail length varies from species to species and, in some cases, between sexes.

Skin and Scales

The skin of a snake is its major protection against a number of physical hazards: mechanical injury, desiccation, and wear and tear for example. Compared with a limbed animal, a snake has an extremely large area of its skin in contact with the surfaces over which it moves, so the skin must be tough. There are three layers of skin, the innermost one being the thickest and containing the pigment cells. The middle layer is very thin and consists of cells that are continually dividing and growing in a plane parallel with the surface of the body. The new cells eventually die and form the horny epidermis that totally encloses the body and consists of (typically) overlapping scales. Unlike the scales of fishes, which are attached to the surface of the skin, snake scales form an integral part of the skin. If a dried snakeskin or a shed skin is examined, it will be seen that the thickened scales are joined together by a much thinner membrane. The scales have evolved from folds in the skin, the thin elastic

This cleared and stained water snake distinctly illustrates the multiplication of vertebrae and ribs typical of all snakes, as well as the slender, loosely attached lower jaws. Photo: Dr. G. Dingerkus.

membranes being between the scales, and the scales themselves being the parts that are presented to the exterior.

Certain groups of scales have particular functions. Those on the belly, for example, are concerned with locomotion, while those covering the eye serve as a protective, transparent spectacle (the brille). Various areas on the snake's body are covered by particular types of scales. Those on the head consist, more often than not, of large, irregularly shaped plates. Those on the dorsal surface are relatively small, usually diamond- to lozenge-shaped and overlapping, while the ventral scales are, in most species, large, broad, and arranged in a single row from the throat to the vent. Those on the underside of the tail (subcaudals) may be arranged in a single or double row, depending on the species.

The type, number, and arrangement of scales on each particular species tend to be fairly constant, and these points are frequently used as

Left: The elongated body allows great flexibility, as shown by this interestingly coiled *Corallus caninus*. Photo: Courtesy Chester Zoo. Right: Close-up of the dorsal scales of a Boa Constrictor, showing the numerous rows present in most pythons and boas. The arrangement of snake scales is known as lepidosis, while the number of each type falls under the category of meristics. Photo: J. K. Langhammer.

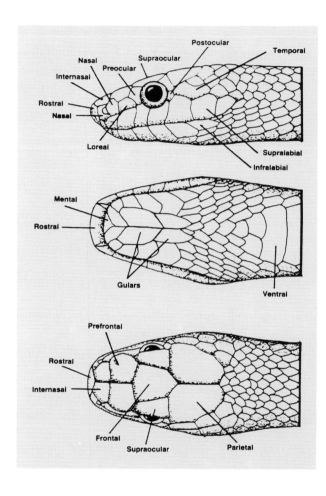

The shed skin of a snake exhibits all the scale characters of the living animal except details of color pattern. Photo: J. Dommers.

The scalation of a snake's head is vital information in identification. Each scale has a name and occurs in a more or less constant position if present. Most important are the scales present and absent, their number, and position relative to other scales. Shown is a fairly typical colubrid snake.

Ventral view of a Boa Constrictor showing the widened ventral scales or scutes. In more typical snakes the ventrals are much wider than in the boids. Photo: J. K. Langhammer.

an aid to the identification and description of species. Field guides and museum catalogues will usually give details of scale counts. Variations in numbers of particular scale types are usually more important in defining species or subspecies than are color patterns. The points of scalation most often used in identification include the arrangement of scales on the head, the number of rows of dorsal scales at midbody, and the numbers of ventral and subcaudal scales. The latter count may also be used to identify the sexes, as male snakes often have longer tails and a correspondingly greater number of subcaudals than do females.

The dorsal scales may also vary from species to species and may be smooth, keeled, or granular. Smooth scales are often shiny and iridescent, often appearing wet, a point that has probably led to the erroneous belief that snakes are slimy. Keeled scales (with a raised central ridge) often appear to have a dry, matt finish, Granular scales are very small, usually roundish, and do not overlap to the extent of other types of scales. Granular scales occur in only one group of snakes, the Acrochordidae (wart snakes).

In many species the dorsal scales possess what are described as apical pits. They appear as minute circular concavities, just visible to the naked eye, near the tips of some or all the dorsal scales. These pits may be arranged singly, in pairs (most commonly), or in groups of three or more (rarely). The pits are caused by localized thinning of the horny scale-covering. The epidermal cells beneath are supplied with bundles of nerve fibers. The function of these apical pits is still not thoroughly understood, but they may have something to do with the sense of touch or temperature detection.

Other scale organs that occur in many species include specialized tactile papillae that may be found in clusters on certain scales on the head, chin, throat, or ventral region. These seem to play a role in the stimulation of courting snakes when the male rubs his chin over the female's body and attempts to get his vent in apposition to hers.

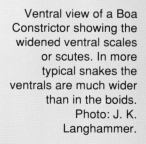

Extreme differences in scalation of snakes. Above is a Rainbow Boa, *Epicrates cenchria*, showing numerous scales on top of the head and numerous rows of dorsal body scales that are extremely smooth and iridescent. Below is a Chinese Moccasin, *Agkistrodon (Deinagkistrodon) acutus*, showing reduced number of large head scales and fewer rows of body scales, each with a large blunt keel. Photos: Above: K. T. Nemuras; Below: Dr. S. Minton.

Sloughing or Shedding

As a snake grows and due to wear and tear on the epidermis, the outer, dead layer of skin must be periodically shed or sloughed. The cells that form the middle layer of the snake's skin do not increase and grow at a uniform rate, but at irregular intervals (depending on age, climatic conditions, and availability of food, for example) a film of exudate is produced that separates the older outer layers from the younger ones beneath. The whole of the skin acquires an opaque appearance, colors become dulled, and the sleekness associated with a normal, healthy snake is temporarily lost. The brille or eye scale becomes affected and takes on a milky or bluish appearance. The snake becomes partially blind, will usually stop feeding, and may hide away. At such times many snakes are more irritable than usual and special care should be taken (especially with venomous species) to avoid the increased likelihood of bites. After a few days the eye clears again and the snake will seek out a rough surface on which it can rub its lips. It is at the lips that the old skin breaks free and can be turned inside out and pushed back over the head and body, somewhat in the manner of a lady removing her stocking. To facilitate the loosening of the skin, the snake will expand and contract its muscles in shivering waves and perhaps attempt to crawl over or between rough-surfaced objects so that purchase is applied.

In healthy snakes the skin should shed in a single piece. The cast skin is almost transparent and shows only a trace of the pigmentation. However, the scales can still easily be seen, and shed skins are often used to identify the presence of a species in a certain habitat.

Young snakes usually shed their skins a couple of days after birth or hatching and almost invariably before their first meal. A snake may shed up to ten times in its first year, when growth is rapid. This number is reduced each year as the rate of growth diminishes. Adult snakes usually shed no more than three or four times per year. An unhealthy snake may have difficulty in shedding its skin completely, which can cause further health problems.

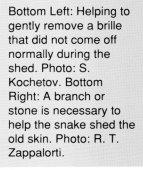

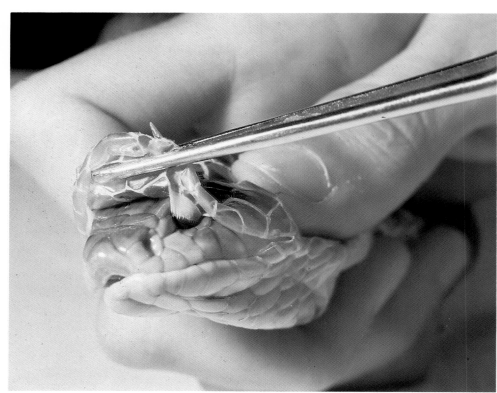

Two gorgeous captive-bred kingsnakes just after shedding. Top: An albino ringed phase California Kingsnake, *Lampropeltis g. californiae*. Bottom: A Gray-banded Kingsnake, *L. alterna*. Photos: K. T. Nemuras.

Sidewinding is a method of locomotion developed by several desert-dwelling snakes. Compare the tracks left by the African Dwarf Puff Adder, *Bitis peringueyi* (top), and the North American Sidewinder, *Crotalus cerastes laterorepens* (bottom right). Photos: K. H. Switak.

Locomotion

The means and apparent ease by which a snake moves have fascinated man for generations. To early man this must have appeared to be an almost supernatural feat. Even today, when snake locomotion has been studied in detail, one cannot help but marvel at how a legless creature can move with such speed, grace, and agility. The flowing locomotion of most snakes is made possible by the accessory articulating facets of the vertebrae that allow the animal to bend considerably in almost any direction. Locomotion in most species is achieved by a combination of lateral undulations produced by the dorsal muscles and rectilinear crawling, though each method can be used individually. Lateral (mainly) undulations of the body allow the scales along the flanks to come into contact with imperfections or objects on the terrain in which it is moving. Most snakes prefer to move through undergrowth or rocky terrain that gives them the opportunity of pushing themselves forward.

However, if moving slowly or pensively (as when stalking prey), rectilinear locomotion alone may be used. In this case, the snake can move in an apparent straight line. It accomplishes this by using the broad ventral scales (or gastrosteges) that are attached to the snake's numerous rib pairs by special muscles. The ribs articulate with the vertebrae and, if one could imagine a snake's skeleton moving, the ribs would walk somewhat in the manner of a centipede. At the same time, the muscles expand and contract and cause the broad ventral scales to move in waves, the posterior edge of each scale pushing against imperfections in the substrate and causing the snake to go forward. Thus if a snake is placed on an unnaturally smooth surface (a sheet of glass or a polished linoleum floor, for example) it will have obvious difficulty in moving forward. Large, heavy snakes (such as pythons, boas, and large viperids) use rectilinear crawling almost exclusively—as if their obesity has caused them to become lazy. Only if alarmed or if swimming is a weighty snake likely to break into undulatory movement.

Terrestrial snakes that sometimes climb tend to push the head up and get a purchase in the neck region before pulling the body up after it. The body is then arranged in a balanced situation before the next step is taken. The snake's body is remarkably synchronized to balance and it rarely falls accidentally. Arboreal snakes have further adaptations to help them move through the trees. The lateral scales are often heavily keeled and the ventrals sharply angled at the edges to help them get a grip on bark, etc. Some snakes have an almost uncanny talent of being able to scale an apparently smooth tree trunk vertically by using these adaptations.

So called "flying snakes," members of the genus *Chrysopelia*, have taken their arboreal talents a little further. In pursuit of prey or when escaping from predators, they can move rapidly through the foliage and launch themselves into the air. By flattening the body dorso-ventrally to form a concave ventral surface and at the same time making undulatory movements, they can glide some considerable distance, though landing at a lower level than that from which they took off.

Aquatic snakes use undulatory movements to swim. Some of the sea snakes even have laterally flattened bodies and paddle-like tails to increase their swimming efficiency. Most of the more aquatic snakes have more or less replaced the broad ventral scales with smaller scales resembling those on the dorsal surface. Most

species of snake appear to be able to swim efficiently should the occasion arise.

Some desert-dwelling species that inhabit terrain with a loose, shifting substrate have developed a specialized means of locomotion known as sidewinding. Being unable to efficiently use lateral undulation or rectilinear crawling due to the shifting nature of the surface over which they must move, they have developed a system of throwing body loops so that the main pressure of movement is directed vertically downward. The snake moves at an angle of about 45 degrees to the line of its own body by raising the head and throwing it forward in the direction of travel. As the head contacts the ground, a loop of the body is raised and moved toward the head, which by this time is beginning its next step. Snakes moving in this manner leave characteristic J-shaped tracks in the soft substrate.

Sidewinding snakes can move surprisingly quickly in this manner and almost appear to walk across the surface of the sand. Snakes from various parts of the world but from similar habitats have developed this method of locomotion. The Sidewinder, *Crotalus cerastes*, of the southwestern USA and Mexico; the Saw-scaled Viper, *Echis carinatus*, from northern and eastern Africa and southwestern Asia; and the Dwarf Puff Adder, *Bitis peringueyi*, from Angola and Namibia, all exhibit the talent and all inhabit areas where this system of locomotion is often necessary. Other species of snakes are able to exhibit sidewinding to a certain extent if the occasion arises, and sidewinders themselves are also able to move in a more conventional manner.

The Senses

It may come as a surprise to some that snakes are extremely sensitive animals that possess all of the senses with which we ourselves are blessed, although some are less efficient and others more efficient than ours. Let us examine the basic senses of snakes and compare them with our own.

Sight: Considering their predatory nature, the eyes of snakes are relatively inefficient, but like other animals with poor eyesight they make up for this apparent disability by having other extremely sharp senses. It is quite feasible that snakes evolved from lizards or lizard-like creatures that had taken to a subterranean existence. A characteristic of most burrowing creatures is the lack of efficient eyes. Eyes are not necessary in a dark world, so during the snake's burrowing period the eyes degenerated to mere vestiges of those possessed by their surface-dwelling ancestors. The primitive burrowing snakes of today are good examples of animals with degenerate eyes. We can assume that when the more advanced snakes returned to the surface and sight again became important, the degenerate eyes had to regenerate, producing eyes of varying efficiency, depending on the species, its habits, and its habitat.

However, in almost all species the eyes have never regained the sophisticated features of those of their ancestors nor have they developed any of the unique efficiency that is exhibited in the birds and the mammals.

In general, a snake's eyesight can be said to be poor when compared with ours or even with that of most lizards. Due to the absence of a retinal fovea they have a reduced ability to focus

The Corn Snake, *Elaphe guttata*, is a typical colubrid showing the round pupil characteristic of unspecialized hunters. Photo: J. Iverson.

Top: The vertical pupil typical of nocturnal hunters is readily seen in this *Echis carinatus*. Photo: R. T. Zappalorti.

Right: A whip snake, *Ahaetulla nasuta*, showing the horizontal figure 8 pupil indicating the presence of binocular vision. Photo: C. Banks.

highly mobile eyelids plus a third eyelid or nictitating membrane, but some burrowing or semi-burrowing forms possess a brille, while others exhibit stages in the development of one. In some cases the center of the still movable lower eyelid is more or less transparent and the reptile is able to see with its eyes closed. In other cases the lower lid with the window remains permanently shut, while in still others the upper and lower lids have become completely fused together.

Hearing: It is a well known fact that snakes do not possess external ears, nor in fact do they possess a tympanum or eardrum (perhaps another clue to the theory that snakes evolved from burrowing ancestors). However, snakes apparently can hear as they react to noises of varying degree and pitch. It can be assumed that a snake's auditory sense is far from efficient when compared with ours or even with that of most lizard species, but it is efficient enough for snake species to be successful. In normal hearing, airborne sound waves cause the typanum to resonate; the vibrations are then transmitted to the inner ear via the small bones in the ear and thence transmitted as nerve impulses via the auditory nerve to the brain. As snakes have lost the outer and middle ears, as well as the Eustachian tube, they cannot receive most airborne sounds, though experiments have shown that they respond to low-frequency waves. The snakes' method of hearing is by picking up vibrations from the solid surfaces on which they rest. The vibrations pass through the snake's jawbone to the quadrate and thence to the stapes, which is in close proximity to it. From there nerve impulses are transmitted to the brain in the usual manner. It is suspected that the lung is also involved in the transmission of sound and other vibrations. This explains why snakes, though they may be by no means scarce, are rarely seen by the average country hiker—the reptiles have picked up the vibrations and fled well before the hiker arrives on the scene.

and their perception of detail is poor. With the exception of a few genera (such as *Ahaetulla* and *Thelotornis*), snakes have difficulty in recognizing stationary objects by sight and thus have to rely on the perception of movement of living prey or have to use other senses to detect dead or immobile prey.

Eye size and efficiency depend on the species's methods of catching prey. Most burrowing species have eyes in various stages of degeneration, while many arboreal and fast-moving diurnal terrestrial species that actively hunt by sight have large eyes; most of these also have circular pupils. A few of the nocturnal, arboreal genera (e.g., *Hapsidophrys*) have extremely large eyes with round pupils, but the majority of the nocturnal genera exhibit vertically slit or elliptical pupils. There are exceptions in that some species with vertical pupils are diurnal, but it is probable that these have evolved from nocturnal ancestors.

The snake species with probably the most advanced eyesight belong to the genera *Ahaetulla* (Oriental Whip Snakes) and *Thelotornis* (Bird Snake). Studies have revealed that the eyes in both these genera possess areas that can be described as retinal fovea. In addition, the eyes are oriented forward and the pupils are in the form of a horizontal figure 8. These properties, coupled with a groove along either side of the snout, give the snake binocular vision and the ability to focus and recognize stationary prey. Several other arboreal snakes have similar modifications.

The eyes of snakes have no movable eyelids, but the cornea is protected by a circular transparent scale (or, in some cases, a transparent part of a larger scale) known as the brille or spectacle. Most lizards have a pair of

Smell and Jacobson's Organ: If an animal is oriented to any particular sense (it is probable that our main sense of orientation is our sight), then the snake is surely oriented by its sense of smell. Although snakes and lizards have a normal sense of smell operated by the sensory epithelium lining the nostrils, this is relatively poorly developed. These reptiles mainly rely on what to us can be regarded as a roundabout way of detecting odors. Situated in the palate just below the nose and corresponding to but not adjoining the nostrils is a pair of domed cavities lined with sensory epithelium connected to a special branch of the olfactory nerve. These vomeronasal pits are known as Jacobson's organs and are used to detect scent particles that are introduced to them by the tongue. In snakes the system is more efficient than in most lizards and it is believed that the tips of the highly mobile forked tongue are designed to fit into the organs. This explains the continual flickering of an active snake's tongue, which it protrudes through a labial notch (making it unneccessary to continuously open the mouth). The scent particles are picked up from the air or solid objects on the tips of the tongue and transferred directly to the inner surfaces of the Jacobson's organs from whence the necessary messages are passed to the brain. This sophisticated sense of smell is highly important to snakes, which use it to find prey, to seek out a mate, and to detect potential enemies. The efficiency of the Jacobson's organ and the modification of the tongue for use with it have probably resulted in a reduction of the sense of taste as in snakes the tongue has relatively few taste buds.

Balance and Touch: The sense of balance in snakes is quite highly developed and arises from both the semicircular canals that respond to head movements and the muscles as they are affected by changing gravitational stresses as other parts of the body are tilted. In spite of its long, cylindrical shape a snake is able to stay the right way up whatever situation it finds itself in, whether moving through the slender branches of

a tree, speeding over uneven ground, burrowing beneath the surface, or swimming in some body of water.

The sense of touch is also highly developed. One has only to lightly touch a resting captive snake on any part of its body and note the reaction, which will range from a twitch of the area touched to angry defensive action or attempt at flight, depending on the species of snake and its degree of tameness. This indicates that the snake's skin is amply supplied with nerve endings. Snakes are thigmotactic; that is, they respond to the stimulus of closeness to solid objects and feel uneasy when caught out in the open with little opportunity for taking refuge. Thus most snake species when at rest squeeze

Top: Interior of the mouth of *Leptophis mexicanus* showing the multiple tooth rows of the upper jaws. Photo: K. T. Nemuras.

Bottom: The tongue in a hatchling *Lampropeltis t. triangulum* (left) and an adult *Elaphe o. rossalleni* (right). Photos: Left: W. B. Allen, Jr.; Right: I. Francais.

Well-developed labial pits are readily seen in the young Emerald Tree Boa, *Corallus caninus*, top, and the Green Tree Python, *Chondropython viridis*, bottom. Photos: Top: R. D. Bartlett; Bottom: R. Anderson.

themselves tightly into whatever cavity is available.

Some snake species and some individuals have a particular home area with a single refuge to which they invariably return after foraging. A good example of this behavior is demonstrated by the Black Mamba, *Dendroaspis angusticeps*, which, if undisturbed, will live for years in some termite mound or tree hollow, only venturing out for the necessary activities of feeding and breeding. Thigmotactism is an important factor in captive snake husbandry. Many snakes that are not provided with a refuge into which they

can tightly squeeze will suffer stress, refuse to feed, and slowly deteriorate in health. The Blood Python, *P. curtus*, and the Royal Python, *P. regius*, are two typical examples of snakes that will steadfastly refuse to feed unless they are able to hide in some tight cavity.

Heat-sensitive Organs: A highly specialized sense organ found only in two families of snakes is the heat-sensitive pit or organ. In the Boidae, all members of the subfamily Pythoninae (except *Aspidites* and *Calabaria*), and the genera *Corallus*, *Epicrates*, and *Sanzinia* of the subfamiliy Boinae have these organs arranged in series along the jaw-line, either within the labial scales (Pythoninae) or between them (Boinae). All members of the family Crotalidae (also known as pit vipers) possess a single pair of prominent pits, each located between the eye and the nostril. These heat receptor pits are extremely sensitive to temperature changes, and snakes possessing them are able to locate the direction of warm-blooded prey, even in complete darkness, and strike at it accurately. Experiments with pit vipers have shown that the facial pits are capable of detecting a temperature variation of as little as 0.003°C. On the other hand, the labial pits of boids are slightly less sensitive and have been shown to be able to detect temperature changes of only 0.026°C. It is believed that snakes possessing heat receptor pits are capable of forming an image of a potential meal; even

specimens which have been experimentally blindfolded are able to locate and capture prey.

Although snakes have a relatively odd shape when compared to other animals, they possess most of the internal organs that are necessary for basic physiological functions, although these have become adapted in one way or another to fit into the elongate form. Let us make a brief examination of the snake's various physiological systems.

Feeding and Digestion: The interior of the mouth contains various glands that help moisten and lubricate the prey in preparation for swallowing. As snakes invariably swallow their prey whole (they have no means of tearing, crushing, or chewing), these lubricatory glands are very important, especially to those species that feed on mammals and birds. There are palatine glands on the roof of the mouth, plus lingual (tongue), sublingual (below the tongue), and labial (lip) glands. These glands all produce mucus (or saliva) that keeps the interior of the mouth moist, as well as enzymes that start the digestive process. When the snake is stimulated by the prospect of a meal (by a combination of the olfactory, optical, and/or heat receptory senses), the oral glands produce an additional quantity of lubricatory mucus in anticipation of the delicacy about to be devoured (in other words, its mouth waters).

The venom glands of poisonous snakes are modifications of a pair of the upper labial glands (glandulae labialis superior) that produce normal saliva as well as protein-containing venom from the Duvernoy's glands (sometimes called parotid glands), which are incorporated within and at the rear of the upper labial glands. There is one situated on each side of the upper jaw, usually just posterior to the eye and extending well into the cheek, though in a few genera the gland extends into the neck or even into the thorax. The venom gland opens into a duct that passes venom through the canal or along the groove contained in the venom fang. Even some snakes without modified injection fangs produce poisonous saliva of variable potency from the upper labial glands; the venom is introduced into the prey via the numerous puncture wounds caused by the sharp teeth. It is therefore advisable to avoid the bites of all snakes, even those that are apparently harmless.

The Teeth: There is a great variety of tooth specialization in the various snake species, a fact that is important to the taxonomist. Typically, teeth are carried on the dentaries of the lower jaw and the maxillae, the pterygoids, and the palatines in the upper jaw. In pythons (subfamily Pythoninae), teeth are also carried on the premaxillae. There are, of course, exceptions. For instance, primitive snakes of the family Leptotyphlopidae have no teeth at all in the upper jaw, while members of the family Typhlopidae have no teeth in the lower jaw, perhaps indicating that, in spite of superficial morphological resemblance, the two families are

only distantly related but represent parallel development.

In general, snake teeth are sharply pointed, strongly recurved, and fused directly into the bones on which they are affixed. The teeth are shed and replaced at regular intervals. Shed teeth often are swallowed with the prey, often appearing in the snake's feces later on (which is surprising when you consider that the teeth of prey animals are usually completely digested). The cycle of tooth replacement ensures that matured teeth and partly grown teeth of various sizes are always available on all the tooth-bearing bones.

In the majority of snake species, including the boids and most of the colubrids, the teeth are solid and fairly uniform in size, though those at the front or the rear part of the maxilla may be somewhat larger. Snakes bearing these simple teeth are known as aglyphic species. Some snakes in the family Colubridae, especially those of the subfamilies Boiginae, Homalopsinae, Aparallactinae, Elachistodontinae, and some of

Copperheads, *Agkistrodon contortrix*, showing the heat-sensitive facial pit typical of all pit vipers. The bottom photo also shows the size and placement of the fangs. Photos: Top: W. B. Allen, Jr.; Bottom: J. Gee.

the Xenodontinae and Natricinae, are known as **rear-fanged** or opisthoglyphic species. In such cases, two or more fangs at the rear of the maxilla are enlarged and are grooved (usually anteriorly) so that venom can be conducted from the venom gland and introduced into the prey.

The majority of rear-fanged snakes are considered to be relatively harmless to man due to the relative impotence of the venom (though it may be perfectly adequate for subduing the specialist prey of the snake) and the difficulty in engaging the venom fangs. However, there are two notable exceptions and a number of suspect ones. The Boomslang, *Dispholidus typus*, and the Twig Snake, *Thelotornis kirtlandi*, both from Africa and of the subfamily Boiginae, have a relatively large gape and long opisthoglyphous fangs set far forward on the maxillae. These facts, coupled with a readiness to bite in defense and a particularly potent venom, have made these two colubrids notorious in causing human fatalities (each of these species has been responsible for the death of at least one famous herpetologist). Many other opisthoglyphic snakes, particularly the larger species, can give painful bites, and sporadic deaths have occurred from envenomation by various species. It is worth emphasizing the point here again—and the author makes no excuse for repeating himself—that it is advisable to avoid the bites of **all** snakes, whether apparently harmless or not.

Members of the venomous families Elapidae and Hydrophiidae are known as proteroglyphic species. The venom fang is canaliculate (really an adaptation of the groove, as the suture or joint can be seen along the anterior surface of the fang) and situated at the front of the maxilla. The pair of fangs is more or less fixed rigidly on the maxillae, though in a few genera (*Dendroaspis*, for example), the maxilla itself is mobile, allowing the fangs to be brought forward.

The contents of the venom gland pass into the

canal of the fang and are injected into the prey as the snake bites, via an aperture near the point of the fang. In a few genera (for example, *Hemachatus*, the Ringhals), the aperture is situated at the front of the relatively short fang and by rapid contraction of the venom gland venom can be sprayed directly at an aggressor, usually in the direction of its eyes. The aim is fairly accurate up to 2 or 3 meters (6-10 ft), and venom in the eyes can cause severe pain, inflammation, and temporary blindness. Goggles should be worn when dealing with such species.

The most efficient and highly advanced venom apparatus in snakes is that possessed by the families Viperidae and Crotalidae, which are known as solenoglyphic species. The hypodermic-like fangs have become completely canaliculate (only a mere vestige of the joining suture can be seen). They are the only teeth present on the maxillae and, unlike the relatively fixed fangs of the proteroglyphs, lie back along the roof of the mouth during normal activity but can be rapidly brought forward by rotation of the maxilla. The fangs of solenoglyphic snakes are usually relatively long, those of a large Gaboon Viper being up to 2.5 cm (1 in) long on the curve.

Dietary Range: All snakes are exclusively carnivorous and only take plant material accidentally during prey consumption. Indeed, many snakes seem to be unable to digest vegetable materials, as can be witnessed by the presence of grain in the feces of a specimen that has recently digested a chicken with a well-filled crop. Many juvenile snakes, as well as adults of the smaller species, eat invertebrates, including worms, molluscs, insects, and spiders. There are even small species that specialize in eating particular invertebrates such as crickets, centipedes, and snails. Larger snakes feed almost exclusively on various vertebrates. Some may feed indiscriminately on whatever is

A fang is any greatly elongated tooth in the jaws of a snake. The Emerald Tree Boa, *Corallus caninus*, to the top right has fangs at the front of both upper and lower jaws, while the Boomslang, *Dispholidus typus*, at the bottom has the fang located below the eye, very far forward for a "rear-fang." Photos: Top: R. S. Simmons; Bottom: J. Visser.

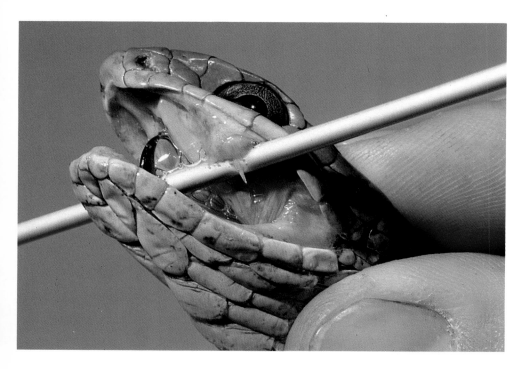

available, although the vast majority of snakes tend to specialize in certain groups of animals that are partially determined by the range of prey available to them in their particular habitat. Thus snakes living in or near water feed predominantly on fish or amphibians; desert-living species feed principally on lizards and small mammals; while arboreal snakes may specialize in feeding on geckos, treefrogs, or nestling birds. Two genera of snakes, *Dasypeltis* of Africa and *Elachistodon* of India, feed exclusively on the eggs of birds.

There are quite a few species that specialize in eating other snakes. Many of the larger burrowing snakes will feed on smaller ones. Perhaps the best known snake-eater among snakes is the King Cobra, *Ophiophagus hannah* (its generic name even means snake-eater). This species will steadfastly refuse to eat anything except other snakes, although it can be maintained for many years in captivity by force-feeding it on other foods. The non-venomous North American kingsnakes of the genus *Lampropeltis* have earned admiration from man for their habit of overpowering by constriction and eating other snakes, including highly venomous rattlesnakes. Another famous snake-eating snake is the Mussurana, *Clelia clelia*, of South America, which has earned respect by feeding on the highly venomous *Bothrops* species.

Catching and Killing Prey: Among snakes, there are those that actively go out hunting in locations where suitable prey is likely to abound, others that lie passively in ambush

waiting hopefully for their prey to pass by, and those that use a combination of these two methods. Snake species have various means of catching and killing prey.

The simplest method is the grab and swallow technique in which the snake, having located its prey by sight, smell, or a combination of both, grabs the prey in its mouth, where it is trapped by the recurved teeth, and begins to swallow it. Many of the primitive burrowing snakes as well as many colubrids, particularly fish- and amphibian-eaters, feed in this manner. It should be noted that in most cases the prey items of snakes using this technique are incapable of putting up much resistance and submit to being swallowed in a resigned manner.

Another method used to overpower prey is constriction, which is used by many colubrids and the boids. The prey is grabbed in the mouth and a reflex action immediately follows as a number of coils of the snake's body are rapidly wound around the prey, quickly immobilizing it. Sufficient pressure from the muscular coils is applied to suffocate the prey animal fairly rapidly but not, as is commonly believed, to crush every bone in its body. Constriction is used as a means of defending the snake from potentially dangerous prey such as reptiles, birds, and mammals capable of defending themselves with tooth, beak, or claw; once the prey is secured in the coils, it is held in such a

Left: The shuddery majesty of a Gaboon Viper's fangs. Is there any doubt why this is considered to be one of the most deadly snakes known? Photo: J. Visser.

Below: Predation works both ways. Top: A Dwarf Puff Adder, *Bitis peringueyi*, prepares to swallow a captured gecko. Bottom: A large centipede has killed and begun eating a small ground snake. Photos: Top: K. H. Switak; Bottom: W. B. Allen, Jr.

Feeding. Top Left: A California Kingsnake, *Lampropeltis getulus californiae*, swallowing a large gopher snake. Bottom Left: An Eastern Hognose, *Heterodon platyrhinos*, killing a toad. Right: A Dwarf Puff Adder, *Bitis peringueyi*, envenomating a gecko. Photos: Right and Top Left: K. H. Switak; Bottom Left: W. B. Allen, Jr.

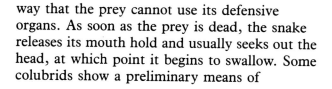

way that the prey cannot use its defensive organs. As soon as the prey is dead, the snake releases its mouth hold and usually seeks out the head, at which point it begins to swallow. Some colubrids show a preliminary means of constriction, in that they subdue the prey by pressing it against a solid surface with part of the body. The author has seen a captive Common Kingsnake, *Lampropeltis getulus*, swallowing a mouse while at the same time

An Eastern Coral Snake, *Micrurus fulvius*, swallowing a garter snake. Photo: R. T. Zappalorti.

restraining two further mice by pressing them against the wall of the terrarium.

The most refined method of overpowering prey practiced by snakes is, of course, envenomation. A venomous snake introduces sufficient poison into its prey to kill it or at least to paralyze it. In some species of rear-fanged snakes and elapids and hydrophiids, the grab and swallow technique is used with the added advantage of the prey being immobilized by envenomation. Some elapids, most viperids, and crotalids bite the prey, inject it with venom, then release it. In such cases the prey often covers a considerable distance before it becomes immobilized by the effect of the envenomation. The snake will pause for a few minutes, making no attempt to pursue the prey, then it will almost leisurely follow the track of the stricken prey, using its olfactory senses. When it finds the dead or dying prey, it will (usually) seek out the head end and begin to swallow it. Like constriction, envenomation is also a method of defending the snake from potentially dangerous prey.

Swallowing: One of a snake's most remarkable properties is its ability to swallow prey several times larger than its own head, thus enabling it to take in up to 400 times its daily nutritional requirements in a single meal! However, there are many grossly exaggerated stories with regard to the size of prey swallowed by some of the larger boids. Let us first look at the mechanism that allows a snake to swallow such large prey. Firstly, most snakes have an extremely large gape and recurved teeth that allow them to catch and retain hold of relatively large animals. Most of the snake's jaw bones are independently movable and, as the mouth is opened, the palatine and pterygoid bones are drawn forward by the relevant muscles. This, in turn, causes the maxillae to slide upward under the prefrontals, and, at the same time, the quadrate swings forward and turns outward, together with the palatal bones, thus enlarging

Feeding. Clockwise from top left: *Epicrates striatus*; *Heterodon nasicus kennerlyi*; *Elaphe guttata*; and *Lampropeltis g. getulus*. Photos (clockwise): J. T. Kellnhauser; K. H. Switak; K. H. Switak; W. B. Allen, Jr.

the buccal cavity. The lower jaw is also thrust forward, each side of the jaw capable of independent movement. The two halves of the lower jaw are connected at the chin by an extremely elastic ligament that allows the dentaries to spread a considerable distance. As the snake clamps its mouth shut over the prey the movable bones reverse and begin to draw the prey into the buccal cavity. In contrast to the highly mobile bones of the jaw and palate, those of the cranium form a very firm and rigid container for the brain, which protects this delicate organ from pressure and damage during the process of swallowing. By alternating movements of the various bones and the elasticity of the skin and muscles, the snake is gradually able to work prey into the gullet, where peristaltic action takes over and the food makes its way to the stomach.

Size of Prey: With regard to the size of prey, one can safely say that most snakes would be unable or at least unwilling to swallow animals more than ten times the volume of their own head. Stories of pythons or boas overpowering and swallowing adult cattle or even elephants can be taken with a grain of salt. However, there are authenticated cases of large pythons swallowing animals as large as a 37 kg (84 lb) goat, a 47 kg (104 lb) donkey, and a 53 kg (117 lb) pig.

Attacks of snakes on man with the intent of procuring a meal are rare, though there is, of course, the usual rash of dubious stories. There are a few semi-authenticated reports of large pythons and anacondas overpowering and attempting to or succeeding in swallowing people, usually children or women. In general, snakes secure prey of a size range suitable for easy swallowing, and there is a lower as well as an upper limit of size. While a captive Indian Python, *P. molurus*, for example, will feed eagerly on mice as a juvenile, there comes a time when such small prey becomes difficult to deal with and the snake has to graduate to rats, rabbits, or chickens. There is no reason to doubt that a similar situation exists in the reptile's natural habitat.

Frequency of Feeding: The fact that most snakes take large meals of whole prey animals that contain all of their nutritional requirements means that snakes feed relatively infrequently. In addition, snakes have a relatively slow rate of metabolism and a correspondingly low energy requirement when compared to many other animals. Being human, we often compare the feeding habits of other animals to ourselves. It therefore comes as a surprise to some that many snakes feed only every two to three weeks and at certain times of the year they may fast for even longer periods. In general, young, rapidly growing snakes will feed more often than adults, perhaps two to three times per week, with

This sequence of a Yellow Rat Snake, *Elaphe obsoleta quadrivittata*, swallowing a nestling bird was taken by R. T. Zappalorti.

Swallowing is an elaborate process in snakes, involving coordination of very flexible jaws with multiple rows of teeth. Photo: R. T. Zappalorti.

frequency of feeding diminishing as the reptile ages. Other factors that affect frequency of feeding include temperature, types of food (small invertebrate-eating snakes feed more frequently than those feeding on vertebrates), and periodic shedding. Some captive snakes seem to go on marathon fasts for no apparent reason. There are documented cases of an African Rock Python, *P. sebae*, fasting for 990 days and a Reticulated Python, *P. reticulatus*, going 679 days without a meal. A 5 m (16 ft) male Anaconda, *Eunectes murinus*, in the author's care once fasted for 420 days then took a muscovy duck; thereafter it continued to feed normally on chickens or ducks at two-week intervals. At the Frankfurt Zoo (Germany), a Gaboon Viper, *Bitis gabonica*, refused to feed for two and a half years, then took a guinea pig.

Digestion: The organs of a snake's digestive system, like most of its other organs, are adapted to fit into the elongate shape. The esophagus is long, with a large number of longitudinal folds allowing for a high degree of distension. Peristaltic action in the esophagus is poorly developed, and it is mainly the muscles of the neck and body that push the food toward the stomach. The stomach is also endowed with a number of longitudinal folds that give it an exceptional capacity for expansion. Muscular action churns the food in the stomach, and it is

here that the main digestive process takes place.

Gastric juices with a high proportion of hydrochloric acid help digest the bones of the prey as well as the softer parts. Time taken to digest prey varies, depending on the type of prey and temperature. In cool conditions it may take a week or more before the prey is completely digested. During digestion in the stomach a large amount of gas is produced that further increases its distension.

When the food has decomposed into a semi-fluid mass, it passes into the small intestine, which is arranged in a great number of coils. The lining of the small intestine consists of numerous folds (villi) of mucous membrane that are amply supplied with blood capillaries. Food is further broken down here and the nutrients are absorbed into the bloodstream. The undigested residue of the food then passes into the wider large intestine where more fluid is extracted and it becomes increasingly more solid in consistency. The fecal matter is compressed into solid pellets and stored at the base of the large intestine until defecation takes place.

The final section of the digestive tract is the cloaca, which also provides an outlet for urine and sexual secretions. The interior of the cloaca is divided into three sections: the coprodeum, where feces is gathered together; the urodeum, where the urinary and sexual passages enter;

and the proctodeum, which leads to the exterior via the vent, which lies transversely across the body. In female snakes the urinary and sexual passages are separate, but in male snakes they are joined to form a common channel emptying into the urodeum.

Various anal glands that produce often foul-smelling (to us) secretions are situated at the junction of the urodeum and proctodeum.

Excretory System and Water Balance: Although a snake's horny skin helps prevent it from losing water through evaporation, it is not completely infallible. In addition, water is lost through the actions of respiration and excretion. A snake therefore has to take in water to counteract these fluid losses. The amount of water required by snakes varies from species to species. Those existing in arid desert regions are adapted to gaining all or most of the fluid they require from that contained in the bodies of their prey, while those existing in less arid regions may drink regularly and frequently. Snakes drink by immersing their mouths into the water and drawing the water in through the labial notch by movements of the cheek and neck muscles. Arboreal and desert species may utilize dew and condensation on the ground, leaves, rocks, and even their own bodies.

Much of the regulation of water balance in the serpent's body is carried out by the kidneys, although the main function of these organs is to remove the nitrogenous products of metabolism.

In snakes as well as other reptiles and birds the highly toxic ammonia produced from the breakdown of proteins is converted in the elongate, lobeless liver to relatively harmless uric acid (urea, in the case of mammals). The uric acid, which is only slightly soluble in water, is transported to the kidneys in the bloodstream. If it were excreted from the body in solution, this would result in an enormous loss of water. Much of the water is therefore removed in the kidneys and the residue is passed to the cloaca, where even more water is removed. The final product is a semi-solid creamy white mass containing very little water. This is passed out through the vent, often together with intestinal feces. This explains the dark and light colored parts in the droppings of reptiles and birds.

Respiratory System: In most snakes the left lung is either vestigial or absent, only the right lung being functional. This is elongated, in some water snakes stretching back almost as far as the vent and acting additionally as a hydrostatic organ. Additional respiratory surfaces are provided by the vascular lining of the lung extending forward onto the roof of the windpipe. In view of the snake's method of feeding, there is a modification of the glottis (entrance to the windpipe) that allows it to be protruded forward over the tongue during the swallowing of large prey. The glottis, like the rest of the trachea, is reinforced with rings of cartilage that prevent it from collapsing under pressure. The snake is thus able to take a protracted bulky meal without danger of suffocation.

Heat Balance and the Circulatory System: In general, a snake's blood has much the same functions as that of other vertebrates. It is a medium of gaseous interchange, provides a means of transporting nutrients to the tissues and removing waste materials, and plays an important part in regulating the body temperature by transferring warmth from the body surface to the various internal organs. As in all of the vertebrates, the snake's heart pumps the blood around the body through a system of arteries, veins, and capillaries. Snakes, like all reptiles (other than the crocodilians, which possess a nearly complete four-chambered heart), have a heart that has two auricles and an incompletely divided ventricle so that in section it appears to have only three chambers. Thus the pulmonary and systematic circulations are only partially separated. Relative peculiarities of the blood vessels in snakes arise, of course, as a result of the extreme elongation of the body and the different sizes (or absence) of some paired organs.

Like all reptiles (and amphibians and fishes), snakes are ectothermic (relying on external heat sources) and poikilothermic (having a variable body temperature). This means that, unlike birds and mammals, they are not able to maintain a constant suitable body temperature

Although prey usually is swallowed head-first, in this case the nestling is being swallowed feet-first. Photo: R. T. Zappalorti.

As the nestling disappears down the rat snake's gullet, notice that the tongue and the glottis are free, allowing the snake to continue breathing. Photo: R. T. Zappalorti.

through normal metabolism. At reduced temperatures snakes become noticeably torpid and do not regain a full capacity to respond to stimuli until they again reach an adequate temperature. In order to continue to survive, the average snake must maintain its body temperature between 4° and 38°C, regardless of climatic conditions. The reptile may be able to survive temperatures just outside this range for short periods, but protracted periods of unsuitable temperatures will result in death or, at the very least, severe injury. Most snakes have a preferred optimum temperature for normal activity, and in most species this ranges between 18-35°C, although, of course, there are extremes, depending on the species and its habitat.

As a snake is unable to control its temperature by physiological means it has to resort to behavioral methods. The habits of various species differ considerably, depending on the climatic conditions. In equatorial conditions, for example, where temperatures remain fairly high and there are constant hours of day and night throughout the year, there is no period of winter hibernation and the chief hazard is overheating in the midday sun. In such cases, many species are nocturnal or burrowing, while those that are diurnal operate in the shade or during the hours of dawn and dusk (crepuscular). At excessively hot or dry times of the year, many species

estivate, becoming inactive for varying periods.

At higher latitudes and altitudes, snakes face the problems of greater ranges of temperature between night and day and more dramatically between summer and winter. In winter the environmental temperature may remain below the snake's activity levels for several months, in which case the reptile can only survive in a state of torpor in a frost-free subterranean refuge. In areas of permafrost, where the subsoil remains frozen throughout the year, no snakes can survive, although a few species reach into surprisingly high latitudes. *Vipera berus*, the Adder, for example, crosses the Arctic Circle,

A typical Vancouver Island Wandering Garter Snake, *Thamnophis elegans vagrans*. Photo: Dr. G. Dingerkus.

In the same population as the garter snake on the previous page, many melanistic specimens occur. This seems to be a response to the cool, humid climate, allowing the species to survive through any extremes of weather. Photo: Dr. G. Dingerkus.

reaching 68° North in Scandinavia, and *Thamnophis sirtalis*, the Common Garter Snake, reaches 67° North in the Yukon. In the Southern Hemisphere, the pit viper *Bothrops ammodytoides* reaches a southern limit for snakes at about 50° South in Argentina. Altitude poses

similar temperature problems for montane species, but again *V. berus* reaches 3000 m (9750 ft) in the Swiss Alps, while *Agkistrodon himalayanus*, the Himalayan Pit Viper, reaches a record altitude of 5000 m (16,250 ft).

Wherever snakes live, they actively seek out areas in which the temperature range allows them to operate at their preferred temperature. Thus snakes from colder climates must bask in the sun to reach their optimum activity temperature, although they will move back into the shade if there is any danger of overheating. Some diurnal snakes may become partially nocturnal on warm summer nights, while some nocturnal species may gain a little extra heat at night by lying on rocks or even roads that have retained heat from the daytime sun.

Snake species are adjusted to the climates to which they are native and usually are unable to satisfactorily acclimate to alien conditions, an important point to bear in mind when considering housing for captive specimens.

The perfect way not to keep or even temporarily cage a snake. Photo of *Lampropeltis getulus holbrooki*: S. C. and H. Miller.

Housing for Captive Snakes

There are several types of accommodations that can be used for keeping captive snakes. A container in which living reptiles or amphibians are kept may be referred to as a vivarium or terrarium. A room or building in which several terraria are kept may be referred to as a reptilarium or serpentarium, while an outdoor enclosure for these animals may be called a reptiliary—or even herptiliary if a selection of amphibians and reptiles are kept together. (Actually, most herp-keepers say they keep

is now possible to purchase ready-made terraria with all systems electronically controlled.

Many enthusiasts, however, prefer to make their own terraria. The great advantage of this is that they can be made to a pattern tailored to the requirements of a particular species and at the same time can be designed to meet the esthetic preferences of the individual. Another plus for making your own terraria is that you usually can save a considerable amount of expense. A terrarium may be manufactured

terraria in reptile rooms or herp rooms—the other terms are considered "quaint" today, at least by American keepers.) At one time a terrarium for snakes consisted of a simple glass-fronted box with an electric light bulb for warmth. This was often left on day and night, week in and week out, so that the reptiles were subjected to constant high temperature, bright light, and low humidity. Although many species may have seemed to do well in such terraria at first, the unnatural conditions would sooner or later contribute to the demise of the reptiles. Our correlation of ecological studies to captive snake-keeping has advanced dramatically and it

Two views of a well-built snake room designed, in this case, for raising tricolored kingsnakes. The closet is used to house the incubator as well as for storage. This type of herp room is easy to heat and allows simple control of the snakes. Photos: R. W. Applegate.

An old-fashioned aquarium tank used as the basic snake terrarium. Although such simple terraria are commonly used by beginners, they are not really the best type of housing for snakes. Photos: J. Dommers.

from a host of different materials and, with a little artistic imagination, can be made into an extremely attractive feature or focal point in the modern home. There is no reason, in fact, for a terrarium to be any less attractive than a colorful exhibit of tropical fish in a planted aquarium. Choice of materials will reflect the habits of the species to be kept; timber, for example, would be unsuitable for an aqua-terrarium or for snakes requiring an excessively humid environment, but would be ideal for desert-dwelling species.

Terrarium shapes are immaterial as long as they provide the various species with conditions suited to their habits. Tree snakes, for example, would require a tall, roomy terrarium with facilities to climb. A long, low terrarium would be more suitable for terrestrial species. Semi-arboreal, active species such as racers would require more space in which to move about. Some of the more languid species, such as pythons and puff adders, can make do with relatively little space. An aqua-terrararium is necessary for semi-aquatic species (such as many water snakes of the subfamily Natricinae), while totally aquatic species, such as those of *Erpeton* and *Acrochordus*, would require an aquarium containing water with little or no land. It is a waste of time to provide many species with more space than they require. A Sand Boa, for example, will soon find a favorite spot and will spend most of its time there, whatever size you make the terrarium. Most snake species actually prefer to live in a confined space. Being thigmotactic, they seek out confined spaces in which to rest and, when not actively hunting or breeding, will spend most of their time there. In the wild, the size of a snake's territory is usually dictated by the availability of food, so if food items are plentiful the reptile's range of movement will be correspondingly small. In captivity the snake is provided with adequate food, so a fairly limited range of movement is required.

Environmental requirements in the terrarium will vary, depending on the wild habitat of the species. Unlike many mammals and birds, which often can adapt quickly to an alien climate providing they receive adequate food, most reptiles find it difficult or impossible to adjust to temperatures and degrees of humidity strange to them. For simplicity, terraria and their environments can be divided loosely into four categories, but a knowledge of the species's wild habitat is important so that additional factors can be taken into account.

Whether a terrarium is heated or not will, of course, depend on where you live as much as where the snake comes from. If, for example, you live in a warm, humid climate and you intend to keep snakes from a warm, humid climate, then your environmental additions to the terrarium will be minimal. But as the majority of snake-keepers seem to dwell in temperate to cool climates, the four basic types will be as follows:

1) *The unheated dry terrarium*: for species that live in cool but relatively dry conditions, such as temperate heathland, steppe, or prairie. The range of temperature change is high, between day and night and between summer and winter. Species from such regions require a period of winter hibernation if their biological cycle is to be kept normal.

2) *The unheated humid terrarium*: for species that live in and around bodies of water or in moist meadow or woodland in cool to warm temperate regions. The range of temperatures is not so great, but such species may also require a winter period of hibernation. The aqua-terrarium is also included in this category.

3) *The heated dry terrarium*: for species that live in subtropical to tropical desert or semi-desert (arid) situations. Temperature ranges for inland or montane species (as opposed to coastal habitats) would still be high, especially between night and day. A short period of hibernation may also be required.

4) *The heated humid terrarium*: for tropical rain-forest species. Temperature and humidity remain relatively high and constant, day and night, throughout the year. Hibernation normally is unnecessary.

There are, of course, many borderline types of terrarium, and the only way to decide what kind of accommodation is suitable for a certain species is to obtain information on the habitat from a climatic atlas or from a fellow herpetologist who is successful with the species in question.

TERRARIA CONSTRUCTED LARGELY FROM TIMBER

Having decided on the snake species to be kept, a terrarium can be purchased or built. Timber is a useful material for constructing terraria that do not sustain a great amount of humidity. If used in moist conditions, timber will, of course, deteriorate more rapidly than other more suitable materials. It should be quite

This simple but well-made wooden terrarium provides all the essentials for keeping a medium-sized snake. Photo: S. C. and H. Miller.

easy for the handyman to make a presentable display terrarium, which is basically a wooden box with a glass viewing panel at the front. The type of timber used can vary from solid hardwood or pine planking to plywood of varying thicknesses. Thin plywood would require a solid framework, but probably the easiest material to use is 12 mm (half-inch) thick, exterior quality plywood that may be glued and tacked together without a frame. Chipboard or hardboard could also be used, but these materials will require a coat of primer followed by an undercoat and a couple of coats of good quality lead-free gloss paint to protect then from moisture. The exterior of a plywood terrarium can be made to look most attractive by staining and varnishing to match or to contrast with the other furniture in the room where you wish to have your display. The interior can also be varnished or painted in colors to compliment the display in the

Although boas and pythons are large snakes, they are inactive and need relatively small cages. Children should never be allowed near a large snake without an adult present to supervise. Photo: S. C. and H. Miller.

terrarium. You must always allow several days for paint, varnish, etc., to thoroughly dry out before adding any animals to cages.

The glass or plexiglass viewing panel, which may also double as an access door (an additional door will be required for dangerous or wild species, as we will discuss later in the text), may be mounted on a hinged frame. It is best to have the hinges on the bottom and let the door swing outward and downward. This helps prevent snakes escaping and also allows you to let the door hang right down during maintenance operations, rather than having to prop it open. Alternatively, the glass may be slid into grooves, horizontally or vertically. In larger terraria it may be necessary to have two or more doors that may be separated by one or more fixed windows.

Adequate ventilation holes should be drilled in the upper third of each end of the terrarium and also in the roof. Remember that the holes must be much smaller in diameter than the smallest snake you intend to keep! To be doubly secure against escapes, the ventilation holes may be covered with a sheet of perforated zinc or wire gauze. Where very small, harmless species are being kept, the ventilation holes can be covered with plastic mesh (insect screening is ideal). The edges of the gauze should be secured and tidied up with a narrow framework made from half-round beading. Provision should be made for concealment of the heating and lighting apparatus, which will be discussed later.

Sometimes it is possible to purchase a plastic base tray (of the type used for cat litter boxes), and the terrarium could be built around the dimensions of this so that you will have a sliding floor tray. Such a tray is hygienic, will hold the substrate material, will prevent moisture from damaging the wooden floor of the cage, and is easy to remove for routine maintenance or cleaning. The tray must be tight-fitting, however, or the snakes will find their way beneath it. It is very difficult to make a cage with a tray bottom truly escape-proof.

TERRARIA CONSTRUCTED LARGELY FROM GLASS

A revolution in the aquarium industry was the advent of silicone rubber sealing compounds of the type used for sealing joints around glass windows, etc. Such material is invaluable to the terrarium keeper. It is relatively inexpensive, and sheets of glass can be cemented together with it to produce a strong, watertight container of almost any desired shape and size. Moreover, sections of glass can be left out at the ends or the back so that ventilated access doors of drilled plywood, plastic sheeting, plexiglass, or framed gauze can be fitted. The sealer is supplied in tubes that can be fitted into a caulking gun to make application easy. It may be obtained from aquarium stores.

As an example, a tall terrarium to house a pair of small tree snakes (*Ahaetulla* or *Chrysopelia* species, for example) can be constructed from 6

With a climbing branch, a decent substrate, a water bowl, and a basking light, most snakes will do well for long periods. The log and the plant provide cover, also a necessity for a happy snake. Photo: S. C. and H. Miller.

mm (quarter-inch) thick tempered glass. Unless you are adept at glass cutting, it is best to get your glass dealer to cut the sheets to size for you. At the same time you can ask him to grind smooth the edges that will be left exposed after construction (such as around the top) to eliminate the risk of cut fingers. For a terrarium 120 cm (48 in) high x 80 cm (32 in) wide x 50 cm (20 in) deep the following sheets of glass will be required: one base 80x50 cm (32x20 in), two sides 120x50 cm (48x20 in), one front 80x120.6 cm (32x48.5 in) (to allow for glass thickness), and two rear panes 80x40 cm (32x16 in). In addition, a sheet of 6 mm (quarter-inch) thick plywood or plexiglass is required for the 80x40cm (32x16 in) access/ventilation door at the rear. This sheet should be symmetrically drilled with a series of small ventilation holes. The door is slid into plastic runners that are cemented to the top and bottom of the open part of the glass at the rear.

The construction should be carried out on a firm, flat surface that preferably is covered with an old blanket or several thicknesses of newspaper. Lay the base sheet down and apply a continuous strip of sealer along the bottom edge of one of the side panels and place this in position on top of one of the base edges. Get an assistant to hold this in position while you apply a further strip of sealer along the outer front edges of the base and side pane, ready to receive the front pane, which then can be held in position with adhesive tape. The other side panel is then cemented into position and secured with adhesive tape. The lower rear pane is then cemented in position and secured with adhesive tape. The whole construction should be left for 24 hours for the sealer to set thoroughly. Then it is turned and laid on its front and the upper rear pane is cemented and taped into position (it will be difficult to do this if the terrarium is standing the right way up as gravity will cause it to slide down). Allow another four hours for this to partially set before applying a continuous strip of sealer along all internal joints for added strength. The sealer can be smoothed over with a wet finger. Any sealer that accidentally gets

onto the viewing panels should be allowed to set before it is scraped off with a razor blade.

When using sealing compounds, be sure to follow the manufacturer's instructions especially with regard to ventilation. The strong acetic acid vapors from the sealing compound can be unpleasant and overpowering. The sealer should be perfectly set after another 24 hours, when the adhesive tape may be removed, the excess sealer scraped away, and the glass thoroughly cleaned and polished from both sides.

The terrarium lid is best made from plywood and is constructed so that it just fits over the top of the main container. The framework of the lid can be placed just below the edges of the lid to form lips to prevent the lid from sliding too far down. The depth of the lid will depend on the type and size of heating and lighting apparatus to be used, but 20 cm (8 in) should be adequate. Small holes (covered) are drilled in the top of the lid for ventilation purposes. The lid can be painted or varnished to make it look more attractive. Strips of plastic or vinyl of a similar color to the lid may be cemented around the bottom of the container to hide the depth of the substrate material.

Acrylic sheeting may also be used for

Left: A simple display terrarium containing live plants as well as a snake. Such a display may look nice, but few snakes can adapt to such constant exposure to light and people. Photo: A. v. d. Nieuwenhuizen.

Below: Currently in vogue are fiberglass cages with sliding acrylic front panels. They are fairly expensive but are easy to maintain and long-lasting. Photos: W. B. Allen, Jr.

A highly decorative bank of snake cages built into a wall and turned into a centerpoint of room decor. Photo: S. C. and H. Miller.

terrarium construction, but a problem with this material is that it scratches easily and will not stand up to regular cleaning without an opaque film of fine scratches forming on the surfaces.

BUILT-IN TERRARIA

One of the most satisfying types of terrarium is one that is made from substantial materials, such as concrete blocks, clay bricks, or timber. Such a permanent display may be built into an alcove or be free-standing in a living area, conservatory, greenhouse, or spare room. The advantage of built-in terraria, which are particularly suitable for larger species such as boids, is that they can be constructed to match the internal decoration or form a focal point. A solid concrete base in the terrarium will mean that a permanent pond can be constructed in the floor, while artificial cliff faces incorporating controllable hiding places can be constructed into the walls. Plant troughs can be built into the decor both in and outside the terrarium. Though there is virtually no limit to the designs that can be used, such a project is a major one and should be planned very carefully from the outset. Many enthusiasts have built some very attractive and functional exhibits that are a credit to a combination of their scientific and artistic talents. Such a display may be a tropical rain-forest exhibit, complete with a waterfall, lush growing plants, and underwater viewing into a stream or pond. Fish or turtles may be kept in the filtered and treated pond water, while tree snakes may populate the planted areas. A good way of getting some ideas with regard to constructing permanent or semi-permanent terraria is to make a point of visiting

zoological gardens with reptile houses. Although such collections may vary from the esthetic standpoint, the creators of such public displays are experts, and most of them will be pleased to discuss their experiences with enthusiastic amateurs.

As an example of a built-in terrarium for large pythons or boas, the following suggestion may give you some ideas. Sizes given will, of course, vary depending on the amount of space available and the size of the reptiles to be kept. Imagine we have an alcove some 3 m (10 ft) long and 1.5 m (5 ft) deep between a wall and a fireplace (for example). This would give us a floor area of 4.5 sq m (50 sq ft), adequate for (say) a pair of Boa Constrictors or Indian Pythons. It is best to raise the floor level of a permanent terrarium (for esthetic as well as practical purposes). **Before making a heavy construction from blocks and concrete, ensure that you have a solid base on which to work.** You would not, for example, set about building a heavy concrete structure on a raised wooden floor or in upper stories! In such cases it is best to make do with timber.

Assuming we have a concrete base on which to work in our alcove, we can first build three walls about 1 m (3.25 ft) high, one abutting each outer wall of the alcove (next to fireplace and at opposite end) and one midway between the two. A sheet (or sheets) of 12 mm (half-inch) shuttering plywood is placed over the three level walls to act as a base for the concrete floor. A few large holes can be drilled into the plywood at the points where it rests on the tops of the walls, to allow the concrete to come into contact with the bricks. A piece of strong plank about

10 cm (4 in) wide is attached to the floorboard all the way along its front length, to hold in the concrete floor when it is poured. The underside of the floorboard should be adequately supported with wooden or metal props (small tubular jacks are ideal).

At the point where the deepest part of the pool is planned, a 2.5 cm (1 in) minimum diameter hole should be drilled to take the pond drainpipe. It should be arranged to take a standard sink or bath drain with a rubber plug or, alternatively, a gate valve can be installed in the pipe below the floor. It is best to direct the pipe into an existing drain, which may mean making a hole near the base of the rear wall of the building. If you have problems in doing this it may be best to seek advice from a plumber. The drainhole should be firmly plugged with newspaper during construction to prevent concrete entering the pipe.

To keep the area waterproof and to help prevent the plywood from rotting after a time, a sheet of heavy construction plastic is placed over the whole area and taken about 15 cm (6 in) up the walls. A small hole will have to be cut for the drainpipe and this can be sealed around the pipe with silicone rubber sealing compound.

A good concrete mix for the floor is one part cement, two parts sharp sand, and four parts gravel, mixed with water to make a pliable consistency. The concrete is poured to form a first layer about 7.5 cm (3 in) thick. For added reinforcement, a panel of welded steel mesh can be placed in the concrete, ensuring that it does not emerge through the surface. The cement can be compacted and levelled by tamping with a piece of flat wood, but the surface should be left fairly rough to form a key for the next layer.

Allow about 24 hours for the first layer to set before preparing another batch of concrete. The pool should be constructed with fairly dry concrete and the surrounding floor should be made to slope gently down into it. In other words, the whole floor is drainable through the pool drain. If gravel is to be used as a substrate, a lip should be formed around the pool and a small pipe should pass through this at the lowest part of the floor. This will stop gravel falling into the pool and facilitate drainage when you are washing down. Ensure that the drainhole for the pool is at its lowest point and make it watertight by using a sealing compound between the outlet and the concrete.

Parts of the floor and the walls can have natural rocks built into them, cementing them together to form shelves, caves, and cliffs.

Alternatively, artificial rocks can be made by sculpturing concrete with a trowel and smoothing it into shape with a paint brush. With a little practice the technique of concrete sculpturing can soon be mastered and some attractive, natural-looking rock formations can be constructed by using old housebricks or concrete blocks and mortar. A final cement wash can be applied over the whole area. This will fill in any tiny cracks and crevices that would harbor dirt and disease as well as providing a relatively smooth, easy to clean finish. A suitable wash can be made by using one part cement, one part sand, and a coloring/plasticizing agent. These are mixed together with water and continually stirred until the mixture has the consistency of thick, smooth pea soup, adding more cement or water to reach the desired consistency. The mixture is applied with a large paintbrush. A bucket of water should be available to wash out the brush each time it becomes clogged, but excess water should be squeezed out of the brush before proceeding. During application the mixture should be stirred at frequent intervals to prevent it from settling. If two or three mixes of different colors are made these can be applied alternatively in patches or streaks, each being subtly blended into the next. Such a technique, with practice, will produce extremely natural-looking artificial rock surfaces.

After doing all this, you will have an open-fronted terrarium. The next job is to construct the front viewing panels. These are best made as a timber framework into which framed glass doors are fitted, either hinged to open outward or fixed to slide in runners.

The space below the terrarium can be concealed behind doors. This can be used as valuable storage space as well as for access to drains, etc.

Facilities for ventilation should be incorporated into the bottom and top of the cage to allow for circulation of air. A convenient method of heating and ventilation, which will also keep the viewing panel demisted in a humid terrarium, is to mount a radiator attached to thermostatically controlled central heating pipes under the terrarium. A space between the front of the floor and the framework is left free and covered with welded wire mesh. This allows warm air from the radiator to rise up the inside of the glass doors and out through ventilation holes in the roof. The doors concealing the space below the terrarium should also have

The interior of one cage in a bank of homemade snake cages. Note that all the comforts of home are present, including retreats for the snake. Photo: J. Gee.

ventilation holes to allow replacement of fresh air and a continuous current. The lighting and accessory radiant heating apparatus can be set into the roof of the cage behind strong mesh.

TERRARIUM HEATING

Most species of snakes will require supplementary heating of one form or another in the terrarium, though in some regions this may only be required in the winter. The main factor to bear in mind is that captive snakes must have temperature ranges similar to those that prevail in their native habitat. There are many different kinds of heating apparatus that may be used in the indoor terrarium, and the types will also vary depending on the size of the cages. For a number of terraria housing snakes from a similar climate, especially those not requiring a high light or radiant heat intensity, it is sufficient to control the temperature of the room itself rather than the individual cages. Such a system is ideal for breeding rooms in which larger numbers of small species or juveniles are kept in small terraria and plastic containers into which adequate ventilation holes have been drilled.

Where several different species are kept and in larger terraria, each terrarium must have its own individual heating system. The heating apparatus must be installed, tested, and found adequate before the decoration is completed and reptiles are introduced to the cage. It is advisable to have a thermometer mounted in each cage (sophisticated modern digital thermometers are ideal) and to have the heating apparatus in operation for at least four hours to ensure that you are producing the correct temperature range. Adjustments may have to be made through trial and error until you have got it right. Remember that most species seek out their preferred body temperature by thermoregulation, so a limited range of temperatures should be provided. This can be achieved by having the major heat source at one end, so that various heat levels are available from one end of the terrarium to the other. A number of hiding places should be provided at the various temperature spots so a snake can select the one in which it feels most comfortable. A snake may also move from one hiding place to another in order to adjust its temperature.

Many species require a temperature reduction at night. In most cases this is simply a matter of switching off the heat source; the room temperature of the average household is adequate for most species. However, where cages are kept in unheated rooms in cold winters, nighttime heating will be necessary. The raising of the daytime temperature and its lowering at night should take place at the same times every day, but allow for seasonal changes. For example, temperatures will drop slowly in the fall, reaching the minimum for the species in midwinter; the reverse will occur from spring to midsummer.

The use of thermostats and time switches will be very useful and will ensure regularity of day/night temperatures that are not so easy to achieve manually—especially if you are frequently away.

Types of Heating Apparatus

Tungsten Lamps: At one time the ordinary tungsten light bulb was the exclusive method of heating and lighting terraria. They are still useful if used in conjunction with other apparatus and they have certain advantages in that they are inexpensive, supply light as well as heat, and come in various sizes. The required temperatures can be produced by experimenting with numbers of bulbs of various wattages. A useful means of nighttime heating is a bulb of low wattage colored blue or red to minimize the light given off. The main disadvantage of these bulbs is that the quality of light they emit is unsuitable for growing plants and breeding many snake species, although they are quite adequate to use for supplementary lighting.

Infrared Lamps: Infrared lamps of the type used in poultry hatcheries and by pig breeders are very useful for larger terraria. Such lamps have built-in reflectors that direct the heat into a limited area and are useful for heating up basking sites or the surface of the substrate in the case of burrowing snakes. Both red-light and white-light emitting lamps are available, and both have their functions (red lamps are useful at night in cold climates). The temperature of the glass bulbs in some of these high-wattage (usually available in 150-500 watt sizes) lamps becomes very high, and care should be taken not to splash them with water when they are switched on as they may shatter. The temperature of the surfaces below the lamps can be lowered or raised simply by moving the lamp up or down.

Ceramic Heaters: Ceramic heaters are very useful as they do not emit visible light. These may come in the shape of a bulb or a curved plate and can be fitted into a simple bulb socket. They release radiant heat, the bulb-type in most directions, the plate-type in the direction in which it is aimed. They are useful for nightheating and should be controlled with a thermostat.

All forms of radiant heat lamps should be installed outside the terrarium with the heat directed through wire mesh, or they should be adequately encased with mesh to prevent the animals from coming into contact with them and getting burned. The thermoregulatory function of some snakes may become disorganized if they are exposed to high temperature sources, and they may attempt to coil around the lamps and be severely burned if not protected. Never direct radiant heat directly onto terrarium plants from nearby or the plants will quickly desiccate and die.

Central Heating: Ordinary domestic oil, coal, or gas central heating systems can be used to heat large terraria or snake rooms. Consult a heating engineer to get advice on how this may best be done. A system of pipes and radiators under cages can be installed in such a way that convection currents of warm air are directed through the terraria from below and out through the top.

Thermostatically controlled valves and a by-pass system will ensure individual temperatures for terraria. These methods are perhaps only suitable for very large herp rooms or public reptile houses.

Heating Cables, Tapes, and Pads: Horticultural electrical heating cables and tapes also have their uses in the terrarium. Cables are useful in heating the substrate for burrowing and desert species, though they should be used in only half the substrate, giving the snakes a chance to seek out a preferred temperature. Tapes are especially useful for running along the bases of a number of small terraria of the type used for rearing juvenile snakes. Heat pads of the type used to heat aquaria or seed trays from below are useful for small aqua-terraria.

Aquarium Heaters: There are many kinds of thermostatically controlled glass-tube aquarium heaters available that are very useful to the snake-keeper. In aqua-terraria, the heater is simply placed in the water and used as it would be in an aquarium. In a humid terrarium the heater may be placed in a concealed jar of water (which should be topped up at regular intervals). Some brands of these heaters can also be used out of water and may be placed in a special cavity of the artificial rockwork to heat up certain areas.

Tofohr Heater: A simple but effective heater and humidifier (known in Germany as the Tofohr Ofen after the person who invented it) consists of a simple tungsten light bulb mounted inside a tin can. Lugs are cut in the top of the can and drilled so that it can be screwed, open top downward, over a hole cut in the terrarium base. The light bulb socket is fixed to a removable bracket beneath the cage so that the bulb will pass partially into the can. A piece of clay drainpipe or a large clay flowerpot is placed over the can and, in the case of the former, a wire mesh lid is placed on top. A small dish of water placed on top of the can will prevent dust burning and provide humidity. The water in the dish should be kept topped up.

LIGHTING

Adequate terrarium lighting is just as essential to snakes as correct heating. Light/dark cycles are necessary for all species, whether nocturnal or diurnal, though strong light is not strictly necessary for the former. Many diurnal species require natural sunlight or a good substitute. When it is considered that the intensity of light produced by a 40-watt tungsten bulb at a distance of 1 meter (approx. 3.25 ft) is only about 1/3,000 of that provided by the full summer sun, it can be seen that finding a good substitute will pose some difficulty. Even the so-called daylight fluorescent bulbs provide only

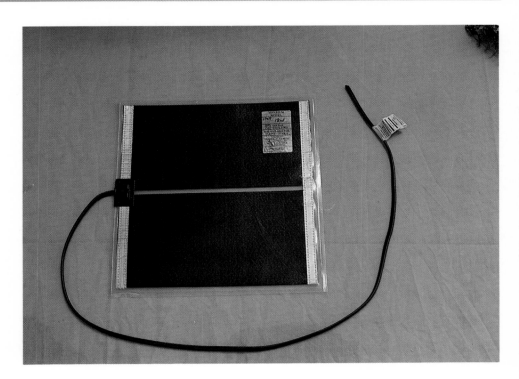

about 1/500 of natural sunlight intensity, while a high-wattage mercury vapor lamp will emit roughly 1/150.

Sunlight: It is almost an impossibility to artificially reproduce natural sunlight intensity in the terrarium. Therefore, wherever possible, natural light should not be totally ignored when choosing a site for your terrarium. It may be placed near a window or even built into a window that receives not more than four hours of natural sunlight per day. Any more than this will bring a danger of overheating unless you can provide an extremely efficient ventilation system. Morning or late afternoon sun is preferable for the confined volume of a terrarium, so an ideal situation would be near a west- or east-facing window. Natural sunlight through glass is of reduced quality, so if you have a portable terrarium with a mesh lid you can move it onto the veranda or into the garden on suitable days, so that natural sunlight reaches the reptiles. (Beware of drafts!)

Ultraviolet Lighting: In recent years, intense experimentation by a number of researchers on the subject has resulted in much improved knowledge of the field of artificial lighting for terraria. The most important parts of sunlight to reptiles are the infrared and ultraviolet rays, the former for heat absorption, the latter to aid in the production of vitamin D_3. A combination of infrared lamps and broad-spectrum fluorescent tubes has been found to give a reasonable sunlight simulation for many species. Infrared lamps have already been discussed in the section on heating, and it is only the white-light type that emits any appreciable light, although all infrared lamps are suitable for use by basking snakes. Ultraviolet lamps in themselves have a limited value in the terrarium, although some herpetoculturists recommend that certain species of diurnal snakes be exposed to ultraviolet rays for a few minutes each week. Exposure to an ultraviolet

Many types of heaters can be used with snakes. Shown is an under-tank heating pad. Photo: S. C. and H. Miller.

Although a paludarium can be very attractive, it also is very difficult to maintain. Photo: B. Kahl.

light should never be for more than 20 minutes at a time and not more than twice per week; prolonged or too frequent exposure can cause incurable damage to the animal's skin and eyes. In small doses, however, ultraviolet rays have proven to enhance the color and general health of many species.

Broad-spectrum Lighting: Originally produced for horticultural use, broad-spectrum fluorescent tubes are much safer to use than ultraviolet lamps. They emit light from the blue end of the spectrum, including small but sufficient quantities of ultraviolet rays of an intensity unlikely to cause any damage to the reptiles' health. In recent years the use of such tubes in the terrarium has considerably improved the maintenance of species that were hitherto regarded as difficult.

Manufacturers of lighting appliances are continually working on improvements, and many have realized the importance of such lighting to the aquarist and terrarium-keeper as well as the horticulturist. The use of such lights in a planted terrarium is almost essential if the plants as well as the animals are to thrive. Manufacturers are usually pleased to provide specification details of lamps available, and it is both useful and interesting to obtain the various information leaflets.

Mercury Vapor and Halogen Lighting: Other forms of lighting that may be considered for large terraria include mercury vapor and quartz halogen lamps, both of which emit a greater intensity of light than most other readily available artificial light forms. Such lamps are extremely powerful and may have wattages of 500 or more. They may emit a high level of radiant heat, so they are unsuitable for small terraria unless suspended well outside the cage. The use of such lamps will promote lush plant growth provided the distance is great enough to prevent desiccation of the foliage.

HUMIDITY

Humidity, or the lack of it, is an important factor for captive snakes. For obvious reasons, snakes that are native to arid environments will not survive for long in a tropical rain-forest terrarium. Conversely, it would be foolish to

expect a creature native to damp woodland to survive for long in a desert terrarium. With regard to humidity, it is probably easier to keep desert creatures than those from humid environments as the forms of heating and lighting in the average terrarium automatically tend to create a dry environment providing only a small drinking water vessel is used.

It is necessary to provide some means of artificial humidification for those species from humid habitats (but remembering that some species come from areas that are humid only at certain times of the year). The creation of correct humidity levels in a terrarium is not quite as difficult as may at first be thought. In small planted terraria, regular mist spraying of the plants and decorations is all that is required, though this may have to be done two or more times per day during dry periods. Spraying is important to many species of small tree snakes that acquire their drinking water solely from droplets on the foliage.

In the aqua-terrarium, where there is a relatively large water surface area, natural evaporation of the water will create its own humidity levels, which will be enhanced by the action of the animals entering and leaving the water. Further slow evaporation of the water can be created by using an aquarium heater in the water and can be further increased by installing an aquarium aerator (at the same time, one could consider using an airlift filter to help keep the water clear).

Small air pumps, filters, etc., can be purchased from aquarium shops and can be used in the aqua-terrarium for increasing humidity, increasing temperature of the airspace, and ventilation, simultaneously. Another method of maintaining humidity is to use a Tofohr heater.

In large brick and concrete terraria, a waterfall running over rocks and controlled by a small circulation pump will not only increase the attractiveness of the display, it can be functional in maintaining higher humidity levels for snakes requiring them.

Whatever kind of humidification is used and even where semi-aquatic snakes are being kept, it is important that the reptiles have dry areas in which to bask or hide. A permanently wet environment can lead to skin diseases breaking out in many species. For snakes that come from areas with well-defined wet and dry seasons, some attempt must be made to reproduce these conditions in the terrarium. Such seasonal changes in humidity may have a bearing on the reproductive cycles of many species.

VENTILATION

Inadequate ventilation in the terrarium can lead to excessive carbon dioxide in the terrarium base, permanent dampness of the substrate, and a possible buildup of harmful microorganisms. In such conditions the animals will suffer stress, lose much of their resistance, and succumb to disease. In basic terrarium construction,

Yes, you can simulate a rain-forest environment in your home if you are careful and can tolerate a lot of maintenance. Vine snakes of various types do well in such aqua-terraria, but most snakes cannot tolerate the constant high humidity. Photos: B. Kahl.

provision must be made for adequate ventilation whether by holes drilled in the walls at varying heights or by mesh-covered panels. The best kind of ventilation is where the air enters the base of a terrarium near a heater or a heated surface and travels upward by convection, leaving near the top. This will allow regular total air exchange in the cage without producing cold drafts.

In some cases it may be necessary to provide additional ventilation apparatus rather than rely on convection currents. An aquarium aerator will provide extra ventilation in a small terrarium, and the air-outlet need not necessarily be immersed in water if a lower humidity is required. For terraria kept in stuffy living rooms, particularly if the owners are smokers, it is advisable to have the fresh air drawn in from outside. It can be passed over an underfloor heater before it enters the terrarium through a special ventilator. In reptile houses or serpentaria it is wise to have an exhaust system so that the whole area surrounding the terraria is adequately ventilated.

Full use should be made of fresh air, which is free and beneficial to animals and plants. On warm days portable terraria may be placed near open windows, outside on the veranda, or in the garden, but be sure to give protection from the sun's rays entering through glass. Green

horticultural shading material can be erected, making a sort of awning over the terrarium to protect it from strong sunlight.

GREENHOUSE OR CONSERVATORY

An exciting concept of snake-keeping is to have the reptiles range free in a greenhouse, conservatory, or tropical house. Done with care and adequate pre-planning, the advantages of this are manyfold and far outweigh the

disadvantages. The main problems will be related to creating the right environment in a large area and preventing escapes and disappearances. However, once the correct conditions are achieved the greenhouse terrarium can create an enormous amount of pleasure. A greenhouse is perhaps most suited to a tropical rain-forest display. A miniature jungle can be created and high levels of humidity can be maintained by the use of a waterfall and regular damping down. If you are more ambitious and can bear the expense, sprinklers can be installed so that rainfall can be regularly produced. Basking areas can be placed in several strategic positions using heat lamps. The background temperature should not fall below 18°C, and the reptiles should be able to select their own preferred temperatures by basking under the lamps or in sunlight. It may be necessary to cover part of the roof or walls with horticultural screening to prevent overheating from the summer sun.

Windows and ventilation holes should be covered with a suitable mesh to prevent escapes. Pipes and other heating appliances should be caged in with mesh to prevent the reptiles from burning themselves and from disappearing into cavities associated with such systems. All hiding places should be accessible and controllable, as it will be necessary to catch the inhabitants from time to time. It should be possible to keep a number of groups of compatible species in such an environment, a combination of aquatic, terrestrial, and arboreal snakes, for example. Venomous species are not suited for such accommodations, for obvious reasons. It may be possible to breed lizards and frogs in the same environment, thus providing almost self-sufficient natural food for many species. The proud owner of such a setup will be able to spend many hours puttering about in his very own jungle, studying the habits of his interesting charges. Breeding of snakes should be easily achieved in such an environment, though eggs may have to be removed for artificial incubation.

OUTDOOR ENCLOSURES

The Reptiliary: One of the most satisfactory methods of keeping snakes in almost natural conditions is in an outdoor reptile house. Species native to the area in which they are kept will have no climatic problems, and it is possible to keep most temperate and subtropical species outside in temperate climates all year around, provided satisfactory frost-free hibernacula are provided. Many snakes will breed more readily in outdoor enclosures than in confined indoor terraria, though it may be necessary to collect any eggs for artificial incubation. Even tropical species will benefit from a period outside in the warmer summer months, providing it does not get too cold at night. Natural sunlight is of great value to the snakes' health.

A basic reptile house consists of a walled enclosure with a firmly packed but well-drained hard-core foundation to a ground depth of at least 50 cm (20 in), to prevent the inmates from burrowing out and escaping. Size of the house will depend on the amount of space available and the number of snakes and species to be kept, but it is better to keep to a smaller, more manageable size than to be overly ambitious. If you intend to keep several species, it is best to construct a number of adjoining but separate enclosures. The enclosure should be placed in a position where it receives maximum benefit from sunlight but at the same time is sheltered from cold, prevailing winds. In the Northern Hemisphere, a reptile house backing onto the south-facing wall of a building is ideal; alternatively, it can be constructed into a south-facing slope, the back being screened with thick shrubbery or a fence.

For most smaller species the wall need be no higher than 90 cm (36 in), but this will of course depend on the species being kept. For longer snakes, it will be necessary to dig a pit so the outer wall is still not too high to prevent comfortable viewing but the inner wall is deep enough to prevent the snakes from crawling over the top. For additional escape prevention, an inward overhang about 15 cm (6 in) wide can be placed all around the top of the wall.

To create better viewing and to gain maximum benefit from the sunlight it is advisable to create a moat about 90 cm (36 cm) wide around the inside of the wall and to keep this free of debris. If waterproofed concrete is used, this can provide a water-filled ditch that will be of benefit to the inmates. The body of earth removed from the foundations and the moat can be piled up to form a mound in the center of the enclosure, bringing it closer to eye-level.

During construction, ponds, waterfalls, rockeries, etc., can be incorporated, as well as hibernacula if necessary. A hibernaculum can be made from a plastic food container, a plastic drum, or similar container laid on its side, the open end pointing slightly downward (to prevent rainwater entering) and buried about 60 cm (24 in) below the surface. The container is loosely packed with dry sphagnum moss, hay, and wood shavings. A length of plastic pipe of sufficient diameter serves as an entrance tunnel and also should slope slightly downward. The entrance to the pipe can be cemented among a number of rocks so it appears to be a natural crevice into which the reptiles can pass.

The reptile house may be decorated with plenty of rocks, flat stones, rotting logs, etc., and planted with suitable ground cover and shrubs. A pond and waterfall also can be incorporated. A number of plant-free sandy areas should be provided for some species to lay eggs. A mound of grass clippings may also be used as an egglaying site by some species, or eggs may be laid under flat rocks or in rotting logs. Close watch should be kept for mating and egglaying activities so that the eggs can be collected as soon as possible for artificial

Samples of various substrates. Every keeper has his own choice for "best" substrate, often based on past experiences, good and bad. Photo: S. C. and H. Miller.

incubation. Maintenance of an outdoor reptile house is minimal and consists mainly of pruning plants back and ensuring that there are no overhanging branches that would provide escape routes for inmates.

The Outdoor Terrarium: This is similar to the indoor terrarium, except that it is open to the elements, being screened on top with mesh to prevent escapes. Outdoor terraria can be built with bricks or concrete blocks and are ideal for a sloping garden. The front is furnished with a large, framed viewing window. Ambitious projects can include a pond at the front so that one can view above and below water level. It is even possible to have a partial roof or a removable roof into which heating apparatus can be installed so that species from warmer climates can be kept.

TERRARIUM DECORATIONS AND PLANTS

There is much disagreement on what items constitute the ideal furnishings for terraria. There are those who favor the natural method, in which the terrarium is planted and decorated to give an indication of the animals' natural habitat, and those who favor the more hygienic clinical system, where a sheet of absorbent paper, a dish of water, a hiding box, and a brick as a shedding aid are provided. The latter method is indeed more hygienic and practical, especially where numbers of snakes are being kept for breeding purposes. To many snake species the difference does not appear to matter as they will breed quite successfully in a clinical environment provided they have the correct environmental conditions. However, most snake-keepers will want to have at least one

decorative terrarium in his living area in which he can put his artistic talents to use in producing a mini-habitat.

Substrate Materials: For small desert or semi-desert species, coarse sand or a mixture of peat and sand can be used as a floor covering. Fine or silver sand should never be used, as this will stick to the skin and cake between the scales (particularly after the reptiles have crawled through water), causing shedding problems later. For burrowing or semi-burrowing snakes the mixture should be relatively deep. One method of keeping small burrowing snakes is to build a glass terrarium that is very narrow from

Perhaps the most simple and cheap setup that will maintain a snake. Not exactly attractive, it can be used as a quarantine cage, hospital cage, or temporary quarters. Photo: W. B. Allen, Jr.

front to back. If this is about three-quarters filled with substrate material, it will be possible to see the snakes in their tunnels. When you are not actually viewing the snakes, the below-substrate area should be covered with a drape so that the snakes are not disoriented by the light entering from the sides.

For larger snakes and for humid terraria, the most hygienic substrate material to use (other than absorbent paper) is gravel or shingle. The size of the gravel should be selected to suit the size of the inmates: ½ cm (¼ in) gravel for small snakes to 2.5 cm (1 in) or more for large pythons. Gravel and shingle are available in many colors, and it is interesting to look around and discover new kinds of substrate material for the terrarium. Gravel should be thoroughly washed and dried out before use. This can be accomplished by placing it in a large sieve placed on four bricks and hosing it through with a strong jet of water, giving it an occasional shake. It is always advisable to have a spare stock of gravel to use at cleaning time (which should be about once per month).

Tree Branches: For most snakes, even those that do not climb a great deal, a tree branch in the terrarium is attractive to look at and will provide exercise and a shedding aid for the inmates. In desert terraria a bleached, gnarled branch or root can look most attractive. Driftwood from the seashore or trapped in snags in rivers is often highly suitable as it will be bleached, weathered, and smoothed down by the action of sun, sand, and water. Alternatively, bizarrely shaped limbs can be lopped directly from the tree (but be sure you have permission if it is not your tree!). All wood collected for the terrarium should be thoroughly scrubbed, washed, and dried before use. It is advisable also to use a wire brush on it to remove pieces of loose bark, etc., that would otherwise make a mess in the terrarium later. One method of producing weathered limbs artificially is to place them in a cement mixer

with a mixture of coarse sand and water and turn them for an hour or so. They can then be left for a day or so in a strong bleach solution and then soaked in clear water, thoroughly dried, and possibly sanded to remove rough areas before use.

Hollow logs and branches are useful as hiding places for some species, but be sure that such hiding places are accessible; it can sometimes be difficult to remove a stubborn snake that has jammed itself into a hollow log. With a little carpentry it is possible to fashion controllable hiding places.

In rain-forest terraria where small arboreal species are being kept, hollow logs can be used to grow epiphytic plants and form an attractive display. In addition, dead branches can be used to support creeping plants as well as provide climbing frames for arboreal snakes. Large climbing snakes, such as boids, will require very strong, robust branches. All branches should be fixed securely in the terrarium so that there is no danger of them collapsing and causing possible injury to the snakes. Branches may be fixed by cementing the bases into the floor in large terraria. In smaller terraria the branches can be subtly tied into position with green gardener's wire.

An interesting idea for arboreal snakes is to suspend the branch from the ceiling of the terrarium with a hook and eye so this will swing gently as the snakes move among the twigs. Corkwood bark of the type used by florists is a useful item and can be used as an attractive wall covering in the terrarium, to conceal plant pots, or to provide hiding places for the snakes.

Rocks: Either natural or artificial rocks can be used in the terrarium to provide basking areas, hiding places, and aids to shedding as well as producing a decorative effect. If you live in a big city where natural rocks are difficult to come by, you may be able to purchase suitable ones from aquarium or garden shops, but it is much more fun to go out and hunt your own free rocks on location.

Whether these are jagged rocks or large weathered pebbles is a matter of taste, but for the most attractive esthetic effect it is best to stick to a single variety in each terrarium. Rocks should be arranged in the terrarium in such a way that they cannot fall down and injure the reptiles. In large terraria, where a great number of rocks are used it is best to cement these together, leaving only controllable hiding places, or great problems will ensue when the snakes must be removed. With a little practice, natural rocks can be cemented together to produce a natural-looking rock-face. Judicious use of cement coloring material can almost make the joints invisible.

Lightweight artificial rocks made from cement-covered styrofoam have proved very useful. Apart from the obvious advantage of a much lighter weight, they can be made to any size or shape required and can be made to fit exactly into corners so that there are no

Artificial rocks can be made in any desired shape and size as required by the cage setting. Photo: S. C. and H. Miller.

uncontrollable hiding places left for elusive snakes or parasites. Styrofoam (expanded polystyrene) is a very light, white, synthetic material used for insulating or packing and is available in sheets of varying sizes and thicknesses. Thicker chunks can be made by passing pieces of stiff wire through several thicknesses of the material and simply bending it over at the ends. The required shape is roughly fashioned by breaking or cutting off pieces. The whole surface is then bound with galvanized wire netting (half-inch chicken wire) that, being extremely malleable, can be shaped into the imperfections on the surfaces. The rock is then covered with a layer of cement mortar about 12 mm (½ in) thick. A suitable mix is one part cement, two parts sand, and a plasticizing agent to the manufacturer's instructions, mixed with water to a pliable consistency. The cement can be trowelled or molded into place with the hands on the exposed surfaces of the styrofoam, ensuring that all of the wire mesh is embedded. The surface can be smoothed into shape with a damp paintbrush and, with skilful use of a trowel, various authentic-looking rock formations can be sculpted. The part fitting into the corners and the base need not necessarily be cemented over, and the job can be done *in situ* or an artificial corner can be made using two planks. Free-standing rocks should be covered on all sides except the base, which will be resting on the terrarium floor.

Some excellent, controllable hiding places can be produced by making two fake rocks to fit exactly on top of each other. A concave hollow of sufficient depth for the snake is made in the top of the lower rock and a couple of access holes left for the snakes to gain entry and exit.

The joint between the two rocks can be sculpted to look like geological strata or a fault with natural crevices. Access to the snake is made by simply lifting off the top rock. Coloring agents can be added to the cement during construction or a combination of color washes can be used to make the rocks look even more natural. The finished rocks should have the texture of fairly smooth sandstone. Allow at least 48 hours in a cool, preferably humid, atmosphere for the cement to set (it may crack if dried out too quickly) before moving the artificial rocks.

Plants and Planting: Although plants can be somewhat problematic in the terrarium, there is no doubt that living plants add that subtle finishing touch to the display terrarium, particularly if it is to be a showpiece in the hall, living room, or den. However, plants are sometimes even more difficult to keep in good condition in the terrarium than the animals. It

All snakes require retreats or hides in which to retire from the world. Most snakes like the feel of walls on their sides, so the hide box should not be roomy but instead on the cramped side. Manufactured hide boxes are available in many sizes and designs, and many common items can be adapted into hides. Shown here are a plastic half-gallon (opaque) jar, a piece of curved pine bark, and a short length of plastic pipe. Photos: W. B. Allen, Jr.

must be remembered that plants also have requirements of temperature, light, humidity, and ventilation; they also must be fed at frequent intervals. There are cases where it is almost impossible to keep living plants. For example, most boids and large colubrids will quickly destroy plants with their sheer weight. In such cases it is best to make do with artificial plants or no plants at all. There are some very realistic looking artificial plants available, but in the author's opinion these still do not constitute a satisfactory substitute for the real thing. In the case of no plants at all, you often can compensate by having a display of plants set outside the terrarium.

For the smaller terrestrial and arboreal snake terrarium, a living plant display does not pose the same problems as it did at one time. The use of broad-spectrum fluorescent tubes or horticultural growth lamps gives the plants lighting conditions they did not receive with the old tungsten bulbs. Many kinds of exotic house plants are suitable for the terrarium, and these should be cared for as recommended by your

supplier. For authenticity, plant species should be used that are native to the same habitat as the snakes being kept, though this is not strictly necessary. A good book on exotic house plants will also give you many ideas on how to care for them in the terrarium. It is best to keep all plants potted, the pots concealed behind rocks or logs. An advantage of using artificial rocks is that you can arrange for cavities in them to fit the pots exactly (do not forget to include drainage holes beneath). The space in and around the top of the pot above the soil can be covered with gravel to hide the edge of the pot and also to help prevent snakes burrowing into the soil and damaging the roots. Another advantage of using potted plants rather than planting them directly into the terrarium substrate is that they can be removed easily at cleaning time. If a second specimen of each plant is kept, you can interchange them at, say, monthly intervals. While one is "on duty" in the terrarium, the other can be taking rest and recreation on the windowsill or in the greenhouse!

Greenery sets off the colors of many attractive snakes and may be worth the difficulties in keeping it fresh and bright. Photo of *Lampropeltis mexicana*: K. T. Nemuras.

General Husbandry and Care

Anyone desiring to keep snakes in captivity should first of all give great consideration to the responsibilities involved. The husbandry and care of any animal begin on the day it is acquired and continue daily on a routine basis. Remember that an animal confined to a cage cannot care for itself—you are responsible for its welfare and all its requirements. Before obtaining any specimens, ensure that you have the time, patience, and ongoing enthusiasm to care for them properly.

Another point to be taken into consideration is that while the potential snake-keeper may be enthusiastic about his newly found hobby, others, including close members of his own family, may not share his enthusiasm. People who like snakes tend to have a "feel" for them, a quality not possessed by most other people. As the famous herpetologist Hans Gadow once wrote: "People who delight in keeping Newts or Frogs, Tortoises or Snakes, are, as a rule, considered eccentric. Once those around you have overcome your eccentricity, you can usually go ahead; but remember that while some people can be converted to like snakes and others can learn to tolerate them provided they are kept locked up, there are a few who will not view them with the slightest favor under any circumstances. The herpetologist should view such people with muted sympathy and on no account should he use his snakes, even in fun, to instil further fear."

Keeping a pair or a few snakes should not be overly time-consuming in maintenance. Once the basic terrarium has been set up, four or five hours per week should be adequate for routine husbandry and care.

SELECTION AND ACQUISITION OF SPECIMENS

Of the 2,700 or so different snake species, relatively few are available on the general pet market at any one time. What is available often depends on such factors as the season, the country in which you live, and the conservation status of the snakes in question, both in your own country and the country of origin. Most countries have their specialist reptile and amphibian dealers, and often pet shops will have a few snake species. It will often pay to shop around for a few days before making a decision.

Always avoid those premises that are obviously dirty and untidy. Fortunately, in most countries with animal welfare legislation the days of the unscrupulous animal dealer are over, but from time to time undesirable premises crop up, with masses of unhealthy specimens crowded together in smelly cages. These, however, are compensated for by a new breed of professional dealer whose premises are kept absolutely spotless and only animals in prime

health are offered for sale. Such animals are always displayed in clean, attractive display terraria, and the dealer is always pleased to give specific advice regarding the habits and care of particular species.

In spite of the fact that the establishment may be apparently faultless, it still pays to examine any prospective purchases most carefully. For obvious reasons, most dealers are unlikely to guarantee the health or life of an apparently healthy specimen once it has been taken from the premises. Look for signs of ectoparasites both on the animals and in the display cages. Ask for a trial handling; if it is your first time, the dealer will be pleased to instruct you.

Choose only those snakes that are plump, sleek, and have an unblemished appearance devoid of any unshed patches of skin. Ensure that the snake is alert (most healthy snakes will initially object to being picked up; others will show interest by tongue flickering) and that its eyes are bright and clear. Examine its mouth and vent for signs of inflammation that could indicate disease. Ask if the snake is feeding and what it is eating. If you know from the outset what the snake has already been eating, it will be a great help. It is often suggested that you actually witness the snake feeding.

Stock may also be obtained from other hobbyists who have bred their snakes or who wish to dispose of excess stock. The best way to find out who may have excess stock for sale is to join a herpetological society at the regional or

Delapidated buildings and trash dumps often are excellent places to look for snakes. Be sure that you get permission to enter any private land you may be hunting in, and be sure you know all the locally applicable laws. Photo: J. Gee.

local level. By regularly attending meetings and reading the publications you will gradually learn who is keeping and breeding what species. Not only will you be able to obtain good stock, you will have firsthand advice on how to look after it. Even if you live too far away to attend regular meetings, most societies publish a newsletter in which members will advertise their excess stock, giving their phone number or contact address. Two big advantages of obtaining home-bred (as opposed to wild-captured) stock are that it is likely to settle more quickly into its new terrarium and is less likely to be diseased or infested with parasites. In addition, you know that another animal has not been taken from the wild.

A third method of obtaining specimens is collection from the wild. This method should be pursued with great caution as many countries now have a total ban on the collection of wild specimens. In some countries certain species may be protected in some states and not in others. It may be illegal to transport certain species from one state or country to another. In addition there may be certain areas, such as national parks and state forests, where the collection or disturbance of any animal or plant is forbidden. In some countries, reptiles may be captured only by licensed collectors.

However, there are some places in some countries where some snakes still may be legally collected, but in some of these the reptiles collected are not allowed to be legally offered for resale. Therefore it is really only ethical (and good conservation practice) to collect only what you require. It is a great temptation to overcollect where species are abundant, but you should only take what you can comfortably care for. One advantage of collection from the wild is

that you can see *exactly* the type of habitat in which the snake lives and prepare the terrarium accordingly.

Before attempting to collect from the wild, always be aware of *all* national and local legislation pertaining to the area and species in question.

FINDING SNAKES IN THE WILD

Whether for purposes of collecting or just for field study or photography, a trip into the wild to find snakes is one of the most thrilling aspects of herpetology. Such a trip should be carefully planned, though occasionally you may discover a good collecting area by accident at short notice. Many herpetologists plan their annual vacation so that they will be near good reptile country, in spite of the fact that their spouses and children may have other desires. In my case I usually select a spot somewhere on the coast that boasts a rugged, serpent-infested hinterland; then while the wife and kids are soaking up the sun on the beach, I am scrabbling around in the vegetation on some distant hillock.

One of the most important pieces of equipment for a field herpetologist is a guide to the snakes found in a particular state or country. First study the distribution maps to find out what species occur in the area. Once a snake is found, you can identify it by checking against the characteristics given in the field guide.

There are various means of finding snakes. With experience, you will develop a sort of special sense for recognizing country that is inhabited by snakes. Active diurnal snakes are often fleetingly spotted just as they make themselves scarce, so you should move as slowly and quietly as possible. You should develop a keen eye for searching through the foliage and brush where many snakes are remarkably camouflaged in their natural habitat. Many species can be found by turning over rocks, logs, and other ground litter. Old rubbish dumps and derelict buildings in country areas are often excellent sites for hunting snakes. In the early morning, before the sun becomes too hot, snakes love to bask under old pieces of corrugated iron, junked car doors, metal drums, etc., and it is worth turning these over to see what is beneath. Anything turned should be gently laid back in its original position so other forms of wildlife are disturbed as little as possible.

If you are in an area where venomous snakes occur you should take the necessary precautions. It is best to wear long trousers and stout boots. Never put your hands under logs or rocks or into crevices before being sure what lurks there. It is best to carry a snake-stick wherever possible. I have found a good multipurpose snake stick to consist of an L-shaped piece of steel attached to a stout (broomstick-like) pole about 1 m (3.25 ft) long. You can have the steel fitting made quite

If you are hunting or even walking where venomous snakes occur, watch your feet. Most venomous snakes, like this Copperhead, are well-camouflaged. Photo: J. Gee.

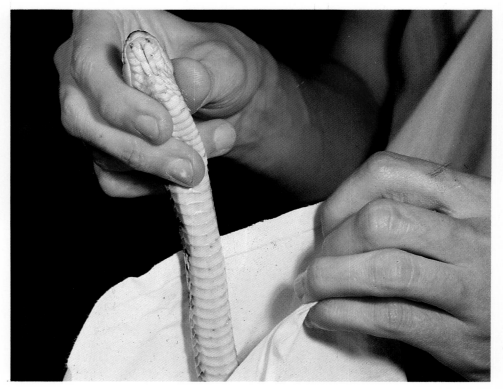

cheaply at your local metalworks. It should have a ferrule so that it will fit over the pole. Holes in the ferrule will allow it to be screwed to the pole. When you are on the move you can use it as a walking stick, the steel end serving as a handle. The true handle of the pole should be slightly concave and covered with a piece of rubber tubing. The stick can be used to turn stones and logs, remove loose bark from trees, and pin snakes to the ground. Other kinds of catching sticks should be used for catching agile venomous snakes.

TRANSPORT OF SPECIMENS

The most satisfactory method of packing snakes for transport is in individual cloth bags in turn placed into stout cardboard or wooden boxes. When packed in cloth bags, snakes tend to settle quickly and can easily breathe through the pores in the cloth. When collecting snakes in the wild, a number of bags of various sizes should be taken.

Old bed linen is ideal for making snake bags, and if you have someone in the family handy with a sewing machine you can soon make up a number of bags quite cheaply. In emergency situations, pillow cases can be used. A narrow cloth strip should be sewn near the neck of the bag so it can be tied shut. Before use, bags should be thoroughly inspected for holes.

Left: A snake stick or hook of some type is essential to correct handling of larger aggressive or venomous snakes. Right: Control of the head is necessary when putting a snake into a bag or removing it. Photos: Left: J. Dommers; Right: S. Kochetov.

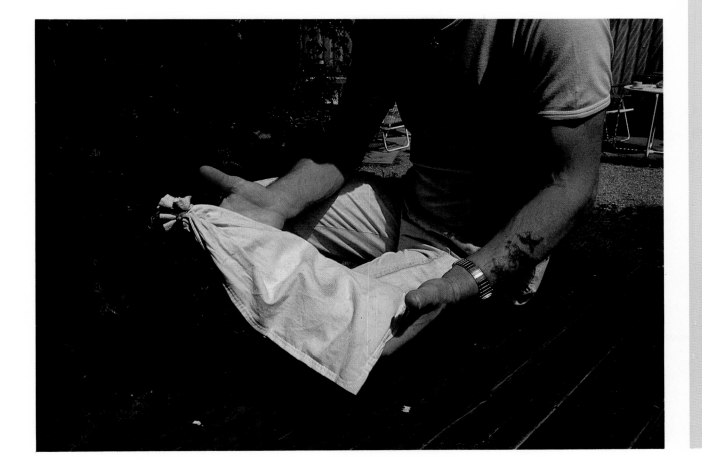

A good snake bag is double-sewn, has a separate tie string, and is made of material that will let the snake breathe while not allowing the teeth to penetrate easily. Photo: S. C. and H. Miller.

The snake stick is used to control the snake by carefully pinning its head or forcing the body to move in the proper direction. It is not used to force the head into the ground or to toss the snake into the proper container. Snakes are delicate. Photos: S. Kochetov.

packing boxes. In cold climates the boxes containing the bags should be lined with an insulating material such as styrofoam, just leaving a few ventilation holes in the lid. Unlike mammals and birds, a snake's oxygen requirements are minimal in cold weather and it is better to insulate rather than over-ventilate during transport.

If for some reason or other you have to send snakes via public transport, always select the quickest and most direct route and not necessarily the cheapest. Snakes may be sent by road, rail, or air, depending on the distance. If you are sending animals from one country to another, be sure that you are complying with the regulations of both the exporting and importing countries. Pack snakes in individual bags and label each bag clearly, stating the species contained in the bag. This is particularly important where venomous snakes are concerned. The bags are packed in wooden boxes with screwed on lids. Due to the low metabolic rate of snakes it is not necessary to supply them with food or water for journeys of less than five days and no journey should take longer with today's modern transport systems. The outer container should be clearly marked with the name and address of both the consignee and the consignor, as well as the telephone number where relevant. The box should also be marked urgent, tropical livestock, please keep warm, or something similar. Snakes cannot be sent through the mails.

If you intend to do a lot of snake transporting, it would be wise to invest in one or more carrying boxes. These are best made of stout timber with ventilation holes drilled in the lid. The lid can also have a number of cup hooks screwed into it on the inside so that bags can be tied up individually; alternatively, you can have several compartments. This is for safety's sake so you do not have to put your hand into a pile of bags containing venomous snakes. Remember that snakes can, and will, bite through cloth.

When purchasing stock from a dealer or a breeder, it is best to pick up the specimens yourself wherever possible rather than have them sent by some form of public transport. The dealer will usually supply bags and/or

QUARANTINE

All new reptiles arriving into a collection should undergo a period of quarantine to reduce the possibility of disease or parasites being introduced into existing stocks. Quarantine cages should preferably be kept in a different room from the main collection and need not be substantially decorated. A simple aquarium with the necessary environmental controls is all that is required. New stock should be kept under close observation for not less than 30 days. If all is well after that time it may be introduced to the permanent collection.

Should a disease break out while the animals are in quarantine, they should receive veterinary treatment and should not be moved until 30 days after a complete cure has been effected.

INSPECTION AND HANDLING

All new arrivals should be thoroughly inspected for signs of diseases and parasites, and if anything is discovered it should be treated accordingly. Thereafter, it is a good idea to inspect the reptiles thoroughly on a monthly basis to ensure they are remaining healthy. Many snakes, especially some of the larger boids and colubrids, soon accept being handled on a regular basis. However, some of the smaller species object to being handled, and there is evidence that overhandling in all snakes can lead to stress and can interfere with breeding cycles. Therefore, unless a snake is to be kept as a pet

it preferably should be handled as little as possible. However, if a snake is to remain tame it should be handled frequently. The choice is yours. Venomous snakes should be handled as infrequently as possible for obvious reasons.

Methods of handling vary with the size and the aggressiveness of the species or individuals, and can be divided into four groups.

Small Nonvenomous Snakes: Aggressive specimens up to 40 cm (16 in) in length can be grasped firmly but gently around the neck, just behind the head, with the thumb and forefinger,

allowing the body to drape over the hand. Nonaggressive or tame specimens simply can be lifted up by placing the fingers under the body and allowing the snake to drape across the hand or twine between the fingers. Bites from small nonvenomous snakes are negligible as the teeth are tiny and are unlikely to break the skin. The worst you can expect is a few very minor pinprick-like punctures that simply can be wiped with a little antiseptic solution or cream.

Medium-sized Nonvenomous Snakes: Snakes from 40-150 cm (16-60 in) come into this

Proper handling of a snake is necessary for both the health of the snake and your own health. You must provide support for the body and control of the head to the extent required by the size and temperament of the snake. Photos: S. C. and H. Miller.

Even the most gentle, tame, highly bred snake will bite if sufficiently provoked. This albino California Kingsnake, *Lampropeltis getulus californiae*, obviously is putting a lot of effort into leaving a few shallow punctures. Photo: J. Wines.

it to thrash its body about as it will be likely to severely injure itself. Tame snakes in this category can be simply lifted up about one-third and two-thirds down the body using both hands. It can then be draped over the arms and restrained occasionally as it crawls about.

Large Nonvenomous Snakes: Specimens in this category, which includes the larger colubrids and many boids in excess of 150 cm (60 in), are capable of giving deep, lacerating bites, and their powers of constriction should also be treated with respect. Bites should receive medical treatment with special efforts to avoid infection. Aggressive specimens should be handled by two or more people, depending on the snake's size. One person grips the snake firmly by the neck just behind the head, while the other(s) restrains its body. Many large boids become remarkably tame, especially if handled frequently from the juvenile stage. Large, docile snakes can be lifted up by the body using both hands and draped around the arms and shoulders. Old clothes or overalls should always be worn when handling nervous snakes, which have a habit of emptying the contents of their cloaca when restrained. The fecal discharges are often foul smelling and can be corrosive to clothing unless washed off fairly quickly.

Venomous Snakes: As far as handling goes, venomous snakes are in a definite category of their own. All venomous snakes (including those rear-fanged species that normally are classed as mildly poisonous) should be treated with the utmost respect. No venomous snakes should be kept by beginners, and any prospective handler of such species should first have had plenty of experience with aggressive nonvenomous varieties in order to be familiar with the type of problems that may occur. If at all possible, it is also advisable to serve a short apprenticeship with somebody experienced with venomous species before obtaining any specimens. The prospective keeper of venomous snakes should be thoroughly familiar with all the rules, regulations, and safety procedures associated with venomous snakes and their venoms.

In general, it can be said that the viperids are somewhat easier to handle than the elapids, but there are exceptions. Many of the heavier viperids, particularly those in the genus *Bitis*, are fairly sluggish and cumbersome, though they can strike in a flash if necessary. These heavy vipers can be picked up with a snake hook that consists of a metal rod with a T- or L-shaped end. The hook end is simply slipped under the center of the snake's body and lifted up. With very heavy vipers it may be necessary to use two snake hooks or a combination of hook and grab (such as Pilstrom tongs). Ensure that the handle of the hook or grab is longer than two-thirds the length of the snake, and always hold the snake well away from the body. When handling venomous snakes it is wise to have as few people as possible in the vicinity. Elapids and rear-fanged colubrids should be handled with a grab. This consists of a long rod with a handle and a

category and, depending on the size of their teeth, some of these are capable of giving deep, painful bites or even lacerations that may require medical treatment. Aggressive or lively snakes should be secured by the neck just behind the head with one hand, while supporting the body with the other. Do not hold the snake by the neck with one hand and allow

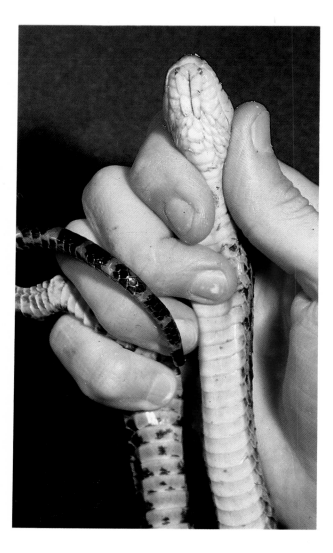

trigger-like grip at one end and a cable-controlled tong at the other. Such instruments as fruit or litter pickers can be converted for snake handling. The tong should be cushioned with rubber tubing or foam rubber to prevent possible injury to the snakes. Special snake grabs or tongs are manufactured by some companies; information on these may be obtained through your herpetological society or your local zoo.

Venomous snakes should only be grasped in the hand for specific examination, medical treatment, or venom extraction (milking). The snake's head should first be pinned to the surface on which it is resting with the T end of a snake stick. Firm pressure must be used, but do not apply so much pressure that the snake is injured. It requires a bit of practice before you get it right. Having secured the snake's head with the stick, the other hand is used to grasp the neck with the thumb and forefinger just behind the head, ensuring that there is not enough neck left free for the snake to turn its head around and bite. The snake stick can then be placed to one side and the other hand can be used to restrain the snake's body.

The technique of handling venomous snakes is one that can never be satisfactorily described

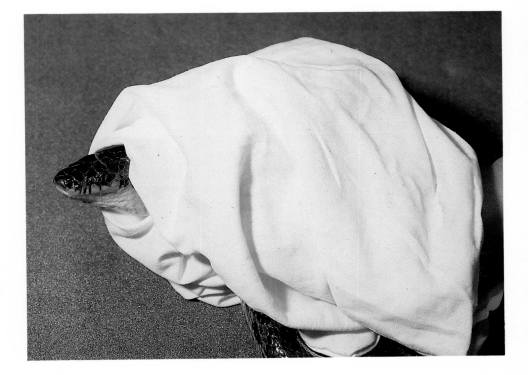

The snake bag can be used to help control a snake. Photo: S. Kochetov.

in writing, and unfortunately the only way to gain experience is to try it out, preferably in the company of somebody already experienced. In any case, a second person should always be

A large and dangerous snake such as the Mangrove Snake, *Boiga dendrophila*, should be carefully controlled when handled. Better yet, don't handle it unless necessity demands it. Photos: S. Kochetov.

within earshot in case of emergency. The appropriate antivenin should always be available, preferably lodged at the surgery of the local medical practitioner or at a local hospital where expert medical attention will be available in case of accidents.

NUTRITION

A balanced diet is important to all animals in order to maintain their bodily functions at an efficient level and thus remain in the best of health. A balanced diet is one that contains the correct variety and quantity of constituents required to keep a given animal in the best of health. Basically, all animals require proteins, carbohydrates, fats, vitamins, minerals, and water in varying quantities. Let us take a brief look at each of the dietary constituents.

Proteins: These are a major dietary requirement of any animal as they form the bulk of muscle and tissue in the body and inner organs. They play a major part in the growth, replacement, and repair of body tissue.

Carbohydrates: These include starches and sugars that are necessary to provide energy.

Fats: These help to insulate the body, act as shock-absorbing material, and are a storage site of nutrients for future use.

Vitamins: There are several kinds of vitamins important to the good health of snakes, including A, B_1, B_2 complex, D, and E.

Minerals: Calcium and phosphorus are important for good bone formation. Trace elements such as iron, sodium, manganese, etc., in small quantities are also important.

Water: Fresh water should always be available to captive snakes. Some small tree snakes will only drink water droplets from the foliage, so a daily misting of the terrarium is important.

Snakes feed largely on whole prey animals

that contain all of the basic dietary constituents. If snakes are fed on healthy prey, then there should be no necessity for any extra dietary supplements. An exception is those snakes (garter snakes, for example) that can be trained to take strips of dead fish. This should only be used as a standby food when other food is not available; it should be used sparingly and should be dusted with a vitamin/mineral supplement.

Freshwater fish should be given in preference to marine varieties as the latter are more likely to contain the enzyme thiaminase, which breaks down vitamin B_1 in the body and will cause a deficiency of this vitamin.

Food Items

Often the species of snakes kept in captivity may be dictated by the types of food items they normally eat. Snakes that specialize in feeding on certain items, for example snails, lizards, or other snakes, are often extremely difficult to tempt with more easily available items. If a ready supply of specialist food items is not available for particular species, then it is perhaps best not to keep those species unless one contemplates a regimen of force-feeding. There are, however, plenty of other species that will take more readily available items.

General Invertebrate Foods: Some of the smallest of snake species and juveniles of many larger ones will feed largely on invertebrates. In many cases a variety of invertebrate food is important. The best way to provide this is to collect insects, spiders, slugs, snails, earthworms, crustaceans, etc., from the wild. Termite nests are an invaluable source of food for some small burrowing snakes, and pieces of nests containing numbers of the insects can be placed in the terrarium. In the temperate winter such food items become scarce, so you will have to rely on the limited number of food species

Common invertebrate foods for snakes. Clockwise from top left: Freshwater shrimp (Photo: B. Kahl); small crayfish (Photo: P. Taborsky); maggots (Photo: M. Gilroy); hornworms, a moth larva (Photo: Dr. G. Dingerkus); sowbug, *Porcellio scaber* (Photo: K. Lucas, Steinhart).

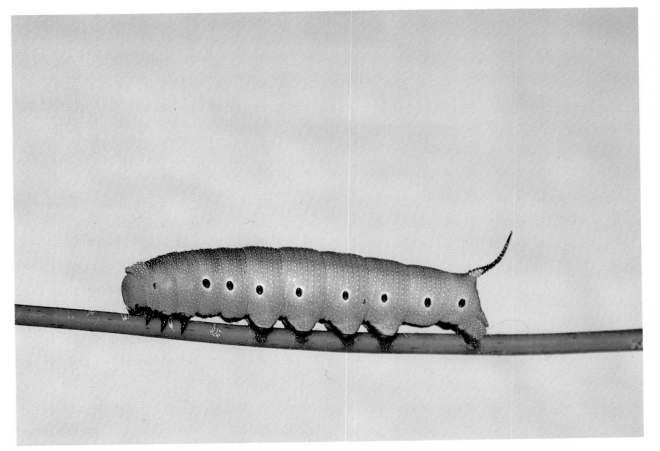

Molluscs are eaten by many types of snakes and often are easily collected at night. Top: A slug, *Limax maximus*. Photo: K. Lucas, Steinhart. Bottom: A garden snail. Photo: A. Norman.

If you live in an area where termites are common, you are in luck. A piece of wood or dirt containing large numbers of workers can be placed in the terrarium for a snake to feed on at its leisure. Be careful that none escape, however. Photos: Left: W. B. Allen, Jr.; Right: Dr. G. Dingerkus.

available from suppliers. These include mealworms, crickets, and locusts.

Mealworms: Almost everybody has heard of mealworms, which are bred commercially as a live food for many kinds of pet animals. They are initially rather expensive to buy but are quite easy to breed from a purchased culture. Only the smallest of snakes are likely to feed on them, but they are useful for this purpose. Mealworms grow to about 2.5 cm (1 in) in length and are the larvae of a kind of flour beetle, *Tenebrio molitor*. Mealworms are a nutritious item, although it is recommended that a mineral supplement containing calcium be dusted over them if they are used in great quantities. In general, they are best used only as a supplement to a varied wild-caught diet.

Mealworms should be kept at room temperature in shallow trays with about 5 cm (2 in) of bran, covered with a piece of sacking. One or two pieces of raw potato, carrot, or apple placed on the sacking will allow the mealworms to collect moisture. Some of the mealworms should be allowed to pupate and mature into adult beetles to ensure an ongoing supply of various sized worms as well as more pupae and beetles, all of which will be eaten by some snakes, especially small burrowing species. At intervals of two or three months, a new culture should be started with fresh bran. After as many worms as possible have been rescued from the old culture it should be discarded. It is best to keep two or three cultures going at various stages of maturity. An alternative to breeding mealworms is to purchase a small amount as and when they are required.

Crickets: All species of cricket and grasshopper are nutritious food items that will be taken readily by some small insectivorous snakes. Indeed, some species, such as *Eirenis rothi*, feed almost exclusively on crickets in the wild. Crickets are also bred commercially, the most usual species being the house cricket, *Gryllus bimaculatus*. They may be kept in a small container, such as a plastic aquarium, with rolls of corrugated cardboard as hiding places. Papier-mache egg cartons also can be used. A small tube of water with cotton wool plugged into the opening or a saucer with a piece of sodden cotton wool will provide moisture for the insects to drink. Do not provide an open water dish or the insects will drown. Crickets can be fed mainly on bran, supplemented with some greens, carrots, or fruit. It is important to keep cricket cultures clean, and uneaten food should be replaced with fresh food at frequent intervals.

The container in which the crickets are kept should be maintained at a temperature 26-30°C, which should allow the crickets to breed readily. They will often lay their eggs in the damp cotton wool, so this should be checked regularly. If eggs are present, the cotton wool should be moved to a smaller container for hatching. The various sized instars and adults provide insects of various sizes to suit the tiniest of juvenile snakes.

Locusts: The migratory locust, *Schistocercus migratoria*, is bred commercially and is another nutritious standby food for insectivorous snakes. These insects require a well-ventilated glass-fronted cage and a temperature range of 26°C (night) to 33°C (day). They can be fed with bran and a fresh daily supply of grass stalks standing in a jar of water, the area around the rim packed with cotton wool to prevent the insects from falling in and drowning. The moist cotton wool will also provide drinking water.

Locusts are a little more difficult to breed than crickets. The best way is to provide test tubes full of sand inserted into the cage floor; the females will lay their eggs in these by inserting their long ovipositors into the sand. If you require only a small quantity of locusts for your snakes it is perhaps best to purchase the occasional batch rather than attempt the difficult and time-consuming task of breeding them.

Earthworms: Various species of earthworm, especially the common angleworms (many available species), are a nutritious food for many small snake species. Garter snakes (*Thamnophis*) will take earthworms almost as a staple diet, but the occasional fish also should be given.

Earthworms are found almost everywhere and are common in most suburban gardens where they may be collected on a regular basis. A layer of dead leaves about 3-5 cm (1-2 in) thick is placed in a secluded corner of the garden and covered with a piece of sacking. This is kept damp by regularly spraying it with water during dry weather. Earthworms will congregate in the damp area to feed on the dead leaves, and they may be collected daily for a period of one to two weeks by lifting the sack and sifting through the leaves. As soon as one area becomes sparse in worms (do not over-collect), a new trap can be set up in another part of the garden. Do not collect again from the original spot until at least 12 months later.

Fish: Many aquatic or semi-aquatic snakes will feed almost exclusively on fish. Some can be trained to take dead fish or even strips of fish meat, but it is best to give live freshwater fish wherever possible. Marine fish should only be given to sea snakes. Readily bred aquarium fishes such as guppies (*Poecilia reticulata*) are a good standby item for small fish-eating snakes. Even lizard- or frog-eaters such as *Ahaetulla* or *Chrysopelia* can be persuaded to take fish if they are offered in a shallow container of water so that the fish flip about. Local small freshwater fish can be netted in rivers, streams, or lakes (check local laws). Another good source of supply is the commercial freshwater fish farm. Live trout, for example, in some areas can be purchased at various ages from tiny fry to adults, and sizes suitable for most fish-eating snakes can be obtained. One problem with trout is that they require cool, highly oxygenated water if they are to live for any length of time, so unless you have such facilities, it is advisable to buy only enough at a time for your snakes' immediate requirements.

Crickets and grasshoppers are excellent foods for many insect-eating snakes, and they are readily cultured or purchased. Top to bottom: *Gryllus,* a common field cricket (Photo: M. Gilroy); mating locusts *Schistocerus migratoria* (Photo: M. Gilroy); crickets feeding on orange slices with bone meal and calcium added (Photo: W. B. Allen, Jr.); *Acheta domestica,* another common cricket (Photo: B. Kahl).

Many snakes take fish, either live (top, a Common Water Snake, *Nerodia sipedon*, feeding on a shiner) or frozen and thawed, but relatively few will take an earthworm (center). Both earthworms and fishes can be raised or purchased. Guppies (bottom) are cheap, available, breed easily, and are of the proper size for many snakes. Photos: Top: R. Everhart; Center: C. O. Masters; Bottom: R. Zukal.

Goldfish always are a good standby item for fish-eating snakes. Many breeders cull large quantities of young fish after the breeding season and retain only those of good enough quality for further breeding. The inferior quality fish are, however, good enough for feeding to snakes! If you know a goldfish breeder you may be lucky enough to be able to get a supply of goldfish for next to nothing.

Amphibians: Many snake species feed almost exclusively on amphibians. Some may feed exclusively on frogs, others exclusively on salamanders, and yet others may prefer a mixture of both. When collecting food amphibians from the wild, ensure you are not breaching any local conservation regulations.

Frog or toad egg masses may be collected in clumps and allowed to hatch. Tadpoles will be taken eagerly by many small aquatic snakes. They also can be grown in aerated, planted aquarium tanks until they metamorphose into young frogs. The froglets can be further grown by feeding them on insects (such as fruitflies), so that you have various sizes for various sizes of snakes. The commercially bred African Clawed Frog, *Xenopus laevis*, is a very useful species as it can be bred all the year around so that a continuous supply of tadpoles and partially grown to adult frogs is available. The Axolotl, *Ambystoma mexicanum*, is a useful aquatic salamander that also breeds readily in captivity.

Reptiles: Some snakes feed partially or exclusively on other reptiles in the wild. Many tree snakes may feed on geckos or chameleons but usually will readily convert to skinks or anoles; some will even take small live fish as a substitute.

A useful food lizard for small lizard-eating snakes is the cosmopolitan House Gecko, *Hemidactylus frenatus*, which will breed readily. A group of these geckos kept free in a warm,

A selection of foods for aquatic snakes. Minnows, such as the Fathead Shiner, *Pimepheles*, top right, and Golden Shiner, *Notemigonus*, are readily purchased. Frogs are more difficult, but cultured African Clawed Frogs, *Xenopus*, may be available. Axolotls, *Ambystoma mexicanum* (bottom), are about the only ecologically safe salamander to feed. Photos: Top: A. Norman; Center Right: D. Schneider; Center Left: K. Lucas, Steinhart; Bottom: P. W. Scott.

dead birds or mammals after a period of training, and you should make it a policy to feed dead prey whenever possible. The main standby for bird-eating snakes is day-old chicks of domestic poultry. These may be obtained cheaply, alive or dead, from hatcheries (many hatcheries dispose of the majority of cock birds). Some specialist companies supply large quantities of deep-frozen chicks that can be thoroughly thawed out and used as necessary. It is useful to keep a few live birds and grow them up to various sizes, depending on the size of the snakes you have to feed. (Zoning laws may prohibit the keeping of chickens and ducks, even those a few days old.) Other useful domestic birds (both chicks and adults) for snakes of various sizes include quail (the chicks of which are very small and suitable for small snakes; quail eggs are also good for egg-eating snakes), pigeons, ducks, geese, turkeys, and guinea fowl. Adult birds of the larger varieties

Many people have qualms about feeding higher vertebrates to snakes, feeling that there is little to be said for killing a lizard or snake by feeding it to another snake. If you must, always use the most common and ecologically stable species for food. Above: *Sceloporus undulatus*, the Fence Lizard. Photo: Dr. G. Dingerkus. Center: A brood of Common Water Snakes, *Nerodia sipedon sipedon*. Photo: W. B. Allen, Jr. Bottom: *Anolis carolinensis*, the Green Anole. Photo M. Gilroy. All these are commonly fed to captive snakes.

humid room or greenhouse (temperature 26-30°C) and given a supply of insects (crickets, mealworms, flies, etc.) to feed on will provide a self-sufficient supply of food lizards after a period of time.

Snake-eating snakes can pose a problem as they will often steadfastly refuse to take any substitute voluntarily. A regular supply of snakes for snake-eaters usually is not available, so force-feeding of substitute foods is often required. The King Cobra, *Ophiophagus hannah*, is a typical example of a difficult feeder, though force-fed specimens have lived for many years. Perhaps the most satisfactory solution to snake-eaters that will not adapt to other foods is not to keep them at all.

Birds: Many snakes will feed on birds of various types. However, when we arrive at the subject of feeding birds and mammals to snakes we touch on a delicate subject. Many people are totally against others keeping captive snakes because they feel sorry for the animals that they must be fed. Fortunately, most snakes will take

are of course suitable only for the larger boids.

The feeding of wild birds to snakes should be done with the greatest of caution. Birds that have been killed by traffic and are not too badly damaged or tainted may be used occasionally. Otherwise only use those birds that are classified as pests and are not protected by law. These may include house sparrows and common starlings, but be sure you are aware of local laws before attempting to catch any (by humane trapping or netting). For obvious reasons, any animals that have been poisoned or shot with shotgun pellets (lead and metal poisoning) should never be used.

Mammals: Laboratory mice and rats are the main mammals used to feed captive snakes. It may pay to keep breeding groups of these animals, which breed prolifically, and ensure a steady supply. Alternatively, they may be purchased as required, which will of course save you the extra time of maintaining the breeding groups, which can often be more time-consuming than the reptiles themselves. Like

day-old chicks, mice and rats may be available deep-frozen from commercial suppliers. Very young mice, sold as "pinkies," are often the best food for small to medium size constrictors. Other mammals useful for larger snakes include rabbits, gerbils, gophers, and guinea pigs, which should always be humanely killed before feeding to the snakes. Needless to say, all animals kept purely as prey animals for snakes should receive kind and hygienic husbandry and should not be neglected because they are just snake food.

FEEDING TECHNIQUES

How frequently one feeds captive snakes is often a matter of trial and error. Many species that feed readily can easily be overfed in the juvenile stage. Massive amounts of fat will build up in the body, eventually diminishing the functions of the internal organs and leading to sterility at the best, early death at the worst. It is also difficult to lay down hard and fast rules

about amounts of food to be given at each meal, and a certain amount of experimentation will be necessary. However, the following generalizations can be made.

Juvenile growing snakes should be fed about twice per week. Small to medium sized snakes can be offered food about once per week, while larger snakes can be fed substantial meals about once per two weeks.

However often you feed your snakes, try to keep similar periods between each feeding. The reptiles will soon learn to expect food at the given times and will be ready and waiting. If two or more snakes are kept together in a cage, keep a close watch at feeding time as two or more snakes may grab the same prey animal, resulting in injury or even one snake swallowing the other. Snakes will not feed during the shedding period, which may occur from three to eight times per annum depending on age and species.

If live prey is given to snakes, careful watch should be kept. If the prey is not overpowered

and eaten in a few minutes, it should be removed from the terrarium and tried again a day or two later. Live mice and rats have been known to gnaw into the body and severely damage an uninterested snake at night. Most snakes can be persuaded to take dead prey, particularly if it is moved about in front of their noses; it is best to do this with a stick to avoid getting bitten. Dead animals may be left in the terrarium overnight, but if uneaten the following morning they should be removed and disposed of by burning. Dead prey will putrefy very quickly in the warm environs of the terrarium.

All snakes consume whole prey animals that they may capture alive or find in carrion form. The fur, feathers, and bones of the prey animals are an important part of the diet and provide roughage as well as valuable minerals for bone-building and organic functions. Although some snakes can be trained to take strips of lean meat, this is not an adequate diet and must be supplemented as often as possible with whole

Mice are perhaps the most common food of captive snakes because so many diverse species will accept mice of various ages and sizes. Pinkie mice, one- to two-day-old hairless babies, are most popular. Photos: Top: *Heterodon nasicus*, S. C. and H. Miller; Center: *Elaphe o. obsoleta*, W. B. Allen, Jr.; Bottom: Colony of adult mice, Dr. H. R. Axelrod.

food animals. With the exception of some fish- and invertebrate-feeders, snakes normally will not require any additional supplements to their diet as they will receive whole prey animals that are a balanced diet in themselves.
Vitamin/mineral supplements in powder form can be dusted onto the meat, fish, or invertebrates being fed to snakes.

Sometimes snakes will steadfastly refuse all food offered. Having ascertained that you are giving the correct food for the species, have tried various kinds of foods, and have offered it dead and alive, during the day and at night, it may be necessary to resort to force-feeding. Before doing this, however, ensure that the reptile is not suffering from any disease or condition that may contribute to it losing its appetite. Mouth rot (necrotic stomatitis), shedding difficulties, internal or external parasites, and many other conditions may affect the appetite, so treatment for such conditions should precede or accompany force-feeding.

There are two methods of force-feeding. The first is to take a whole prey animal of suitable size. Opening the snake's mouth by gently pulling on the loose skin below the jaw, the

animal is pushed head-first into the mouth. Sometimes the snake will then start swallowing the prey of its own accord, in which case it can be released. If not, it will be necessary to work the prey down into the gullet and massage it into the stomach. The handle of a wooden spoon (lubricated with animal fat, glycerine, or mineral oil) or something similar can also be used to gently push the prey home. The second, more effective method of force-feeding is to liquefy the dead prey animal in a food processor, then place it in a large syringe with a smooth-ended rubber or plastic tube of suitable diameter and length pushed over the nozzle. The tube is lubricated with animal fat, glycerine, or mineral oil and pushed into the labial notch of the snake's mouth and then down into the stomach (approximately one-third the length of the snake). The contents of the syringe are then simply squeezed out. In order to get all of the food out of the tube and into the stomach, the food should be in a slurry with water. Some of the more difficult feeders can be maintained for long periods using these methods, which seem to do them little harm; indeed, some appear not only to get used to it but come to look forward to this method of feeding almost to the point of voluntarily opening the mouth for the tube to be introduced.

Another method of trying to induce snakes to take types of prey that normally are alien to them is as follows. If we are trying to get a snake that normally feeds on frogs to take mice, we can take a mouse and coat it with the mucus from a frog's skin. This will impart a froggy flavor to the mouse, and the snake may then take it readily. After this has been done a few times the snake often will begin to take mice that have not been treated. Snake-eating snakes can sometimes be persuaded to eat mice or chicks that have been wrapped in the shed skin of another snake.

HYGIENE

In order to minimize the risk of disease and to retain our snake specimens in prime health, good hygienic practices are essential. If snakes are kept on absorbent paper, this can be easily changed each time it is soiled. If the reptiles are kept on other kinds of substrate the fecal pellets can be scooped out as they appear by using a large spoon or a small long-handled shovel. The droppings of healthy snakes normally are fairly solid and leave little mess behind once you have scooped them out. At approximately monthly intervals the snakes should be removed to a spare cage or temporarily placed in a secure container (a clean trash can is ideal). All materials should be taken from the cage and either discarded and replaced or scrubbed clean. The inside of the cage and its contents should be scrubbed out with warm, soapy water, followed by a weak solution of bleach, and finally swilled out with clean water before being dried and refurnished. Domestic disinfectants other than bleach or povidone-iodine should never be used.

Drinking and bathing water should always be scrupulously clean and changed frequently. Many snake species seem to delight in defecating in the water bath (often just after it has been cleaned!), so cleanliness is essential. The glass viewing panels of the terrarium should be crystal-clear at all times; there is little worse in destroying the esthetic effect than having the viewing glass smeared with filth. All these regular chores are a little time-consuming but

should be well worth the effort.

Personal hygiene is also of utmost importance when dealing with captive animals. Although snakes are not notorious for passing diseases on to humans, there is no need for unnecessary risks. Always wash your hands thoroughly after handling snakes and their accommodations. It would be wise to have overalls or old clothes specially for use when you are dealing with your snakes.

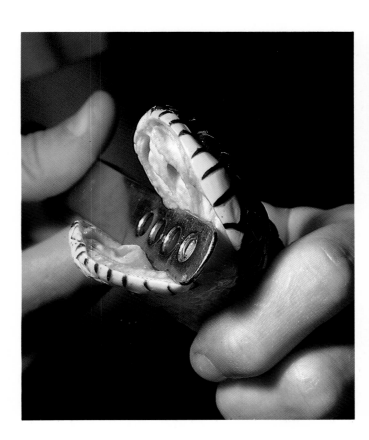

Force-feeding a *Boiga dendrophila* using a specially made tool, a flat piece of steel with holes to stabilize the feeding tube. Because a snake's mouth is delicate and even one or two broken teeth can lead to serious infections, force-feeding always is a risky step to take when trying to save a snake. Photos: S. Kochetov.

Top: Sometimes snakes require help in shedding, but such a step can be dangerous. Be sure the snake has exhausted all natural ways of shedding and be prepared to give supplements and prevent possible dehydration. Photo: S. Kochetov.

Right: Egg-binding is not uncommon in snakes that are not given correct substrates in which to lay. The large egg size of some snakes, such as this *Spalerosophis diadema*, the Diadem Snake, increases the possibility of serious blockages. Photo: R. T. Zappalorti.

Diseases and Treatment

Disease prevention is always better than cure, and this applies to snakes just as much as it does to humans and other animals. New arrivals to a collection, from whatever source, should be quarantined for a period before introduction to existing stock. Any snakes that become sick should be isolated immediately, preferably in a special hospital cage with minimum furnishings. This is best kept in a room separate from the main collection.

Veterinary advice should be sought whenever possible. Many snakes are expensive and valuable and deserve professional treatment. The layman should not attempt to diagnose and treat diseases without veterinary advice. In recent years the veterinary profession has taken a more active interest in exotic pets, including snakes and their diseases, that had hitherto been somewhat neglected. There are vets who show an active interest in reptiles and their diseases and are willing to advise your local veterinarian through the appropriate veterinary associations. In addition, it is important to be up to date with regular advances and changes in the various drugs used in the treatment of sick reptiles.

Any cages that have contained diseased snakes should be thoroughly disinfected by using a strong sodium hypochlorite or formalin solution, ensuring that all parts of the cage, its surrounding areas, utensils, and furnishings are treated. Dead snakes preferably should be sent for an autopsy. There are a number of institutions and pathologists prepared to perform such examinations free of charge or at a small fee in the interests of science. Your local zoo, college, or museum may know where the snake may be sent for autopsy. If a reptile dies from a known disease or if it is impractical to send it for a post-mortem examination, it should be incinerated. A dead snake saved for examination should be placed in a plastic bag tied at the neck and then placed in another bag. If it is likely to be some time before it reaches the laboratory it should be injected with formalin in several parts of the body, including the thoracic and abdominal cavities and the fleshy part of the tail. This will delay putrefaction of the organs.

Types of diseases may be loosely divided into two categories, non-communicable and communicable. The former are conditions caused by such things as incorrect environmental conditions, inadequate diet, and mechanical injuries, none of which can be transmitted from one reptile to the next. The latter are infectious diseases caused by various organisms that can be passed from one animal to the next if not kept under control.

NON-COMMUNICABLE DISEASES

Environmental Deficiencies: Optimum conditions for captive snakes are those in which the captive environment resembles that found in the natural habitat as closely as possible. If the temperature is too low, the snake may refuse to feed or may regurgitate recently consumed food. Digestion may be too slow, resulting in putrefaction of the prey in the snake's body and food poisoning. If the temperature is too high, heat prostration with renal constipation will result in death. Relative humidity levels too high for some species will result in blister disease, particularly to the belly scales, while a relative humidity that is too low may result in shedding problems, including retained spectacles. Photoperiod, quality of light, and seasonal environmental variations can also affect the natural cyclical activities such as mating, shedding, and hibernation. Life support systems in the terrarium should be checked and maintained to be continuously suitable for the individual species.

Water snakes cannot be kept in water for long periods, as most will develop bacterial lesions on the ventral scales that can become severely infected. With few exceptions, never keep a snake in a cage that has little access to dry basking areas. Photo: W. B. Allen, Jr.

Stress: This is a problem normally associated with human beings suffering from a hard time of one sort or another. Many will be surprised to hear that stress can affect all animals. Newly captured snakes are most susceptible to stress; the trauma of being captured, transported, and placed in an alien environment can take a toll on the reptiles's health and resistance to disease. Stress reduces resistance, and organisms that normally live in harmless symbiosis with the snakes can suddenly become pathogenic. Stress therefore should be minimized. Newly arrived specimens should be treated with the utmost care and respect and handled as little as possible. Sudden movements in front of the cage should be avoided; in fact, it would be wise to cover the glass viewing panel for a few days until the reptile gets used to its new environment. As snakes are very much creatures of habit, they soon learn exactly where the various basking areas, hiding places, water bowls, and other furnishings are situated.

Therefore, once the initial terrarium has been set up it would be unfair to the snakes to change the furnishings around each time the cage is cleaned out.

Nutritional Disturbances: Most snakes that are feeding readily, even on substitute diets, are not likely to suffer from serious nutritional disturbances. An exception concerns those snakes that may be fed on fish or pieces of fish meat. The flesh of many fish, but mainly saltwater species, contains the enzyme thiaminase, which destroys the B_1 vitamin (thiamine) in the body and can result in a deficiency of this vitamin (hypovitaminosis B_1). This deficiency can result in disorientation, loss of balance, and convulsions. If fish is heated to 80°C for about 5 minutes the thiaminase is destroyed and the balance returned. The fish of course should be allowed to cool to room temperature before being fed to the snakes. Snakes that have starved for protracted periods for various reasons will be emaciated and obviously deficient in vitamins and minerals. If the snake begins to feed again or is force-fed on

In the case of severe cuts or bite wounds, a veterinarian can literally stitch a large snake back together. Snakes have excellent healing powers and can recover from major injuries if infections do not set in. Photo: W. B. Allen, Jr.

a regular basis, the balance is restored. In severe cases the veterinarian may recommend the addition of a vitamin/mineral supplement to the food to speed up the return of a diet balance.

Shedding Problems: One of the most frequently encountered problems in captive snakes is difficulty in shedding or sloughing satisfactorily. All snakes shed their skins at regular intervals, the frequency depending on species, age, and seasonal influences, but most snakes shed on an average three to eight times per annum. Sloughing problems frequently arise when the relative humidity in the cage is too low (when snakes normally accustomed to humid habitats are those most likely to suffer) or if the snake is suffering from an infestation of skin mites. Normal shedding is usually preceded by a lack of luster in the skin, a fading of color and

pattern, and a milkiness of the brille (eye spectacle) that indicates a secretion of lubricating fluid between the old and the new skin beneath. During this period, snakes usually will not feed. Within 48 hours of these signs the snake should commence shedding, and this should be completed in an hour or so. The snake first rubs its lips against a rough surface, thus loosening the skin at this area. A healthy snake will then literally crawl out of its old skin (this being turned inside-out in the process) and emerge as a sleek, colorful improvement of its former self.

In an unhealthy specimen, or where the air is too dry, the skin may break off in pieces, allowing the lubricating fluid to dry under the unshed pieces. Such unshed skin must be removed, as infection can quickly set in beneath, creating further health hazards. The affected reptile should be placed in a container of lukewarm water in such a way that it is completely submerged (but allowed to breathe of course) and allowed to soak for a couple of hours, after which some of the loose skin should float away and the remainder can be gently peeled off with the fingers.

Occasionally the old eye spectacle is particularly stubborn and may remain on the snake long after the remainder of the skin has been shed. In some severe cases a snake may have two or more spectacles left on an eye from previous sheddings. After shedding, the spectacles should be examined to see if they have been shed (if not, this can usually be detected by the presence of a slightly ragged edge). An obstinate eye spectacle can be lubricated with glycerine or mineral oil over a period of two to three days, after which it usually can be gently lifted with the fingernail, taking great care not to damage the new brille beneath. On no account should a metal instrument be used to do this. Another method that can be tried is to wind a piece of adhesive tape around the finger, sticky side out, then gently dab at the brille in the hope that it will adhere to the tape.

After a troublesome shedding occurs, the conditions should be improved in order to diminish the possibility of it recurring.

Mechanical Injuries: Wounds may be suffered as a result of injury due to fighting, attempting to escape, striking against the terrarium glass, etc. Such wounds are susceptible to infection, particularly in the case of newly captured specimens suffering from stress. Open lesions should be treated as soon as possible by bathing them with an antiseptic solution such as povidone-iodine and, if extensive, stitched with an everting mattress suture (by a veterinarian). Healing of such wounds is often prolonged in snakes, and a regular course of antiseptic bathing should be carried out until visible healing begins. In some cases antibiotic treatment may be required. Bactericidal antibiotics can be used in snakes for both prophylaxis and treatment.

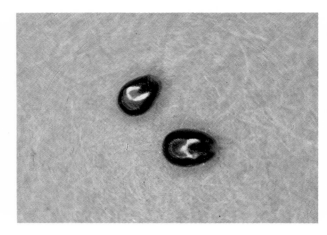

COMMUNICABLE DISEASES

Ectoparasites: Bloodsucking ticks and mites are most commonly found on wild-caught snakes and if not removed can cause epidemics of serious proportions in captive stocks. Additionally, bloodsucking parasites can transmit blood-borne parasitic diseases and *Aeromonas* septicemia. Ticks of one or more species attached to newly caught specimens can usually be found quite easily. Up to 5 mm (1/5 in) in length, ticks fasten themselves with their piercing mouthparts to the snake's skin, usually between the scales and often at secluded parts of the body, such as in the loose folds below the jaw, around the vent, or between the ventral and subcaudal scales. Manual removal of ticks should be preceded by dabbing with alcohol to relax the mouthparts, otherwise there is a danger of the head being left embedded in the skin, which can result in sepsis. Newly arrived snakes should be inspected carefully for ticks, and these should be removed and destroyed.

Mites of several species, but particularly those of the genus *Ophionyssus*, are common and can be a serious problem in the terrarium unless checked in time. Being highly mobile, mites can also quickly move from reptile to reptile and terrarium to terrarium, and large numbers of them can cause stress, anemia, difficulties in shedding, loss of appetite, and eventual death. Unlike ticks, mites do not live on the body of the host but hide in crevices during the day, coming out to suck the reptile's blood at night. Mites are about the size of a pinhead, roughly globular in shape, and normally brown in color, but become red when bloated with blood. Mites often can be seen moving over a reptile's body or attached to the skin if the terrarium lights are turned on suddenly at night. In severe infestations, mites also may be seen during the

Ticks are not uncommon on wild-caught boids and other larger snakes. If present in large enough numbers they can be a drain on the snake's health, and they also can carry several serious diseases. They should be removed as soon as possible and the site of attachment treated with an antibiotic cream. Photos: Top Left: Removing a tick from *Python sebae*; W. B. Allen, Jr.; Top Right: Ticks engorged with blood; M. Gilroy; Bottom: Tick attached above the eye of *Dromicus typhlus*; B. Kahl.

day. Another sign of a mite infestation is the appearance of their dust-like, silvery feces on the reptile's skin or on surfaces in the terrarium. Infected reptiles should be moved to a clean terrarium in which is suspended a small piece of dichlorvos insecticidal strip and left for a period of four days. About 1 sq cm per 10 liters (⅕ in per cu ft) of air space is adequate. The strip preferably should be suspended inside a perforated container so that the reptiles cannot come into direct contact with the insecticide. All free-moving mites will be destroyed by the vapors emitted by the strip. The treatment should be repeated after ten days to destroy any nymphs that hatch from eggs in the interim period. Vacated infected terraria should be thoroughly cleaned, scrubbed, and disinfected.

Endoparasites: Parasitic organisms living in the internal parts of the body are known as endoparasites. The most important

into a dead prey animal. The following anthelminthics and dosages have been recommnended as suitable for snakes:
For **roundworm** treatment:
Albendazole: 50 milligrams per kilogram orally.
Fenbendazole: 50mg/kg orally.
Levamisole: 200mg/kg orally or 50mg/kg by injection.
Mebendazole: 100mg/kg orally.
For **tapeworm** treatment:
Bunamide: 25mg/kg orally.
Dichlorphen; 200mg/kg orally.
Niclosamide: 150mg/kg orally.
Praziquantel: 20-30mg/kg orally or 3.5-7mg/kg by injection.

Other internal parasites less commonly encountered include flukes that infect the buccal cavity and upper respiratory tract. These normally respond to treatment with orally

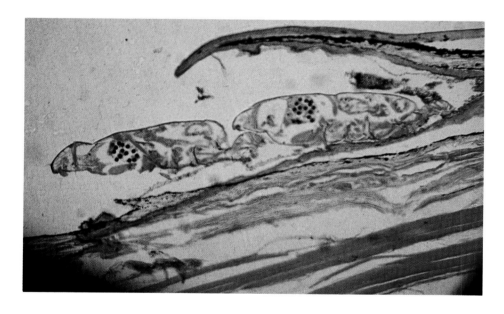
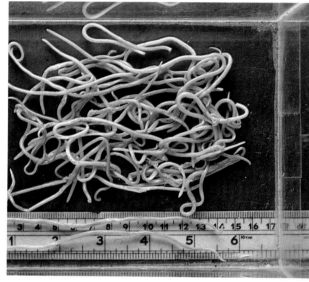

Left: Cross-section of a snake mite, *Ophionyssus natricis*, attached under the scale of a Common Garter Snake. Right: A group of roundworms, *Polydelphis quadricornus*, from *Python molurus*. Photos: E. Elkan.

endoparasites of concern to the snake-keeper are those known as helminths. Those most commonly found are various species of roundworm and tapeworm. Most wild snakes play host to one or more species of intestinal worm. Under normal conditions complications are rare, although some researchers regard tapeworms in small fish-eating snakes to be pathogenic. Worm infestations also can become a problem in snakes suffering from stress, resulting in an unnatural buildup of parasite size or numbers. This can lead to anemia and general malaise and can eventually lead to death. Signs of severe endoparasitic infection include loss of appetite, emaciation, and the presence of worms, their eggs, or segments of tapeworms in the feces. Routine microscopic examination of feces samples (which can be arranged by a veterinarian) will provide evidence of infection.

Anthelminthic preparations are available through your veterinarian, whose advice should be sought with regard to worm infections. These may be given via stomach tube or, if the snake is feeding readily, by injecting the vermicide

administered (by stomach tube) praziquantel at a dosage rate of 100mg/kg. Degenerate arthropods known as pentastomes, also (but fortunately rarely) found in the respiratory tract, can be highly pathogenic to their hosts but are difficult to treat.

Protozoan Infections: Cases of dysentery in captive snakes have been caused by the protozoan *Entamoeba invadens*. Symptoms include general debilitation and watery, slimy feces. Untreated, this can rapidly reach epizootic proportions in a captive collection. Treatment with metronidazole, orally administered at a dosage rate of 160-400mg/kg, has proven effective.

Intestinal flagellates are common in snakes but usually appear to be non-pathogenic, though they may sometimes be responsible for diarrhea. Treatment with metronidazole has proved effective in such cases.

Bacterial Infections: Cases of infective salmonellosis have occurred in snakes. As some of these organisms can be pathogenic to humans, it emphasizes the need for good

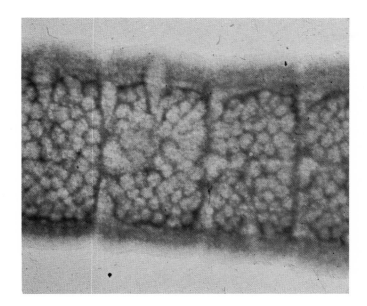

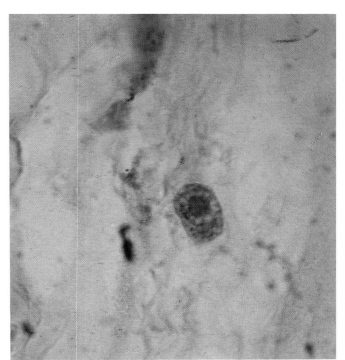

invasion of the mucous membranes in the mouth. In severe cases, the mucous membranes of the jaw margins swell to such an extent that the mouth cannot be properly closed, the bones of the jaw eventually may become infected, and death will ensue. Death is often caused by a combination of starvation (as a snake with this condition will not feed) and the toxic products of the bacterial infection. It is important to catch this disease in its early stages. Any swelling of the mouth should be investigated. The disease manifests itself in inflamed mucous membranes, with a gray, paste-like mass adhering to areas around the teeth. The mouth should be held open and swabbed out with povidone-iodine (cotton swabs are ideal for this) or hydrogen peroxide, taking particular care to remove the paste. Swabbing may be required daily over a period of several days, and it may be necessary to force-feed the snake during treatment. In advanced cases, the veterinarian may advise the surgical removal of infected tissue and bone under general anesthetic. Such treatment will usually be accompanied by a course of antibiotics.

Respiratory Infections: These are uncommon in snakes that are kept in optimum

Top Left: Segments (proglottids) of a typical tapeworm. Bottom Left: *Entamoeba invadens*, a common cause of dysentery in snakes. Photos: E. Elkan.

Mouthrot in snakes. Top Right: Infected tissue around the fangs of a Puff Adder, *Bitis arietans.* Bottom Right: Severe, possibly terminal, necrotic stomatitis in a Boa Constrictor. Photos: W. B. Allen, Jr.

hygienic practices. Infective salmonellosis manifests itself in watery, often greenish, foul-smelling feces. Treatment with antibiotics, as advised by your vet, often proves effective.

Abscesses and Cysts: Soft or hard lumps appearing on a snake's body under the skin are often attributable to bacterial invasion, usually as a result of a previous break in the skin that apparently may have healed. Large abscesses or cysts can be opened surgically under anesthetic by a qualified veterinarian. The wound is cleaned out and swabbed with povidone-iodine and treated with an antibiotic before being sutured. Further antibiotic treatment by injection may be required during the healing process.

Mouth Rot: This condition (or as it is more correctly termed, necrotic stomatitis) is unfortunately one of the commonest forms of malaise in captive snakes and is frequently fatal. Newly captured specimens suffering stress are particularly susceptible. Nervous snakes that strike against the terrarium glass and injure the mouth and jaw are susceptible to bacterial conditions. Symptoms include difficulty in breathing, blocked nostrils, and a mucous discharge. These conditions often can be alleviated and cured by moving the reptile to warmer, drier, well-ventilated conditions. In severe cases your veterinarian may recommend a course of antibiotic treatment.

VETERINARY TREATMENT

Although many simple treatments may be administered by the snake-keeper, it is emphasized here that veterinary advice should be sought at any time there is the slightest doubt about the efficacy of the proposed treatment. The layman can quite easily diagnose a disease falsely and carry out the wrong treatment, which can in itself be a hazard to the health of the snake. In addition, there are laws in many countries that prohibit the administration of certain treatments to animals by anyone other than veterinarians or licensed animal technicians.

Anesthesia: All surgical operations on snakes should be accompanied by anesthesia. It is advisable that snakes not be fed for 96 hours prior to anesthesia. A reliable anesthetic for snakes has proven to be a cyclohexylamine, ketamine hydrochloride, given by intramuscular injection at a dosage rate of 50mg/kg. In cases where the initial dose is insufficient, the level of anesthesia can be deepened by a halothane/oxygen mixture applied via a small face mask (a small plastic funnel has been found to be a suitable substitute). Ketamine can be dangerous to debilitated individuals, in which case a halothane/oxygen or methoxyflurane/oxygen mixture can be given in an induction chamber to produce a satisfactory level of anesthesia. Obviously a competent vet must administer anesthesia.

Euthanasia: Unfortunately it sometimes becomes necessary to kill a specimen that is diseased or injured beyond repair. This preferably should be carried out by a veterinarian. Snakes can be killed by injecting with an overdose of barbiturates, by decapitation, or by cooling and eventual death by subsequent deep-freezing.

Drug Administration: Snakes usually are injected intramuscularly in the middle third of the body just to the side of the spinal column. The needle is inserted under a scale and pushed in an anterior direction. Where rapid absorption of the drug is less urgent, it is somewhat safer to inject intramuscularly into the fleshy part of the tail.

Many drugs can be administered orally to snakes by using a syringe and stomach tube. The head of the snake is held firmly and the rounded end of the lubricated stomach tube is pushed through the labial notch. At least one-third of the snake is held vertically and the tube is passed down through the esophagus to the stomach. The drug, which is in solution or suspension in the syringe, is allowed to descend into the stomach by gravity.

Surgery: Recent advances in veterinary techniques with regard to the lower vertebrates have led to a better understanding of anesthesia and surgery in captive reptiles. Many surgical operations, including removal of tumors, repair of wounds, and even hysterectomies, can now be safely carried out.

HIBERNATION

The subject of hibernation in captive reptiles is one that in the past has roused a certain amount of controversy. Many snakes have been kept at constant high temperatures, day and night, year in and year out, without any regard to their natural climatic requirements. Snakes are relatively non-adaptive to conditions alien to them, and, although a reptile from a temperate habitat may appear to thrive and feed summer and winter under artificial heat, its life will be considerably shortened and its cyclic rhythms will be disturbed. Snakes kept in such conditions are unlikely to breed.

Temperate to subtropical snakes require seasonal changes in temperature and photoperiod as well as a period of immobility during the winter months. In the wild such periods of immobility occur when the temperature is inadequate to permit normal activity. Hibernation also plays an important part in seasonal reproductive activity, which normally takes place in the spring. Wild snakes usually hibernate deep in the ground in fissures, hollow roots, or burrows of various animals; some species congregate in large numbers in suitable hibernacula.

Hibernating a captive snake for several months of the year may seem a boring proposition. However, an adequate alternative to hibernation seems to be a short rest period at a much reduced temperature. This can be achieved by first ensuring that the reptile is adequately fed and has built up enough body to be able to withstand a prolonged period of fasting. Feeding is then stopped and the temperature in the terrarium is reduced progressively over a period of about 14 days. The terrarium is best kept in an unheated but frost-free room at this time. When the temperature is reduced to 4-6°C, the reptiles can be allowed to hibernate in the terrarium (under cover in their hiding places) or can be placed in a ventilated container loosely packed with dry sphagnum moss. The reptiles are kept at this low temperature for four to eight weeks, after which the process is reversed—a gradual increase to 20-28°C over a period of 14 days, but still reducing the night temperature to around 15°C. Such treatment will usually trigger a natural breeding response from snakes that normally hibernate in the wild.

Reproduction and Propagation

Perhaps the most satisfying and exciting aspect of keeping snakes is encouraging the reptiles to reproduce. However, only those specimens that are kept in optimum conditions are likely to make any effort to court and mate, and it is essential to have a knowledge of a species's natural habitat and environment before a serious breeding program is commenced.

SEX DETERMINATION

Perhaps the most obvious requirement for captive breeding success is to have a male and a female of the species to be bred. In general, it can be said that it is not easy to distinguish the sexes of snakes as in most species there is very little sexual dimorphism. One notable exception is the genus *Langaha*, in which the complex nasal extensions of male and female differ in structure. In some snake families the tail (being the distance from the posterior edge of the anal scale to the tail tip) is longer and stouter in males (because of the hemipenes) than in the females. This difference is particularly marked in the Viperidae and most members of the Boidae. Determination of the sexes of members of the genus *Bitis* is relatively easy in that the female has a short, sharply tapering tail, while that of the male is four to five times longer. Subcaudal scale counts are a fairly reliable method of sexing many species, the scales below the tail being greater in number in males than in females. (Such counts seldom are completely accurate in distinguishing individuals, instead representing mathematical trends within a species.) In most snake species the adult females

are larger and more robust than the corresponding males, though there are exceptions; of course, this is little help if you are dealing with immature specimens.

The most reliable method of determining the sexes of snakes has become probing with a sexing probe. When not sexually active, the hemipenes of the male snake lie inverted (inside-out) in sheaths situated in the base of the tail just posterior to the vent. By inserting a probe into either side of the vent and pushing it gently in the direction of the tail tip, it is possible to pass it inside the inverted male hemipenis to a distance several times greater than that possible in a female. The distance varies from species to species, but it normally is possible to pass the probe for up to ten subcaudal scales in the male, but seldom more than two or three in the female. Sexing probes

Top: External sexing of Corn Snakes. The male has a longer tail than the female, and the tail is distinctly thicker, especially at the base. Photo: J. Gee. Bottom Left: A pair of Emerald Tree Boas, *Corallus caninus*; the male is the smaller animal. Photo: S. Kochetov. Bottom Right: Careful use of a stainless steel sexing probe to determine sex. This is a male Corn Snake. Photo: J. Gee.

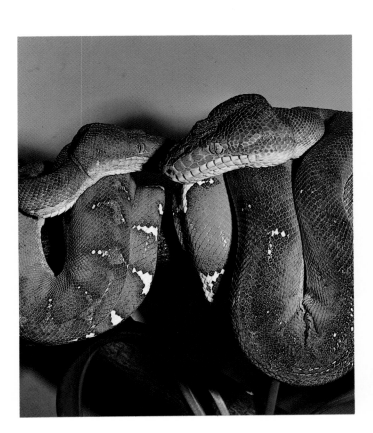

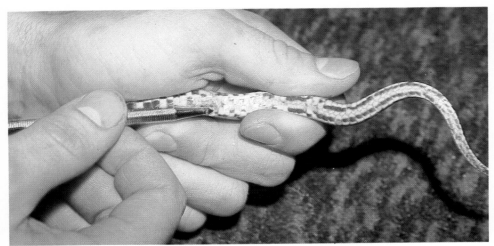

can be obtained from specialist suppliers (ask at your local zoo or herpetological society) and are usually available in sets of various sizes suitable for small to large species or individuals. They may be manufactured from stainless steel or synthetic material and basically resemble a knitting needle with a little ball at the tip. Before use, the tip should be lubricated with a little petroleum jelly or mineral oil. The snake must be restrained (you may require help). Insertion into the vent should be carried out with great care so as not to cause injury. If one probe does not slide in easily, try a smaller one. Never force a probe home. With a little practice, the use of probes for sexing snakes becomes easy.

Further methods of sex determination in snakes include surgical sexing and hormone investigation of fecal or blood samples. Such methods may be carried out by zoological gardens or research establishments and are usually out of reach of the amateur snake-keeper. However, such methods are reliable, and if the means and facilities are available in your area they should not be discounted. Information may be obtained from reptile curators or specialist veterinarians.

REPRODUCTIVE CYCLES

The snake's reproductive cycle is affected by environment and seasonal changes. If kept in conditions alien to that of the natural habitat the

A mating pair of Womas, *Aspidites ramsayi*. Photo: R. T. Hoser.

reproductive cycle will be severely impaired, resulting in few breeding successes. I make no excuse for repeating the fact that it is most important to have a knowledge of a species's natural biotope. The provision of seasonal changes in the terrarium will greatly enhance the chances of successful propagation.

Most snake species breed once per year upon reaching sexual maturity. Breeding condition is brought about in response to climatic conditions at certain times of the year. For example, species from temperate climates will benefit from a period of hibernation followed by a progressive increase in temperature and photoperiod. Species from dry subtropical climates will still require seasonal changes in temperature and photoperiod, even if not hibernated. Some species may benefit from a period of estivation, others from variations in humidity. Many rain-, montane-, or monsoon-forest species lay their eggs to coincide with seasonal periods of high humidity in order to facilitate satisfactory development of the embryo. By experimenting with heaters, lights, timers, and humidifiers, it is possible to emulate the native habitat, resulting in the successful breeding of most species.

COURTSHIP

Most snakes are fairly solitary outside the breeding season. An exception is those that hibernate communally in suitable sites—an advantage of this of course is that the sexes are near each other in the spring breeding season. Most snakes, however, find their mates initially by chance as their paths cross. Of course, the natural breeding stimulus in the appropriate season will also make the snakes more active in seeking a mate. Scent plays an important part in attracting the male to the female, the Jacobson organ having a significant function. A sexually mature female will emit secretions from the anal gland and leave a scent trail that is attractive to the male. In addition, female snakes that have recently shed release a pheromone called vitellogen on the skin surface from between the scales that also stimulates male sexual activity. A male finding a female scent trail will follow the trail with great determination, flickering his tongue at frequent intervals. Taking the correct direction along a scent trail is presumably decided by the progressive increase in concentration of the scent. As a male approaches a female along the trail, he will flick his tongue at increasing intervals and the excitement in his movements becomes obvious to the onlooker.

As most snakes normally are solitary, the greatest breeding successes are attained when the sexes are kept separately for most of the year, introducing females to males at breeding time. Those specimens that are physiologically prepared through optimum climatic conditions will normally commence courtship almost immediately after introduction. In the wild, several males may converge on a receptive female after following her scent trail, and in some species a combat ritual will take place in which rival males vie for the attentions of the female. A combat ritual is a form of serpentine wrestling in which males, with bodies entwined, will attempt to force the heads of their adversaries to the ground. Four, five, or even more males may participate, though two is more usual. Injuries rarely occur during these battles, as the weaker, exhausted males will eventually concede defeat and crawl off to try their luck elsewhere. The dominant male will then court and mate the female without interference from other males, but his task is far from complete.

Female snakes usually remain fairly passive during male combat rituals and may even crawl off while the suitors are doing battle. Having found the female again, the dominant male needs to persuade her to mate. The male approaches the female in short, jerky movements while continually flickering the tongue in and out. He will nudge and taste the region of her vent, from whence sexually

Top: The cloacal region of an Emerald Tree Boa showing the anal scale and the spurs of the male. Photo: S. Kochetov. Center: During courtship and mating the male Milksnake, *Lampropeltis triangulum gentilis*, grasps the female at the back of the head. Photo: L. Trutnau. Bottom: Detail of an anal spur in a male *Epicrates striatus*. Photo: J. Dodd.

no cause for concern as such injuries usually heal completely without mishap.

A single pair of snakes kept together in a terrarium or introduced together at breeding time will often show no apparent tendency to mate, even when one has steadfastly endeavored to produce optimum conditions. In such cases a mating response can often be achieved by

stimulating scents emerge. Eventually he will move his head slowly and jerkily along the female's body in the direction of her head and will endeavor to entwine his body with hers (which is not always easy when the female is not immediately receptive). He stimulates her body with his tongue and, when in the correct position, will attempt to bring his cloaca into apposition with hers. At this stage some of the more primitive snakes with ventral spurs will use these to further stimulate the female in the region of the vent. If receptive, the female will obligingly lift her tail clear of the ground to give the male easier access.

Eventually, with tails and bodies entwined, the male is able to force one of his engorged hemipenes into the female's cloaca and copulation commences. Copulation in snakes may take from 30 minutes to several hours. In some cases the female often loses interest and may try to crawl off dragging the male by his hemipenis. This sometimes results in minor injuries either to the hemipenis or to the interior of the female cloaca, but small amounts of blood left on the substrate during or after mating are

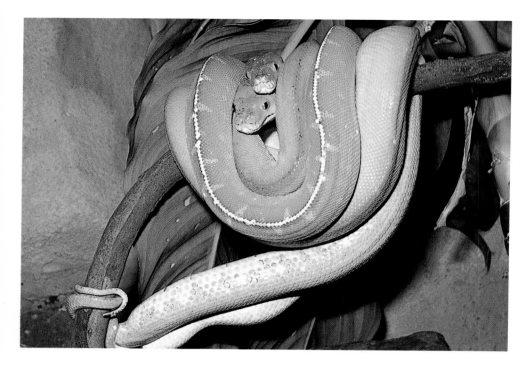

even be supplemented by small cartiliginous processes or spines that help anchor the organ firmly in the female cloaca.

The paired testes lie in the posterior part of the abdominal cavity, the right organ being situated further forward than the left and both being situated anterior to the kidneys. Spermatozoa produced in the testes pass along the seminal vessels and join with the urinary vessels from the kidneys before emptying into a common chamber of the cloaca through the papilla urogenitalis. The base of this papilla continues as a groove along which the semen is conducted to the erect hemipenis and thus introduced into the female cloaca during copulation.

The female ovaries are also paired and are situated in the part of the body corresponding to the position of the male testes. Only in the family Typhlopidae has the left ovary and its accompanying oviduct become vestigial. Ova are produced in the ovary, ripen, and are then actually released into the body cavity. During ovulation in the body cavity, the follicles surrounding the ova burst and the generative cells migrate to the funnel-like mouths of the paired oviducts, which open just posterior to the liver. The ova pass through the oviducts, where they are fertilized by the male spermatozoa during copulation and are then stored in the uterus (which is the posterior part of the ovary). The thin but muscular walls of the oviduct and the somewhat thicker walls of the uterus are furnished on the interior with ciliate cells for transporting semen and with various glands for the production of egg-building secretions. The right and left oviducts may join first or enter the cloaca separately, depending on the species.

Copulation in three species of snake. Notice that the vents of the snakes are in contact, with the bodies variously twisted to permit copulation. Top: *Chondropython viridis.* Photo: C. Banks. Center: *Lampropeltis triangulum sinaloae.* Photo: L. Trutnau. Bottom: *Lampropeltis alterna.* Photo: R. W. Applegate.

introducing a second or even a third male to induce the combat ritual, after which the victorious male will not hesitate to commence courtship. Keep a close watch on the proceedings and then carefully remove the vanquished males from the terrarium, allowing the pair to mate in peace. Under normal circumstances, copulating snakes should be left undisturbed.

THE REPRODUCTIVE SYSTEM

The male snake possesses a pair of hemipenes (literally: half-penises), each of which is capable of operating independently of the other (an attribute shared only with the lizards). During non-sexual activity these organs lie inside-out in sheaths inside the tail base. Unlike the true penis of mammals, there is no seminal duct, but a simple external groove forms the path along which sperm is conducted. This groove normally is inside the sheathed hemipenis but reaches the outer surface when the organ is everted through the vent for sexual activity. The structure of the hemipenes is usually complex and varies greatly from species to species. Many are furnished with numerous spines that may

THE GRAVID FEMALE

In a successfully mated female snake, the fertilized eggs are stored in the lower part of the oviduct (the uterus), where they develop for a shorter or longer period, depending on the species and its method of reproduction. A female snake containing fertilized eggs at any stage of development is said to be gravid. Snakes may be oviparous or ovoviviparous. In the former case (egglayers) the mother lays eggs containing poorly developed embryos with a large supply of nutritive yolk for the further development of the embryos within the egg but outside the maternal body. In contrast, an ovoviviparous (livebearing) species retains the eggs in the uterus for a much longer period and full term embryonal development takes place within the maternal body. In simple terms, the two groups can be described as egglaying and livebearing, respectively, although in the latter case the embryos still develop in an egg sac that ruptures at birth or shortly thereafter. Some oviparous species show varying degrees of development toward ovoviviparity in that the embryos develop to a fairly advanced but not complete stage before oviposition. Thus, among the various oviparous species, the period of gravidity may range from 25-70 days before the eggs are deposited, while the gestation period in ovoviviparous species may take 100 days or more.

An additional factor that must be borne in mind with regard to periods of gravidity is that the females of some species evidently are able to store viable sperm in the seminal receptaculum (situated near to the head of the oviduct) for months or even years. This explains the fact that a female snake that has been kept for a long period in captive isolation may suddenly become gravid and eventually lay a clutch of fertile eggs. In some rare cases snakes have been known to lay two or more fertile clutches over a period of several years without having been in contact with a male since the first mating.

Parthenogenicity (a method of reproduction in which the ova develop without fertilization by the male gamete and produce offspring identical to the female parent) has been discovered in some lizard species and in the blind wormsnake *Ramphotyphlops* (= *Typhlina*) *bramina*. It has not yet been proved in a few other snakes though there is a likelihood that it may exist.

In an advanced state, gravid females take on a plump appearance, particularly toward the posterior part of the body, and the outline of the developing eggs usually can be clearly seen as bulges on either side of the abdomen. At an early stage in its gravidity, a female snake may refuse to feed until after egglaying or birth of the young; this is a natural phenomenon that should give no cause for concern. However, she will drink frequently and profusely, so fresh water must be available at all times. It is also important that optimum climatic conditions are available at this time as a gravid female often will bask in order to absorb added warmth for

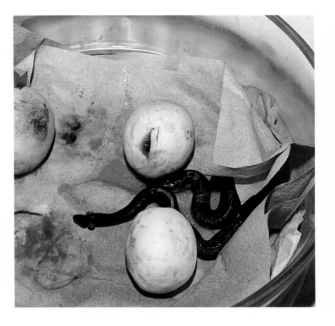

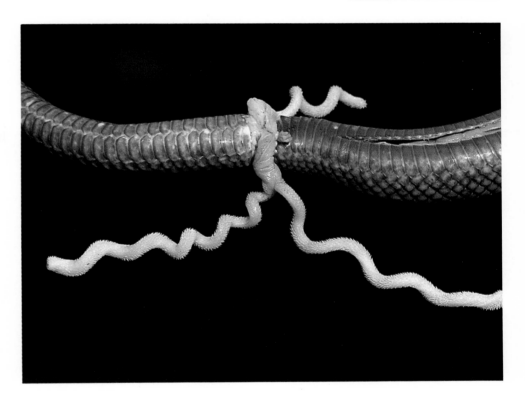

Hemipenes. Top: Partially everted hemipenes of a hatchling cobra, *Naja* sp. Photo: W. B. Allen, Jr. Center: Deeply forked hemipenes of the Mole Snake, *Pseudaspis cana*. Photo: J. Visser. Bottom: Hemipenes removed from the rattlesnake *Crotalus viridis*. Photo: J. Visser.

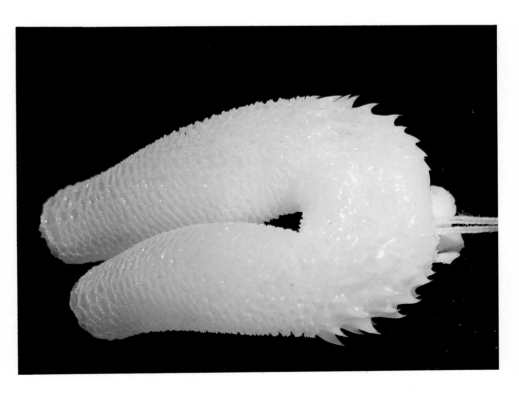

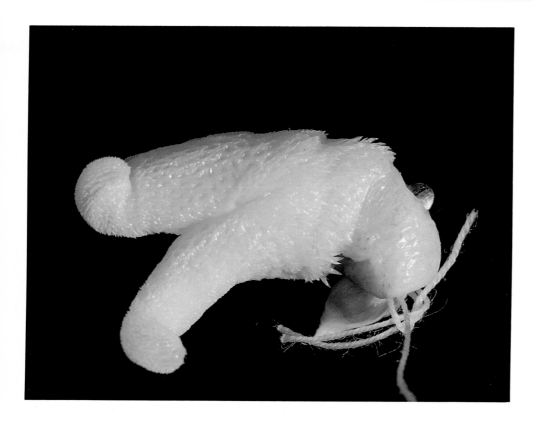

Hemipenes removed from the cobra *Naja nivea* and inflated with fluid to retain their erected shape. Photo: J. Visser.

Obviously gravid Diadem Snake, *Spalerosophis diadema*, and a partial clutch of eggs. Photo: R. T. Zappalorti.

sex ratio in a clutch, the optimum temperature producing a fairly equal mixture of males and females, but deviations slightly above or below the optimum producing predominantly one sex or the other.

A snake in its natural, wild habitat will have a choice of prospective egglaying sites and, as the time for oviposition approaches, will spend up to several days searching for the ideal spot. This may be beneath a flattish stone, under a log, in a rotten log, in loose soil, or among rotting vegetation. The garden compost heap or the farm manure heap is often chosen as an egglaying site by common snakes living in suburban or agricultural areas. Often suitable egglaying sites may be few and far between, resulting in several snakes using the same site. Communal nests containing hundreds, even thousands, of eggs are occasionally recorded. The interior of termite mounds is often a favored egglaying site for many snake species, the microclimate contained therein being ideal for embryo development.

In the terrarium, the choice of egglaying sites is limited, but it is important to try and provide something that is acceptable to the snake. Egglaying chambers seem to offer a reasonable compromise for many species. Such a chamber can easily be made by using a plastic margarine or ice cream tub or a similar container compatible with the size of the snake. Holes of a diameter just large enough for the snake to gain entry are cut in one or two sides of the tub. The interior of the tub is loosely filled with slightly damp sphagnum moss. If two or more such chambers are offered in the heated terrarium there is a good chance that a gravid female will select one in which to lay her eggs. Sometimes, however, a snake will not be satisfied with anything you offer and will end up scattering the eggs haphazardly about the substrate or even in the water bath. A close watch should be kept at egglaying time so that such eggs can be quickly rescued. With the exception of those species that incubate their eggs (e.g., pythons), the eggs should be removed as soon as possible for artificial incubation.

the developing embryos.

You should refrain from handling a gravid female unless it becomes absolutely necessary, as undue disturbance may result in stress and affect the satisfactory development of the embryos.

OVIPOSITION

Oviposition or egglaying in oviparous species usually takes place in a spot specially selected by the female as being ideal for the welfare and further development of the embryos. The major factors for this seem to be concealment and optimum temperature and humidity.

Recent research has shown that in many reptile species temperature can determine the

Ovoviviparous species are less selective and tend to give birth to their young or hatching eggs wherever they happen to be at the time, though there is evidence to suggest that they will seek a secluded spot if possible. The young usually are brought forth each in a transparent membrane that they will break open during or shortly after birth. Occasionally, usually in hot, dry conditions, the membrane will dry out too quickly and the young snakes will have difficulty in escaping. In such cases, the membrane can be carefully snipped open with a pair of surgical scissors.

In most cases, young snakes are immediately active and will soon seek out hiding or basking places. Little or no maternal interest is shown by ovoviviparous snakes toward their young once they have given birth. Indeed, they may

Actual egg-laying in a Diadem Snake. This species has an exceptionally large egg for the size of the adult female. Photos: R. T. Zappalorti.

Egg-laying in *Cyclagras gigas* (Top Left) and *Pituophis melanoleucus catenifer* (Top Right). Photos: Top Left: C. Banks; Top Right: W. B. Allen, Jr.

Guarding of an egg clutch or nest by a female Burmese Python, *Python molurus bivittatus*. Notice that hatching has begun. Photo: B. Kahl.

Birth. Top Left: Birth of a Puff Adder, *Bitis arietans*. Photo: C. Banks. Other photos, top to bottom: Birth of a Copperhead, *Agkistrodon contortrix*. Notice the yellow tail tip and remnant of the birth membrane on the young at the bottom. Photos: R. T. Zappalorti.

Top: A natural nest of Corn Snake, *Elaphe guttata*, eggs in the process of hatching. Photo: R. T. Zappalorti. Center: New-born Boa Constrictors with membranes and cords, including still-born young. Photo: W. B. Allen, Jr. Bottom: A female Milksnake, *Lampropeltis triangulum sinaloae*, wrapped around her eggs. Photo: L. Trutnau.

even regard them as a tasty addition to the menu. After an adult snake has given birth, it is best to remove the young to separate containers.

INCUBATION

In almost all cases, the best breeding results occur when the eggs of captive snakes are removed from the laying site and incubated artificially. An exception is when native snakes are being kept in an outdoor reptile house in a suitable climate, but even then it can be somewhat of a hit and miss affair. In the past, the most difficult part of snake breeding has been the satisfactory incubation of the eggs. Keepers have seen their excitement mount as the snakes mate, go through a period of gravidity, and lay their eggs, only to be sorely disappointed as the eggs slowly shrivel away and fail to hatch. In the last 20 or 30 years, however, a better understanding of the conditions and techniques required by developing eggs has brought the possibility of reasonable success to the serious enthusiast.

The eggs of all oviparous snakes are typically egg-shaped to elongate. They are white to cream in color and possess a soft, leathery shell designed to absorb moisture from the material in which they are incubating. Newly laid eggs often have a collapsed or dimpled appearance but soon will fill out and become taut as moisture is absorbed. Eggs laid in the terrarium or in egglaying chambers should be carefully removed and, preferably, always kept the same way up. They should be arranged in rows and buried in hollows to about half their diameter in an incubation medium contained in a plastic box, thus allowing for regular inspection without undue disturbance.

Occasionally eggs may be laid in a clump. If not discovered and separated before the surface mucus dries out, it will be impossible to separate them without damaging them. In such cases the clump should be partially buried in the incubation medium so that as many as possible are visible.

Many methods of artificial incubation have

been recommended, ranging from placing the eggs on moist absorbant paper to burying them in slightly damp sand, peat, sphagnum moss, or a whole range of other materials. In recent years a most satisfactory incubation material has been found to be vermiculite, an inert mineral that is available commercially from plant nurseries. It is sterile, retains moisture, and comes in various grades. For incubation purposes a fine grade is suitable. This can be mixed with roughly an equal amount (by weight) of water, which will be completely absorbed. If sand is used, it should be washed and sterilized, then partially dried out. Peat is best avoided as an incubation material as the acidity may impair normal development of the embryos.

Plastic lunch or refrigerator boxes are ideal for holding the incubation medium. Holes can be drilled in the lid to allow air circulation (mild ventilation is also important to incubating eggs, but **not** cold drafts). The incubation box should be placed in an incubator that is maintained at 25-30°C. The type of incubator is immaterial as long as the correct temperature can be maintained. An incubator suitable for hatching bird eggs can be used, but a simple and efficient incubator can be quite easily made at home. A ventilated wooden box with a glass door on the front and heated by a simple lightbulb controlled by a thermostat is all that is required. It is recommended that a blue or red bulb be used to minimize the amount of light produced. Alternatively, a heat cable, a heating pad, or a porcelain heat bulb can be used.

Most eggs will develop satisfactorily in a temperature range of 25-30°C, and variation in that range will do little harm. Indeed, such variations will correspond to natural temperature fluctuations and should help produce a satisfactory ratio of sexes. During development, the eggs will absorb moisture from the surrounding medium and increase in weight. Eggs that fail to absorb moisture are usually infertile but should not be discarded until this is absolutely certain. The contents of infertile eggs will putrefy and become discolored; as soon as this happens they should be removed and discarded. Sometimes mold

Snake egg clutches must be incubated. The substrate may vary from vermiculite (top left and bottom), preferred by many breeders, to mulch (top right) or even just damp paper towels (center). Photos: W. B. Allen, Jr; Bottom: J. Gee.

may form on the exposed surface of a developing egg. This appears to do no harm, but to be on the safe side the mold can be brushed away gently with a fine camel-hair brush. The eggs should be inspected daily but should otherwise be left undisturbed in their original positions and should never be turned as one would turn

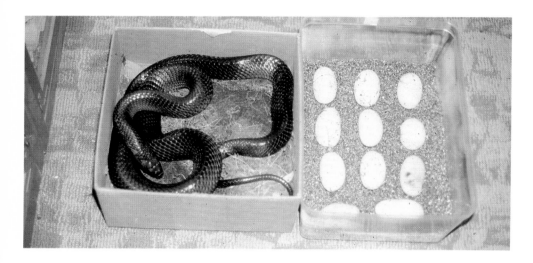

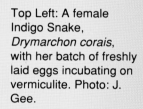

Top Left: A female Indigo Snake, *Drymarchon corais*, with her batch of freshly laid eggs incubating on vermiculite. Photo: J. Gee.

bird eggs. (Many herpetoculturists now believe that a bit of turning will do no harm, but perhaps it is best to play safe and not disturb eggs unless necessary.) After a few days, fertile eggs will show well-defined blood vessels through the shell; if held up to the light (do not do this too often), the developing embryo will be seen as a dark shadow.

The period of incubation varies from species to species and also depends on the temperature. Incubation at slightly lower temperatures will take longer that at higher ones. The incubation time for most oviparous species ranges from 40 to 70 days. The beginner to snake breeding is often excited and frustrated at the same time while waiting for the eggs to hatch, but his patience will be rewarded when he sees the first signs of hatching. As the fully developed embryo begins to absorb the bulk of the yolk, the shell may again collapse. The young snake

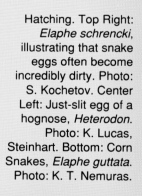

Hatching. Top Right: *Elaphe schrencki*, illustrating that snake eggs often become incredibly dirty. Photo: S. Kochetov. Center Left: Just-slit egg of a hognose, *Heterodon*. Photo: K. Lucas, Steinhart. Bottom: Corn Snakes, *Elaphe guttata*. Photo: K. T. Nemuras.

possesses a single egg-tooth on its snout that it uses to slit open the shell from the inside. Small slits in the shell are the first signs of hatching. There may be a great variation in the amount of time from when the first slit appears to full hatching. Certain snakes may crawl out of the shell almost immediately after making the slit, while others may take two or three days to emerge from the egg. Occasionally a snake may stick its head and neck out of the shell but rapidly withdraw to the safety of the shell if disturbed. Sometimes it is a great temptation to help babies that appear to be taking a long time to hatch, but this is a natural process and normally must be left to the reptiles themselves. They still may be absorbing the remaining contents of the yolk sac, which is attached at the lower abdomen, as well as developing the use of the lung. On rare occasions the albumen surrounding the hatchling will dry out too quickly, causing the snake to adhere to the shell. In such cases the snake can be released by gently dissolving the dried albumen with lukewarm water on a piece of cotton or paper towel.

REARING

The rearing of young snakes often poses difficulties, especially the young of specialist feeders. The successful rearing of some species can constitute a challenge requiring a great deal of patience and time.

As soon as the hatchlings are free-moving and detached from the eggshell, they should be removed from the incubation chamber. No attempt should be made to remove the yolk sac that still may be attached to the abdomen; this will soon shrivel up, dry, and detach itself. The tiny scar left on the belly soon will heal without treatment though it will do no harm to dab it with a mild solution of medical antiseptic.

The young are best housed in small, ventilated, individual containers such as plastic lunch boxes or plastic aquaria. The containers themselves can be kept in a heated room or within a heated terrarium. The necessary

climatic requirements should be provided for the species in question. Rearing containers should be simply furnished. Absorbent paper (such as kitchen towels) can be used for a substrate and changed each time it becomes soiled. A small hiding box, a climbing branch, a rock, and a dish of water will suffice as decorations, as it will be necessary to have easy access to the youngsters for inspection.

Juvenile snakes normally will not feed until after the first shed, which occurs in the first few days after birth. The frequency with which

Hatching. Top: *Python molurus bivittatus.* Photo: B. Kahl. Bottom Left: *Cerastes cerastes;* note that the "horns" are fully developed. Photo: K. H. Switak. Bottom Right: *Python regius.* Photo: R. W. Applegate.

the first six weeks or so, reducing feedings to once per week thereafter. Small snakes can be given baby (pink) mice or even parts of dead adult mice (tail or limbs).

Ideally, specimens should be weighed regularly and the feeding strategy adjusted so that all snakes from a particular hatching grow at a similar rate. Bear in mind that wild snakes have to hunt for food and may sometimes have to go for quite long periods without catching any. Captive feeding is unnatural, so a compromise strategy must be formulated.

The age at which snakes reach sexual maturity varies from species to species and individual to individual, and may depend on such factors as availability of food, temperature, and other

Top: Hatchling Common Kingsnakes, *Lampropeltis g. getulus*. These soon will be moved to individual rearing cages. Photo: J. Gee.

Right: Mutations and freaks are not always "improvements," as witnessed by this two-headed melanistic embryo of *Rhabdophis tigrinus*. Photo: S. Kochetov.

Bottom: However, many mutations are worth working to preserve. This *Python regius* has a solid gold vertebral stripe. Photo: R. D. Bartlett.

juvenile snakes feed varies immensely from species to species and even from individual to individual, consequently some specimens grow relatively faster than others. Quite often it will be difficult to get a young snake to feed, particularly in the case of specialist feeders, when every effort must be made to obtain natural food. The important thing is to get it over the first few months. Experimentation with different foods can begin when the snake is growing strongly. Some juvenile snakes of certain species will take food very readily indeed, and a mistake that many beginners make is to overfeed such specimens, which will become obese and malformed. Not only will these be of doubtful use for breeding, they will probably die prematurely due to a buildup of excessive fat in the internal organs. Juvenile snakes that readily take mice or chicks, for example, should be fed about twice per week for

climatic influences. In captivity, most species will reach breeding condition in one to three years if kept in optimum conditions.

RECORD KEEPING

Reptile keeping and breeding, which can be termed herpetoculture, is a science that is still in its infancy when compared with, say, tropical fish keeping. There are still many gaps in our knowledge regarding the reproduction and habits of many snake species, and it is therefore important that records be kept of all relevant details (and even those that may appear to be irrelevant at the time). Such records should be made available to other enthusiasts through the medium of society journals or by personal communication. It is only by combined effort and experience that progress is made in any science. Methods of record keeping will vary from individual to individual. You may prefer a

system of record cards or a diary in which daily happenings are recorded. A home computer is ideal for record keeping, especially when you like to have facts at your fingertips almost instantly.

As some species occur in very small numbers in captivity and legislation may prevent the collection of further specimens from the wild, it is obvious that an alarming amount of inbreeding is likely to occur. It is only by the

keeping of records and mutual cooperation among snake-breeders that such inbreeding can be kept to a minimum by spreading the available genes as widely as possible throughout the captive stock. With some of the rarer or endangered species it would certainly be a good idea to have a pedigree system or an international studbook that could perhaps be organized by a consortium of herpetological societies. With increasing success in the

Mutations in captive-bred snakes. Top: Black vertebral stripe, *Python regius*. Photo: R. D. Bartlett. Center: Albino *Lampropeltis g. californiae*. Photo: A. Kerstitch. Bottom: Golden (? albino) *Python molurus bivittatus*. Photo: R. D. Bartlett.

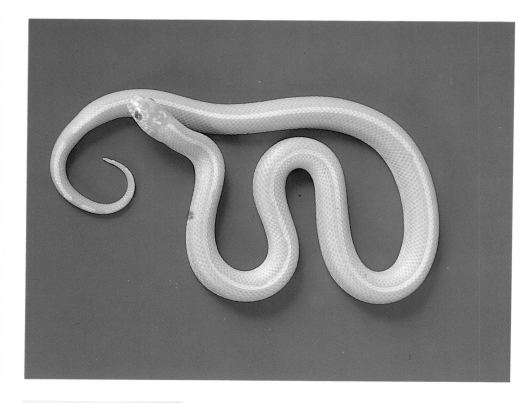

numbers of snakes being bred, it is not hard to believe that the breeding of color varieties will become popular. This is widely practiced among all keepers of semidomestic animals in one form or another, so why not by snake-keepers, too. Many species exhibit melanism, albinism, or leucism, so the time will come when varieties are specially produced by captive breeding. This, in fact, already is true of several species of *Elaphe* and *Lampropeltis*.

The most important records to be kept are those related to breeding, such as mating behavior, frequency of copulation, and periods of gravidity. Individual clutch records should be kept, with data pertaining to the quantity, weight, and dimensions (length and breadth in mm, preferably measured with calipers) of eggs. Incubation times, temperatures, and methods should be recorded. Hatching behavior should be noted and a record should be kept of the feeding, shedding, and growth (regular weighing and measuring) of the juveniles.

Albinos currently are very popular and are becoming very common. Perhaps the two most popular albinos are those of the Common Kingsnake and the Corn Snake. Above is an albino striped *Lampropeltis getulus californiae*, one of the earliest mass-produced albinos. To the right is the "snow corn" albino of *Elaphe guttata*. Breeders have shown that many different types of albinos occur in snakes. Photos: Top: R. Hunziker; Right: J. Wines.

Corn Snakes, *Elaphe guttata,* are now available in over two dozen patterns and colors. The most common mutant is the amelanistic albino, lacking black in the body coloration and with a red eye. The hatchlings at the top include both normals and amelanistics, resulting from a mating of heterozygous parents. Below, an amelanistic is compared with a normal reddish phase Corn; note the lack of the black line around the red saddles. Photos: Top: K. T. Nemuras; Bottom: R. Everhart.

Snakes of the World

HOW TO USE THIS SECTION

The suborder Serpentes is arranged systematically from infraorder to subfamily rank. For ease of reference the genera are arranged in alphabetical order within each subfamily. In polytypic (containing more than one species) genera, typical generic characteristics are first described, Then one or more species examples are briefly described. In monotypic genera (containing only one species), the generic and specific characteristics are included in the species description. In both generic and specific descriptions, the name of the original author and the year of first decription are given, thus giving the reader an easier starting point for further research. An attempt has been made to follow generic spellings and dates in Williams and Wallach, 1989, when possible; this has resulted in several changes from the information accepted in many earlier terrarium works. Common English names have only been used where these are in general use as they can vary tremendously from one English-speaking area to the next.

Many genera and species are only sparsely treated in the literature, and in such cases it is indicated that the biology is poorly known and that further research is urgently required. The descriptions include brief notes on geographical distribution, habitats, habits, general appearance, and care. Geographical distributions and habitats given will provide a clue to the conditions required in the terrarium. Information on climatic conditions in certain areas can be gleaned from the climatic graphs of a world atlas. For example, a species that inhabits lowland rain forest of Malaya will require a temperature range of 26-32°C throughout the year, with very slight cooling at night (never less than 20°C) and a high humidity throughout the year. The species descriptions are not intended to be other than a cursory clue to identification. Field guides or specific descriptive papers should be used to positively identify species. A number of these are listed in the bibliography. Further information on research material can be obtained from herpetological societies and major libraries.

Masticophis flagellum piceus, juvenile, Red Coachwhip. Photo: K. Lucas, Steinhart.

Infraorder Scolecophidia

The infraorder Scolecophidia contains three families with a total of some ten genera and about 300 species of blind snakes that have a circumtropical distribution. The differences of the species of this infraorder from those of the other infraorders include a more compact skull and unique tooth arrangements. All have a rudimentary pelvic girdle at various stages of reduction. The species are found mainly in dryer habitats, but sometimes in rain forest or montane rain forest.

The maximum length is 70 cm (28 in), and all species are circular in body section. The head is flattened and there is often a shovel-like rostral shield to aid in burrowing. The eyes are completely covered with ocular scales and the body scales are very smooth. The extremely short tail often ends with a thorn-like scale. Most species are earthen or sand colored to match their subterranean habitat, occasionally with darker or lighter spots or flecks. There usually is no significant difference in the colors of the dorsal and ventral surfaces. Most species live in subterranean burrows, but some also may be found in ant nests or termite mounds.

To date, blind snakes have found little popularity with the terrarium fraternity, probably due to their retiring habits. For this reason, relatively little is known about their biology, and further research is required. Any prospective terrarium-keeper looking for subjects for biological research would do well to choose species from this category. The blind snakes are best kept in narrow glass aquaria filled with soil or a soil substitute. They may be fed on earthworms and other subterranean creatures, including termites and ants (some species are specialized feeders and further research is required). In the wild, the reptiles come to the surface after heavy rain, often in order to drink. The substrate therefore should be watered about once per week with a watering can so that some water runs into the burrows and drains off into the gravel (but do not waterlog completely). If you have one or two concave stones on the surface, the water will gather in the cavities and the reptiles will then find free water to drink when they come to the surface.

Family Typhlopidae— Blind Snakes

Containing about 240 species that formerly were placed in the single genus *Typhlops*, modern herpetologists now recognize at least three genera. The species are found in most of the warmer areas of the earth but are most abundant in Africa and Asia. The rostral scales are large and often overhang the mouth, forming a robust, shovel-like burrowing structure. The eyes are covered with enlarged scales. Teeth occur in the upper jaw only. The short tail ends with a thorn-like scale. Most species are oviparous, but a few are ovoviviparous.

Ramphotyphlops bramina. Photo: Dr. S. Minton.

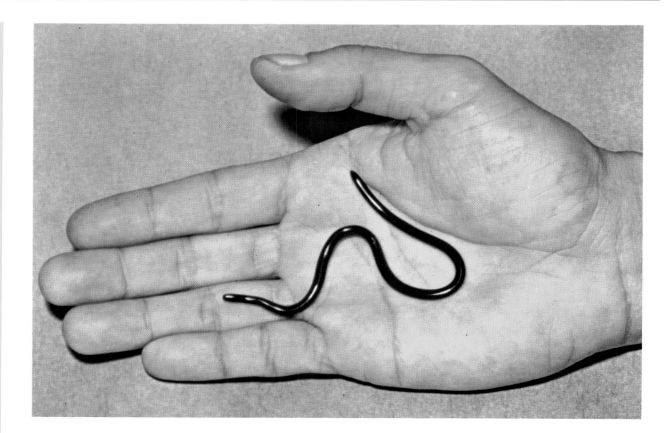

Top:*Ramphotyphlops bramina*. Photo: R. E. Kuntz. Center: *R. bramina*. Photo: A. Kerstitch. Bottom: *Ramphotyphlops nigrescens*. Photo: C. Banks.

• *Ramphotyphlops* Fitzinger, 1843: A genus containing some 30 species. Found in Central America, Africa, S.E. Asia, and Australia. Formerly known as *Typhlina* Wagler, a name preoccupied by the generic name of a rotifer.

R. bramina (Daudin, 1803): **Bootlace Snake, Brahminy Blind Snake.** Has a very wide, circumtropical range including E. Africa, Madagascar, S.E. Asia, and Central America (where introduced). Common name derived from erroneous belief of British soldiers in Asia that it disguises itself as a bootlace, ready to attack in the mornings when donning one's boots! Of course, it is completely harmless. Length to 17 cm (7 in). Glossy dark brown to black. Feeds on termites, ants, and other small invertebrates. Recently has been shown to be parthenogenetic. Now established in Florida and Hawaii.

R. broomi (Boulenger): **Striate Blind Snake.** Northern and eastern Australia. Light brown above with longitudinal reddish brown streaks. Length to 25 cm (10 in).

• *Rhinotyphlops* Fitzinger, 1843: A genus containing about 25 species found in Africa south of the Sahara. Often with a pointed but very large rostral shield. Length to 80 cm (32 in).

R. lalandei (Schlegel, 1839): Southern Africa.

R. schlegeli (Bianconi, 1847): Eastern and S.E. Africa. Four subspecies, *R. s. dinga* being the largest snake of the family, growing to 80 cm (32 in).

- ***Typhlops*** Oppel, 1811: A genus containing about 180 species of typical blind snakes found in most tropical and sub-tropical countries; absent from Australia.

Species range from 10-70 cm (4-28 in) in length. Most feed on termites, ants, and other subterranean invertebrates. It is thought that some species suck out the contents of the insects's bodies and discard the chitinous exoskeleton.

T. diardi Schlegel, 1839: **Diard's Blind Snake.** Found from eastern India through Burma to the Malayan peninsula. To 50 cm (20 in). Dark brown on dorsal surface, lighter beneath. Ovoviviparous, producing up to 16 young. Two subspecies.

T. lumbricalis (Linnaeus, 1758): **Earthworm Blind Snake.** Found in Cuba and the Bahamas mainly in forest clearings. To 40 cm (16 in).

T. punctatus (Leach, 1819): **Spotted Blind Snake.** Found in tropical Africa in savannah and forest margins. One of the largest species, reaching 65 cm (26 in). Glossy brown, spotted or marbled with paler brown or yellow. Three subspecies.

T. reuteri (Boettger, 1881): **Reuter's Blind Snake.** Madagascar. The smallest species in the genus at 10 cm (4 in).

T. vermicularis Merrem, 1820: **Eurasian Blind Snake.** Southeastern Europe (the Balkans) to Middle East and N.E. Egypt. To 35 cm (14 in). Worm-like, glossy pale brown. Oviparous, laying up to eight elongate eggs.

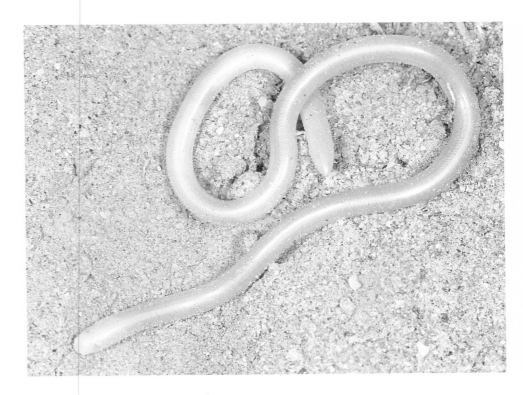

Top: *Rhinotyphlops schinzi*. Photo: P. Freed. Center: *Typhlops arenarius*. Photo: P. Freed. Bottom: *Typhlops richardi*. Photo: J. Iverson.

Top: *Typhlops biminiensis*. Photo: R. D. Bartlett. Center: *Typhlops vermicularis*. Photo: S. Kochetov. Bottom: *Typhlops bibroni*. Photo: J. Visser.

Family Anomalepidae— American Blind Snakes

A family with four genera and some 20 species found in Central and South America. Similar to Typhlopidae, but some species possess a single tooth in the lower jaw.

- *Anomalepis* Jan, 1860: A genus containing four species. Found from Mexico to Ecuador and Peru. Length to 30 cm (12 in). Single tooth in either side of lower jaw.

  A. mexicanus Jan, 1861: Mexico to Panama.

- *Helminthophis* Peters, 1860: A genus containing three species found in Central and northern South America. Length to 25 cm (10 in). No teeth in lower jaw.

  H. frontalis (Peters, 1860): Costa Rica.

- *Liotyphlops* Peters, 1881: A genus containing some 12 species found from Costa Rica to Paraguay. Single tooth on lower jaw.

  L. albirostris (Peters, 1857): Costa Rica to Brazil and Paraguay.

- *Typhlophis* Fitzinger, 1843: A genus containing a single species found in N.E. South America.

  T. squamosus (Schlegel, 1839): N.E. South America (including Trinidad). Length to 30 cm (12 in). No teeth in lower jaw.

Top: *Liotyphlops albirostris*. Photo: P. Freed. Center: *Leptotyphlops dulcis dissecta*. Photo: G. Pisani. Bottom: *Leptotyphlops dulcis dulcis*. Photo: Dr. S. Minton.

Above: *Leptotyphlops hamulirostris*. Photo: Dr. S. Minton. Below: *Leptotyphlops humilis*. Photo: A. Kerstitch.

Below Left: *Leptotyphlops weyrauchi*. Photo: S. Holley. Below Right: *Leptotyphlops humilis segregatus*. Photo: K. Lucas, Steinhart.

Family Leptotyphlopidae—Worm Snakes

A family containing two genera (revision urgently required) and about 41 species. Found in the Americas, Africa, and Asia as far as India (absent from Europe, eastern Asia, and Australasia). Inhabit arid areas to rain forest and montane rain forest, often in termite mounds, ant nests, or in the root balls of epiphytes. Vary from 8-30 cm (3-12 in) in length. Round in section; very slender and worm-like. No teeth in upper jaw. Most feed on termites or ants, their larvae and pupae.

- ***Leptotyphlops*** Fitzinger, 1843: A genus containing some 40 species of worm snakes.

  L. dulcis (Baird & Girard, 1853): **Texas Blind Snake.** From Texas to Mexico in arid areas. Shiny reddish brown to pinkish. Length to 25 cm (10 in). Oviparous, laying two to seven elongate eggs that are guarded by the female. Two subspecies.

  L. humilis (Baird & Girard, 1853): **Western Blind Snake.** From California into Mexico, in arid areas. Glossy brown to purplish. Length to 40 cm (16 in). Oviparous, laying two to six elongate eggs, often in communal nests guarded by several females. Four subspecies.

  L. sundevalli (Jan, 1862): **Sundevall's Worm Snake.** Tropical West Africa in humid areas. Length to 10 cm (4 in).

  L. macrorhynchus (Jan, 1862): **Long-nosed Worm Snake.** Turkey to Pakistan in arid areas. Length to 17 cm (7 in).

  L. tesselatus (Tschudi, 1845): Peru, in montane rain forest. One of the smallest species at 8 cm (3 in).

- ***Rhinoleptus*** Orejas-Miranda, Roux-Esteve & Guibe, 1970: A genus containing a single species in Africa.

  R. koniagui (Villiers, 1962): West Africa; tropical rain forest. Has a hook-like rostral shield. Largest member of the family at 50 cm (20 in).

Infraorder Henophidia

The infraorder Henophidia contains five families with a total of 36 genera and about 137 species with a circumtropical distribution. Snakes in this group have an enormous size differential, ranging from 40 cm (16 in) to 10 m (33 ft). Habit and habitat are also extremely varied, ranging from burrowing to arboreal species. Almost all species in the infraorder possess a vestigial pelvic girdle that in some species is visible as cloacal spurs. In most species the body is relatively muscular and round in section. Similarities in the group include points of skull and tooth structure.

Family Aniliidae— Cylinder Snakes

A family containing three genera and about ten species found in South America and S.E. Asia. (*Anomochilus* and *Cylindrophis* often are placed in the Uropeltidae by specialists.) Most are found in forested tropical areas. Further research is required into the evolution of the family. Length to 90 cm (36 in). Most have the body round to slightly triangular in section. Burrowing or semi-burrowing habit. All possess cloacal spurs and all are ovoviviparous. Food consists of various small vertebrate animals, especially amphibians and reptiles.

Cylinder snakes should be kept in a heated tropical terrarium with a deep, well-drained substrate for burrowing. Narrow glass containers will provide better possibilities for observation. Further research into biology and captive husbandry is required.

● *Anilius* Oken, 1816: A genus containing a single species found in northern South America.

A. scytale (Linnaeus, 1758): **Scarlet Pipe Snake, Coral Cylinder Snake.** Found in the Amazon and Orinoco Basins and the Mato Grosso. Inhabits rain forest and dryer forested areas. Length to 90 cm (36 in). The very small eye is covered by an ocular scale. The tail is very short. Ground color is red, with black transverse bands, vaguely like a coral snake but lacking the white or yellow bands. A nocturnal burrowing snake usually found near water. Feeds on fish, frogs, lizards, and snakes. Ovoviviparous, producing 9-16 young.

● *Anomochilus* Berg, 1901: A genus containing a single species native to Sumatra. Formerly called *Anomalochilus* van Lidth de Jeude, preoccupied by a beetle.

A. weberi (van Lidth de Jeude, 1890-91): **Weber's Cylinder Snake.** A (presumably) very rare species from western Sumatra in tropical rain forest. Length to 25 cm (10 in). Body round in section; head small and snout blunt. Dorsal surface brown with longitudinal rows of darker flecks. White line along flanks. Little appears to be known about the biology of this burrowing species.

● *Cylindrophis* Wagler, 1828: A genus containing eight species of Asian cylinder snakes found from India and Sri Lanka into Indo-China and S.E. Asia to the Aru Islands (Indonesia). Found mainly in rain forest or montane rain forest, though *C. rufus* is commonly found in agricultural areas. Length to 75 cm (30 in). Upper side of skull covered with large scales. Broad tail flattened dorso-ventrally. When threatened, members of the genus conceal the head in the body coils and raise the enlarged tail (brightly colored on the underside in black and white or red) as a defense gesture. In general, the species have a

dark ground color with whitish, yellowish, or reddish flecks or broken bands. The habitat is usually damp substrate, some even in mud. They feed on small vertebrates (frogs, lizards) or invertebrates (worms, slugs, etc.). In captivity they can be trained to take whole fish, strips of dead fish, and meat. They require a warm, humid, rain-forest terrarium with facilities for burrowing and a large water container.

C. aruensis Boulenger, 1820: **Aru Cylinder Snake.** Found in the Aru Islands of eastern Indonesia, this is the easternmost species of the genus.

C. maculatus (Linnaeus, 1754): **Ceylonese Cylinder Snake.** Native to Sri Lanka, where very common in the montane rain forests.

C. rufus (Laurenti, 1768): **Red Cylinder Snake.** Best known cylinder snake. Found throughout Indo-China and S.E. Asia. Length to 75 cm (30 in).

Top: *Cylindrophis rufus.*
Photo: R. D. Bartlett.
Bottom: *Anilius scytale.*
Photo: Dr. S. Minton.

Family Acrochordidae— Wart, File, or Elephant's Trunk Snakes

A family containing two genera with three species found from India through S.E. Asia to New Guinea, the Solomon Islands, and northern Australia. (Almost all current workers consider *Chersydrus* a synonym of *Acrochordus*.) Almost totally aquatic species that may be found in fresh or brackish water, sometimes in sea water. Length to 2.5 m (8 ft). The head and body are covered with small, finely keeled and pointed scales with a rasp-like texture. There are no enlarged belly scales. The whole skin is somewhat flabby, hanging loosely on the body. The head and mouth are broad, and the small eyes and valved nostrils are on the top of the head. The tail is prehensile. All species are ovoviviparous.

Acrochordidae should be kept in large heated aquaria with underwater landscaping (rocks and branches) so that the reptiles have something to hang onto with their tails. A little salt added to the water will be beneficial. Feed on live fish. Newly captured specimens are often reluctant to feed, so force-feeding may be necessary.

- ***Acrochordus*** Hornstedt, 1787: A genus containing two species found from India to northern Australia.

  A. javanicus Hornstedt, 1787: **Javan File (Wart) Snake, Elephant's Trunk Snake.** Native to coastal areas from India to northern Australia. Length of female to 2.5 m (8 ft), male to 1.4 m (4.6 ft). Common in mangrove swamps, estuaries, and brackish waters. Gray to dark brown above with broad darker reticulations. Underside is whitish with dark reticulations extending from the dorsal surface onto the belly. Very loose skin. Appears almost helpless when removed from water. Gives birth to live young, probably out of the water. Juveniles in captivity should be provided with land areas, because they are not fully aquatic.

- ***Chersydrus*** Cuvier, 1817: A genus containing a single species found from India to northern Australia. Often synonymized with *Acrochordus*.

  C. granulatus (Schneider, 1799): **Marine File (Wart) Snake, Little File (Wart) Snake.** Found from S.E. Asia to northern Australia. Length to 120 cm (48 in). Flattened tail. Gray, brown, or almost black above, with narrow, indefinite whitish to fawn crossbands. Lighter beneath. Skin not quite so flabby as in *A. javanicus*. Produces 7-12 live young.

Top and Upper Center: *Acrochordus arafurae*. Photos: C. Banks. Lower Center: *Acrochordus javanicus*. Photo: H. Bleher. Bottom: *Chersydrus granulatus*. Photo: C. Banks.

A juvenile *Acrochordus javanicus*. The numerous small, very rough scales have led to the name filesnake for this and related species. Photos: K. T. Nemuras.

Top: A juvenile *Acrochordus javanicus* illustrating the high eye-set and very fine head scalation. Photo: K. T. Nemuras. Bottom: A juvenile *Chersydrus granulatus* with an exceptionally vivid color pattern, lost in adults. Photo: R. D. Bartlett.

Loxocemus bicolor.
Photos: Top: R. D.
Bartlett; Bottom: Dr. S.
Minton.

Family Boidae—Pythons and Boas

A family containing five subfamilies, 23 genera, and some 79 species distributed throughout the tropics. The range of size is enormous, from 45 cm (18 in) to 10 m (33 ft), and the group includes the world's largest snake species. All species possess a vestigial pelvic girdle almost always visible as a pair of short, claw-like spurs situated on either side of the vent. The jaws are furnished with many strong teeth. They overcome their prey by constriction. They are oviparous or ovoviviparous, and some of the former exhibit maternal care (brooding) to a greater or lesser extent.

Many authorities do not believe the Boidae is a natural family and would recognize several smaller families instead. These smaller families would include Loxocemidae, Bolyeriidae, and Tropidopheidae (for *Exiliboa, Tropidophis, Trachyboa,* and *Ungaliophis*).

In view of their size, beauty, and their readiness to become tame, many species in this family are extremely popular terrarium subjects. However, some of the larger species will soon outgrow their accommodations, so unless you have the space to provide a relatively large terrarium you should perhaps elect to keep smaller species. Additionally, many local laws restrict the keeping of boids by private individuals.

SUBFAMILY LOXOCEMINAE— MEXICAN DWARF BOAS

Contains only a single genus.
● *Loxocemus* Cope, 1861: Contains only a single species.

L. bicolor Cope, 1861: **Mexican Burrowing Python.** Found in S. Mexico and N. Costa Rica, inhabiting dampish woodland usually under leaf-litter, etc. Length to 120 cm (48 in). Head shields are relatively large. Brownish and iridescent with irregular light blotches.

Classification long has been problematic, and this snake has been included in the family Aniliidae or the subfamily Pythoninae or Erycinae in the past. However, it is probably a closer relative of *Calabaria* than *Eryx*. Subfamily status within the Boidae is now widely accepted. Its biology is poorly known. In captivity it will take small mammals (mice, rats). Husbandry similar to that described for *Calabaria*.

SUBFAMILY PYTHONINAE— PYTHONS

This subfamily contains six genera and 22 species found in tropical Africa, Asia, and Australasia. Many are the giants of the snake world and require voluminous accommodations, including a large heated water container for bathing.

- *Aspidites* Peters, 1877: A genus containing two species native to central N. Australia. Crepuscular and terrestrial with limited climbing ability. Strictly protected in the wild.

A. *melanocephalus* (Krefft, 1864): **Black-headed Python.** Widely distributed in the northern half of Australia except for the most arid regions. Habitats vary from wet forest to semi-arid grassland. Length to 2.5 m (8 ft). Light to dark brown above with darker crossbands, lighter on the flanks. Head, neck, and throat black, underside whitish. Feeds on small mammals, birds, and reptiles, including venomous snakes.

A. *ramsayi* (Macleay, 1882): **Woma.** Widely distributed in arid central Australia. Shelters during the day in hollow logs, animal burrows or thick vegetation. Length to 2.5 m (8 ft). Gray to brown or reddish above with darker crossbands. Head not black as in preceding species, but juveniles may have a black patch on the snout. Feeds on small mammals, birds, and reptiles.

Top: *Aspidites melanocephalus*. Photo: C. Banks. Center: *Aspidites ramsayi*. Photo: C. Banks. Bottom: *Aspidites melanocephalus*. Photo: R. D. Bartlett.

Top: *Aspidites ramsayi*.
Photo: R. T. Hoser.
Bottom: *Aspidites ramsayi* with exceptional amount of dark head pigment.
Photo: R. D. Bartlett.

refer many *Liasis* species to *Python* or *Morelia*, and the taxonomy and nomenclature of the Australasian pythons should be considered unstable at best. As used here, *Liasis* contains species seemingly allied to *L. childreni*, *Morelia* contains only the carpet pythons, and *Python* contains the remaining (possibly unrelated) species. The Amethystine Python often is placed in *Python* rather than *Liasis* as used here. The status of several recently described Australian *Liasis* species is very uncertain.

Left: An adult *Chondropython viridis* with an orange newborn and an older yellow juvenile. Photo: L. Porras.

Below: *Calabaria reinhardtii*. Photos: P. J. Stafford.

- **Calabaria** Gray, 1858: A genus containing only a single species.
  C. reinhardtii (Schlegel, 1851): **Calabar Ground Python.** Native to tropical western and central Africa, where it inhabits forest and savannah regions, burrowing into preferably damp substrate. Length to 110 cm (43 in). Narrow head with blunt snout; short, blunt tail. When alarmed; it conceals its head in its coils and presents the tail as a false head. Color is warm reddish brown with a few lighter specks.
  In the wild, it is presumed to feed on small rodents and lizards. Should be provided with a humid terrarium with adequate burrowing facilities (a mixture of peat and bark chippings is ideal). Feed on mice.
- **Chondropython** Meyer, 1875: A genus containing only a single species.
  C. viridis (Schlegel, 1872): **Green Tree Python, Jamomong.** Native to New Guinea, N. Australia (Cape York Peninsula), Aru Archipelago, Solomon Islands, where it inhabits tropical rain forest. Length to 180 cm (72 in) (but usually somewhat shorter). Body triangular in section. Head relatively large, with narrow neck. The front teeth are very long (to aid in catching birds). Bears a striking similarity in appearance and habits to the unrelated *Corallus caninus*, the Emerald Tree Boa, presenting an example of convergent evolution. Leaf-green in color with a yellow or white broken vertebral stripe. Blue specimens (lacking yellow pigment) are sometimes found. Juveniles are yellow, orange, or reddish brown, changing to adult coloration in about 12 months. Rests with the coils draped over a thick branch. Feeds on frogs, lizards, birds, and small mammals (including bats). Oviparous (maternal brooding).
  In captivity it requires a roomy, well-ventilated tropical rain-forest terrarium with facilities to climb and bask. Robust plants (*Ficus, Monstera*, etc.) can be used for decoration. Feed on mice or small birds.
- **Liasis** Gray, 1842: A genus containing ten species of pythons. Native to Indonesia, New Guinea and Australia. Taxonomy requires further research. Currently some authorities

Chondropython viridis. Top Left: Yellow juvenile. Photo: B. Kahl. Top Right: Detail of enlarged nasals. Photo: P. J. Stafford. Bottom Left: Normal green adult. Photo: W. Tomey. Bottom Right: Blue phase adult. Photo: P. J. Stafford.

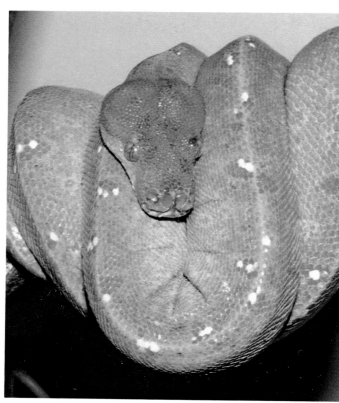

Top Left: *Liasis albertisi*. Photo: C. Banks. Top Right: *Liasis amethystinus*. Photo: C. Banks.

L. albertisi Peters & Doria (1878): **White-lipped Python.** Native to New Guinea and Australian islands in the Torres Strait, where it is found in a variety of habitats from primary monsoon forest to secondary forest and coastal swampland. Length to 3 m (10 ft).

Relatively slender, with a narrow neck. Color grayish to reddish brown, somewhat iridescent. Labials white to cream. Some specimens have a darker head. Captive specimens require a roomy humid terrarium with facilities to climb and bathe, including robust plants. Feed on small mammals, birds, and lizards.

L. amethystinus (Schneider, 1801): **Amethystine Python.** Moluccas, Timor, New Guinea, Solomon Islands, N. Australia (eastern side of Cape York Peninsula). Found in a variety of habitats

Above: *Liasis amethystinus*, male. Photo: C. Banks. Bottom Left: *Liasis albertisi*, hatchlings. Photo: C. Banks. Bottom Right: Detail of head of *Liasis amethystinus*. Photo: R. T. Hoser.

from coastal and island scrub to rain forest. The giant of the genus, the record length being 8.5 m (over 27 ft), but averages 3.5 m (11 ft). A powerful though somewhat slender snake for its size. Iridescent olive-yellow to brown above with numerous irregular broken dark crossbands, usually connected along the flanks to form an almost continuous stripe. Underside is white or cream. In captivity it requires voluminous accommodations with facilities to climb and bathe. Feeds on a variety of vertebrates.

L. childreni Gray, 1842: **Children's Python.** Distributed throughout the northern three-quarters of Australia and found in a wide range of habitats from central deserts to coastal rain forests. Primarily terrestrial but climbs well. Length to 150 cm (60 in), but usually shorter. Usually light brown above, lighter on the flanks. Has a series of irregular

Top: *Liasis* aff. *amethystinus*, New Guinea Scrub Python phase. Photo: K. H. Switak. Center: *Liasis* aff. *childreni*, phase known as *gilberti*. Photo: C. Banks. Bottom: *Liasis amethystinus*, juvenile. Photo: M. J. Cox.

purplish brown patches along the back and often a dark streak through each eye. Feeds on small mammals, birds, and reptiles.

Keep in a relatively dry, warm terrarium with gravel substrate and climbing facilities. Will use a water bath. A small (50 cm, 20 in) version of this species from S.W. Australia is given specific status (*L. perthensis*).

L. fuscus Peters, 1879: **Water Python.** Native to Timor, eastern New Guinea, and northern Australia (from the Kimberley region to eastern Queensland). Usually found in the vicinity of streams, rivers, or lakes, into which it flees when

Top: *Liasis* aff. *childreni*, phase known as *L. stimsoni orientalis*, a taxon of uncertain status. Photo: C. Banks. Center: *Liasis (Bothrochilus) boa*, juvenile. Photo: P. Freed. Bottom Left: *Liasis childreni*. Photo: C. Banks. Bottom Right: *Liasis* aff. *childreni*, phase known as *gilberti*. Photo: C. Banks.

Liasis fuscus is closely related to *L. mackloti*, and some authorities think them to be the same species. Top and Bottom: *Liasis fuscus*. Center: *Liasis mackloti*. Photos: Top: Courtesy London Zoo; Center: P. J. Stafford. Bottom: R. T. Hoser.

Top: *Liasis olivaceus*. Photo: C. Banks. Center: *Liasis fuscus*. Photo: Dr. S. Minton. Bottom: *Liasis papuanus*. Photo: R. D. Bartlett.

Top Left and Right:
Liasis perthensis.
Photos: R. T. Hoser.

alarmed; swims well. Length to 3 m (10 ft), usually shorter. Uniform dark to sooty brown above, iridescent. Yellowish beneath, the throat creamy white. Feeds on a variety of vertebrates including fish and young crocodiles. In captivity it must have a large heated water bath. Feed on small mammals and birds.

L. olivaceus Gray, 1842: **Olive Python.** Found in New Guinea and northern Australia (from coastal W. Australia to western half of Cape York Peninsula). Inhabits a range of biotopes from coastal forest to rocky outcrops and hills in the interior. Length to 4 m (13 ft), usually shorter. Uniform pale fawn to olive or dark brown above, lighter along the flanks. Underside whitish. Labials paler than rest of head. Feeds on a variety of vertebrates. Two subspecies. Requires a large, airy, heated terrarium with facilities for climbing (rocks and branches) and bathing.

● *Morelia* Gray, 1842: **Diamond and Carpet Pythons.** A genus containing a single species. *M. spilotes* (Lacepede, 1804): **Diamond Python, Carpet Python.** Widely distributed throughout Australia except the far west and southern Victoria; also New Guinea. Found in a great variety of habitats, from eastern coastal rain forest to central desert areas. Terrestrial, living in burrows of other animals, but often arboreal, living in hollow limbs. Mainly crepuscular or nocturnal, feeding on a variety of vertebrates. Length to 4 m (13 ft), average 2 m (6.5 ft).

Right: *Morelia spilotes*, hatchling. Photo: P. Freed.

Two distinctive subspecies (considered by many to be population variants): *M. s. spilotes*, the **Diamond Python**, found in S.E. Australia, is usually olive black above, with cream or yellow spots on many of the

individual scales forming an indistinct pattern of diamond shapes. The underside is cream or yellowish, variegated with dark gray. *M. s. variegata*, the **Carpet Python**, is found throughout the rest of the range. It has an enormous variety of colors and patterns, the ground color being light to dark brown marked with blackish (sometimes lighter centered) variegations; underside as for *M. s. spilotes*.

In captivity the species requires a roomy terrarium with facilities for hiding, bathing, and climbing. Feed on mice or chicks

Top Left: *Morelia spilotes spilotes*. Photo: C. Banks. Top Right: *Morelia spilotes variegata*, female, Atherton Tableland phase. Photo: C. Banks. Center: *Morelia spilotes variegata*. Photo: Dr. S. Minton. Bottom: *Morelia spilotes spilotes*. Photo: P. J. Stafford.

Top: *Morelia spilotes spilotes*. Photo: P. J. Stafford. Center: *Morelia spilotes variegata*, pale Northern Australia phase. Photo: R. T. Hoser. Bottom: *Morelia* aff. *spilotes*, phase named *bredli*, of uncertain status, from Central Australia. Photos: C. Banks.

(juveniles), rats or chickens (adults).

● ***Python*** Daudin, 1803: **Typical Pythons.** A genus containing at least ten species of mostly large, typical pythons found in Africa and Asia. Status relative to *Liasis* unclear and often revised.

P. anchietae Bocage, 1887: **Angolan Python.** Found in southern Africa (Angola, Namibia), where it usually is confined to rocky localities. The smallest species of the genus, with a maximum length of 180 cm (71 in), though specimens of this length are rare. The upper surface is pale reddish brown with black-edged yellowish spots and bands. The top of the head has a large triangular dark brown patch that is edged with a pale, dark-edged band and is centered with a small whitish spot. The ventral surface is yellowish

Top: *Python anchietae.* Photo: K. H. Switak. Center: *Python anchietae.* Photo: W. R. Branch. Bottom: *Python boeleni,* currently one of the most expensive and hard to obtain species. Photos: K. H. Switak.

often been persuaded to dine voluntarily by providing them with a container of mud in which to wallow, a messy business but it seems to work!

P. molurus (Linnaeus, 1758): **Indian Python, Burmese Python, Tiger Python.** Native to India, Indo-China, S. China, and Malayan Archipelago. Found in a variety of habitats, from dry, rocky terrain to tropical rain forest. Length to 5 m (16.5 ft); adult male considerably shorter and slimmer than female.

Two subspecies: ***P. m. molurus***, **Light Phase Indian Python** (India and Sri Lanka), which is light brown or buff, marked with a network of dark-bordered cream bands; and ***P. m. bivittatus***, **Burmese** or **Dark Phase Indian Python** (from the remainder of the range) with similar markings but richer and darker coloration, including a pointed "spearhead" on the head.

Top: Portrait of *Python boeleni.* Photo: R. D. Bartlett. Right: *Python molurus bivittatus.* Photo: B. Kahl. Bottom: *Python curtus.* Photo: C. Banks.

with scattered brown spots toward the sides. In captivity it requires a warm, semi-arid terrarium, but with bathing facilities. It should be provided with rocks and hiding places. Feed on small vertebrates, especially birds.

P. curtus Schlegel, 1827: **Blood Python.** Found in Malaya, Sumatra, Borneo. Almost always found in the vicinity of or in water; swamp-dwelling. Length to 2.7 m (9 ft), but usually shorter. A plump-bodied species with a relatively narrow head and a short tail. Ground color is pinkish to reddish, broken with irregular bands and patches of black and yellowish gray. The underside is lighter.

In captivity *P. curtus* is initially difficult, often refusing to feed voluntarily. It is also one of the most aggressive and difficult to tame members of the genus and bites readily. It requires a warm, humid terrarium with a large water container. Difficult feeders have

One of the most popular python species for the terrarium-keeper. Tames and breeds readily and is popular with snake dancers and other exhibitionists. Captive-bred specimens usually are available. Feeds on a variety of vertebrates but will thrive on a staple diet of mice (juveniles), rats, and chickens. Requires a large terrarium with facilities to bathe and climb.

P. regius (Shaw, 1802): **Royal Python, Ball Python.** Native to western and central Africa, where found in a range of habitats but usually in thick undergrowth near or below ground level. Nocturnal, often hunting in the burrows

Top: *Python curtus brongersmai*, perhaps the most brilliantly colored python. Photo: P. J. Stafford. Bottom: Reticulated color pattern variant of *Python molurus bivittatus*. Photo: M. J. Cox.

of small mammals. When threatened, it rolls its coils into a ball with its head protected. Length to 190 cm (75 in), but averages 120 cm (48 in). A small, robust species. The body is chocolate to golden brown with an attractive pattern of large cream or yellowish buff blotches.

Requires a medium sized humid terrarium with facilities to bathe and climb. Tight-fitting hiding places are essential. Often difficult to feed in the early stages, but once used to feeding on mice and/or small rats this docile species makes an excellent terrarium subject.

P. reticulatus (Schneider, 1801): **Reticulated Python.** Found throughout tropical Indo-China and Indonesia to the Phillipines, usually inhabiting tropical rain-forest areas, especially near rivers, lakes,

Python molurus molurus. Photos: Top: Courtesy Cotswold Park; Center: S. Kochetov; Bottom: Dr. S. Minton.

Top: *Python oenpelliensis*. Photo: R. T. Hoser. Center: Axanthic (no yellow) variant of *Python regius*. Photo: R. D. Bartlett. Bottom Left: *Python regius*. Photo: S. Kochetov. Bottom Right: Adult and hatchling *Python regius*. Photo: S. C. and H. Miller.

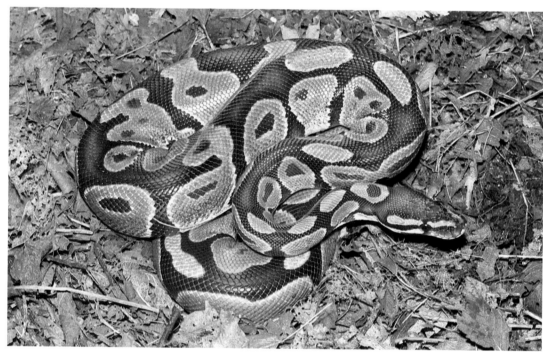

Python regius. Photos:
Top: R. T. Zappalorti;
Center: P. J. Stafford;
Bottom: J. Dodd.

etc. Competes with *Eunectes murinus* (Anaconda) for the distinction of being the world's largest Recent snake. Length to 10 m (32 ft), but average adult size more likely to be 5-6 m (16-20 ft). Relatively slender when compared to *E. murinus*.

Large terraria with extra large heated water container and facilities for climbing required. Wild specimens are aggressive, and large ones can be dangerous, constricting and biting. Tamest terrarium inmates are those reared from hatchlings. Feed on a variety of vertebrates. Large specimens can be fed on rabbits, chickens, ducks, geese, or even turkeys.

P. sebae (Gmelin, 1789): **African Rock Python.** Native to many parts of Africa south of the Sahara, this species is found in a range of habitats from savannah to forest but

especially brushland and rocky outcrops. Length to 5 m (16.5 ft). Similar in shape and size to *P. molurus* (with which it frequently hybridizes in captivity), but slightly more aggressive. Color is reddish to grayish brown above with a pattern of dark bands and patches. The underside is whitish with dark flecks. Requires a large, semi-humid terrarium with rocks, branches, and a large bathing container. Feeds on rats and chickens.

P. timorensis (Peters, 1876): **Timor Python.** Found on the islands of Timor and Flores in the Indonesian Archipelago, where it inhabits rain forest. A slender, diurnal python, one of the least known of the genus. Little appears to be documented on its husbandry. It is likely to require similar but less voluminous accommodations than that described for *P. reticulatus*.

Python reticulatus. Top Left: Female incubating eggs. Photo: W. B. Allen, Jr. Bottom Left: Dark phase. Photo: S. Kochetov. Right: Juvenile. Photo: P. J. Stafford.

Top: *Python sebae natalensis*. Photo: W. R. Branch. Bottom: Portrait of *Python reticulatus*. Photo: K. T. Nemuras.

SUBFAMILY BOINAE—TYPICAL BOAS

The subfamily Boinae contains 11 genera and some 41 species found mainly in the New World but also in Madagascar, New Guinea, and some Pacific Islands. All are ovoviviparous.

● *Acrantophis* Jan, 1860: **Madagascar Boas.** A genus containing two species of Old World boas, native only to Madagascar (Malagasy Republic). Similar in appearance and habit to the New World *Boa*. Mainly terrestrial and nocturnal or crepuscular, resting in hollows during the day. Require medium-sized heated accommodations with facilities to hide and bathe. Feed on small invertebrates.

Top: *Python sebae*, partially striped variant. Photo: R. D. Bartlett. Center: *Python sebae*, young. Photo: P. Freed. Bottom: *Acrantophis dumerili*. Photo: K. Lucas, Steinhart.

Top Left: *Acrantophis dumerili*, female. Top Right and Bottom: *Acrantophis madagascariensis*. Photos: K. H. Switak.

A. dumerili Jan, 1860: **Dumeril's Ground Boa.** Northern Madagascar in damp forested areas. Length to 3.5 m (11 ft), usually shorter.
A. madagascariensis (Dumeril & Bibron, 1884): **Madagascar Ground Boa.** Southern Madagascar in drier brushland. Length to 4.5 m (14 ft), usually shorter.
• *Boa* Linnaeus, 1758: **Boa Constrictors.** A genus containing a single species and several subspecies in Central and South America. Found in a variety of habitats, but seem to

Boa constrictor. Top: Surinam red-tailed phase. Photo: R. D. Bartlett. Center: Aberrant striped pattern. Photo: J. Coborn. Bottom Left: Pale Mexican phase. Photo: B. Kahl. Bottom Right: *Boa constrictor occidentalis.* Photo: M. Freiberg.

prefer drier areas. Primarily terrestrial but climb well. Mainly nocturnal. Range of size from 2.5 m to 4 m (8-13 ft). Wide variations in color and pattern are possible, but usually variations on cream-buff with large uneven but distinct blotches of dark brown that sometimes become progressively more reddish toward the tail. Require a large dry terrarium with facilities to climb and bathe. Occasionally bred in captivity, producing 15-40 young per birth. Feed on mammals and birds.

B. constrictor constrictor Linnaeus, 1758: **Common Boa.** Found in E. Ecuador through Peru, Bolivia, and Colombia to N. Brazil, Venezuela, the Guianas, and Trinidad and Tobago.

B. c. occidentalis Philippi, 1873: **Argentine Boa.** Native to Paraguay and Argentina; the southernmost race. Relatively dark colored.

Boa constrictor. Top: *Boa constrictor constrictor.* Photo: P. J. Stafford. Center Left: *Boa constrictor amarali.* Photo: M. Freiberg. Center Right: *Boa constrictor occidentalis.* Photo: M. Freiberg. Bottom: *Boa constrictor occidentalis.* Photo: S. Kochetov.

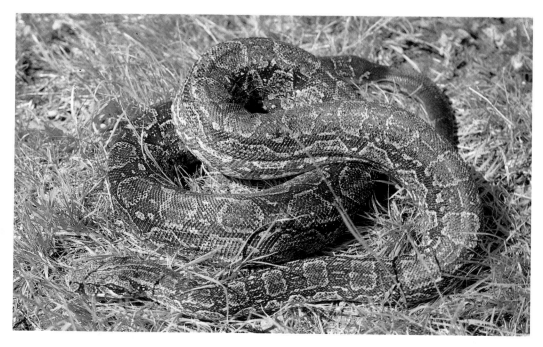

Portrait of *Boa constrictor constrictor*. Photo: P. J. Stafford.

Left: Red-tailed *Boa constrictor*. Photo: J. K. Langhammer. Right: *Boa constrictor*, Hog Island phase. Photo: R. D. Bartlett.

Right: *Boa constrictor melanogaster*. Photo: J. K. Langhammer.

B. c. nebulosa (Lazell, 1964): **Clouded Boa.** Dominica and the Lesser Antilles.
B. c. imperator Daudin, 1803: **Imperial Boa.** Mexico to N.W. South America.
B. c. ortoni Cope, 1878: **Orton's Boa.** N.W. Peru.
• *Corallus* Daudin, 1803: **Tree Boas.** A genus containing three species of nocturnal arboreal boas native to Central and northern South

Above: *Corallus annulatus*. Photo: W. B. Allen, Jr. Right: *Corallus caninus*, adult. Photo: H. Hansen.

America. All are laterally compressed and
have a relatively large triangular head and
narrow neck. The front teeth of the upper jaw
are exceptionally long and recurved. All
species require a tall, preferably planted,
tropical rain-forest terrarium with robust
climbing branches.

C. annulatus (Cope, 1876): **Ringed Tree
Boa.** Nicaragua to Colombia, in forested
areas, but also found in gardens and
agricultural areas. Length to 130 cm (51 in).
Brownish olive with darker, indistinct ring
markings. Three subspecies. Feeds on small
mammals and birds, also frogs and lizards.

C. caninus (Linnaeus, 1758): **Emerald Tree
Boa.** Native to the Amazon basin, from Peru
and Bolivia through Brazil to the Guianas.
Length to 2.2 m (7 ft 3 in). Leaf-green with a
broken white dorsal stripe. Yellow beneath.
Feeds on birds and mammals (including bats).

Top: Portrait of *Corallus
caninus*. Photo: B. Kahl.
Bottom: Orange young
of *Corallus caninus*.
Photo: S. Kochetov.

Top Left: *Corallus enydris enydris*, red juvenile. Photo: R. D. Bartlett. Top Right: *Corallus caninus.* Photo: Courtesy Chester Zoo. Bottom: Newborn *Corallus enydris cookii.* Photo: P. J. Stafford.

Corallus enydris.
Photos: Top: B. Kahl;
Center: Dark phase *C. e. cookii*, P. J. Stafford;
Bottom Left: S. Kochetov; Bottom Right: Dr. G. Dingerkus.

Often difficult to settle in the terrarium, and initial force-feeding (with mice, small birds, etc.) may be necessary. Bears a striking resemblance to *Chondropython viridis*.

C. enydris (Linnaeus, 1758): **Garden Tree Boa.** Nicaragua to Peru and the Guianas. Tends to avoid thickly forested areas, more common in scrub and secondary forest, also gardens and agricultural land. Length to 180 cm (71 in). Light brown with darker spots and blotches.

● *Epicrates* Wagler, 1830: **Slender Boas.** A genus containing about ten species of relatively slender boas found in Central and South America and the West Indies. Most are crepuscular and semi-arboreal, being at home in the trees as well as on the ground.

Require a roomy terrarium with facilities to climb and bathe. Several of the endangered island species are subject to captive breeding

Top: Newborn *Corallus e. enydris*. Photo: R. A. Winstel. Center: *Epicrates cenchria maurus*. Photo: J. Dodd. Bottom: *Epicrates angulifer*. Photos: Left: P. J. Stafford; Right: S. Kochetov.

Epicrates cenchria.
Top: Juvenile. Photo:
Dr. G. Dingerkus.
Center Left: *Epicrates cenchria maurus.*
Photo: B. Kahl. Bottom
Left: Juvenile. Photo:
Dr. G. Dingerkus.
Bottom Right: *Epicrates cenchria alvarezi.*
Photo: R. D. Bartlett.

Epicrates cenchria.
Top: *Epicrates cenchria alvarezi.* Photo: M. Freiberg. Center: *Epicrates cenchria maurus.* Photo: P. J. Stafford. Bottom Left: *Epicrates cenchria cenchria.* Photo: R. S. Simmons. Bottom Right: *Epicrates cenchria crassus.* Photo: M. Freiberg.

Top: Newborn *Epicrates cenchria cenchria*. Bottom: *Epicrates chrysogaster chrysogaster*, striped phase. Photos: R. D. Bartlett.

Top Left: *Epicrates fordi fordi*. Photo: P. J. Stafford. Top Right: *Epicrates striatus striatus*. Photo: L. Edmonds. Center: *Epicrates chrysogaster reliquus*. Photo: R. D. Bartlett. Bottom: *Epicrates fordi*. Photo: R. D. Bartlett.

Top: *Epicrates gracilis.*
Photo: R. D. Bartlett.
Center: *Epicrates inornatus.* Photo: Dr. S. Minton. Bottom: *Epicrates inornatus.*
Photo: R. D. Bartlett.

Epicrates striatus. Photos: Top Left: P. J. Stafford; Top Right: L. Edmonds; Bottom: J. Dodd.

programs for conservation purposes.

E. angulifer Bibron, 1843: **Cuban
Boa.** Island of Cuba. Length to 4.5 m (15 ft),
the longest of the genus. Light brown with
darker or reddish reticulations.

E. cenchria (Linnaeus, 1758): **Rainbow
Boa.** Costa Rica to N.E. Argentina and
Paraguay. Length to 2.5 m (8 ft). Ten
subspecies with a great variation in color from
light yellowish brown to bronze, with or
without darker circular markings. All show
the characteristic smooth, close-set, iridescent
scalation. Highly popular and docile terrarium
subjects regularly bred in captivity.

E. inornatus (Reinhardt, 1843): **Puerto
Rican Boa.** Puerto Rico, Haiti, and adjacent
islands. Length 75 cm (30 in), making it the
smallest in the genus. Three subspecies.

E. striatus (Fischer, 1856): **Haitian
Boa.** Haiti, Bahamas. Length to 2.5 m (8 ft).
Light brown with darker reddish brown
broken bands. Five subspecies.

   Other species in the genus include **E.
exsul**, **Abaco Island Boa**; **E. fordi**, **Ford's
Boa**; and **E. subflavus**, **Jamaican Boa.**

● **Eunectes** Wagler, 1830: **Anacondas.** A
genus containing four species native to South
America. Large, semi-aquatic boas never
found far from bodies of water. Robust species
requiring very large accommodations with
heated bathing facilities.

Epicrates subflavus.
Photos: R. D. Bartlett.

E. murinus (Linnaeus, 1758): **Anaconda.** Native to Amazon and Orinoco Basins. Semi-aquatic and mainly nocturnal, preying on aquatic and semi-aquatic animals including fish, caimans, capybaras, and water birds. Length to at least 9 m (29 ft); world's heaviest snake if not the

Top Left: *Eunectes murinus.* Photo: Dr. G. Dingerkus. Top Right: *Epicrates striatus.* Photo: C. Banks. Bottom: *Eunectes murinus.* Photo: B. Kahl.

longest (see *Python reticulatus*); some specimens may have a central body diameter in excess of 30 cm (12 in). Head narrow, with eyes and nostrils set on top; relatively thick neck. Olive green to bronze-brown, marked with almost circular dark brown to black blotches along the back. Similar blotches on the sides with yellow-ochre centers.

Remains aggressive in captivity, and large specimens must be handled with care. Reared juveniles make the best terrarium subjects. Feed on mice, rats, and chicks (juveniles); rabbits, ducks, geese, etc. (adults).

Top: *Eunectes murinus*, juvenile. Photo: J. Dodd. Center: *Eunectes murinus*. Photo: K. T. Nemuras. Bottom Left: *Eunectes murinus*. Photo: Dr. G. Dingerkus. Bottom Right: *Eunectes notaeus*. Photo: Courtesy London Zoo.

E. notaeus Cope, 1862: **Southern or Yellow Anaconda.** N. Argentina, Paraguay. Semi-aquatic. Length to 3.5 m (11 ft). Yellowish to yellowish green with dark blotches. In view of its smaller size, more suited to the home terrarium than *E. murinus*.

● ***Exiliboa*** Bogert, 1968: **Mexican Dwarf Boas.** A genus containing a single species. ***E. placata*** Bogert, 1968: **Oaxacan Dwarf Boa.** Found in the Oaxaca area of Mexico to an altitude of 2500 m (8125 ft). Nocturnal and arboreal; hides under logs, rocks, etc., during the day. Length to 45 cm (18 in). Head distinctly set off from body; very short tail. Uniform blackish above and beneath, except for a white spot on the vent. A rare species, thought to feed largely on frogs.

● ***Lichanura*** Cope, 1861: **Rosy Boas.** A genus containing two species native to western North America. Found mainly in semi-arid brushland. Largely nocturnal; they climb about in shrubs, feeding on birds and small mammals. Head narrow and tail short. Require a medium-sized dry terrarium with facilities for climbing. Produce six to ten young.

L. roseofusca Cope, 1868: **Coastal Rosy Boa.** S.W. California into Baja Mexico. Length to 100 cm (39 in). Pinkish to rose-red with darker stripes.

L. trivirgata Cope, 1861: **Mexican Rosy Boa.** Arizona into Mexico. Length to 106 cm (42 in). Darker in color than *roseofusca*. The relationship of these taxa is confused and currently under study.

Top: *Lichanura roseofusca*. Photo: I. Francais. Bottom: *Eunectes notaeus*. Photo: B. Kahl.

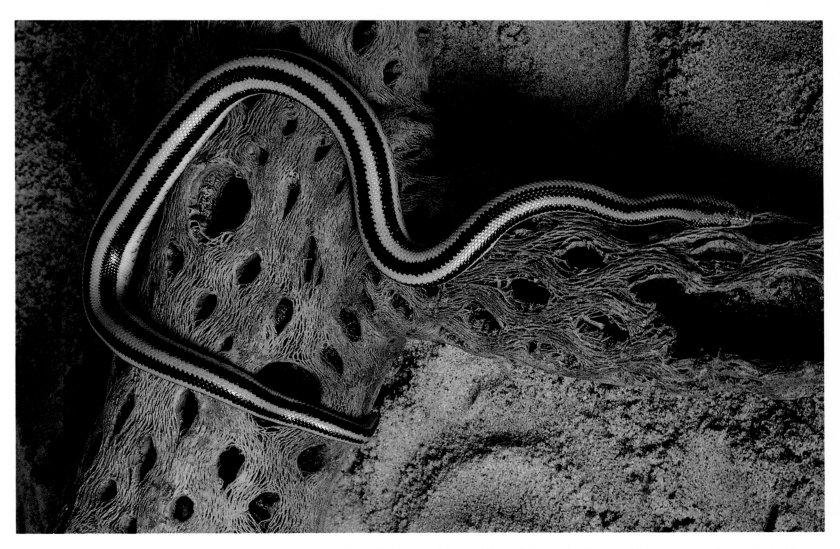

Top: *Lichanura trivirgata*. Photo: I. Francais. Bottom: *Lichanura roseofusca*. Photo: K. Lucas, Steinhart.

Sanzinia madagascariensis. Top: Juvenile. Photo: R. D. Bartlett. Center: Adult. Photo: Courtesy Chester Zoo. Bottom: Juvenile. Photo: P. Freed.

- ***Sanzinia*** Gray, 1849: **Madagascar Tree Boas.** A genus containing a single species. ***S. madagascariensis*** (Dumeril & Bibron, 1844): **Madagascar Tree Boa.** Madagascar (Malagasy Republic) with the exception of the southwestern part. Rain-forest species, mainly arboreal. Length to 2.5 m (8 ft). Greenish to brownish, marked with whitish centered darker patches. Requires a tall, tropical rain-forest terrarium with adequate facilities for climbing. Feeds largely on birds.

- ***Trachyboa*** Peters, 1860: **Rough Boas.** A genus containing two species native to N.W. South America in rain-forest areas. Nocturnal and crepuscular terrestrial snakes usually found near water. Relatively small, with a maximum length of 45 cm (18 in). The scales on the head and body are rough to the touch. Rarely seen in captivity, there is little information available on captive husbandry, but they should be kept in a moderately heated, humid terrarium with facilities to bathe. Usually will take only frogs as food.
  T. gularis Peters, 1860: Ecuador.
  T. boulengeri Peracca, 1910: Panama to Ecuador.

- ***Tropidophis*** Bibron, 1843: **Wood Snakes, Dwarf Boas.** A genus containing some 15 species native to N. South America and the West Indies. Reaching a maximum length of 100 cm (39 cm), all are terrestrial and crepuscular, hiding in the day under logs or leaf litter, usually in damp situations and rarely far from water. They feed mainly on frogs. Most are various shades of yellow to brown with darker markings. They require a heated, humid terrarium with facilities to bathe and climb.

T. canus (Cope, 1868): Bahamas. Four subspecies.

T. caymanensis Battersby, 1838: Cayman Islands. Three subspecies.

T. haetianus (Cope, 1879): Cuba, Haiti, and Jamaica. Three subspecies.

T. maculatus (Bibron, 1843): Western Cuba, Isle of Pines.

T. melanurus (Schlegel, 1837): Cuba, Isle of Pines, Navassa Islands. Four subspecies.

T. pardalis (Gundlach, 1840): Cuba, Isle of Pines.

T. taczanowskyi (Steindachner, 1880): Peru, Ecuador, and Amazon Basin.

Top: *Trachyboa boulengeri*. Photo: P. Freed. Center: *Trachyboa gularis*. Photo: R. D. Bartlett. Bottom: *Tropidophis canus curtus*. Photo: R. D. Bartlett.

Top: *Tropidophis greenwayi*. Photo: Dr. S. Minton. Center: *Tropidophis melanurus*. Photo: S. Kochetov. Bottom: *Tropidophis melanurus melanurus*. Photo: R. D. Bartlett.

● ***Ungaliophis*** Mueller, 1882: **Banana Boas.** A genus containing two species found from S. Mexico to Colombia in montane rain forest. Length to 75 cm (30 in). Closely related to *Trachyboa* and *Tropidophis* and with similar habits. Feed largely on frogs.
U. continentalis Mueller, 1880: Mexico to Honduras.
U. panamensis Schmidt, 1933: S. Nicaragua to W. Colombia.

SUBFAMILY BOLYERIINAE—ROUND ISLAND BOAS
Contains two monotypic genera.

Top: *Tropidophis semicinctus*, preserved. Photo: P. J. Stafford. Center: *Ungaliophis continentalis*. Photo: R. D. Bartlett. Bottom: *Ungaliophis panamensis*, preserved. Photo: P. J. Stafford.

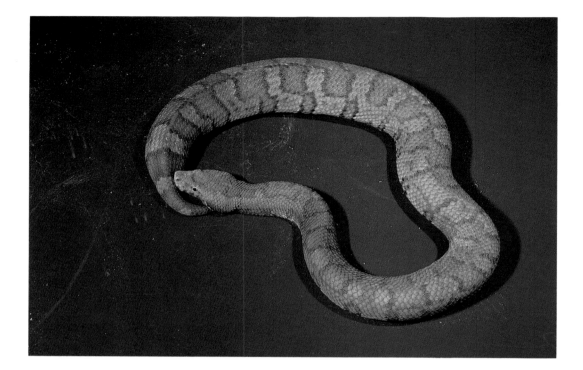

Candoia aspera. Top: Adult. Photo: B. Kahl. Center: Hatchling. Photo: P. Freed. Bottom: Adult. Photo: B. Kahl.

• ***Bolyeria*** Gray, 1842: **Round Island Burrowing Boas.** A genus containing a single species found only on Round Island off Mauritius, Indian Ocean.

B. multocarinata (Boie, 1827): **Round Island Burrowing Boa.** Found in tropical forest areas. Terrestrial and burrowing. Length to 150 cm (60 in). Snout pointed, head not distinctly set off from neck; short, blunt tail. Brownish with irregular network of darker markings. Feeds largely on frogs and lizards. Subject to captive breeding program for conservation purposes. Virtually extinct in the wild.

• ***Casarea*** Gray, 1842: **Round Island Ground Boa.** A genus containing a single species found only on Round Island.

C. dussumieri (Schlegel, 1837): **Round Island Ground Boa.** Found in tropical forest areas. Nocturnal and terrestrial. Length to 150 cm (60 in). Head distinctly set off from neck and tail tapered. Uniform brownish with broken stripe along flanks; lyre-shaped head

marking. Feeds on small mammals, frogs and lizards. Subject to captive breeding program. Virtually extinct in nature.

SUBFAMILY ERYCINAE—SAND BOAS

Contains three genera and about 14 species of sand, rubber, and Pacific boas. Taxonomy requires further research.

● ***Candoia*** Gray, 1842: **Pacific Boas.** A genus containing three species native to the Moluccas, New Guinea, and some Pacific Islands. Inhabit woodland. Semi-arboreal or terrestrial. Length to 150 cm (60 in). Body lightly compressed laterally. Keeled scales. Triangular head distinctly set off from neck. Require a heated tropical terrarium with

Top Left: *Candoia bibroni*. Photo: R. D. Bartlett. Top Right: *Candoia carinata*, adult. Photo: Courtesy Chester Zoo. Bottom: *Candoia carinata*, juvenile. Photo: J. Gee.

Right: *Candoia carinata paulsoni*. Photo: R. D. Bartlett. Upper Center: *Eryx colubrinus loveridgei*. Photo: L. Parras. Lower Center: *Charina bottae*. Photo: K. H. Switak. Bottom: *Eryx colubrinus loveridgei*. Photo: P. J. Stafford.

facilities to climb and bathe. Feed on small mammals, lizards, frogs.

C. aspera (Guenther, 1877): Moluccas, New Guinea, and Solomon and Tokelau Islands. Light reddish brown with darker bands.

C. bibroni (Dumeril & Bibron, 1839): Seram archipelago and adjacent islands. Brown with very small darker irregular spots.

C. carinata (Schneider, 1801): Celebes, New Guinea, Solomon and Tokelau islands. Two subspecies. Brown with darker irregular banding.

● ***Charina*** Gray, 1849: **Rubber Boas.** A genus containing a single species native to western North America.

C. bottae (Blainville, 1835): **Rubber Boa.** British Columbia to southern California, inland to Wyoming, found in grassland and forest edges (especially conifers). Nocturnal and terrestrial, found under logs, rocks, etc. Length to 70 cm (28 in). Head indistinct from

Charina bottae. Photo:
K. Lucas, Steinhart.

Top: *Eryx colubrinus loveridgei*. Photo: R. T. Zappalorti. Bottom: *Eryx conicus*, juvenile. Photo: P. J. Stafford.

Top: *Eryx jaculus turcicus*, female. Photo: P. Freed. Center Left: *Eryx jaculus*. Photo: C. Banks. Center Right: *Eryx conicus*. Photo: C. Banks. Bottom: *Eryx conicus*. Photo: R. T. Zappalorti.

Top Left: *Eryx jaculus*. Photo: Dr. S. Minton. Top Right: *Eryx miliaris*. Photo: S. Kochetov. Center: *Eryx tataricus*. Photo: Dr. S. Minton. Lower Left: *Eryx johni*. Photo: B. Kahl. Lower Right: *Eryx johni johni*. Photo: J. P. Swaak.

neck; short, blunt tail. Uniform brown, lighter beneath. Produces two to eight live young. Requires temperate terrarium with facilities to burrow. Hibernation period recommended. Feed on small mammals and lizards.

- *Eryx* Daudin, 1803: **Sand Boas.** A genus containing about ten species native to S.E. Europe and northern and central Africa through the Middle East to India. Mostly found in desert and steppe areas. Length 50-100 cm (18-39 in). Head not distinctly set off from neck. Small eyes set on top of head. Short, sometimes blunt, tail. Burrow into sand or loose earth and also utilize small mammal burrows. Mainly crepuscular. Colors vary through various shades of brown and yellow with darker blotches or diamonds along dorsal surface. Feed on small mammals, birds, and lizards. Require a dry desert terrarium with adequate loose substrate for burrowing.

E. conicus (Schneider, 1801): **Rough-tailed Sand Boa.** Pakistan through India to Sri Lanka. Length to 100 cm (39 in). Most colorful species in the genus, with rich black-bordered, red-brown markings on buff background. Two subspecies.

E. jaculus (Linnaeus, 1758): **Javelin Sand Boa, European Sand Boa.** The Balkan penisula through Asia Minor to N. Africa. Length to 70 cm (28 in). Pale gray to buff with darker bars and blotches. Three subspecies.

E. johni (Russell, 1801): **Indian Sand Boa.** Iran to W. Bengal. Length to 100 cm (39 in). Very short, blunt tail.

E. miliaris (Pallas, 1783): **Desert Sand Boa.** Central Asia to Mongolia.

E. tataricus (Lichtenstein, 1823): **Tatar Sand Boa.** East coast of Caspian Sea to W. China. Three subspecies.

Top: *Eryx johni*, subadult. Photo: J. Wines. Bottom: *Eryx tataricus*. Photo: S. Kochetov.

Family Uropeltidae—
Shieldtail Snakes

A family of burrowing snakes containing eight genera and some 44 species found only in the southern part of India and Ceylon (Sri Lanka). The cylindrical body is covered with smooth scales that are somewhat larger on the ventral than on the dorsal surface. The pointed head tapers into the body with no obvious constriction at the neck. With the exception of one genus (*Platyplectrurus*), the barely functional eye is covered with an ocular scale. In most species the short tail ends with an enlarged shield that may be covered with tubercles and even may be adorned with spines. The function of the tail appears to be to anchor the animal in its burrow (for example when dealing with prey). Teeth are present on the upper and lower jaws. These feed mainly on invertebrates, particularly earthworms and burrowing insect larvae. Ovoviviparous, producing 3-15 relatively large young.

As they are not frequently kept in captivity, little is known of their husbandry. A tall, narrow, all-glass terrarium is recommended. This should be filled with a loose, well-drained substrate (peat and sand mixture).

- *Brachyophidium* Wall, 1921: A genus containing only a single species.
  B. rhodogaster Wall, 1921: Found in the Palni Range in southern India, inhabiting tropical rain forest. Most primitive member of the family. Length to 21 cm (8 in) and only 7 mm in diameter. The tail shield is not highly developed, the tail ending in a point. Dark brown above, reddish below.
- *Melanophidium* Guenther, 1864: A genus containing three rare species native to southern India. Found in forested mountainous country, usually between 900-1500 m (3000-5000 ft). Maximum length 60 cm (24 in). The edge of the tail shield is toothed like a saw. Iridescent dark brown to black with lighter stripes or spots.
  M. wynaudense (Beddome, 1863): Southern India.
- *Platyplectrurus* Guenther, 1868: A genus containing two species native to southern India and Sri Lanka. Unlike other genera in the family, the small eyes are not covered with an ocular shield. The tail shield is warty and ends in a spine.
  P. madurensis Beddome, 1877: Travancore, southern India and Sri Lanka. Mountain forest to 1800 m (5800 ft). Length to 45 cm (18 in).
  P. trilineatus Beddome, 1867: Anamalai Hills, Travancore, southern India. Length to 40 cm (16 in). Reddish brown with three darker stripes.
- *Plectrurus* Dumeril & Dumeril, 1851: A genus containing four species native to southern India. Length to 45 cm (18 in) and only 1 cm in diameter. The caudal scales are keeled. The tail shield is relatively small, ending with a pair of spines. Colors range from iridescent reddish to purplish brown, often with darker flecks and stripes.
  P. perroteti Dumeril & Bibron, 1854: Nilgiri Range, southern India. Between 1300 and 1800 m (4250-5800 ft).
- *Pseudotyphlops* Schlegel, 1839: A genus containing a single species.
  P. philippinus Schlegel, 1839: Found in the plains of Sri Lanka. Length to 30 cm (12 in), but with a diameter of 2.2 cm, the most thickset species in the family. Tail shield almost perfectly circular, with a radial arrangement of tubercles. Uniform brown in color. The scientific name arose from a mistake, and the species does not occur in the Philippines.
- *Rhinophis* Hemprich, 1820: A genus containing ten species native to southern India and Sri Lanka. Length from 18-55 cm (7-22 in). Tail shield relatively large and with tubercles; no tail spines. Colors vary from blue-gray through reddish or dark brown, with a variety of darker or lighter flecks, bands, or stripes.
  R. drummondhayi Wall, 1921: Sri Lanka to an altitude of 1200 m (3900 ft).
  R. oxyrhynchus (Schneider, 1801): Sri Lanka on the northern plains. Largest member of family, reaching 55 cm (22 in).
  R. sanguineus (Beddome, 1863): Southern India, especially in the Nilgiri Range.
  R. travancoricus Boulenger, 1893: Travancore Ranges, southern India.
  R. trevelyanus (Kelaart, 1853): Sri Lanka in

hilly, forested country to 1200 m (3900 ft).
- *Teretrurus* Beddome, 1886: A genus containing a single species.
  T. sanguineus (Beddome, 1867): Southern India. Length to 23 cm (9 in). Brown to reddish purple.
- *Uropeltis* Cuvier, 1829: A genus containing about 22 species native to southern India and Sri Lanka. Length from 20-50 cm (8-20 in). Snout pointed and short; cylindrical tail covered with small keeled scales. The tail shield is relatively small and ends with a pair of spines. Colors vary from uniform brown to blackish or reddish, some with darker or lighter markings.
  U. beddomei (Guenther, 1862): Anamalai Hills, southern India.
  U. ceylonicus Cocteau, 1833: Anamalai Hills, southern India, but not Sri Lanka as its scientific name may suggest.
  U. melanogaster (Gray, 1858): Sri Lanka in the hills of the interior.
  U. ocellatus (Beddome, 1863): Southern India, especially in the Anamalai and Nilgiri Hills.
  U. woodmasoni (Theobold, 1876): Palni Range, southern India at an altitude of 1800 m (5800 ft).

Xenopeltis unicolor. Photos: Top: Dr. S. Minton; Bottom: R. D. Bartlett.

Family Xenopeltidae—
Sunbeam Snake

A family containing only a single genus.
- *Xenopeltis* Reinhardt, 1827: A genus containing only a single species.
  X. unicolor Reinhardt, 1827: Burma to southern China, Indo-China, Malayan Archipelago, and Indonesia. Found in and around the margins of monsoon rain forest. Length to 100 cm (39 in). Roundish head set off indistinctly from body. Scales smooth and highly iridescent. Relatively short but tapered tail. Unusual in having two functional lungs. Terrestrial, nocturnal, and secretive, but quickly becomes tame in captivity, feeding on frogs, lizards, and small mammals. In the wild will feed on other snakes. Requires a warm, humid terrarium with adequate hiding places and a large water bath.

Infraorder Caenophidia

The infraorder Caenophidia contains five families of advanced snakes with a total of about 380 genera and well over 2,000 species. It is found throughout the world in tropical, subtropical, and temperate climates. Range of length is from 20-550 cm (8 in - 18 ft). The majority of species are slender and agile and possess large, efficient eyes. The teeth are variable depending on the method of capturing prey. The body scales are highly variable depending on the species. The tail ranges from short to extremely long and may be prehensile (arboreal species) or laterally flattened (sea snakes). Habit and habitat are highly variable, and arboreal, terrestrial, burrowing, and marine forms occur.

The large numbers of species, especially in the family Colubridae, constantly require systematic and taxonomic revision.

Family Colubridae— Typical Snakes

The family Colubridae is the largest and most complex in the suborder Serpentes, containing some 14 subfamilies, 290 genera, and about 2,000 species found in tropical, subtropical, and temperate regions throughout the world. Size range is 20–400 cm (8 in–13 ft). Habit and habitat are extremely variable. They may be diurnal, nocturnal, terrestrial, arboreal, aquatic, or burrowing species. Reproduction may be oviparous or ovoviviparous.

SUBFAMILY XENODERMINAE

The Xenoderminae contains the most primitive colubrids that show certain (probably superficial) resemblances to the wart snakes (Acrochordidae), possessing a mixture of overlapping and non-overlapping scales. There are seven genera and about 12 species native to Southeast Asia and Central and South America. Usually found in humid areas, in swamps or tropical rain forests. The biology of the members of this subfamily is poorly known, and there are opportunities for the terrarium-keeper to contribute to further research.

- *Achalinus* Peters, 1869: A genus containing five species native to Southeast Asia (S. China, Japan, Indo-China). Length to 50 cm (20 in). The head is set off distinctly from the neck, and the snout is pointed. The dorsal scales are strongly keeled and the upper surface is a uniform gray to reddish brown. Nocturnal, hiding during the day under leaf litter and logs or among tree roots. They feed on earthworms, slugs, and frogs. Oviparous, laying four to eight eggs. They require a small, humid terrarium with ample hiding places.

A. rufescens Boulenger, 1888: Southern China to Hong Kong and Vietnam, in hilly areas. Average length 37 cm (15 in). Reddish brown above with lighter underside.

A. spinalis Peters, 1869: Japan and China to an altitude of 2000 m (6500 ft).

- *Cercaspis* Wagler, 1830: A genus containing only a single species.

C. carinatus Kuhl, 1820: Sri Lanka to altitudes of 1200 m (3900 ft). Length to 75 cm (30 in). Elongate head and strongly keeled dorsal scales. Blackish ground color broken with whitish to yellowish rings that become narrower as the snake ages. Biology of this species is poorly known.

- *Fimbrios* Smith, 1920: A genus containing only a single species.

F. klossi Smith, 1920: Indo-China in wooded hills between 1000 and 1800 m (3250-5850 ft). Length to 40 cm (16 in). The head is barely distinct from the neck. A characteristic of this species is the extension of the lower labial scales, giving the snake the appearance of having a beard; the function of these extended scales is unknown. The dorsal scales are strongly keeled. There is only a single row of subcaudals. The color is a uniform gray to olive. Terrestrial and nocturnal. Its biology is poorly known. Feeds on invertebrates (earthworms, slugs, etc.) and frogs. Requires a cool (20°C), humid terrarium with ample hiding places.

- *Nothopsis* Cope, 1871: A genus containing only a single species.

N. rugosus Cope, 1871: Atlantic coastal strip from Nicaragua to Panama and through to Pacific coast of Colombia and Ecuador. Inhabits tropical rain forest. Length to 70 cm (28 in). Rough-scaled. Little is documented on the biology of this species.

- *Stoliczkia* Jerdon, 1870: A genus containing two species native to India and Borneo in hill forest to 1200 m (3900 ft). Length 50-70 cm (20-28 in). Head narrow, distinctly set off from neck. Keeled dorsal scales. The body is slightly flattened laterally and the tail is relatively long. Require a cool, humid rain-forest terrarium. Feed on frogs, worms, slugs, etc. The biology of these species is sparsely documented.

S. borneensis Boulenger, 1899: North

Xenopholis scalaris.
Photo: P. Freed.

Borneo (Sabah) in area of Mount Kinabalu. Enlarged scales along vertebral ridge. Reddish above with three broken longitudinal stripes.
S. khasiensis Jerdon, 1870: Found in the Khase Range in the Indian state of Meghalaya. Uniform reddish brown above, whitish beneath.

- ***Xenodermus*** Reinhardt, 1836: A genus containing a single species.
X. javanicus Reinhardt, 1836: Malayan Archipelago from mainland to Borneo. Found in marshy areas of the rain forests to an altitude of 1100 m. Often found in paddy fields. Length to 65 cm (26 in). Unique arrangement of dorsal scales—three rows of enlarged keeled scales are placed in a chain-like arrangement among smaller keeled scales along the dorsal ridge. A border of smooth, small, mosaic-like scales is followed by a further longitudinal row of larger keeled scales. Color is dark and light brown arranged in broken bands along the body. Amphibious and requires a warm aqua-terrarium. Food is mainly frogs. Oviparous, laying two to six eggs.
- ***Xenopholis*** Peters, 1869: A genus containing a single species.
X. scalaris (Wucherer, 1861): Amazon basin in Bolivia, Peru, Ecuador, and Brazil in tropical rain forest. A small terrestrial species. Biology virtually unknown.

SUBFAMILY SIBYNOPHINAE—MANY-TOOTHED SNAKES

A subfamily containing three genera and about 17 species native to Southeast Asia, Madagascar, and Central America. Found in rain forest and hill forest. Length from 30-80 cm (12-32 in). The head is not set off distinctly from the neck. A characteristic of the family is the numerous fragile teeth, 25-56 on each maxilla, that are flattened and dagger-like, an adaptation connected with a diet of hard-scaled lizards such as skinks.

- ***Liophidium*** Boulenger, 1896: A genus containing five species native to Madagascar, Reunion, and the Comores in tropical rain forest or dryer brushland. Length 30-50 cm (12-20 in). Head barely distinct from neck. Nocturnal and secretive. Biology poorly documented.
L. mayottensis (Peters, 1873): Mayotte and Comores in rain forest.
L. torquatus (Boulenger, 1888): Eastern Madagascar in rain forest.
L. vaillanti (Mocquard, 1901): Madagascar and Reunion.

Liophidium vaillanti.
Photo: P. Freed.

Top: *Scaphiodontophis albonuchalis*. Photo: Dr. S. Minton. Bottom: *Scaphiodontophis annulatus*. Photo: P. Freed.

● *Scaphiodontophis* Taylor & Smith, 1943: A genus containing five species native to Central America. Length to 70 cm (28 in). Some species show coral snake mimicry, having black, white, and red bands. Nocturnal and secretive. Feed on lizards, frogs, and other snakes. Require a moderately heated rain-forest terrarium.
S. annulatus (Dumeril, Bibron & Dumeril, 1854): Mexico (Yucatan peninsula) southward to Honduras.

● *Sibynophis* Fitzinger, 1843: A genus containing seven species ranging from the Himalayan foothills through India and Sri Lanka, and Indo-China to southern China (including Taiwan) and the Malayan Archipelago. May be found in rain forest, including monsoon forest and bamboo forest, some species to an altitude of 3000 m (9750 ft). Length 30-80 cm (12-32 in). Slender and agile. Feed on lizards and snakes. Oviparous, laying two to six eggs. Require a cool (20-25°C), humid terrarium.
S. chinensis (Guenther, 1889): Indo-China to southern China and Taiwan. Found in forests at lower altitudes. Yellowish brown with a dark and light collar.
S. collaris (Gray, 1853): Southern China and Taiwan to Malaysia in rain forest to altitudes of 3000 m (9750 ft). Length to 70 cm (28 in). Slightly triangular head. Gray-brown to brown with three indistinct blackish longitudinal stripes. Broad black band across back of head, followed by a narrower cream to light brown band.
S. geminatus (Boie, 1826): Thailand, Malaysia, Indonesia. Montane rain forest to 1300 m (4225 ft). Reddish brown with blackish crossbands.
S. subpunctatus (Dumeril & Bibron, 1854): Monsoon forests of India and Sri Lanka.

SUBFAMILY XENODONTINAE

This subfamily contains 27 genera and about 193 species all native to the Americas. The species are small to medium in size, some with well-developed opisthoglyph fangs (rear-fanged, venomous). The subfamily contains species of highly varying forms and habits. All species in the subfamily appear to be oviparous.

- **Alsophis** Fitzinger, 1843: A genus containing ten species ranging from the West Indies through northern and western South America to the Galapagos Islands. Found mainly in dryer secondary forest and brushland though never far from water. Length to 60 cm (24 in). Feed on lizards and frogs. Require a well ventilated, semi-dry terrarium.

  A. antillensis (Schlegel, 1837): Lesser Antilles. Six subspecies.

  A. biserialis (Guenther, 1860): Galapagos Islands. Two subspecies.

  A. cantherigerus (Bibron, 1840): Cuba, Cayman Islands. Eight subspecies.

  A. chamissonis (Wiegmann, 1835): Central Chile. Probably a *Philodryas*.

  A. occidentalis Van Denburgh, 1912: Galapagos Islands.

  A. portoricensis Reinhardt & Luetken, 1863: Puerto Rico and adjacent islands. Seven subspecies.

  A. slevini Van Denburgh, 1912: Galapagos Islands.

  A. steindachneri Van Denburgh, 1912: Galapagos Islands.

  A. vudii Cope, 1863: Bahamian Racer. Bahamas. Five subspecies.

- **Antillophis** Maglio, 1970: A genus containing species native to Cuba and Haiti. Formerly classified under *Leimadophis* or *Dromicus*. Form and habit similar to these genera.

  A. andreai (Reinhardt & Luetken, 1863): Cuba. Six subspecies.

  A. parvifrons (Cope, 1863): Haiti and adjacent islands.

- **Arrhyton** Guenther, 1858: A genus containing seven species native to the West Indian islands.

Top: *Alsophis vudii picticeps*. Photo: R. D. Bartlett. Bottom: *Alsophis vudii*. Photo: Dr. S. Minton.

but held distinct by many workers.

C. gigas (Dumeril, Bibron & Dumeril, 1854): **False Water Cobra.** Eastern Bolivia through Brazil to northern Argentina. Found in rain forest and secondary forest, usually in or near water. Length to 210 cm (84 in). Robustly built snake with head distinctly set off from neck. Yellowish brown to chestnut with darker irregular crossbands. The female usually has lighter markings than the male. When threatened this species flattens its neck somewhat in the manner of a cobra, hence its common name. A spectacular and popular terrarium subject. Requires a large aqua-terrarium. Feed on fish, frogs, reptiles, birds,

A. exiguum (Cope, 1863): Puerto Rico and adjacent islands. Three subspecies.

A. funereum (Cope, 1863): Jamaica.

A. vittatum (Gundlach & Peters, 1862): Cuba and Isle of Pines. Two subspecies.

• **Conophis** Peters, 1860: A genus containing four species found from Mexico to Costa Rica in arid to semi-desert areas. Length to 70 cm (28 in). Mostly uniform sandy brown with or without indistinct lateral striping. Feed mainly on lizards. Require a semi-arid terrarium with daytime temperatures to 30°C, reduced at night to 20°C.

C. lineatus (Dumeril, Bibron & Dumeril, 1854): Mexico (Yucatan Peninsula) to Costa Rica. Three subspecies.

• **Cyclagras** Cope, 1885: **False Water Cobra.** A genus containing a single species. Often considered a synonym of *Hydrodynastes*,

and small mammals. Oviparous, laying up to 40 eggs.

- ***Darlingtonia*** Cochran, 1935: A genus containing a single species.

  D. haetiana Cochran, 1935: Haiti. Length to 30 cm (12 in). Head distinctly set off from neck. Terrestrial. Biology poorly documented.

- ***Ditaxodon*** Hoge, 1958: A genus containing a single species.

  D. taeniatus (Hensel, 1868): Southeastern Brazil. Formerly classified as a *Philodryas*, to which it has many similarities.

- ***Dromicus*** Bibron, 1843: A genus containing approximately 12 species native to South America. Much systematic confusion, and some species may be included among *Alsophis*, *Antillophis*, *Arrhyton*, or *Leimadophis*. Many authorities consider *Dromicus* to be a synonym of *Liophis*. Urgent revision required. Length to 50 cm (20 in). Diurnal and terrestrial species found mainly near water, feeding largly on frogs. Require a small aqua-terrarium; temperature 25-30°C.

  D. melanotus (Shaw, 1802): Colombia through Venezuela to Trinidad and Tobago and Granada.

- ***Heterodon*** Latreille, 1801: **Hognose Snakes.** A genus containing three species found from eastern North America to northeastern Mexico in a variety of habitats, from prairie to marshland. Sharply upturned and pointed snout. Stout body with broad neck. When threatened they spread the neck and hiss; if further threatened, they will roll over onto their back and feign death. However, if placed on the belly, they will again roll over onto the back!

  H. nasicus Baird & Girard, 1852: **Western Hognose Snake.** From central southern Canada through the midwestern USA into Mexico. In sand and gravel prairie to river floodplains. Length to 90 cm (36 in). Active primarily during morning or late afternoon; burrows to avoid extremes of temperature. Light brown to gray or yellowish gray above with darker patches along back. Underside

Top: *Cyclagras gigas*. Photo: K. T. Nemuras. Center: *Dromicus typhlus*. Photo: B. Kahl. Bottom Left: *Dromicus typhlus*. Photo: J. Kellnhauser. Bottom Right: *Heterodon nasicus*. Photo: R. T. Zappalorti.

Top Left: *Heterodon nasicus*. Photo: K. T. Nemuras. Top Right: *Heterodon platyrhinos*, albino hatchling. Photo: P. A. Vargas. Bottom: *Heterodon nasicus kennerlyi*. Photo: K. Lucas, Steinhart.

Top: *Heterodon platyrhinos*, feigning death. Photo: J. Iverson. Bottom Left: *Heterodon nasicus kennerlyi*. Photo: K. H. Switak. Bottom Right: *Heterodon simus*. Photo: R. T. Zappalorti.

Top Left: *Heterodon platyrhinos*, hood spread. Photo: R. Anderson. Top Right: *Heterodon simus*. Photo: W. B. Allen, Jr. Bottom: *Heterodon platyrhinos*. Photo: R. T. Zappalorti.

patterned with black blotches. Oviparous, laying 5-25 eggs. Requires a dry, moderately heated terrarium (with basking areas), but with facilities to bathe. Needs a deep, sandy substrate for burrowing. Feeds on frogs, toads, lizards. Three subspecies.

H. platyrhinos (Latreille, 1801): **Eastern**

Hognose Snake. Eastern half of the USA south of the Great Lakes, in open, sandy soil areas including agricultural land. Length to 115 cm (46 in). Snout not so dramatically upturned as in preceding species. Color very variable: yellow, tan, brown, reddish, or gray with squarish dark blotches. Melanistic (all

black) individuals relatively common.
Oviparous, laying up to 60 eggs. Care as
described for preceding species. Feeds almost
exclusively on toads, so hard to maintain.

● ***Hypsirhynchus*** Guenther, 1858: A genus
containing a single species.
H. ferox Guenther, 1858: Haiti and adjacent
islands. Length to 100 cm (39 in). Biology
poorly known.

● ***Ialtris*** Cope, 1862: A genus containing two
species native to Haiti and adjacent islands.
Length to 75 cm (30 in). Terrestrial. Well-
developed opisthoglyph fangs. Biology poorly
known.
I. dorsalis (Guenther, 1858): Haiti. Brown
with darker flecks. W-shaped marking at rear
of head.

● ***Leimadophis*** Fitzinger, 1843: A genus
containing 30 species found from southern
Central America to Argentina. Much
systematic confusion, some species in the
genus being regarded as belonging to *Alsophis*,
Arrhyton, *Dromicus*, or *Antillophis* by some
authorities. As with *Dromicus*, many workers
consider *Leimadophis* to be a synonym of
Liophis. Varied habitats, from tropical rain

Top: *Heterodon simus*.
Photo: J. Iverson.
Bottom: *Leimadophis
epinephalus*. Photo: K.
T. Nemuras.

Top: *Leimadophis reginae*. Photo: R. S. Simmons. Center: *Leimadophis poecilogyrus*. Photo: M. Freiberg. Bottom: *Leimadophis reginae*. Photo: R. S. Simmons.

Prefer damp areas near water and can swim well. Length 60-80 cm (24-32 in). Feed on fish, frogs, and possibly invertebrates. Require a warm aqua-terrarium. Oviparous, laying four to ten eggs.

L. cobella (Linnaeus, 1758): South America east of the Andes.

L. miliaris (Linnaeus, 1758): Brazil to Argentina.

- *Lygophis* Fitzinger, 1843: A genus (often considered a synonym of *Liophis*) containing eight species native to South America in tropical rain forest, especially the more humid areas. Length 35-75 cm (14-30 in). Slender, with a narrow head. Climb reasonably well. Require a warm terrarium with large water vessel and facilities to climb and bask. Feed on lizards and frogs.

forest to pampas. Length 25-50 cm (10-20 in). Diurnal and terrestrial. Feed on frogs, lizards, and small mammals. Require aqua-terrarium but with dry basking areas.

L. reginae (Linnaeus, 1758): Northern South America. Two subspecies.

L. poecilogyrus (Wied, 1823): Brazil to Argentina. 12 subspecies.

- *Lioheterophis* Amaral, 1934: A genus containing a single species.

L. iheringi Amaral, 1934: State of Paraiba in N.E. Brazil in low altitude forest. Length to 40 cm. Require a warm aqua-terrarium; feed on frogs.

- *Liophis* Wagler, 1830: A genus containing about 25 species native to South America.

Top: *Liophis anomalus*. Center Left: *Liophis jaegeri*. Center Right: *Liophis miliaris*. Bottom: *Liophis elegantissima*. Photos: M. Freiberg.

Top: *Liophis miliaris.* Photo: F. Achaval. Center Left: *Liophis sagittifer.* Photo: H. Piacentini. Center Right: *Lygophis lineatus.* Photo: M. Freiberg. Bottom Left: *Lygophis lineatus.* Photo: M. Freiberg. Bottom Right: *Lystrophis dorbignyi.* Photo: F. Achaval.

L. coralliventris (Boulenger, 1894): S.E. Brazil and Paraguay. Upper surface olive-green to bluish gray, belly whitish; underside of tail red with black spots.

L. lineatus (Linnaeus, 1758): From Panama to northern Argentina. Three subspecies. Dorsal surface yellowish to olive, with a dark and light broken vertebral stripe and dark stripes along the flanks.

- **Lystrophis** Cope, 1885: **South American Hognoses.** A genus of about 3 species native to southern South America in open forests and plains. The general body shape and upturned snout are similar to *Heterodon*. 30 to 75 cm.

L. dorbignyi (Dumeril, Bibron and Dumeril, 1854): Argentina to southeastern Brazil. Feeds largely on toads.

Top: *Lystrophis dorbignyi*. Photo: F. Achaval. Center: *Lystrophis semicinctus*. Photo: R. S. Simmons. Bottom: *Lystrophis semicinctus*. Photo: M. Freiberg.

Top: *Philodryas aestivus subcarinatus*. Photo: M. Freiberg. Center: *Philodryas baroni*. Photo: H. Piacentini. Bottom: *Philodryas baroni fuscoflavescens*. Photo: M. Freiberg.

Top: *Philodryas baroni fuscoflavescens.* Photo: M. Freiberg. Center: *Philodryas burmeisteri.* Photo: H. Piacentini. Bottom: *Philodryas olfersi.* Photo: M. Freiberg.

Top: *Philodryas patagoniensis*. Photo: L. C. deZolessi. Bottom: *Philodryas psammophideus*. Photo: M. Freiberg.

● **Paroxyrhopus** Schenkel, 1901: A genus containing three species native to the Amazon Basin and Paraguay. Found in various forested habitats. Length to 75 cm (30 in). Enlarged rear fangs. Terrestrial. Biology poorly documented. Considered by some to be a synonym of *Xenopholis*.

P. atropunctatus Amaral, 1923: Brazil (Minas Gerais).

P. reticulatus Schenkel, 1901: Paraguay.

P. undulatus (Jensen, 1900): Amazon Basin to Mato Grosso.

● **Philodryas** Wagler, 1830: A genus containing 15 species native to South America in rain forest. Mainly arboreal. Length 100-140 cm (39-56 in). Slender, with head distinctly set off from neck. Tail relatively long. Mostly uniform green. Require a tall rain-forest terrarium with ample climbing facilities (robust plants) and a basking area. Feed on lizards and frogs.

P. aestivus (Dumeril, Bibron & Dumeril, 1854): Brazil (Mato Grosso). Green. Two subspecies.

P. olfersi (Lichtenstein, 1823): Eastern Peru and western Brazil into Argentina. Green.

P. psammophideus Guenther, 1872: Eastern Bolivia, S.W. Brazil into Argentina. Semi-arboreal. Brownish with darker markings.

P. viridissimus (Linnaeus, 1758): Amazon Basin. Green.

● **Platyinion** Amaral, 1923: A genus containing a single species.

P. lividum Amaral, 1923: Mato Grosso in tropical rain forest. Length to 75 cm (30 in). Head not distinctly set off from neck. Well-developed opisthoglyph fangs. Only five teeth on upper jaw anterior to the fangs. Upper side

Top: *Rhadinaea brevirostris*. Photo: P. Freed. Bottom: *Rhadinaea flavilata*. Photo: J. Iverson.

Rhadinaea laureata.
Photo: Dr. S. Minton.

bluish gray with darker blotches. A burrowing snake. Biology barely researched.

- **Rhadinaea** Cope, 1863: A genus containing about 40 species. Taxonomy disputed (Boiginae or Xenodontinae, but here included among the latter). Some species of this genus now are included in **Urotheca;** see the discussion of *Pliocercus* in the Natricinae. Found from S.E. USA to Uruguay and Argentina. Varied habitats from swamps to rain forest and agricultural areas (especially banana plantations). Length 35-60 cm (14-24 in). Mainly brownish, some species with longitudinal stripes. Diurnal. Feed on lizards, salamanders, and frogs. Require a warm terrarium with large water container.

R. brevirostris (Peters, 1863): Amazon Basin.

R. flavilata (Cope, 1871): **Pine Woods Snake.** S.E. USA, from North Carolina to S. Florida and west to Louisiana. Found in low marshy areas and damp pine flatwoods, also coastal islands. Length to 40 cm (16 in). Golden to reddish brown above, head darker than body; underside yellowish white.

Oviparous, laying two to four relatively large (2.5 cm - 1 in) eggs.

R. poecilopogon Cope, 1863: S. Brazil, Uruguay, and Argentina.

- **Rhadinella** Smith, 1941: A genus containing a single species.

R. schistosa Smith, 1941: E. Mexico. Closely related to *Rhadinaea* and recently synonymized with it.

- **Sordellina** Procter, 1923: A genus containing a single species.

S. punctata (Peters, 1880): Eastern Brazil in lowland tropical forest, usually near water. Length to 20 cm (8 in). Brown with longitudinal darker blotches and spots. Feeds mainly on frogs and their larvae. Oviparous.

- **Synophis** Peracca, 1896: A genus containing three species native to the upper Amazon Basin (Ecuador and Colombia). Partially aquatic and feeding upon fish and amphibians. Length to 75 cm (30 in). Relatively long head and narrow neck. Mostly uniform brown to olive above, lighter below. Require a moderately heated aqua-terrarium.

S. bicolor Peracca, 1896: Ecuador. Dark

brown above, much lighter beneath.

S. lasallei (Niceforo Maria, 1950): Colombia and Ecuador.

● ***Tretanorhinus*** Dumeril & Bibron, 1854: A genus containing four species native to Central and South America and some Caribbean islands. Amphibious snakes rarely found far from and usually in water. Feed largely on fish and frogs. Require a heated aqua-terrarium.

T. nigroluteus Cope, 1861: Mexico to Panama and Costa Rica. Three subspecies.

T. taeniatus Boulenger, 1903: Coastal lowlands of Colombia and Ecuador.

T. variabilis Dumeril & Bibron, 1854: **Caribbean Water Snake.** Cuba, Isle of Pines, Cayman Islands.

● ***Umbrivaga*** Roze, 1964: A genus containing three species native to northern South America. Tropical rain forest. Length 30-40 cm (12-16 in). Terrestrial, feeding on small amphibians, reptiles, and invertebrates.

U. mertensi Roze, 1964: Venezuela.

U. pygmaeus (Cope, 1868): Upper Amazon region (Colombia and Ecuador).

Top: *Tretanorhinus* cf. *nigroluteus*. Photo: S. Kochetov. Bottom: *Rhadinaea montana*. Photo: J. Iverson.

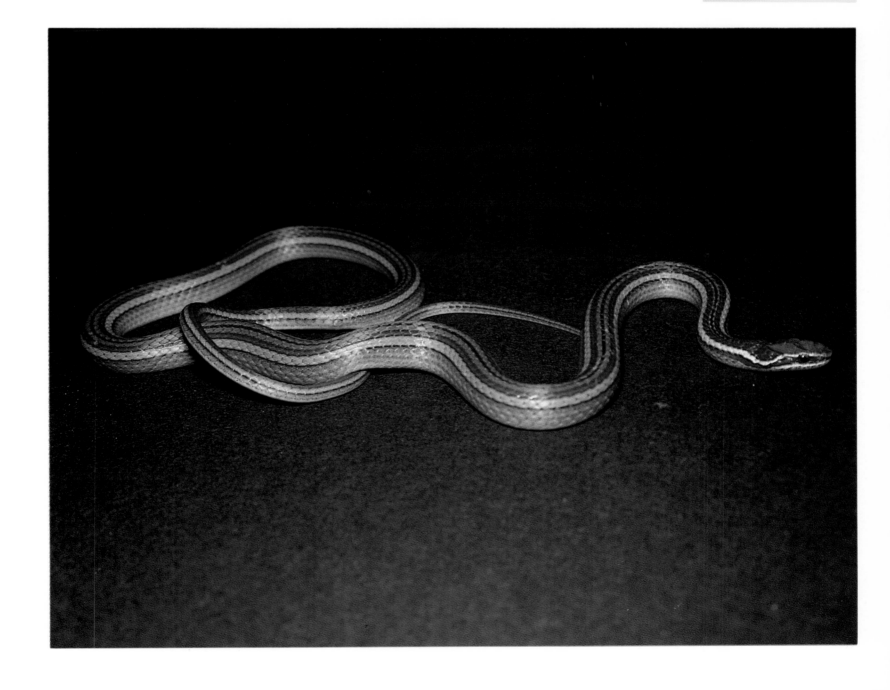

Top: *Tretanorhinus variabilis lewisi*. Photo: Dr. S Minton. Bottom: *Uromacer dorsalis*. Photo: R. S. Simmons.

Top: *Uromacer dorsalis*.
Photo: R. S. Simmons.
Bottom: *Uromacer oxyrhynchus*. Photo: C. Banks.

- ***Uromacer*** Dumeril & Bibron, 1854: **Haitian Vine Snakes.** A genus containing four species native to Haiti and adjacent islands, inhabiting dry brushland. 120-200 cm (48-80 in). Head set off distinctly from narrow neck. Snout pointed. Diurnal and partially arboreal (especially *U. oxyrhynchus*). Color green to bluish green, lighter beneath. Feed mainly on lizards, sometimes frogs. Opisthoglyphs (rear-fanged, venomous). Effect of venom on man uncertain. Oviparous, laying 6-12 eggs. Require a large heated semi-humid terrarium with dry basking areas and facilities to climb.
  U. catesbyi (Schlegel, 1837): Eight subspecies.
  U. oxyrhynchus Dumeril & Bibron, 1854.
- ***Uromacerina*** Amaral, 1930: A genus containing a single species.
  U. ricardini (Peracca, 1897): Sao Paulo state in S.E. Brazil. Form and habit similar to *Uromacer*.
- ***Xenodon*** Boie, 1826: **False Vipers.** A genus containing eight species occurring from Mexico to Argentina (found only east of the Andes). Found mainly in tropical rain forest. Length to 140 cm (56 in). Relatively large head and broad neck. Body broad and dorso-laterally flattened. Short, sharply tapered tail. Juveniles marked with broad dark bands on lighter ground color; adults uniformly brownish. May be active by day or night. Usually found in damp areas near water, where they feed largely on frogs and toads, sometimes birds and mammals. If threatened,

they flatten the neck and body, hiss loudly, and feign attacks. Although the enlarged rear fangs are ungrooved, it is thought that the saliva may contain venomous secretions, so handle with care! Require a warm (daytime to 30°C, reduced to 22-23°C at night), humid terrarium with large water vessel.
X. merremi (Wagler, 1824): From the Guianas to Argentina. Often placed in ***Waglerophis***.
X. rhabdocephalus (Wied, 1824): Mexico south to Bolivia. Two subspecies.
X. severus (Linnaeus, 1758): Amazon Basin.

SUBFAMILY CALAMARINAE

This subfamily contains nine genera and some 65 species distributed from India to New Guinea and the Philippines. They are found mainly in rain forest and montane rain forest to an altitude of 1800 m (5850 ft). Length from 15-75 cm (6-30 in). Most have the head indistinct from the neck and have a pointed or shovel-shaped snout. The rostral shield usually extends forward over the mouth. Relatively short tail, usually ending with a spine. All species are subterranean, living in burrows and emerging only at night or after heavy rain. Food consists mainly of earthworms and other invertebrates and their larvae. Some species live in termite mounds and feed on the termites and their nymphs. All are best kept in glass terraria suitable for burrowing snakes. None are regularly available in the hobby, few have ever been kept in the Western World, and the taxonomy is poorly understood.

Xenodon (Waglerophis) merremi. Photos: Top and Bottom: M. Freiberg; Center: F. Achaval.

- *Agrophis* F. Mueller, 1894: A genus containing three species native to the Celebes and Borneo. Length 20-25 cm (8-10 in). Only 15 rows of scales around midbody. Color iridescent chestnut-brown. Often considered a synonym of *Pseudorabdion*.
  A. sarasinorum F. Mueller, 1894: Celebes, in montane rain forest to 1700 m (5525 ft).
- *Brachyorrhos* Kuhl, 1826: A genus containing a single species.
  B. albus (Linnaeus, 1758): Java, Moluccas, New Guinea. Length to 75 cm (30 in) (largest member of subfamily). Brown with darker longitudinal stripes.
- *Calamaria* Boie, 1827: A genus containing 52 species distributed from Assam and Burma through Malaysia and Indonesia to the

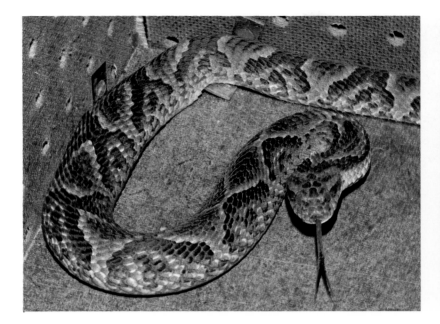

Moluccas. Length 20-60 cm (8-24 in). Only 13 rows of scales at midbody. Mainly iridescent dark brown, some species with darker blotches or stripes.

C. agamensis Bleeker, 1860: Sumatra, Java, Borneo.

C. leucocephala Dumeril & Bibron, 1854: Malaya, Sumatra, Java, Borneo, Bali.

C. lumbricoidea Boie, 1827: Sumatra, Java, Borneo, Celebes. Two subspecies.

C. pavimentata Dumeril & Bibron, 1854: Assam to S. China, south to Java. Two subspecies.

C. vermiformis Dumeril & Bibron, 1854: Thailand through Malayan Peninsula into Sumatra, Java, and Borneo.

● *Calamorhabdium* Boettger, 1898: A genus containing two species found in the Celebes and on Batjan. Length 20 cm (8 in). Iridescent dark brown. Prominent spine at tail tip.

C. kuekenthali Boettger, 1898: Batjan.

● *Etheridgeum* Wallach, 1988: A genus containing only a single species. Formerly called *Padangia* Werner, preoccupied by a mollusk.

E. pulchra (Werner, 1924): Sumatra. Biology hardly known.

● *Idiopholis* Mocquard, 1892: A genus containing two species native to Borneo. Length 15-19 cm (6-7.5 in); smallest species in the subfamily. Dark, uniform ground color with light neckband or light head and neck. Some workers consider this a synonym of *Pseudorabdion*.

I. collaris Mocquard, 1892: N.E. Borneo.

● *Pseudorabdion* Jan, 1862: A genus containing two species ranging from Thailand through Malaysia and Indonesia to the Philippines. Length to 25 cm (10 in). Iridescent sooty brown with a narrow yellow collar. Often misspelled *Pseudorhabdion*.

P. longipes (Cantor, 1847): Widely distributed throughout generic range.

● *Rabdion* Dumeril, 1853: A genus containing only a single species. Formerly called

Top Left: *Xenodon rhabdocephalus*. Photo: J. Kellnhauser. Top Right: *Xenodon suspectus*. Photo: J. Kellnhauser. Bottom: *Xenodon rhabdocephalus*. Photo: K. T. Nemuras.

Rhabdophidium Boulenger, 1894.
R. forsteni (Dumeril & Bibron, 1854): Celebes. Length to 45 cm (18 in). Pointed snout and extended rostral scale. Iridescent blackish brown. Biology poorly known.

- *Typhlogeophis* Guenther, 1879: A genus containing a single species. Like several other genera in this group, now considered a synonym of *Pseudorabdion* by specialists.
T. brevis Guenther, 1879: Philippines. Length to 35 cm (14 in). Pointed snout and extremely short tail. Burrowing species; biology poorly known.

SUBFAMILY COLUBRINAE

This subfamily contains about 50 genera and some 300 species. The greatest number of genera occur in Africa, Asia, and the Americas, with a few in Europe and only a single genus in Australia. Most of the species are relatively long (from 150-300 cm—60-120 in—total adult length). They are what can be described as typical snakes, most of them being slender and agile. None of them possess venom fangs, although there are some really aggressive species in the group. Methods of prey capture include "grab and swallow" and constriction. Some of the genera are specialized in certain prey (e.g., snail-eaters).

Arizona elegans. Photo: B. Kahl.

Top: *Arizona elegans*. Photo: B. Kahl. Bottom: *Arizona elegans philipi*. Photo: G. Pisani.

● *Arizona* Kennicott, 1859: A genus containing a single species.

A. elegans Kennicott, 1859: **Glossy Snake, Faded Snake.** Western and central USA and Mexico, in various dry habitats from coastal chaparral to sagebrush flats and oak-hickory woodland from sea level to 1700 m (5525 ft). Length to 140 cm (56 in). Somewhat similar in appearance to *Pituophis*, but has smooth, unkeeled scales without any rows of keeled scales. Snout somewhat pointed. Light brown above with variable broken black-bordered brown or gray blotches. An adept burrower that may be active day or night. Usually found on the surface in early mornings or evenings. Feeds mainly on lizards, sometimes small mammals. Requires a dry terrarium with high daytime temperature (to 30°C) cooled to 18-20°C at night. Oviparous, laying from 5-25 eggs. Nine subspecies.

● *Cemophora* Cope, 1860: A genus containing a single species.

C. coccinea (Blumenbach, 1788): **Scarlet Snake.** Southern USA including Florida. Found in deciduous, mixed, or coniferous forest and adjacent areas with well-drained

Top: *Arizona elegans*. Photo: J. K. Langhammer. Bottom: *Cemophora coccinea*. Photo: J. Iverson.

Top: *Chilomeniscus cinctus*. Photo: G. Pisani. Bottom: *Cemophora coccinea*. Photo: J. Iverson.

Top: *Cemophora coccinea.* Photo: R. D. Bartlett. Bottom: *Chilomeniscus cinctus.* Photo: Dr. S. Minton.

dry terrarium with adequate hiding places and loose, dry substrate. Oviparous, laying four to eight elongate eggs. Three subspecies.

● *Chilomeniscus* Cope, 1860: **Sand Snakes.** A genus containing two species native to S.W. USA and N.W. Mexico. Found in desert areas at altitudes to 1000 m (3250 ft). Length to 25 cm (10 in). Burrowing and nocturnal. Feed on various invertebrates. Require a dry terrarium with loose substrate suitable for burrowing.

C. cinctus Cope, 1861: **Banded Sand Snake.** Central and S.W. Arizona, south into Baja California and Sonora, Mexico. Flattened, shovel-like snout. Head and neck same width. Pale yellow to pinkish above with dark brown or black crossbands. Oviparous, laying small clutches of eggs. Biology poorly known.

C. stramineus Cope, 1860: Found only at the southern tip of Baja peninsula.

● *Chionactis* Cope, 1860: **Shovel-nosed Snakes.** A genus containing two species native to S.W. USA and N.W. Mexico in various dry habitats including sandy desert areas. Length 35-40 cm (10-16 in). Burrowing and nocturnal, with a shovel-like snout. Feed

soils. Length to 80 cm (32 in). Due to its brilliant coloration of red, black, and creamy white saddles, it is often confused with coral snakes. Terrestrial and mainly nocturnal. Feeds on lizards, small snakes, and especially reptile eggs. Requires a moderately heated,

Top: *Chilomeniscus cinctus*. Photo: J. Iverson. Below: *Chionactis occipitalis klauberi*. Photo: G. Pisani.

Top: *Chionactis occipitalis annulata.* Photo: Dr. S. Minton.
Bottom: *Chionactis palarostris.* Photo: R. Holland.

on a variety of invertebrates, including scorpions and centipedes. Require a dry terrarium with facilities for burrowing.

C. occipitalis (Hallowell, 1854): **Western Shovel-nosed Snake.** Southern Nevada south into Baja California and Sonora, Mexico. Length to 40 cm (16 in). Glossy, whitish to yellow with well defined black bands along body and tail. Oviparous, laying two to four eggs. Four subspecies.

C. palarostris (Klauber, 1937): **Sonora Shovel-nosed Snake.** S.W. Arizona into Sonora, Mexico. Length to 35 cm (14 in). Yellow with alternating black and red saddle-shaped crossbands. Habits poorly known. Two subspecies.

- ***Chironius*** Fitzinger, 1826: A genus containing 14 species found from Central America to northern South America in tropical or montane rain forest. Length to 230 cm (92 in). Very slender, with head distinct from neck and very large eyes. Range from brown to greenish, uniform or with blotches and/or bands. Mainly nocturnal and terrestrial. Feed largely on frogs. Require a heated rain-forest terrarium. Oviparous, laying 10-15 eggs.

Top Left: *Chionactis occipitalis klauberi.* Photo: Dr. S. Minton. Top Right: *Chironius fuscus*, juvenile. Photo: P. Freed. Center: *Chironius fuscus.* Photo: J. Kellnhauser. Bottom: *Coluber constrictor constrictor*, female. Photo: R. T. Zappalorti.

Coluber constrictor.
Top: *C. c. foxi.* Photo: J.
K. Langhammer.
Center: *C. c.
constrictor.* Photo: W.
B. Allen, Jr. Bottom: *C.
c. mormon.* Photo: K. H.
Switak.

C. carinatus (Linnaeus, 1758): Nicaragua to Brazil.
C. fuscus (Linnaeus, 1758): Panama to central Brazil, the Guianas, and Peru.
C. scurulus (Wagler, 1824): Amazon Basin.
● ***Coluber*** Linnaeus, 1758: **Racers.**
A genus containing 30 species found in the tropical, subtropical, and temperate regions of the Northern Hemisphere. Found in a variety of usually fairly dry habitats. Length 60-250 cm (24-100 in). Slender, agile, and fast-moving. Head usually set off distinctly from neck, the eyes large. Diurnal and terrestrial, though many climb well. Feed on small mammals, birds and their eggs, lizards, and snakes. All are oviparous, with clutch sizes to 45. Some species are extremely aggressive, hissing and biting repeatedly when threatened or captured, though they are harmless to man and eventually tame quite well. Require a roomy, warm, dry terrarium with facilities to climb and bathe. Temperate species require a period of winter hibernation.

The contents of *Coluber* are unclear, and some workers feel the genus should be restricted to just *Coluber constrictor*, the type species. The Eurasian species then would be placed in one or several genera, the exact names and contents undetermined. The name **Haemorrhois** Boie, 1827, often is used for *ravergieri* and similar steppe species. **Hierophis** Fitzinger, 1834, has been used to include *viridiflavus* and allies.
Argyrogena Werner, 1924, is used for the Banded Racer, *A. fasciolatus*, of India.

C. algirus (Werner 1894): **Algerian Whip Snake.** North Africa and Malta. Length to 100 cm (39 in). Slender, with well-defined

Coluber constrictor constrictor. Adult at lower right. Photos: Top: J. Iverson; Bottom: R. T. Zappalorti.

Top: *Coluber gemonensis*. Photo: B. Kahl. Center: *Coluber jugularis*. Photo: J. Coborn. Bottom: *Coluber hippocrepis*. Photo: J. Kellnhauser.

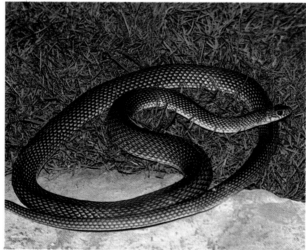

head. Gray or brown with darker collar. Series of dark bars along back and dark spots along flanks.

C. constrictor (Linnaeus, 1758): **Northern Racer.** S.W. Canada, through USA (found in all mainland states except Alaska) into Mexico in a variety of habitats, but prefers plains, grasslands, and partially wooded country at altitudes from 0-2150 m (0-7000 ft). Length to 200 cm (78 in). May be uniform black, bluish, brown, or greenish above, and white or yellowish to gray below. Young typically gray with dark spots. Oviparous, laying 5-28 eggs. About ten poorly defined subspecies.

C. hippocrepis Linnaeus, 1758: **Horseshoe Snake.** Balkan Peninsula, Sardinia, Pantelleria, and N.W. Africa in warm, dry habitats, usually with some plant cover. Diurnal. Length to 150 cm (60 in). Ground color olive, yellowish, or reddish with bold pattern of dark-edged brown blotches.

C. jugularis Gmelin, 1789: **Large Whip Snake.** Balkan Peninsula, S.W. USSR, Romania, Hungary, and Yugoslavia. Also S.W. Asia. Diurnal. Length to 300 cm (120 in). Well-defined but smallish head. Yellowish brown to olive brown with weak pattern of

Top Left: *Coluber hippocrepis*. Photo: C. Banks. Others: *Coluber jugularis*. Photos: S. Kochetov (Center Right), B. Kahl.

Top: *Coluber jugularis.* Center: *Coluber karelini.* Bottom Left: *Coluber ravergieri,* young. Bottom Right: *Coluber ravergieri,* female. Photos: S. Kochetov.

narrow stripes. Underside light yellow to orange. Young gray to brown with dark bars along back. Four subspecies.

C. najadum (Eichwald, 1831): **Dahl's Whip Snake.** Southern Balkan Peninsula, north to S. Bulgaria and S. Yugoslavia. Also Caucasus and S.W. Asia as far as Iran. Diurnal and

mainly terrestrial in dry, rocky habitats, usually with some plant cover. Length to 135 cm (54 in). Very slender snake with narrow, well-defined head and large eyes. Gray-green to olive-brown at front, becoming browner or reddish brown toward the tail. A large row of

dark spots along side of neck, often surrounded by concentric light and dark rings. Markings more pronounced in juveniles. Feeds mainly on lizards. The common subspecies is *C. n. dahli.*

C. ravergieri Menetries, 1832: **Spotted Whip Snake.** Western to Central Asia. Length to 120 cm (48 in). Three subspecies.

C. viridiflavus Lacepede, 1789: **Green Whip Snake.** Southern Europe from Iberia to Sicily and Malta. Diurnal and mainly terrestrial, though climbs well in rocky or bushy habitats. Length to 150 cm (60 in). Slender, with relatively small head set off distinctly from neck. Greenish yellow, marked with dark green or black indistinct crossbars. Underside yellowish to grayish. Juveniles more distinctly marked.

- ***Conopsis*** Guenther, 1858: A genus containing two species native to central Mexico. Length to 35 cm (14 in). Pointed snout. Grayish brown with darker spots. Terrestrial. Biology poorly documented.
C. nasutus Guenther, 1858: Central Mexican plateau.

- ***Contia*** Girard, 1853: A genus containing a single species.
C. tenuis Baird & Girard, 1853: **Sharp-tailed Snake.** Coastal California north into Oregon, Washington, and British Columbia, usually in moist areas in coniferous forest. Nocturnal, usually hiding under stones and logs during the day. Length to 45 cm (18 in). Short, spine-tipped tail. Uniform shiny reddish brown above, with black and white banded underside. Requires a moderately heated humid terrarium.

- ***Coronella*** Laurenti, 1768: **Smooth Snakes.** A genus containing two species native to Europe, N.W. Africa, and W.Asia in dryer areas, including temperate heathland. Length to 70 cm (28 in). Head barely distinct from neck, eyes relatively small. Yellowish to grayish brown with dark flecks and broken stripes. Feed largely on lizards. Require a moderately heated, dry terrarium. A winter period of hibernation is recommended.
C. austriaca Laurenti, 1768: **Smooth Snake.** S. England, France, N. Spain, S. Scandinavia, east to USSR, south to Italy, Sicily, and Greece, also Asia Minor to Iran. Diurnal. Length to 70 cm (28 in).

Top: *Coluber karelini mintonorum*. Bottom: *Coluber najadum dahli*. Photos: Dr. S. Minton.

Top Left: *Coluber spinalis*. Photo: S. Kochetov. Top Right: *Coluber viridiflavus*, juvenile. Photo: B. Kahl. Center: *Coluber viridiflavus*. Photo: Courtesy Dr. D. Terver. Bottom: *Coluber rhodorachis*. Photo: Dr. S. Minton.

Top: *Contia tenuis*. Photo: K. Lucas, Steinhart. Bottom: *Coluber ventromaculatus*. Photo: Dr. S. Minton.

Right: *Coronella girondica*. Photo: Dr. D. Terver.

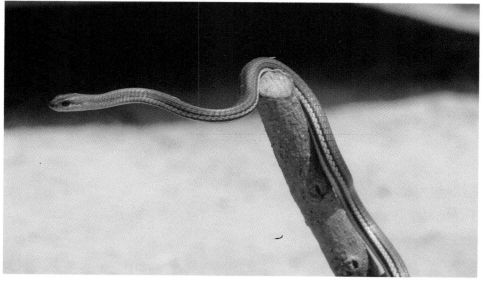

Dendrelaphis caudolineata. Photo: M. J. Cox.

Left: *Coluber ravergieri*. Photo: S. Kochetov. Top Right: *Coronella austriaca*. Photo: Dr. D. Terver. Bottom Right: *Coronella girondica*. Photo: Dr. D. Terver.

Ovoviviparous, producing up to 15 young.
C. girondica (Daudin, 1803): **Southern Smooth Snake.** Spain, S. France, Italy, and N.W. Africa. Crepuscular. Length 50 cm (20 in). Oviparous, laying five to seven eggs.

• **Dendrelaphis** Boulenger, 1890: **Bronze-backed Snakes.** A genus containing 12 species native to S.E. Asia in monsoon forest, rain forest, and montane rain forest. Arboreal. Length 60-130 cm (24-52 in). Head distinctly set off from narrow neck. Eyes large. Body and tail extremely slender. Mainly bronzy with longitudinal stripes. Skin between scales pale blue. Feed on frogs and lizards. Require a warm, well-planted, rain-forest terrarium with facilities to bathe.
D. calligaster (Guenther, 1867): **Northern Tree Snake.** New Guinea and adjacent islands to N. Australia (Cape York). Length 120 cm (48 in). Oviparous, laying three to six elongate eggs. Three subspecies.

Coronella austriaca.
Photos: Top: B. Kahl;
Bottom: S. Kochetov.

Top: *Coronella austriaca*. Photo: Dr. D. Terver. Bottom: *Dendrelaphis calligaster*. Photo: Dr. S. Minton.

Top: *Dendrelaphis pictus*. Photo: Dr. S. Minton. Center: *Dendrelaphis punctulatus*. Photo: C. Banks. Bottom: *Dendrelaphis* aff. *striatus*. Photo: M. J. Cox.

Top: *Drymarchon corais corais*. Photo: R. D. Bartlett. Bottom: *Dendrelaphis punctulatus*. Photo: C. Banks.

D. caudolineata (Gray, 1834): Malaya through Indonesia to Philippines. Three subspecies.

D. picta (Gmelin, 1789): **Common (Indonesian) Bronze-back.** Southern Asia from Himalayan foothills to S. China and Malaysia and Indonesia to Timor. Four subspecies.

D. punctulata (Jacquinot & Guichenot, 1842): **Common Tree Snake.** New Guinea and adjacent islands, northern and eastern Australia. Oviparous, laying 5-12 eggs. Two subspecies.

D. tristis (Daudin, 1803): India, from Darjeeling south to Sri Lanka.

• **Dendrophidion** Fitzinger, 1843: A genus containing eight species found from Mexico to northern South America. Tropical rain forest. Length 70-110 cm (28-44 in). Extremely slender with long, fragile tail. Diurnal to crepuscular, terrestrial or semi-arboreal. Feed mainly on frogs. Aggressive and bite readily. Require a warm, planted, rain-forest terrarium. Oviparous, laying up to 15 eggs.

D. dendrophis (Schlegel, 1837): Guatemala to Ecuador. Olive green to brown with darker blotches.

• **Drymarchon** Fitzinger, 1843: **Indigo Snakes.** A genus containing a single species.

Drymarchon corais.
Top: *D. c. couperi,*
male. Photo: R. T.
Zappalorti. Center: *D. c.
melanurus.* Photo: K. T.
Nemuras. Bottom Left:
D. c. couperi. Photo: R.
D. Bartlett. Bottom
Right: *D. c. couperi.*
Photo: R. T. Zappalorti.

Top: *Drymarchon corais rubidus*. Photo: R. D. Bartlett. Bottom: *Drymobius margaritiferus*. Photo: B. Kahl.

D. corais (Boie, 1827): **Indigo Snake.** Southern USA (Florida and Texas) to Argentina, in varied habitats. Length to 260 cm (100 in). Robust snake with almost triangular body section. Lustrous blue-black or mixed brown and black. Throat and sides of neck suffused with red, orange, or cream.

Subspecies *D. c. couperi* from S.E. Georgia and Florida is uniformly glossy blue-black. This attractive snake has an excellent temperament and is relatively easy to maintain in captivity, hence it has become a prize item for the terrarium-keeper. In the USA wild specimens are now strictly protected. Fortunately, captive-bred specimens are now sporadically available. Feeds on frogs, lizards, other snakes (including venomous species), young turtles, small mammals, and birds. Requires a roomy terrarium with facilities for climbing and bathing. Oviparous, laying 6-12 eggs. Eight subspecies.

● ***Drymobius*** Fitzinger, 1843: **Tropical Racers.** A genus containing four species

Drymobius margaritiferus. Photos: B. Kahl.

ranging from southern USA (Texas) as far as Peru. Found in varying habitats. Length to 130 cm (52 in). Slender, with head distinctly set off from neck. Relatively large eyes. Extremely fast and agile. Diurnal and terrestrial. Feed largely on frogs. Require a large terrarium with facilities for bathing and climbing.

D. margaritiferus (Schlegel, 1837): **Speckled Racer.** Texas to N. South America. Length to 125 cm (50 in). Bluish black speckled with yellow. Four subspecies.

D. rhombifer (Guenther, 1860): Nicaragua to Peru. Length to 130 cm (52 in).

• **Drymoluber** Amaral, 1930: A genus containing two species native to tropical South America east of the Andes. Found in dryer

Duberria lutrix. Photo:
J. Visser

woodland areas. Length to 100 cm (39 in).
Slender, with narrow head indistinctly set off
from neck. Diurnal and arboreal. Feed largely
on lizards. Require a warm, dry terrarium
with facilities for bathing and climbing.
D. dichrous (Peters, 1863): Colombia,
Ecuador, Peru, Brazil, and Venezuela.
- ***Duberria*** Fitzinger, 1826: **African Snail-
eating Snakes.** A genus containing two
species native to eastern Africa from Ethiopia
to the Cape. Found in savannahs and lower
mountain slopes (to 3000 m - 9750 ft). Length
30-45 cm (12-18 in). Small head, barely
distinct from neck. Smooth scales. Short,
blunt tail. Uniformly reddish brown to
blackish, with or without irregular spots and

patches. Nocturnal, hiding under rocks, etc.,
during the day. Feed on slugs and snails, the
latter being pulled out of the shells. Require a
warm, dry terrarium with reduced
temperature at night.
D. lutrix (Linnaeus, 1759): Ethiopia to the
Cape. Three subspecies.
- ***Eirenis*** Jan, 1863: A genus containing 14
species ranging from N.E. Africa through the

Eirenis collaris. Photos:
S. Kochetov.

Top: *Eirenis rothi.*
Bottom: *Eirenis punctatolineatus.*
Photos: Dr. S. Minton.

Top: *Eirenis rothi*.
Photo: J. Coborn.
Bottom: *Elaphe
bimaculata*, striped
phase. Photo: S. C. and
H. Miller.

Middle East to N.W. India. Found in a range of dry habitats. Length 30-60 cm (12-24 in). Small and slender. Usually grayish to yellowish brown, some with markings. Crepuscular and secretive, hiding under stones, etc. Feed largely on invertebrates, particularly crickets and scorpions; larger species take small lizards. Kill larger prey by constriction. Require a small, warm, dry terrarium with nighttime reduction in temperature. Oviparous, laying two to eight relatively large, elongate eggs.

E. collaris (Menetries, 1832): **Collared Dwarf Racer.** Middle East, from Asia Minor to Arabia. Length to 30 cm (12 in). Yellowish brown with black collar. Feeds greedily on crickets.

E. modestus Martin, 1838: Middle East, from Asia Minor to Persia. Length to 60 cm (24 in). Two subspecies.

E. persicus (Anderson, 1872): Turkey to N.W. India. Length to 40 cm (16 in). Three subspecies.

E. punctatolineatus (Boettger, 1892): **Dotted Dwarf Racer.** Turkey, Iraq, Iran. Two subspecies.

● **Elaphe** Fitzinger, 1833: **Ratsnakes.** A genus containing some 50 species of medium sized colubrines, many of which are popular terrarium subjects. Widely distributed throughout the Northern Hemisphere and found in a great range of habitats. Length 60-250 cm (24-100 in). Head set off distinctly from neck in most species. Eyes relatively large. Smooth dorsal scales or central rows weakly keeled. Wide ventrals often keeled to aid in climbing. Mainly crepuscular or nocturnal. Require a roomy, well-ventilated terrarium with moderate temperatures (22-28°C, reduced slightly at night). Temperate species require a period of hibernation. Most are oviparous, but a few produce live young.

E. dione (Pallas, 1773): **Steppes Ratsnake.** Ukraine to Korea and N.E. China. Length 100 cm (39 in). Broadish head, distinctly set off from narrow neck. Black-

Top Left: *Elaphe obsoleta bairdi*, male. Photo: R. D. Bartlett. Right: *Elaphe carinata*, juvenile. Photo: R. D. Bartlett. Bottom: *Elaphe carinata*. Photo R. Everhart.

bordered dark gray diamond markings on light gray ground.

E. guttata (Linnaeus, 1766): **Corn Snake, Red Ratsnake.** Central USA into Mexico. Common in cultivated areas, where it usually is welcome as a predator of rodent pests. Length to 180 cm (72 in), but usually shorter. Brilliantly colored with black-bordered red blotches on a beige to pink background. Popular and hardy terrarium subject that will feed largely on mice. Reproduces freely in the terrarium, given the correct conditions, and has produced many color varieties under domestication. Hibernation period recommended. Oviparous, laying 5-25 eggs. Two or three subspecies.

E. longissima (Linnaeus, 1766): **Aesculapean Snake.** Central France,

Top: *Elaphe dione*. Photo: S. Kochetov. Center: *Elaphe flavirufa pardalina*, hatchling. Photo: P. Freed. Bottom: *Elaphe flavirufa pardalina*. Photo: R. D. Bartlett.

S. Switzerland, S. Austria, Czechoslovakia, S. Poland, and S.W. USSR, south to N.E. Spain, Sicily, and S. Greece, across Turkey to N. Iran. Isolated populations in Germany are said to have been introduced by the Romans. Found in dry, sunny woods and among shrubby vegetation. Length to 180 cm (72 in). Slender, with rather narrow but well-defined head. Usually a uniform gray-buff to olive-brown, sometimes with a vague pattern of dark or light longitudinal stripes. Underside off-white. Juveniles more vividly marked. Terrestrial but climbs well. May sometimes be seen basking. Feeds on small mammals. Requires a large, roomy terrarium with facilities to climb. Period of hibernation recommended. Oviparous, laying 5-15 eggs. Three subspecies.

Top: *Elaphe carinata*. Photo: R. Everhart. Bottom: *Elaphe guttata*, female. Photo: R. T. Zappalorti.

Top: *Elaphe guttata*, hatchling. Photo: R. T. Zappalorti. Bottom Left: *Elaphe climacophora*. Photo: S. Kochetov. Bottom Right: *Elaphe flavolineata*. Photo: M. J. Cox.

E. mandarinus (Cantor, 1842): **Mandarin Ratsnake.** Burma to W. China. Very colorful species.

E. moellendorffi (Boettger, 1886): **Flower Snake.** China. Head coppery red, contrasting to rest of body color.

E. obsoleta (Say, 1823): **American Ratsnakes.** Eastern USA to N.E. Mexico in a variety of habitats. Length to 250 cm (100 in). Nine more or less distinct subspecies, including: ***E. o. obsoleta*, Black Ratsnake—** mainly black with traces of white between scales; ***E. o. bairdi*, Baird's Ratsnake—**

brown to orange-brown with four longitudinal dark stripes (often considered a full species); ***E. o. lindheimeri*, Texas Ratsnake—** yellowish to grayish, with brown to blackish blotches often with traces of orange between scales; ***E. o. quadrivittata*, Yellow Ratsnake**—yellow to yellow-buff or orange, with four distinct longitudinal dark stripes. Require a roomy, well-ventilated terrarium with facilities for bathing and climbing. Oviparous, laying 5-30 eggs. Breed readily in captivity, given suitable conditions. Period of hibernation recommended.

Elaphe guttata. Top: Albino juvenile. Photo: J. Visser. Bottom: E. g. guttata. Photo: R. Everhart.

Top Left: *Elaphe longissima*. Photo: R. D. Bartlett. Top Right: *Elaphe mandarinus*. Photo: P. Freed. Bottom: *Elaphe guttata emoryi*. Photo: J. Iverson.

Top: *Elaphe guttata*, albino female. Photo: R. T. Zappalorti. Bottom: *Elaphe longissima*, damaged head scales. Photo: B. Kahl.

Top: *Elaphe mandarinus*. Photo: R. D. Bartlett. Bottom Left: *Elaphe moellendorffi*. Photo: K. H. Switak. Bottom Right: *Elaphe moellendorffi*. Photo: R. D. Bartlett.

E. quadrivirgata (Boie, 1826): Japan. Feeds mainly on frogs.

E. quatuorlineata (Lacepede, 1789): **Four-lined Ratsnake.** S.E. Europe, north to Istria and S.W. USSR; central and S. Italy, Sicily; Balkans and adjacent islands into S.W. Asia. Length to 250 cm (100 in). Robust snake with long head and somewhat pointed snout. Two subspecies or color phases: the western *E. q. quatuorlineata* is yellowish to pale brown or gray with four dark longitudinal stripes and a dark streak along the side of the head; the eastern *E. q. sauromates* lacks the longitudinal stripes and has indistinct, darker blotches. Juveniles of both phases are covered with irregular dark spots on a lighter background. Care is as for *E. obsoleta*.

E. radiata (Schlegel, 1837): **Radiated Ratsnake.** From Burma to S. China and south through Indo-Australian Archipelago. Length to 150 cm (60 in). Bronzy with black

Top: *Elaphe moellendorffi*. Photo: S. Kochetov. Center: *Elaphe moellendorffi*. Photo: Dr. G. Dingerkus. Bottom: *Elaphe obsoleta spiloides*. Photo: R. T. Zappalorti.

stripes on front half of body only. Aggressive, with a spectacular threat display including spreading the neck vertically and opening the mouth. Fast-moving. Feeds on small mammals, birds, and lizards. Requires a dry, warm terrarium.

E. rufodorsata (Cantor, 1842): E. USSR, N.E. China, Korea. Length to 60 cm (24 in). Small and slender. Head well-defined. Ground color buff with broken dark-bordered brownish red stripes along body. Amphibious, feeding on fish and frogs. Requires a moderately warm aqua-terrarium and period of winter hibernation.

E. scalaris (Schinz, 1822): **Ladder Snake.** Mediterranean France and Iberian Peninsula. Largely diurnal and found in sunny, often stony terrain. Length to 160 cm (64 in). Adults fairly uniform in color, yellowish gray to brown with pair of faint dark stripes along back. Young boldly marked

Top: *Elaphe obsoleta obsoleta*. Photo: B. Kahl. Bottom: *Elaphe obsoleta quadrivittata*. Photo: R. Everhart.

Top: *Elaphe porphyracea*. Photo: R. E. Kuntz. Bottom: *Elaphe obsoleta obsoleta*. Photo: R. Everhart.

Top: *Elaphe obsoleta quadrivittata*. Photo: B. Kahl. Bottom Left: *Elaphe porphyracea*. Photo: R. E. Kuntz. Bottom Right: *Elaphe quadrivirgata*. Photo: S. Kochetov.

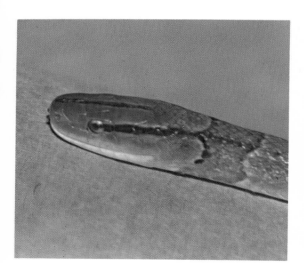

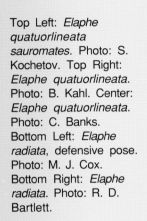

Top Left: *Elaphe
quatuorlineata
sauromates*. Photo: S.
Kochetov. Top Right:
Elaphe quatuorlineata.
Photo: B. Kahl. Center:
Elaphe quatuorlineata.
Photo: C. Banks.
Bottom Left: *Elaphe
radiata*, defensive pose.
Photo: M. J. Cox.
Bottom Right: *Elaphe
radiata*. Photo: R. D.
Bartlett.

with ladder-shaped pattern along back. Feeds
on small mammals and birds. Requires a
large, semi-dry terrarium with facilities for
bathing, climbing, and basking. Oviparous,
laying 6-12 eggs.
E. schrencki (Strauch, 1873): **Amur
Ratsnake, Siberian (Russian)
Ratsnake.** N. E. China, Korea, and eastern
USSR. Length to 170 cm (68 in). A sturdy

species with well-defined head. Dark brown with irregular and broken buff to bright yellow bands. Docile and relatively easy terrarium subject. Two subspecies.

E. situla (Linnaeus, 1758): **Leopard Snake.** Southern Italy, Balkans, and Asia Minor to Crimea. A terrestrial and diurnal sun-loving species usually found in rocky, brushland terrain. Length to 100 cm (39 in). A slender snake with rather narrow but well-defined head. Adults retain juvenile pattern that consists of a series of irregular but generally paired black-bordered red to reddish brown patches arranged along the back and flanks. Ground color yellowish, grayish, or buff. Underside is yellowish white at anterior end but becomes heavily marked toward tail so that middle and posterior underside are mainly black. Feeds largely on lizards. Oviparous, laying two to seven eggs.

E. subocularis (Brown, 1901): **Trans-Pecos Ratsnake.** Southern New Mexico and Texas

Top: *Elaphe radiata*. Photo: P. Freed. Center: *Elaphe rosaliae*. Photo: K. Lucas, Steinhart. Bottom: *Elaphe rufodorsata*. Photo: R. D. Bartlett.

Top Left: *Elaphe schrencki*. Photo: S. Kochetov. Top Right: *Elaphe rufodorsata*. Photo: P. Freed. Center: *Elaphe schrencki*. Photo: R. D. Bartlett. Bottom: *Elaphe scalaris*. Photo: Dr. D. Terver.

Top: *Elaphe situla*. Photo: K. Knaack. Center: *Elaphe taeniurus*. Photo: R. E. Kuntz. Bottom: *Elaphe schrencki*. Photo: Dr. S. Minton.

Top: *Elaphe subocularis.* Photo: K. Lucas, Steinhart. Bottom: *Elaphe taeniurus friesei.* Photo: R. D. Bartlett.

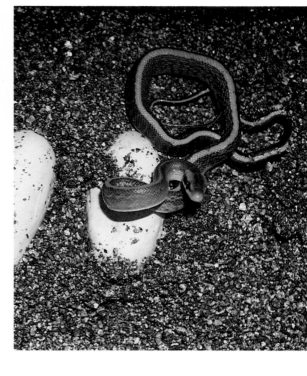

Top Left: *Elaphe taeniurus ridleyi*. Photo: M. J. Cox. Top Right: *Elaphe taeniurus ridleyi*, hatchling. Photo: P. Freed. Bottom: *Elaphe taeniurus taeniurus*. Photo: R. D. Bartlett.

south into Mexico, found in desert and creosote bush scrub and rocky, treed areas. Length to 170 cm (68 in). Long, well-defined head and exceptionally large eyes. Yellowish brown to olive-yellow, marked with a series of dark brown H-shaped blotches. Mainly crepuscular to nocturnal, hiding during the day in rock crevices or abandoned burrows. Feeds on small mammals, birds, and lizards. Oviparous, laying two to seven eggs. Recently placed in the new genus *Bogertophis*.

Top: *Elaphe taeniurus* cf. *yunnanensis*. Photo: R. D. Bartlett. Center: *Elaphe triaspis*. Photo: G. Pisani. Bottom: *Elaphe triaspis intermedia*. Photo: R. D. Bartlett.

marshland. Length to 180 cm (72 in). Light brown to yellowish with series of bold chocolate-brown to black blotches along back and tail. Feeds on small mammals, birds, and eggs. Oviparous, laying 6-30 eggs.

● *Eurypholis* Hallowell, 1860: **Asian Green Snakes.** A genus containing eight species native to S.E. Asia from Indo-China to China and Japan. Mainly found in damp montane forest, especially bamboo forest. Length to 120 cm (48 in). Terrestrial to semi-arboreal. Diurnal. Feed on invertebrates (including earthworms) and frogs. Require a moderately heated, humid terrarium with facilities to climb. Oviparous, laying 6-13 eggs. Many recent workers prefer to use the name *Entechinus* Cope, 1895, for this genus, believing *Eurypholis* to be preoccupied by a fish.

E. major (Guenther, 1858): **Chinese Green Snake.** Southern China, Taiwan, N. Vietnam. Length 100 cm (39 in). Narrow, oval head. Smooth scales. Upper body uniformly dark green, underside yellow to yellowish green.

E. multicinctus (Roux, 1907): N. Indo-China to S. China.

● *Gastropyxis* Cope, 1860: A genus containing a single species. Thought by some to be a

E. taeniurus Cope, 1860: **Beauty Snake.** From Assam to N. China and southward through Indo-Australian Archipelago in a wide range of habitats. Length to 250 cm (100 in). Triangular head with rounded snout. General ground color is olive-yellow to grayish yellow. Irregular dark blotches, some with light centers, arranged along the top of the front two-thirds of body. Posterior end of body plain above, markings merging into unbroken stripe along posterior flanks and sides of tail. Underside yellowish. Feeds on small mammals and birds. Given the right conditions it settles well into the terrarium.

E. vulpina (Baird & Girard, 1853): **Fox Snake.** USA, Great Lakes region west to S.E. South Dakota, E. Nebraska, and N. Missouri. Found on prairies, farms, wooded valleys, and

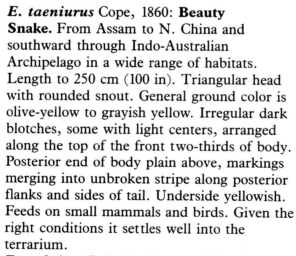

synonym of *Hapsidophrys.*

G. smaragdina (Schlegel, 1837): Tropical Africa, from Guinea to Angola and east to Uganda. Inhabits rain forest. Length to 120 cm (48 in). Very slender; head distinct from neck. Eyes very large. Uniformly leaf-green above, underside yellow. Arboreal and diurnal to crepuscular. Feeds on frogs and lizards. Requires a planted, humid terrarium.

● *Gonyophis* Boulenger, 1891: A genus containing a single species.

G. margeritatus (Peters, 1871): Malayan

Peninsula and Borneo, in hills to 900 m (3000 ft). Length to 160 cm (64 in). Narrow head with large eyes. Keeled dorsal scales. Brownish, with black-bordered yellowish green blotches running into transverse orange bands toward the posterior end of the body and the tail. Terrestrial; usually found near water. Feeds largely on frogs. Requires a warm rain-forest terrarium.

- ***Hapsidophrys*** Fischer, 1856: A genus containing a single species.

  *H. **lineata*** Fischer, 1856: Tropical Africa between Guinea and Angola, east to Kenya, Uganda, and Tanzania. In rain forest to 2000 m (6500 ft). Length to 100 cm (39 in). Extremely slender, with well-defined head and huge, liquid eyes. Keeled dorsal scales. Bright green with narrow black lace pattern. Skin between scales and inside of mouth and tongue bright cobalt-blue. Underside light green. Arboreal. Feeds mainly on frogs. Requires a well-planted, humid, rain-forest terrarium.

- ***Hydrablabes*** Boulenger, 1891: A genus containing two species native to Borneo in tropical rain forest. Length to 50 cm (20 in). Head barely distinct from neck, with rounded snout and small eyes. Blunt tail. Burrowing species. Biology poorly known. Should be provided with burrowing facilities.

  *H. **periops*** (Guenther, 1872): Olive-brown with a yellowish stripe along each flank.

- ***Iguanognathus*** Boulenger, 1898: A genus containing a single species.

  *I. **werneri*** Boulenger, 1898: Sumatra. Length 30 cm. Burrowing snake of the tropical rain forest. Biology barely known.

Eurypholis major.
Photos: Top: R. D. Bartlett; Center and Bottom: R. E. Kuntz.

Top Left: *Lampropeltis calligaster calligaster.* Photo: W. B. Allen, Jr. Top Right: *Hapsidophrys lineata.* Photo: J. Coborn. Center: *Lampropeltis getulus californiae,* ringed phase. Photo: B. Kahl. Bottom: *Lampropeltis alterna.* Photo: G. Pisani.

● ***Lampropeltis*** Fitzinger,
1843: **Kingsnakes.** A genus containing about
eight species native to North and Central
America in varying habitats from arid areas to
marshland. Length 35-200 cm (14-79 in).
Often robustly built constricting snakes. Some
of the larger species have earned a good
reputation as destroyers of venomous snakes,
including rattlesnakes. Some species have a
remarkable similarity in color pattern to
certain coral snakes. Due to their often vivid
coloration and their docility, they are popular
terrarium subjects. They require a medium-
sized dry terrarium with facilities to climb and
bathe. Food varies depending on the species,
but the larger ones will soon settle to a diet of
mice, small rats, and young chickens.
L. getulus (Linnaeus, 1766): **Common
Kingsnake.** USA from coast to coast in a
variety of habitats. Length to 200 cm (79 in).
Some eight mostly well-defined subspecies,
several popular with the terrarium-keeper.
These include ***L. g. getulus,* Eastern
Kingsnake**—chocolate-brown to black with
bold yellowish chain-like pattern; ***L. g.***

Top: *Lampropeltis
alterna.* Photo: R. W.
Applegate. Center:
*Lampropeltis calligaster
rhombomaculata.*
Photo: R. Anderson.
Bottom: *Lampropeltis
getulus californiae,*
striped phase. Photo:
W. B. Allen, Jr.

Top: *Lampropeltis getulus californiae*, ringed phase. Photo: A. Kerstitch. Center: *Lampropeltis getulus californiae*, brown ringed phase. Photo: K. Lucas, Steinhart. Bottom: *Lampropeltis getulus floridana*. Photo: K. T. Nemuras.

Top: *Lampropeltis getulus floridana* Photo: R. Everhart. Bottom: *Lampropeltis getulus getulus*, eating *Ophisaurus*. Photo: R. T. Zappalorti.

Top: *Lampropeltis getulus getulus*. Bottom: *Lampropeltis getulus holbrooki*. Photos: J. Iverson.

Top: *Lampropeltis getulus getulus*. Photo: W. B. Allen, Jr. Bottom: *Lampropeltis getulus holbrooki*. Photo: S. C. and H. Miller.

Top: *Lampropeltis mexicana, greeri* phase. Bottom: *Lampropeltis mexicana, thayeri* phase. Photos: K. T. Nemuras.

Top: *Lampropeltis pyromelana*. Photo: B. E. Baur. Bottom: *Lampropeltis triangulum annulata*. Photo: B. Kahl.

Top: *Lampropeltis pyromelana pyromelana*. Photo: L. Porras. Center: *Lampropeltis triangulum campbelli*. Photo: W. B. Allen, Jr. Bottom: *Lampropeltis triangulum elapsoides*. Photo: W. B. Allen, Jr.

Top: *Lampropeltis triangulum hondurensis*. Photo: K. T. Nemuras.
Bottom: *Lampropeltis triangulum sinaloae*. Photo: B. Kahl.

Top: *Lampropeltis triangulum triangulum*. Photo: K. T. Nemuras.
Bottom: *Lampropeltis zonata parvirubra*. Photo: B. E. Baur.

californiae, **California Kingsnake**—chocolate-brown to black with bold light crossbands or stripes; *L. g. floridana,* **Florida Kingsnake**—chocolate-brown-tipped yellowish scales and obscure pattern of narrow crossbands; *L. g. holbrooki,* **Speckled Kingsnake**—dark brown to black, speckled with yellow or whitish; *L. g. niger,* **Black Kingsnake**—shiny black with faint whitish dots; *L. g. nigritus,* **Desert Black Kingsnake**—black with small whitish spots, mainly on flanks; *L. g. splendida,* **Desert Kingsnake**—dark brown to black with narrow light crossbands and speckles along flanks. Mainly crepuscular but many become fully nocturnal in warmer months. Oviparous, laying 3-24 eggs. A period of hibernation is recommended during the winter.

L. pyromelana (Cope, 1866): **Sonoran Mountain Kingsnake.** Utah and Arizona south into Mexico. Length to 105 cm (41 in). Tricolored with red, black, and cream bands. Top of head black, snout whitish. Feeds largely on lizards. Oviparous, laying three to six elongate eggs. Three subspecies.

L. triangulum (Lacepede, 1788): **Milk Snake.** Central and eastern USA south into Central America. Length to 180 cm (72 in). A highly variable coral snake mimic. Red with narrow yellow or white bands bordered with black. Top of head black; tip of snout usually blackish. Feeds on small mammals, birds, lizards, and other snakes. Oviparous, laying 3-18 elongate eggs. Over 20 subspecies. The common name arises from the erroneous belief that it sucks the milk from the udders of cows.

L. zonata (Lockington, 1876): **California Mountain Kingsnake.** Montane regions of California and Baja California. Length to 100 cm (40 in). Body ringed with black, white,

Top: *Lampropeltis triangulum syspila*. Photo: K. Lucas, Steinhart. Bottom: *Lampropeltis zonata parvirubra*. Photo: B. Kahl.

Top Left: *Lampropeltis zonata multifasciata.* Photo: B. E. Baur. Top Right: *Leptophis ahaetulla.* Photo: R. S. Simmons. Bottom: *Leptophis ahaetulla.* Photo: R. S. Simmons.

and red. Top of head black and snout all black or with white or red flecks. Feeds on lizards, snakes, birds, and their eggs. Oviparous, laying three to eight eggs.

● ***Leptodrymus*** Amaral, 1927: A genus containing a single species.

L. pulcherrimus (Cope, 1874): In Central American lowlands of Guatemala, Nicaragua, Honduras, and Costa Rica. Found mainly in dry brushland and secondary forest. Length to 120 cm (48 in). Olive-brown with two to four longitudinal black stripes. Terrestrial, feeding on small mammals, birds, and lizards. Requires a medium-sized dry terrarium.

● ***Leptophis*** Bell, 1825: A genus containing seven species found from Mexico to Argentina. Found in dryer brushland. Length to 140 cm (52 in). Very slender body and elongate head. Greenish to bluish green in color. Diurnal and terrestrial. Require a well-heated dry woodland terrarium. Oviparous, laying 5-15 eggs.

L. ahaetulla (Linnaeus, 1758): Mexico to Argentina. 12 subspecies.

L. mexicanus (Dumeril, Bibron & Dumeril, 1854): Southern Mexico to Costa Rica. Two subspecies.

● ***Liopeltis*** Fitzinger, 1843: A genus

Top: *Leptodrymus pulcherrimus*, juvenile. Photo: P. Freed. Center and Bottom: *Leptophis mexicanus*. Photos: K. T. Nemuras.

containing about nine species found from the southern Himalayan foothills through Burma and most of Indo-China. Also south to Sri Lanka and the Indo-Australian Archipelago. Length to 80 cm (32 in). Head barely distinct from neck. Slender body. Terrestrial, feeding on small lizards and invertebrates. Require a warm rain-forest terrarium with adequate hiding places.

L. baliodiris (Boie, 1827): Malaya, Java, Sumatra, and Borneo. Monsoon forest. Brown with dark barring.

L. calamaria (Guenther, 1858): Mountains of Sri Lanka to 2000 m (6500 ft). Brown with dark longitudinal stripes.

L. frenatus (Guenther, 1860): Assam through Burma to Laos. Montane rain forest to 2000 m (6500 ft). Brown with dark stripes.

L. rappi (Guenther, 1860): Southern Himalayan region. Brown with dark barring.

L. tricolor (Schlegel, 1837): Malaya, Sumatra, Java, Borneo. Montane rain forest to 1200 m (3900 ft). Light and dark brown with blackish longitudinal stripes.

Lytorhynchus maynardi.
Photo: Dr. S. Minton.

● *Lytorhynchus* Peters, 1862: A genus containing a few species native to N. Africa and the Middle East to Turkmenistan (USSR). Found in dry habitats to altitudes of 2000 m (6500 ft). Length 35-45 cm (14-18 in). The pointed and swollen snout overhangs the mouth. Slender body. Crepuscular and partially nocturnal. Feed mainly on lizards (especially geckos) and their eggs; also invertebrates. Require a heated, dry terrarium with ample hiding places. Cooler at night. Provide a winter rest period at reduced temperatures.

L. diadema (Dumeril & Bibron, 1854): Algeria east to Arabia and Iran. Yellowish brown with darker blotches or bands.

L. ridgewayi Boulenger, 1887: Iran, Turkmenistan, Afghanistan, and S.W. Pakistan. Length to 36 cm (15 in). Buff, with dorsal row of brownish to reddish brown patches, interspersed with a further row of dark spots along the upper flanks.

● *Masticophis* Baird, 1853: **Coachwhips.** A genus containing eight species found from southern half of USA into Central America and northern South America, often to altitudes of 3000 m (9750 ft). Length 75-250 cm (30-100 in). Very slender, long-tailed, fast and agile terrestrial snakes resembling *Coluber* in form and habit.

M. flagellum (Shaw, 1802): **Coachwhip.** Southern half of USA to central Mexico in a variety of habitats including dry, relatively open situations, pinewoods, rocky hillsides, prairie, and scrub and thorn forest. Length to 250 cm (100 in). Six to eight subspecies with enormous amount of color variation. Western forms range through tan, brown, gray, or pinkish; eastern forms from dark brown to black at the front, fading to light brown toward the rear half of the body. Mainly terrestrial but also climbs well, often taking to a tree if threatened. Feeds on a variety of invertebrates, lizards, other snakes, and small mammals. Requires a large, dry terrarium with climbing and bathing facilities. Winter rest period at reduced temperature recommended. Oviparous, laying 4-16 eggs.

M. mentovarius (Dumeril, Bibron and Dumeril, 1854): Mexico to Colombia and Venezuela. Three subspecies.

● *Mastigodryas* Amaral, 1934: A genus containing 11 species native to Central and South America. Found in various habitats, from dry, semi-desert areas to rain-forest margins. Length to 180 cm (72 in). Closely related in form and habitat to *Coluber* and *Masticophis*. Most species marked with black-bordered bands of contrasting yellows and browns. Terrestrial, but climb well. Feed on a

Top: *Lytorhynchus paradoxus*. Bottom: *Lytorhynchus ridgewayi*. Photos: Dr. S. Minton.

Top: *Masticophis
flagellum flagellum*.
Photo: R. T. Zappalorti.
Bottom: *Masticophis
bilineatus*. Photo: Dr. S.
Minton.

Masticophis bilineatus.
Photo: B. Kahl.

Top: *Masticophis flagellum flagellum*. Photo: R. T. Zappalorti. Bottom Left: *Masticophis flagellum testaceus*. Photo: R. D. Bartlett. Bottom Right: *Masticophis flagellum*, immature. Photo: B. Kahl.

Top Left: *Masticophis lateralis euryxanthus*. Photo: K. H. Switak. Top Right: *Masticophis lateralis*. Photo: J. Dodd. Bottom: *Masticophis taeniatus*. Photo: R. Everhart.

Top Left: *Mastigodryas bifossatus*. Photo: M. Freiberg. Top Right: *Masticophis taeniatus taeniatus*. Photo: R. Holland. Center: *Mastigodryas bifossatus*. Photo: M. Freiberg. Bottom: *Masticophis taeniatus ruthveni*. Photo: Dr. S. Minton.

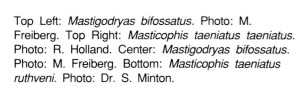

Top: *Masticophis taeniatus schotti*. Photo: Dr. S. Minton. Bottom: *Opheodrys aestivus*. Photo: R. T. Zappalorti.

Top: *Opheodrys vernalis*. Photo: R. T. Zappalorti. Bottom Left: *Opheodrys aestivus*. Photo: H. Bielfeld. Bottom Right: *Opheodrys aestivus*. Photo: R. Anderson.

variety of small vertebrates and eggs. Oviparous, laying 8-12 eggs. Require a large, dry terrarium with facilities to climb, bask, and bathe.

M. bifossatus (Raddi, 1820): Venezuela and Colombia to N. Argentina. Four subspecies.

M. boddaerti (Sentzen, 1796): Colombia and Venezuela to W. Brazil.

M. melanolomus (Cope, 1868): Mexico to Panama. Seven subspecies.

- **Meizodon** Fischer, 1856: A genus containing four species native to tropical Africa. Found in savannah and thorny brushland. Related to *Coronella*, in which they formerly were included. Length to 80 cm. Mostly uniform olive-brown to blackish. Juveniles may show light bands at the back of the head and the neck. Nocturnal and terrestrial, hiding during the day under logs and in leaf litter. Feed mainly on lizards but also on small mammals. Oviparous, laying two to four eggs. Require a medium-sized dry terrarium with adequate hiding places.

M. semiornatus (Peters, 1854): Senegal east to Kenya, Uganda, and Tanzania, south to Mozambique and Zimbabwe. Mostly uniform black. Two subspecies.

M. coronatus (Schlegel, 1837): Senegal east to Sudan and Kenya. Dark brown with three or four lighter bands.

● *Opheodrys* Fitzinger, 1843: **Green Snakes.** A genus containing two species found in the eastern and central USA in shrubs and vegetation often near water. Length 30-110 cm (12-44 in). Slender. Grass-green above, whitish to yellow below. Feed on invertebrates, especially grasshoppers, crickets, and spiders. Require a medium-sized warm, humid terrarium with plants in which they can climb and a large water container. Oviparous, laying 3-12 eggs.

O. aestivus (Linnaeus, 1766): **Rough Green Snake.** S.E. USA and N.E. Mexico. Length to 110 cm (44 in). Keeled scales. Diurnal and arboreal. Swims well and may take to water when disturbed.

O. vernalis (Harlan, 1827): **Smooth Green Snake.** From S.E. Canada and N.E. USA to Texas. Length to 65 cm (26 in). Smooth scales.

● *Philothamnus* A. Smith, 1847: **Green Bush Snakes.** A genus containing seven species native to Africa south of the Sahara in rain forest and riverine woodland. Length 80-130 cm (32-52 in). Oval head distinctly set off from neck; large eyes. Slender. Uniform leaf-green above, whitish or yellowish below. Often with a bluish tinge along flanks, the skin between scales black. Diurnal and crepuscular. Largely arboreal but descend to the ground in search of prey, which consists mainly of frogs and lizards. Swim well and often are found near water. Require a medium sized tropical rain-forest terrarium with robust plants and a large water container.

P. irregularis (Leach, 1819): **Northern Green Bush Snake.** Senegal to Sudan and south to South Africa. Common in reed beds, where it preys on nestling birds in addition to more usual lizard and frog prey. Length to 120 cm (48 in). Uniformly green above.

P. semivariegatus (A. Smith, 1840): **Spotted Bush Snake.** Sudan and Ethiopia south to the Cape in open forest or brushland. Length to 120 cm (48 in). Bright green to olive-green above, sometimes uniform but usually with black to dark blue spots or bars scattered on front half of body. Swift and very adept climber, able to negotiate apparently smooth tree trunks with the assistance of keeled ventral and subcaudal scales.

● *Phyllorhynchus* Stejneger, 1890: **Leaf-nosed Snakes.** A genus containing two species native to S.W. USA and N.W. Mexico. Found in dry semi-desert to desert areas. Length to 50 cm (20 in). Head small, indistinctly set off from neck. Common name

Top Left: *Opheodrys vernalis*. Photo: R. T. Zappalorti. Top Right: *Philothamnus hoplogaster*. Photo: R. D. Bartlett. Bottom: *Philothamnus semivariegatus*. Photo: J. Visser.

Top: *Phyllorhynchus browni*. Photo: J. Iverson. Center: *Phyllorhynchus browni lucidus*. Photo: K. H. Switak. Bottom: *Phyllorhynchus decurtatus perkinsi*. Photo: K. H. Switak.

arises from the enlarged rostral shield that extends forward and then curves back over the snout, an adaptation for burrowing. Burrowing, but come to surface on warm, moist nights. Feed largely on lizards. Habits

poorly known. Require typical burrowing snake terrarium with deep substrate. Oviparous, laying two to five relatively large eggs.

P. browni Stejneger, 1890: **Saddled Leaf-nosed Snake.** South-central Arizona into Mexico. Length to 50 cm (20 in). Pinkish to creamish with fewer than 17 large, dark-edged, brown saddle-shaped blotches along body. Three subspecies.

P. decurtatus (Cope, 1868): **Spotted Leaf-nosed Snake.** S. Nevada south through S.E. California and Arizona to tip of Baja Peninsula and Sinaloa, Mexico. Length to 50 cm (20 in). Pinkish, gray, or tan, with more than 17 dark patches arranged along back and tail. Four subspecies.

● ***Pituophis*** Holbrook, 1842: **Pine, Bull, and Gopher Snakes.** A genus containing some three to four species (taxonomy of some species still unsettled, several subspecies possibly species) native to North and Central America. Found in dry, coniferous forest to sparsely wooded prairie and rocky hillsides to 2750 m (9000 ft). Also found in cultivated areas. Length to 250 cm (100 in). Powerfully

Top: *Pituophis deppei jani.* Photo: P. Freed. Bottom: *Phyllorhynchus browni.* Photo: J. Iverson.

Top: *Pituophis deppei*. Photo: Dr. S. Minton. Bottom: *Pituophis melanoleucus annectens*, albino adult. Photo: K. H. Switak.

Facing Page: Top: *Pituophis melanoleucus bimaris*. Photo: K. H. Switak. Bottom: *Pituophis melanoleucus catenifer*. Photo: K. Lucas, Steinhart.

built with smallish head distinctly set off from neck. Keeled (often weakly) dorsal scales. Great variety of colors and patterns in browns, yellows, and blacks. Semi-arboreal and mainly diurnal. Feed largely on small mammals. Require a warm woodland terrarium with adequate climbing facilities.

P. lineaticollis (Cope, 1861): Mexico to Guatemala.

P. melanoleucus (Daudin, 1803): **Pine, Bull, and Gopher Snakes.** Southern Canada and most of the USA to Mexico. Length to 250 cm (100 in). About ten (disputed) subspecies with enormous variety of pattern, for example: ***P. m. melanoleucus*, Northern Pine Snake**—whitish, pale gray, or yellowish, with black blotches along body; ***P. m. affinis*, Sonora Gopher Snake**—reddish brown blotches at front of body,

Top: *Pituophis melanoleucus melanoleucus*, female in nest chamber. Photo: R. T. Zappalorti.
Center: *Pituophis melanoleucus melanoleucus*, male. Photo: R. T. Zappalorti.
Bottom: *Pituophis melanoleucus sayi*. Photo: J. Iverson.

Top: *Pituophis melanoleucus mugitus*. Photo: J. Iverson. Bottom: *Pituophis melanoleucus melanoleucus*. Photo: R. T. Zappalorti.

Top: *Pituophis melanoleucus mugitus.* Photo: W. B. Allen, Jr.
Bottom: *Pituophis melanoleucus sayi*, female with eggs.
Photo: R. T. Zappalorti.

darker at rear; ***P. m. annectans*, San Diego Gopher Snake**—fused dark blotches on anterior dorsal surface; ***P. m catenifer*, Pacific Gopher Snake**—separate dark brown to black blotches on forepart of body; **Great Basin Gopher Snake, *P. m. deserticola***—large black blotches on forepart of body connected with side blotches and creating isolated light patches along back; ***P. m. lodingi*, Black Pine Snake**—almost uniformly dark brown to black; ***P. m. mugitus*, Florida Pine Snake**—gray at front to rusty brown at rear, indistinct blotches; ***P. m. pumilus*, Santa Cruz Gopher Snake**—dwarf subspecies (to 80 cm - 32 in) resembling ***P. m. annectans*** in color and pattern; ***P. m. ruthveni*, Louisiana Pine Snake**—obscure dark brown blotches on front part of body, distinct lighter to reddish brown blotches at rear; ***P. m. sayi*, Bullsnake**—yellowish, with blackish, brown, or reddish brown blotches. Oviparous, laying 4-25 eggs.

- ***Prosymna*** Gray, 1849: **Shovel-nosed Snakes.** A genus containing about 12 species native to Africa south of the Sahara, in savannah and woodland. Length to 40 cm (16 in). Head indistinct from neck. Cylindrical body. Usually brownish with darker pattern, lighter beneath. Characteristic shovel-like snout produced by enlarged rostral shield. Biology poorly known. Said to feed largely on buried eggs of small reptiles (geckos, skinks,

etc.), but also on invertebrates. Should be kept in a terrarium suitable for burrowing species (deep, loose substrate).
  P. sundevalli (A. Smith, 1849): **Sundevall's Shovel-nosed Snake.** Zimbabwe and Mozambique south into Republic of South Africa, preferring

Top: *Pituophis melanoleucus sayi*, albino female. Photo: R. T. Zappalorti. Bottom: *Prosymna bivittata*. Photo: J. Visser.

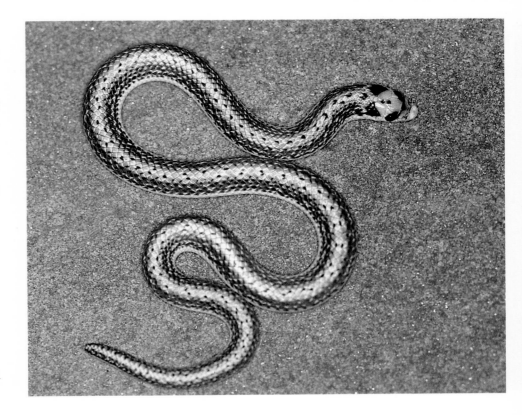

but usually somewhat less. Robust snake with head indistinct from broad neck. Usually uniform brown to gray or yellowish brown above, yellowish with dark markings beneath. The common name is derived from its predation on moles, which along with other rodents, birds, and lizards form its varied diet. Usually settles well in captivity, losing its aggressiveness and becoming tame and affectionate. Requires a large heated terrarium with facilities to bathe. Viviparous, producing 30-50 live young.

● *Pseudoficimia* Bocourt, 1883: A genus containing two species native to W. Mexico. Length to 30 cm (12 in). Possess a shovel-

Top: *Prosymna frontalis*. Photo: P. Freed. Center: *Pseudaspis cana*. Photo: C. Banks. Bottom: *Pseudaspis cana*, juvenile. Photo: K. H. Switak.

sandy localities. Length to 40 cm (16 in). Oviparous, laying three to four relatively large, elongate eggs.

● *Pseudaspis* Fitzinger, 1843: **Mole Snakes.** A genus containing a single species. *P. cana* (Linnaeus, 1758): **Mole Snake.** From Kenya and Angola to the Cape in a wide range of habitats, including cultivated areas where it is welcomed due to its predation on rodents. One of the most numerous snakes in the dryer parts of southern Africa. Length to 200 cm (80 in),

shaped snout for burrowing. Biology poorly known.

P. frontalis (Cope, 1864): Brownish with three darker stripes along the body.

● *Pseustes* Fitzinger, 1843: A genus containing four species found from Mexico to S.E. Brazil. Inhabit brushland and forest edges. Length to 280 cm (112 in). Slender, almost triangular in section. Mainly brown to yellowish brown with darker markings. Semi-arboreal, nocturnal or crepuscular. Inflate throat and vibrate tail when alarmed. Require a large semi-humid terrarium with facilities for climbing and bathing. Feed largely on small mammals.

Top: *Pseustes poecilonotus*, juvenile. Photo: K. T. Nemuras. Center and Bottom: *Pseudaspis cana*, adult. Photos: Dr. G. Dingerkus.

Top Left: *Pseustes poecilonotus*. Photo: J. Kellnhauser. Top Right: *Pseustes sulphureus*. Photo: J. Kellnhauser. Center: *Pseustes shropshirei*, juvenile. Photo: J. Kellnhauser. Bottom: *Ptyas korros*. Photo: R. D. Bartlett.

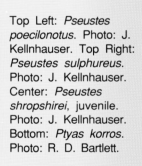

P. poecilonotus (Guenther, 1858): Mexico to N. South America. Four subspecies.

P. sulphureus (Wagler, 1824): N. South America (rain forest). Four subspecies.

● ***Ptyas*** Fitzinger, 1843: **Asiatic Ratsnakes.** A genus containing three species from central, eastern, and S.E. Asia. Usually in more humid areas close to rivers and lakes or in rain-forest areas. Length to 360 cm (144 in), making them the largest colubrids. Distinct head, robust body. Mostly uniformly brown to blackish. Diurnal and crepuscular. Terrestrial but climb well. Feed on a variety of vertebrates, including amphibians, reptiles (including other snakes), birds, and mammals to the size of a rabbit. Popular in the terrarium, soon taming and long-lived given the right conditions. Require a large, semi-humid terrarium with facilities to climb and bathe. Oviparous, laying 6-20 eggs.

Top: *Ptyas korros.* Photo: S. Kochetov. Center: *Ptyas mucosus.* Photo: R. T. Zappalorti. Bottom: *Ptyas mucosus.* Photos: Left: C. Banks; Right: R. T. Zappalorti.

Top Left: *Rhinocheilus antoni*. Photo: K. H. Switak. Top Right: *Ptyas mucosus*. Photo: C. Banks. Bottom: *Rhinocheilus lecontei lecontei*. Photo: K. Lucas, Steinhart.

P. korros (Schlegel, 1837): **Chinese Ratsnake.** Burma, Indo-China, and S. China, into Malaysian Archipelago. Three subspecies.
P. mucosus (Linnaeus, 1758): **Dhaman, Oriental Ratsnake.** Southern USSR through Afghanistan and Pakistan and across India and Burma to S. China and the Malaysian Archipelago. Two subspecies.

● ***Rhinocheilus*** Girard, 1853: **Long-nosed Snakes.** A genus containing one or two species found in S.W. USA and Mexico in dry prairie and desert areas. Length to 100 cm (39 in). Rostral scale projects well over lower jaw, giving the snake a long, pointed snout. Tan to cream with light-bordered black patches interspersed with blotches of pink or red.

*Rhinocheilus lecontei
lecontei.* Photo: B. Kahl.

Top: *Rhinocheilus lecontei lecontei*, "*clarus*" phase. Photo: J. Iverson. Bottom: *Rhinocheilus lecontei tessellatus*. Photo: G. Pisani.

Burrowing snakes emerging at night to feed on small vertebrates and eggs of reptiles and birds. Require a warm, dry terrarium with deep substrate or artificial tunnels.

R. lecontei Baird & Girard, 1853: **Long-nosed Snake.** California, Utah, Arizona.

R. antoni Duges, 1886: Mexico. Considered by virtually all authorities as a color morph of *R. lecontei*.

● **Rhynchophis** Mocquard, 1897: A genus containing a single species.

R. boulengeri Mocquard, 1897: Indo-China and S. China in montane forest and rocky ravines. Length to 130 cm (52 in). Slender, with head distinct from neck. Long, pointed, slightly upturned snout projecting well beyond lower jaw. The extension is covered in small scales and has an unknown function. Resembles *Ahaetulla*, but pupils round. Uniform leaf-green. Biology little known. Arboreal, probably feeding on frogs and lizards.

● **Salvadora** Baird, 1853: **Patch-nosed Snakes.** A genus containing eight species found from S.W. USA to central Mexico in arid areas and mountains to 2400 m (7800 ft). Length 50-120 cm (20-48 in). Longish head with large rostral shield curved back over snout. Brownish with darker stripes along body. Diurnal, quickly taking cover in burrows when disturbed. Feed mainly on lizards but may take small mammals. Require a heated, dry terrarium with nighttime reduction in temperature. Can tolerate relatively high daytime temperatures.

S. deserticola Schmidt, 1940: **Big Bend Patch-nosed Snake.** Big Bend region of Texas into New Mexico, S.E. Arizona, and N.W. Mexico. Length to 100 cm (39 in). Brownish orange middorsal stripe bordered wth narrow black dorso-lateral stripes. Oviparous, laying five to ten eggs.

S. grahamiae Baird & Girard, 1853: **Mountain Patch-nosed Snake.** S.E. California into N. Texas and Mexico. Length to 120 cm (48 in). Whitish to yellowish middorsal stripe bordered with dark brown to black dorso-lateral stripes. Oviparous, laying six to ten eggs. Two subspecies.

S. hexalepis (Cope, 1866): **Western Patch-nosed Snake.** S. California, W. and S. Nevada, S.W. Utah, and through Arizona into Mexico. Length to 115 cm (46 in). Grayish tan to gray; yellowish middorsal stripe bordered by dark dorso-lateral stripes. Oviparous, laying four to ten eggs.

● *Scaphiophis* Peters, 1870: **African Shovel-nosed Snakes.** A genus containing a single species.

S. albopunctatus Peters, 1870: **African Shovel-nosed Snake.** Central Africa from Mali to Tanzania. Found in dryer savannah regions. Length to 160 cm (64 in). Relatively large, roundish head set off indistinctly from neck. Large rostral shield overlapping lower

Top: *Rhinocheilus lecontei tessellatus.* Photo: R. T. Zappalorti. Center: *Salvadora deserticola.* Photo: G. Pisani. Bottom: *Salvadora deserticola.* Photo: J. Iverson.

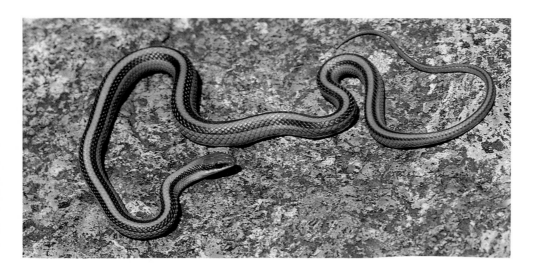

jaw to form a shovel-shaped snout. Smooth scaled. Dark brown with blackish spots. Burrowing snake often found in termite mounds. Feeds on a variety of invertebrates (including termites) and vertebrates. Should be provided with deep substrate in which to burrow in the terrarium. Oviparous, laying up to 50 eggs.

- ***Simophis*** Peters, 1860: A genus containing two species native to central South America. Usually found in open areas (pampas and cleared woodland). Length to 75 cm (30 in). Head indistinctly set off from body. Horn-

Top: *Salvadora grahamiae grahamiae.* Photo: K. H. Switak. Center: *Salvadora hexalepis mojavensis.* Photo: J. Dodd. Bottom: *Spalerosophis arenarius.* Photo: Dr. S. Minton.

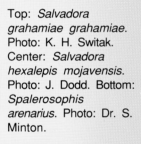

Top: *Salvadora hexalepis* cf. *virgultea*. Photo: B. Kahl.
Bottom: *Salvadora mexicanum*. Photo: R. D. Bartlett.

like, slightly upturned snout similar to *Heterodon*. Terrestrial, feeding largely on small mammals.

S. rhinostoma (Schlegel, 1837): **Sao Paulo False Coral Snake.** Brazil.

S. rhodei (Boettger, 1885): Paraguay.

● ***Spalerosophis*** Jan, 1865: **Diadem Snakes.** A genus containing one or a few species. Taxonomy requires further research.

S. diadema (Schlegel, 1837): **Diadem Snake.** North Africa through Arabia to

Top: *Spalerosophis atriceps*. Photo: Dr. S. Minton. Center: *Spilotes pullatus*. Photo: H. Hansen. Bottom: *Spalerosophis diadema*. Photo: R. T. Zappalorti.

central Asia. Length to 150 cm (60 in). Head set off distinctly from body. Brownish to grayish with irregular dark and light patches along back. Terrestrial and diurnal, active on even the hottest days, hunting for lizards, other snakes, birds, and small mammals.

Top Left: *Spilotes pullatus.* Photo: K. T. Nemuras. Top Right: *Spilotes pullatus.* Photo: M. Freiberg. Bottom: *Spalerosophis diadema cliffordi.* Photo: Dr. S. Minton.

Requires a heated (to 35°C, reduced at night), dry terrarium with adequate hiding places.

- ***Spilotes*** Wagler, 1830: **Chicken Snakes.** A genus containing a single species.

S. pullatus (Linnaeus, 1758): **Chicken Snake.** From S. Mexico to N. Argentina in various habitats, from rain forest to cultivated areas. Length to 250 cm (100 in). Robust, with head set off distinctly from neck and body. Relatively large dorsal scales. Yellowish with darker markings. Terrestrial to semi-

Top: *Spilotes pullatus mexicanus*. Photo: J. Kellnhauser. Center: *Stilosoma extenuatum*. Photo: Dr. S. Minton. Bottom: *Stilosoma extenuatum*, dull phase. Photo: J. Iverson.

arboreal. Swim well. Feed on birds and small mammals. Aggressive when first captured but soon become tame and settle well into captivity. Require a large terrarium with ample climbing and bathing facilities. Oviparous, laying 12-26 eggs. Five subspecies.

- ***Stilosoma*** Brown, 1890: **Short-tailed Snakes.** A genus containing a single species. ***S. extenuatum*** Brown, 1890: **Short-tailed Snake.** Central Florida (USA) in dry, high pineland and upland hammocks. Length to 65 cm (26 in). Slender, cylindrical body with a very short tail. Grayish above with dark brown blotches separated by yellow, orange, or red areas. Undersides whitish, with brownish black blotching. Semi-burrowing. Oviparous. Biology poorly known. Requires a terrarium with sandy substrate, grass clumps, etc.

- ***Thrasops*** Hallowell, 1857: **Black Tree Snakes.** A genus containing four species found in tropical Africa. In rain forest to 2800 m (9000 ft). Length to 230 cm (92 in). Head set off distinctly from body, which is slightly compressed laterally. Large eyes. Mainly black in color. Diurnal and crepuscular arboreal species hunting a variety of vertebrates, especially frogs and lizards. Require a large planted rain-forest terrarium with facilities to bathe. Oviparous, laying 12-20 eggs.
T. aethiopissa (Guenther, 1862): East and C. Africa. Unlike other members of the genus, this species is predominantly green. Two subspecies.
T. jacksoni Guenther, 1895: East Africa. Two subspecies.
T. flavigularis (Hallowell, 1852): Central West Africa.

- ***Zaocys*** Cope, 1861: A genus containing six species native to S.E. Asia from India through Indo-China and S. China through the Malaysian Archipelago to the Philippines. In dryer areas but rarely far from water. Also in

montane regions to 2400 m (7800 ft). Length to 300 cm (120 in). Slender but robust. Tail approximately one-third of total length. Longish head set off distinctly from body; large eyes. Adults mainly dull brown to black with faint striping; juveniles light brown with yellowish blotches and dark stripes. Terrestrial. Excellent swimmers feeding largely on frogs, but will take other vertebrates of suitable size. Usually settle well into captivity, soon losing their initial nervousness. Require a large, well-heated, rain-forest terrarium with facilities to bathe and dry spots to bask and rest.
Z. carinatus (Guenther, 1858): From eastern India through Burma and Malayan Peninsula into Indonesia to Java and Borneo. Largest species, reaching 300 cm (120 in).
Z. dhumnades (Cantor, 1842): China, especially in region of Yangtze Kiang River. Length to 200 cm (80 in). Two subspecies.
Z. nigromarginatus (Blyth, 1854): Southern Himalayan foothills (including Nepal, Sikkim) to Burma and W. China. Length to 220 cm (88 in).

Zaocys dhumnades.
Photos: R. D. Bartlett.

SUBFAMILY DASYPELTINAE
The subfamily contains only a single genus.

- ***Dasypeltis*** Wagler, 1830: **African Egg-eating Snakes.** A genus containing six species native to Africa and Arabia. Found mainly in savannah, brushland, and secondary woodland to altitudes of 2000 m (6500 ft). Length to 80 cm (32 in). Head set off distinctly from neck and body. Eyes relatively large. Teeth absent from front of upper and lower jaws and on the palate but with small teeth on rear parts of jaws. Feed exclusively on eggs and able to spread their jaws to an enormous extent. The egg is swallowed whole, but on reaching the throat region the shell is pierced by sharp extensions of the neck vertebrae that extend into the esophagus. The tips of these prominences are capped with dense, dentine-like bone. The combination of the piercing and muscular contractions causes

Top: *Dasypeltis scabra,* mother and hatchling. Photo: P. Freed. Center: *Dasypeltis inornata.* Photo: J. Visser. Bottom: *Dasypeltis scabra,* beginning to swallow an egg. Photo: W. B. Allen, Jr.

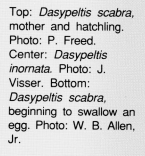

the egg to completely collapse. The contents are swallowed and the collapsed shell is regurgitated. The scales along the flanks are strongly keeled and saw-edged, thus allowing the reptile to coil and rasp, much in the manner of the venomous Saw-scaled Vipers (*Echis*), which they imitate even in color and pattern, which consists of varied buffs and browns, strongly or only faintly marked with lighter or darker patterns. Mainly nocturnal, hiding during the day under rocks and logs. Require a medium sized dry terrarium with temperature reduction at night. Depending on the size of the snakes, they should be fed on budgerigar, finch, pigeon, or quail eggs. Adult specimens should be capable of swallowing small domestic chicken eggs.

D. fasciata (A. Smith, 1849): **Central African Egg-eating Snake.** From the Gambia to Uganda in dryer areas.

D. inornata (A. Smith, 1849): **Southern Brown Egg-eating Snake.** S.E. coastal regions of S. Africa.

D. scabra (Linnaeus, 1758): **Common Egg-eating Snake.** Virtually all of Africa and also Arabia.

SUBFAMILY LYCODONTINAE

This subfamily contains 51 genera and about 325 species found mainly in Africa and Asia but with a few genera (doubtfully placed here and probably better put in the Natricinae or Colubrinae) in North and South America. Small to medium snakes. The subfamily status revolves largely around the teeth arrangement. Large recurved teeth designed for catching and holding prey are arranged in groups at the front and back of the upper jaw and at the front of the

lower jaw, an arrangement that has given the common name of Wolf Snakes to many of the species. In addition, there are numerous smaller gripping teeth. There are no venom fangs.

● ***Adelphicos*** Jan, 1862: A genus containing two species native to Central America. Closely related to *Atractus* and with similar habits. Length to 40 cm (16 in). Striped.

A. quadrivirgatus Jan, 1863: Mexico to Guatemala.

● ***Anoplohydrus*** Werner, 1909: A genus containing a single species.

A. aemulans Werner, 1909: Western Sumatra in tropical rain forest. Length to 45

Top: *Dasypeltis scabra*, egg being slit in distended esophagus. Photo: W. B. Allen, Jr. Bottom: *Dasypeltis scabra*, black phase. Photo: R. T. Zappalorti.

Top Left: *Boaedon fuliginosus*, hatching. Photo: J. Visser. Top Right: *Boaedon fuliginosus*, adult. Photo: Dr. G. Dingerkus. Bottom: *Boaedon fuliginosus*. Photo: S. Kochetov.

cm (18 in). Nocturnal and terrestrial, but biology poorly known .

● *Aspidura* Wagler, 1830: A genus containing five species, native to Sri Lanka and the Maldive Archipelago. In montane forest to over 2000 m (6500 ft). Length 20-45 cm (8-18 in). Head indistinct from body; snout pointed. Tail short, ending with a spine. Nocturnal and terrestrial, feeding on invertebrates (worms, insects, etc.). Require a small heated, humid terrarium with deep substrate (leaf litter). Oviparous, laying 5-20 eggs.

A. brachyorrhus (Boie, 1827): Sri Lanka. Yellowish to reddish brown with four longitudinal stripes.

A. trachyprocta Cope, 1860: Sri Lanka and Maldives. Brown with dark broken stripes.

● *Atractus* Wagler, 1828: A genus containing about 70 species found from Panama to Peru, largest concentrations of species in the N.W. Amazon basin and the rain-forest foothills of the eastern Andes. Lengths range from 20-70 cm (8-28 in). Head set off indistinctly from neck; rounded snout. Great variety of colors and markings, but many are uniformly dark with a wide pale collar. Nocturnal and terrestrial burrowing snakes feeding mainly on earthworms and insect larvae. Require a terrarium with a deep substrate for burrowing.

A. major Boulenger, 1893: Ecuador, Colombia, Venezuela, and Brazil. Light brown with darker patches.

A. elaps (Guenther, 1858): Foothills of the Andes, from Colombia to Peru. Black with red bands.

A. occipitoalbus (Jan, 1862): Ecuador. Dark gray with yellowish white collar.

● *Blythia* Theobald, 1868: A genus containing a single species.

B. reticulata (Blyth, 1854): Assam and Burma in tropical rain forest. Length to 40 cm (16 in). Head set off indistinctly from neck. Olive-brown to black with smooth iridescent scales. Terrestrial. Requires a terrarium with deep (leaf litter) substrate.

● *Boaedon* Dumeril & Bibron, 1854: **House Snakes.** A genus containing eight species native to Africa and Arabia. Found largely in dryer situations, often in cultivated areas. Length 50-130 cm (20-52 in). Head fairly distinct from body. Smooth scales. Great variety of colors and patterns even within species. Nocturnal and terrestrial, feeding on a variety of small vertebrates. Good terrarium subjects, rapidly becoming tame and feeding on mice. Require a medium-sized dry terrarium with hiding places and facilities to bathe. Very similar to *Lamprophis* and considered a synonym of that genus by some workers.

B. fulginosus (Boie, 1827): **Brown House Snake.** Africa south of the Sahara, excluding forest regions. Length to 130 cm (52 in). Light brown to reddish or blackish brown, with two pale stripes extending along neck and into forepart of body. Very common in and around human habitations, where it usually is welcome as a predator of mice. Oviparous, laying up to 16 eggs.

B. lineatus Dumeril & Bibron, 1854: **Striped House Snake.** Senegal to Sudan and south to northern South Africa.

B. olivaceus Dumeril, 1856: **Olive House Snake.** Central Africa in tropical rain forest to 1800 m (6000 ft). Require more humid facilities than other members of the genus.

• ***Bothrolycus*** Guenther, 1874: A genus containing a single species.

B. ater Guenther, 1874: Tropical central Africa in rain forest. Length to 50 cm (20 in). Head distinctly set off from body. Uniformly dark brown. Nocturnal and terrestrial, feeding primarily on frogs. Require a heated rain-forest terrarium with adequate hiding places.

• ***Bothrophthalmus*** Peters, 1863: A genus containing a single species.

B. lineatus (Schlegel, 1837): Guinea to Uganda in tropical rain forest and montane forest to 2000 m (6500 ft). Length to 125 cm (50 in). Head distinctly set off from body; snout squarish. Light brown head running into blue-black color of body. Three reddish longitudinal stripes. Underside uniform bright red. Nocturnal and terrestrial, feeding largely on small mammals. An uncommon but attractive terrarium subject requiring heated rain-forest accommodations. Oviparous, laying three to six eggs. Two subspecies.

• ***Chamaelycus*** Boulenger, 1919: A genus containing two species native to tropical central Africa in rain forest. Length to 35 cm (14 in). Head set off indistinctly from body. Brownish with irregular dark bands and/or blotches. Burrowing snakes requiring a terrarium with deep, loose substrate.

C. fasciatum (Guenther, 1858): Sierra Leone to Gabon and Congo Basin.

Top: *Dinodon rufozonatum*. Photo: R. E. Kuntz. Bottom: *Boaedon fuliginosus*. Photo: Dr. G. Dingerkus.

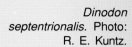
Dinodon septentrionalis. Photo: R. E. Kuntz.

C. parkeri (Angel, 1934): Congo Basin.
- **Compsophis** Mocquard, 1894: A genus containing a single species.
  C. albiventris Mocquard, 1894: N. Madagascar. Length to 17 cm (7 in). Relatively large head set off distinctly from neck. Smooth dorsal scales. Brown with a single vertebral stripe. Biology poorly known.
- **Cryptolycus** Broadley, 1968: A genus containing a single species.
  C. nanus Broadley, 1968: Mozambique in dryer areas. Terrestrial species. Biology poorly known.

- **Cyclocorus** Dumeril, 1853: A genus containing a single species.
  C. lineatus (Reinhardt, 1843): Philippines in tropical rain forest. Length to 50 cm (20 in). Head set off indistinctly from body. Smallish eyes. Brownish with three darker longitudinal stripes running to tail. Nocturnal and terrestrial, feeding largely on other snakes. Requires a warm, humid, planted terrarium.
- **Dendrolycus** Laurent, 1956: A genus containing a single species.
  D. elapoides (Guenther, 1874): Cameroons of West Africa in tropical rain forest. Length to 50 cm (20 in). Slender and slightly compressed laterally. Dark bands on a light background. Arboreal, feeding on frogs and lizards. Requires a tall, planted, rain-forest terrarium.
- **Dinodon** Dumeril, Bibron & Dumeril, 1854: A genus containing eight species native to the eastern Himalayas and eastward to China and Japan. Found in moist, densely vegetated habitats. Length 70-140 cm (28-56 in). Oval head set off distinctly from body. Smooth to lightly keeled dorsal scales. Most species are brownish with darker crossbands, some with a lighter collar. Nocturnal and terrestrial or semi-aquatic, feeding on fish, frogs, lizards, and other snakes. Require a cool, planted terrarium with a large water container.
  D. flavozonatus Pope, 1928: Burma to W. China. Length to 140 cm (56 in), the largest species in the genus.
  D. orientale Hilgendorf, 1880: Japan. Length to 70 cm (28 in).
  D. rufozonatum Cantor, 1842: China, Taiwan, and Korea, into USSR. Length to 100 cm (39 in). Reddish brown with black bands.

Top: *Dinodon rufozonatum.* Bottom: *Dinodon septentrionalis.* Photos: R. E. Kuntz.

Semi-aquatic, feeding on frogs and fish.
D. septentrionalis (Guenther,
1875): Eastern Himalayas to Indo-China and
China. Length to 120 cm (48 in). Gray-brown
to chocolate with brown to blackish brown
crossbars.

● **Dromicodryas** Boulenger, 1893: A genus
containing two species native to Madagascar.
Length to 120 cm (48 in). Patterned with light
and dark stripes. Terrestrial. Biology poorly
known.
D. berneari (Dumeril & Bibron,
1854): Western and southern Madagascar.
D. quadrilineatus (Dumeril & Bibron,
1854): Eastern and southern Madagascar.

● **Dryocalamus** Guenther, 1858: **Wood-Reed
Snakes.** A genus containing five species
native to southern Asia, from India and Sri
Lanka to the Malayan Archipelago and
Philippines. Inhabit monsoon forests and rain
forests. Length 35-90 cm (14-36 in). Closely
related to and similar to *Lycodon*. Nocturnal
and arboreal, feeding on invertebrates, frogs,
and lizards. Require a tall, planted, rain-forest
terrarium.
D. subannulatus (Dumeril & Bibron,
1854): Malaya and Sumatra. Light brown with
black flecks.

Top: *Farancia abacura*. Photo: R. T. Zappalorti. Bottom: *Dryocalamus davisonii*. Photo: Dr. S. Minton.

D. tristrigatus Guenther, 1858: Borneo and adjacent islands, in montane forest to 600 m (2000 ft). Dark brown with three white stripes along the body.

- ***Elapoidis*** Boie, 1827: A genus containing a single species. Often misspelled ***Elapoides***. ***E. fuscus*** Boie, 1827: Sumatra, Java, and Borneo in montane rain forest between 1000 and 1800 m (3250-5850 ft). Length to 50 cm (20 in). Head set off indistinctly from body. Very small eyes. Dark brown with yellow markings. Burrowing species requiring a terrarium with deep substrate. Biology poorly known. Probably feeds largely on invertebrates.

- ***Farancia*** Gray, 1842: **Mud Snakes.** A genus containing two species native to S.E. USA. Head set off indistinctly from body. Tail

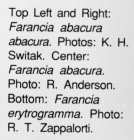

Top Left and Right: *Farancia abacura abacura*. Photos: K. H. Switak. Center: *Farancia abacura*. Photo: R. Anderson. Bottom: *Farancia erytrogramma*. Photo: R. T. Zappalorti.

Farancia erytrogramma.
Top: Ventral pattern.
Photo: Dr. S. Minton.
Bottom: Juvenile.
Photo: J. Iverson.

tipped with a sharp spine. Dorsal scales smooth and iridescent.

F. abacura (Holbrook, 1836): **Mud Snake.** S.E. Virginia to S. Florida and westward to Texas and the central Mississippi Valley. Found in swampy, weedy lake margins, muddy streams, and flood plains. Length to 200 cm (80 in). Glossy black above, cinnabar red beneath, the red often extending as bars into lower flanks. Nocturnal and secretive, feeding largely on salamanders, but will take tadpoles, fish, and frogs. Requires a large aqua-terrarium. Oviparous, laying up to 100 eggs (communal nesting?) in moist cavity. Female often coils around eggs until they hatch.

F. erytrogramma (Latreille, 1802): **Rainbow Snake.** S. Maryland to central Florida and westward to eastern Louisiana; largely along coastal plain. Burrows into sandy or muddy soil near water's

Lamprophis aurora, juvenile. Photo: K. H. Switak.

edge. Length to 165 cm (66 in). Glossy black to blue-black with three narrow red stripes running along body. Underside red with black spots. Feeds largely on eels, but will take other fish, frogs, and salamanders. Requires a large aqua-terrarium. Oviparous, laying up to 50 eggs.

● **Geagras** Cope, 1876: A genus containing a single species.

G. redimitus Cope, 1876: Isthmus of Tehuantepec in Mexico. Dry woodland to semi-desert. Length to 20 cm (8 in). Head set off indistinctly from neck. Extended rostral shield forms a shovel-like snout. Very small eyes and relatively short tail. A subterranean burrowing species requiring a terrarium with a deep substrate. Feeds largely on invertebrates.

● **Geatractus** Duges, 1898: A genus containing a single species. Closely related to and similar

to *Tropidodipsas* and often synonymized with it.

G. tecpanecus (Duges, 1896): Pacific coastal area of Mexico (Guerrero). Biology poorly known.

● **Geophis** Wagler, 1830: A genus containing about 35 species found from Mexico to N.W. Colombia. Many species have very small areas of distribution. Mostly found in dryer areas, especially cactus desert and secondary forest. Length 25-40 cm (10-16 in). Longish head, set off indistinctly from body. Small eyes. Dorsal scales smooth or, in some species, keeled on the posterior half of the body. Irregular dark blotches on a brownish ground color. Nocturnal and terrestrial, feeding on a variety of invetebrates and small vertebrates. Require a dry, desert terrarium with facilities to hide.

G. bicolor Guenther, 1868: Near Mexico City.

G. championi Boulenger, 1894: Panama.

G. dubius (Peters, 1861): Mexican Highlands.

G. hoffmani (Peters, 1859): Honduras to Panama.

G. nasalis (Cope, 1886): Guatemalan Highlands. Common in coffee plantations.

G. semidoliatus (Dumeril, Bibron & Dumeril, 1854): Central eastern Mexico.

● **Glypholycus** Guenther, 1894: A genus containing a single species. Often considered a synonym of *Lycodonomorphus*.

G. bicolor Guenther, 1893: Central Africa; common around Lake Tanganyika. Length to 60 cm (24 in). Head fairly distinct from body. Uniform brown above, whitish below. Very aquatic, feeding largely on fish (cichlids). Requires a heated aqua-terrarium with large body of water.

● **Gonionotophis** Boulenger, 1893: A genus containing four species native to W. Africa in tropical rain forest. Length 45-50 cm (18-20 in). Head distinct from body. Keeled dorsal scales. Mostly uniform brownish. Nocturnal and terrestrial, feeding on frogs and lizards.

G. brussauxi (Mocquard, 1889): Guinea-Bissau to the Congo Basin.

● **Haplocercus** Guenther, 1858: A genus containing a single species.

H. ceylonensis Guenther, 1858: Sri Lanka in montane rain forest to 1800 m (6000 ft). Length to 45 cm (18 in). Head indistinct from neck and body. Brown with dark vertebral stripe. Terrestrial. Biology poorly known.

● **Haplonodon** Griffin, 1910: A genus containing a single species. Possibly a synonym of *Lycodon*.

H. philippinensis Griffin, 1910: Philippines in tropical lowland forest. Length to 80 cm (32 in). Head distinct from neck. Vertical pupils. Marked with narrow white and broad brown bands. Nocturnal and terrestrial. Biology poorly known.

● **Heteroliodon** Boettger, 1913: A genus

containing a single species.

H. torquatus (Boettger, 1913): Eastern Madagascar. Length to 32 cm (13 in). Biology poorly known.

- **Hormonotus** Hallowell, 1857: A genus containing a single species.

H. modestus (Dumeril & Bibron, 1854): Central Africa from Guinea to Uganda in tropical woodland. Length to 85 cm (34 in). Head distinct from body. Uniform yellowish above, whitish below. Nocturnal and terrestrial, feeding on small vertebrates. Requires a heated rain-forest terrarium.

- **Lamprophis** Fitzinger, 1843: A genus of five or six species native to E. and S. Africa. Inhabit savannah and cultivated areas. Length 40-110 cm (16-44 in).

L. aurora (Linnaeus, 1758): **Aurora House Snake.** S. Africa. Length to 90 cm (36 in). Head indistinct from body. Olive to green above with a narrow red to yellow vertebral stripe. Underside yellowish to greenish white. Nocturnal and terrestrial. Feeds on small mammals and lizards that are overpowered by constriction. Requires a heated, dry terrarium with adequate hiding places. An attractive terrarium subject that soon settles into captivity. Oviparous, laying eight to ten eggs. Other species in the genus are **L. fiskii**, Fisk's House Snake; **L. fuscus**, Yellow-bellied House Snake; **L. inornatus**, Black House Snake; and **L. swazicus**, Swaziland House Snake.

- **Lepturophis** Boulenger, 1900: A genus containing a single species.

L. borneensis Boulenger, 1900: Borneo, in tropical rain forest. Length to 140 cm (56 in). Head distinct from body. Keeled dorsal

Top: *Lamprophis aurora*, adult. Photo: K. H. Switak. Center: *Lamprophis fiskii*. Photo: P. Freed. Bottom: *Lamprophis guttatus*. Photo: K. H. Switak.

scales. Uniformly brown. Tree-dweller. Biology poorly known.

• **Leioheterodon** Jan, 1863: A genus containing three species native to Madagascar. Found in tropical rain forest. Length 120-140 cm (48-56 in). Robustly built species with wide, flattish head indistinct from body. Large eyes protected by overhanging supraocular shield. Smooth dorsal scales. Mainly brown above with faint darker patterns. Terrestrial, feeding largely on frogs. Require a tropical rain-forest terrarium with dry hiding places. Often misspelled **Lioheterodon.**

L. madagascariensis (Dumeril & Bibron, 1854): Perhaps the most common and most widely distributed snake species in Madagascar.

L. modestus (Guenther, 1863): Western Madagascar.

Top: *Leioheterodon geayi*. Photo: P. Freed. Center: *Leioheterodon geayi*. Photo: K. H. Switak. Bottom Left: *Leioheterodon modestus*. Photo: P. Freed. Bottom Right: *Leioheterodon geayi*. Photo: K. H. Switak.

- ***Liopholidophis*** Mocquard, 1904: A genus containing five species native to Madagascar. Length 60-100 cm (24-39 in). Narrow head with relatively large eyes. Most species are patterned in yellow and brown. Biology poorly documented.

  L. lateralis (Dumeril & Bibron, 1854): Fairly abundant all over Madagascar.

  L. sexlineatus (Guenther, 1882): Central Madagascar.

- ***Lycodon*** Boie, 1826: **Asian Wolf Snakes.** A genus containing about 16 species native to Asia in varied dry habitats from steppe to rain-forest margins. Length 40-100 cm (16-39 in). Head distinct or indistinct from body. Rounded snout. Smooth dorsal scales. Mostly brownish with or without neck collar and body pattern. Nocturnal and terrestrial, hiding during the day under rocks, fallen logs, etc. Feed on large invertebrates to small vertebrates, sometimes other snakes. Oviparous, laying two to eight relatively large eggs. Require a well-heated dry terrarium with choice of hiding places and a reduced temperature at night.

  L. aulicus (Linnaeus, 1758): India and Sri Lanka eastward to S. China and the Malayan Archipelago to the Philippines; has colonized Mauritius. Length to 80 cm (32 in).

  L. striatus (Shaw, 1802): Soviet Central Asia

Top: *Leioheterodon modestus*. Photo: H. Hansen. Center Left: *Liopholidophis stumpffi*. Photo: P. Freed. Center Right: *Liopholidophis sexlineatus*. Photo: P. Freed. Bottom: *Lycodon aulicus*. Photo: M. J. Cox.

Top: *Lycodon striatus bicolor*. Photo: B. Kahl.
Bottom: *Lycodon subcinctus*, juvenile. Photo: M. J. Cox.

to Central India. Length to 40 cm (16 in). *L. s. bicolor* is beautifully colored with black and golden yellow bands.

L. subcinctus Boie, 1827: Indo-China, S. China, and Malayan Archipelago. Length to 100 cm (39 in).

• *Lycodonomorphus* Fitzinger, 1843: A genus containing three species native to Africa south of the Equator. Length to 110 cm (44 in). Head distinct from body. Large eyes. Slender, with smooth scales. Amphibious, feeding on frogs and fish. Require a heated aqua-terrarium. Oviparous.

L. rufulus (Lichtenstein, 1823): S.E. and S. Africa. Uniformly brown.

• *Lycognathophis* Boulenger, 1893: A genus containing a single species.

L. seychellensis (Schlegel, 1837): Seychelle Islands (Indian Ocean). Length to 100 cm (39 in). Head distinct from body. Keeled dorsal scales. Grayish brown with darker markings; a distinct dark stripe passing from the eye toward back of head. Terrestrial and diurnal. Biology poorly known.

• *Lycophidion* Fitzinger, 1843: **African Wolf Snakes.** A genus containing six species native to tropical and southern Africa. Found in savannah and montane country to 3000 m (10000 ft). Length 25-75 cm (10-30 in). Longish head set off distinctly from body. Squarish snout. Extremely large fangs in the upper and lower jaws are designed to catch slippery prey such as skinks. Nocturnal and terrestrial. Require a dry, heated terrarium with adequate hiding places.

L. capense (A. Smith, 1831): **Cape Wolf Snake.** Ethiopia to the Cape and westward to the Congo Basin. Length to 75 cm (30 in). Brown to reddish brown, often with silvery markings. Oviparous, laying six to eight eggs. Other members of the genus include *L. hellmichi*, Hellmich's Wolf Snake; *L. semiannule*, Eastern Wolf Snake; and *L.*

Top: *Lycodonomorphus whytii.* Photo: J. Visser. Center: *Lycophidion capense.* Photo: J. Visser. Bottom: *Mehelya capensis.* Photo: K H. Switak.

Top Left: *Mehelya crossi*. Photo: K. H. Switak. Top Right: *Ninia sebae*. Photo: P. Freed. Bottom: *Oligodon ornatus*. Photo: R. E. Kuntz.

variegatum, Variegated Wolf Snake.
- *Mehelya* Csiki, 1903: **File Snakes.** A genus containing eight species native to tropical and southern Africa. Length 35-175 cm (14-70 in). Squarish head distinct from body. Body triangular in cross-section, the dorsal scales heavily keeled (giving rise to the common name). Most species in the genus are brown to olive, some with a lighter vertebral stripe. Nocturnal and arboreal, feeding mainly on lizards and other snakes (including venomous species). Can be cannibalistic, so specimens should be kept singly in the terrarium other than in the breeding season, when a careful watch should be kept on the snakes. Require a heated semi-humid terrarium with adequate climbing and hiding facilities. Oviparous, laying five to eight large, elongate eggs.
  M. capensis (A. Smith, 1847): **Common or Cape File Snake.** Tanzania to South Africa. Length to 175 cm (70 in). Gray to purplish brown above with an off-white vertebral stripe. Other species in the genus include *M. nyassae*, Black File Snake, and *M. vernayi*, Angola File Snake.
- *Micropisthodon* Mocquard, 1894: A genus containing a single species.
  M. ochraceus Mocquard, 1894: Northern Madagascar and the island of Nossi-Be. Length to 70 cm (28 in). Head indistinct from body. Body slightly compressed laterally. Light brown with dark V mark on neck. Biology poorly documented.
- *Ninia* Girard, 1853: A genus containing about eight species found from Mexico to Venezuela, Colombia, and Ecuador. Length 40-60 cm (16-24 in). Biology poorly known. Probably nocturnal and terrestrial.
  N. atrata (Hallowell, 1845): Costa Rica to Ecuador. Uniformly black in color.
  N. diademata Baird & Girard, 1853: Mexico to Guatemala.

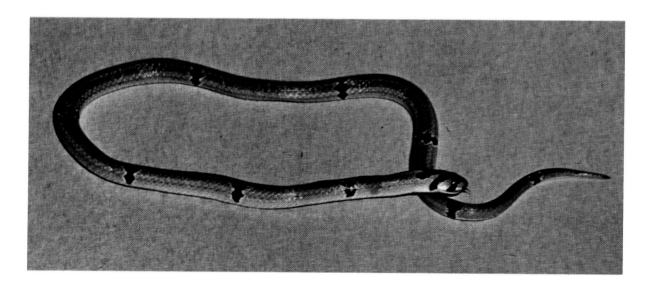

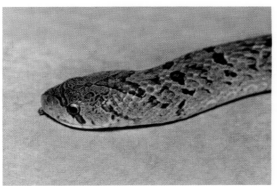

Top and Center Left: *Oligodon formosanus*. Center Right: *Oligodon ornatus*. Photos: R. E. Kuntz. Bottom: *Oligodon taeniatus*. Photo: M. J. Cox.

● *Oligodon* Boie, 1826: **Kukuri Snakes.** A genus containing about 56 species ranging from Turkmenistan (USSR) through Iran and eastward to China and the Indonesian Archipelago. In varied drier habitats, from semi-desert to rain-forest margins. Length 25-100 cm (10-39 in). Head indistinct from body. Large upturned rostral shield. Smooth dorsal scales. Colors range through grays and browns to reddish and yellowish marked with various patterns of lighter and darker colors. Nocturnal and terrestrial, hiding under stones, logs, etc., during the day. Feed largely on lizards. Oviparous, laying up to 16 eggs, but usually less. Require a heated, dry terrarium with adequate hiding places. Provide a reduced temperature at night for species from more extreme climates.

O. bitorquatus Boie, 1826: Sumatra to Sumbawa. Southernmost species in the genus.

O. calamarius (Linnaeus, 1758): Sri Lanka in montane areas to altitudes of 1000 to 1300 m (3250-4225 ft). Length to 25 cm (10 in), the smallest species in the genus.

O. cyclurus (Cantor, 1839): Assam to Thailand. Length to 100 cm (39 in), the largest species in the genus.

O. taeniolatus (Jerdon, 1853): **Streaked Kukuri Snake.** Turkmenistan (USSR) to Sri Lanka. Most widely distributed species of the genus. Length to 60 cm (24 in). Pinkish gray with widely spaced light gray, slightly diagonal crossbands. Narrow chevron mark across head, wider chevron mark across neck.

● *Opisthotropis* Guenther, 1872: A genus containing 11 species found from Indo-China to S.W. China and the island of Hainan; also in Sumatra and Borneo. Found in moist areas of monsoon forest. Length 25-80 cm (10-32 in). Long, squarish head distinct from body. Dorsal scales smooth or keeled. Uniformly colored or with light and dark crossbanding. Amphibious to semi-amphibious, feeding on crustaceans, frogs, and fish. Require a medium sized heated aqua-terrarium with large, planted water area.

O. balteatus (Cope, 1895): Kampuchea to S. China and Hainan. Length to 80 cm (32 in), largest member of genus. Banded.

O. jacobi Angel & Bourret, 1933: N. Vietnam.

O. latouchi (Boulenger, 1899): S. China. Longitudinal stripes.

O. rugosa (van Lidth de Jeude, 1891): Sumatra. Uniformly olive-brown.

O. typica (Mocquard, 1890): N. Borneo (Mount Kinabalu Range). Uniformly olive.

● *Oreocalamus* Boulenger, 1899: A genus containing a single species. Subfamilial status undecided, but generally included here among the Lycodontinae.

O. hanitschi Boulenger, 1899: N. Borneo (Mt. Kinabalu) to 1400 m (4500 ft) in montane rain forest. Length to 40 cm (16 in). Flattish head indistinct from neck; pointed snout. Eyes small. Smooth dorsal scales. Very short tail. Uniformly blackish brown. The biology of this rare species is poorly known.

● *Pararhadinaea* Boettger, 1898: A genus with a single species.

Oligodon taeniolatus.
Photo: Dr. S. Minton.

P. melanogaster Boettger,
1898: Madagascar (Nossi-Be) in rain forest.
Length 25 cm (10 in). Extended rostral shield.
Small eyes. A burrowing species whose
biology is poorly known.

● **Plagiopholis** Boulenger, 1893: A genus
containing three species found in N. Indo-
China and S. China. Length about 40 cm (16
in). Nocturnal and terrestrial. Similar to
Trachischium in form and habit.
   P. blakewayi Boulenger, 1893: Burma.
   P. nuchalis (Boulenger, 1893): Burma and
   N. Thailand.

● **Pseudoxyrhopus** Guenther, 1881: A genus
containing eight species native to Madagascar.
Length 35-110 cm (14-44 in). Longish, oval
head distinctly set off from body. Small,
upward oriented eyes. Short tail. Uniform
brownish or light and dark striped. Biology
poorly known.
   P. quinquelineatus (Guenther, 1881).
   P. microps (Guenther, 1881).

● **Rhabdops** Boulenger, 1893: A genus
containing two species ranging from India to
China. Length to 80 cm (32 in). Squarish
head distinct from body. Nocturnal and
terrestrial, hiding during the day under
ground litter. Feed on earthworms, slugs, and
other invertebrates. Require a warm, humid
terrarium.
   R. olivaceus (Beddome, 1863): S. India.
   Olive-brown with four longitudinal rows of
   small dark flecks.
   R. bicolor (Blyth, 1854): Assam east through
   Burma to S.W. China. Dark brown to black
   back sharply divided along flanks from
   yellowish white underside.

● **Rhynchocalamus** Guenther, 1864: A genus
containing two species found from Arabia to
the Caucasus. Inhabit steppe and semi-desert
areas to altitudes of 1100 m (3575 ft). Length
to 40 cm (16 in). Nocturnal and terrestrial,
hiding under rocks, etc., during the day. Feed

Top: *Rhynchocalamus
melanocephalus*.
Photo: Dr. S. Minton.
Center: *Stegonotus* sp.
Photo: K. H. Switak.
Bottom: *Stegonotus
cucullatus*. Photo: C.
Banks.

on various invertebrates and small lizards. Require a heated, dry (semi-desert) terrarium with ample hiding places (flat stones or pieces of cork bark) and temperature reduction at night.

R. melanocephalus (Jan, 1862): Israel, Turkey, Iran, and Armenian USSR. Reddish to pinkish orange body with black or black and white banded head.

R. arabicus Schmidt, 1933: Arabian Peninsula.

● *Stegonotus* Dumeril, Bibron & Dumeril, 1854: A genus containing about nine species. Sometimes included in the Natricinae. Found in N.E. Australia, New Guinea, the Molluccas, and the Philippines. Inhabit riverine forest from sea level to altitudes of 1000 m (3250 ft). Length 60-140 cm (24-56 in). Head distinct from body. Small eyes with vertical pupils. Smooth dorsal scales. Uniformly brown or with darker markings. Crepuscular to nocturnal, terrestrial to semi-arboreal or semi-aquatic. Usually found near water. Feed largely on frogs. Require a heated aqua-terrarium with facilities for climbing.

S. batjanensis (Guenther, 1865): Halmahera to Batjan. Length to 150 cm (60 in).

S. cucullatus (Dumeril, Bibron & Dumeril, 1853): **Slaty-gray Snake.** N. Australia and New Guinea. Length to 130 cm (52 in). Uniformly brown to slaty-gray. Underside white or cream, sometimes with dark blotches.

S. modestus (Schlegel, 1837): New Guinea to Samoa. Length to 120 cm (48 in).

S. plumbeus (Macleay, 1884): New Guinea. Length to 140 cm (56 in).

● *Tetralepis* Boettger, 1892: A genus containing a single species. Sometimes included in the Natricinae.

T. fruhstorferi Boettger, 1892: Java, in tropical rain forest to 1200 m (3900 ft). Length to 50 cm (20 in). Dark reddish brown with darker dorsal stripe. Biology poorly known.

● *Trachischium* Guenther, 1858: A genus containing five species found in the southern foothills of the Himalayas from 100-2300 m (325-7500 ft). Length 25-70 cm (10-28 in). Head indistinct from body. Smooth dorsal scales, but the males in most species have keeled scales along the posterior flanks and tail. Mostly dark, iridescent brown. Terrestrial and nocturnal, hiding under ground litter during the day. Feed largely on invertebrates. Oviparous, laying three to six eggs. Require a cool (20°C), humid terrarium.

T. monticola (Cantor, 1839): Assam to Bengal. Length 25 cm (10 in).

T. guentheri Boulenger, 1890: Sikkim and Bengal. Length to 50 cm (20 in).

● *Tropidodipsas* Guenther, 1858: A genus containing ten species native to tropical Central America (Mexico to Guatemala). Found in lowland forest. Length 30-65 cm (12-26 in). Head distinct from neck and body.

Slender. Large eyes with vertical pupils. Dorsal scales smooth to lightly keeled. Most species are light brownish with varied dark patterns. Nocturnal and terrestrial to semi-arboreal. Biology poorly known.

Exelencophis Smith, 1942 (for the single species *annulifera* Boulenger) is now accepted as a synonym.

T. fasciata Guenther, 1858: Mexico to Guatemala.

T. philippi (Jan, 1863): Mexico.

T. sartorii Cope, 1863: Mexico to Guatemala.

● *Xylophis* Beddome, 1878: A genus containing two species native to southern India. In montane regions. Length 25-60 cm (10-24 in). Head indistinct from body. Pointed snout. Small eyes. Dark brown with or without darker longitudinal stripes. Semi-burrowing. Biology poorly known.

X. perroteti (Dumeril & Bibron, 1854): Length to 60 cm (24 in).

X. stenorhynchus (Guenther, 1875): Length to 25 cm (10 in).

SUBFAMILY NATRICINAE—WATER SNAKES

The subfamily Natricinae contains about 37 genera and some 185 species, representatives of which are found in most temperate, subtropical, and tropical parts of the world. Although generally referred to as water snakes, many of the species are only semi-aquatic, with some terrestrial, burrowing, or even semi-arboreal. Lengths range from about 30-250 cm (12-100 in). Typical subfamily characteristics include arrangements of the head and body scales, but there is a remarkable lack of uniformity in areas such as tooth arrangement, some species being opisthoglyphs (rear-fanged) and others being totally non-venomous.

● *Adelophis* Duges, 1879: A genus containing a single species.

A. copei Duges, 1879: Mexico, in damp areas. Length to 35 cm (14 in). Smooth dorsal scales. Feed on invertebrates. Require a warm, humid terrarium.

● *Afronatrix* Rossman & Eberle, 1977: A genus containing a single species.

A. anoscopus (Cope, 1861): Guinea to Cameroons, W. Africa, in and around water. Length to 75 cm (30 in). Feeds on fish and frogs and requires a heated aqua-terrarium with a large body of water.

● *Amastridium* Cope, 1861: A genus containing a single species.

A. veliferum Cope, 1861: Southern Mexico to Panama. Length to 40 cm (16 in). Head distinct from body. Enlarged rear fangs. Terrestrial. Biology poorly known.

● *Amphiesma* Dumeril, Bibron & Dumeril, 1854: A genus containing some 40 species found from E. and S.E. Asia to New Guinea and N. Australia in temperate to tropical and

montane rain forest to altitudes of 2000 m
(6500 ft). Length 50-100 cm (20-39 in). Head
fairly distinct from body. Scales strongly
keeled. Enlarged rear fangs present in upper
jaw, but believed to be non-venomous under
normal circumstances.

A. mairi (Gray, 1841): **Keelback.** New
Guinea, N. and E. Australia. Length to 100
cm (39 in). Gray, brown, olive, reddish, or
blackish above, often with irregular darker
crossbands. Undersides cream to yellowish
green or pinkish. Feeds mainly on frogs.
Requires heated aqua-terrarium with dry
basking and resting areas. Oviparous, laying
5-12 eggs.

A. stolata (Linnaeus, 1758): **Striped
Keelback.** India, Sri Lanka, Indo-China, and
S. China. Very variable in color and pattern.

Top: *Amphiesma mairi*.
Photo: K. H. Switak.
Center: *Amphiesma
mairi*. Photo: C. Banks.
Bottom: *Amphiesma
sauteri*. Photo: R. E.
Kuntz.

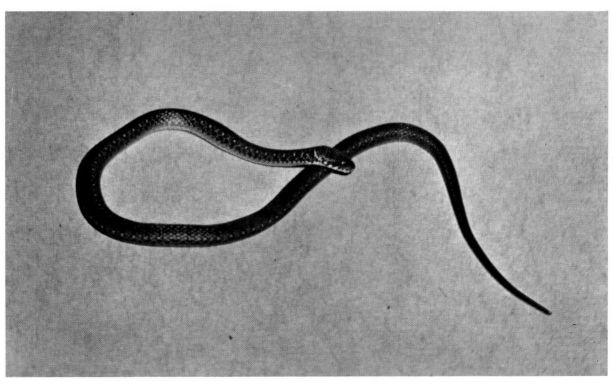

More terrestrial than *A. mairi*, but requires
ample water container.
A. vibakari (Boie, 1827): Far eastern USSR,
Korea, E. China, Japan. Length to 55 cm (22
in). Reddish brown above, yellowish below.
Small dark spots along flanks. Feeds largely
on earthworms. Requires cool (to 22°C),
humid, woodland terrarium.
● **Atretium** Cope, 1861: A genus containing
two species found in S. and E. Asia. Length
to 90 cm (36 in). Elongate head distinct from
body. Strongly keeled dorsal scales.
Uniformly olive-brown to greenish. Semi-
aquatic, feeding on fish and frogs. Require
heated aqua-terrarium. Oviparous, laying 12-
30 eggs.
A. schistosum (Daudin, 1803): S. India and
Sri Lanka. To altitudes of 1000 m (3250 ft).

A. yunnanensis Anderson, 1879: Yunnan,
S.W. China, at altitudes of 600-1500 m (2000-
5000 ft).
● **Balanophis** Smith, 1938: A genus
containing a single species.
B. ceylonensis (Guenther, 1858): Montane
rain forest of Sri Lanka. Length to 60 cm (24
in). Triangular head, distinct from neck.
Opisthoglyphic (rear-fanged), venomous.
Strongly keeled dorsal scales. Olive-brown
with a pattern of yellow, reddish, and black.
A rare species. Biology poorly known.
● **Carphophis** Gervais, 1843: A genus
containing a single species.
C. amoenus (Say, 1825): **Worm
Snake.** Eastern and central USA, from Texas
to the Atlantic coast. Found in damp, hilly
woodlands or grasslands, rarely far from

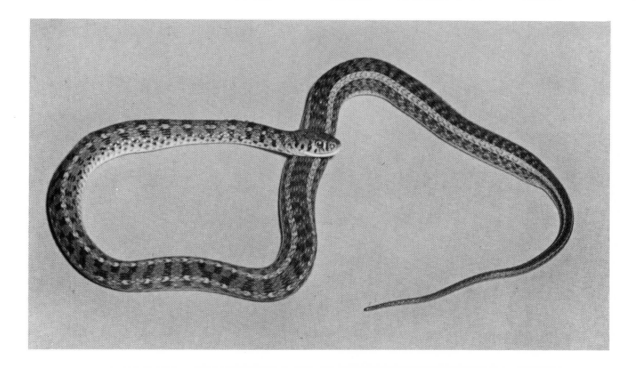

Top: *Amphiesma stolata*. Photo: R. E. Kuntz. Center and Bottom: *Carphophis amoenus amoenus*. Photos: R. T. Zappalorti.

Top: *Diadophis punctatus amabilis*. Photo: K. Lucas, Steinhart. Center: *Diadophis punctatus arnyi*. Photo: J. Iverson. Bottom: *Carphophis amoenus*. Photo: Dr. G. Dingerkus.

water. Length to 37.5 cm (15 in). Head indistinct from body. Short, spine-tipped tail. Brown, gray, or black above with bright reddish pink underside. Secretive, hiding in damp ground litter. Feeds on earthworms. Requires a humid terrarium with deep, loose substrate. Oviparous, laying one to eight elongate eggs.

- ***Chersodromus*** Reinhardt, 1860: A genus containing a single species. Taxonomy

disputed, but probably in Natricinae.
C. liebmanni Reinhardt, 1860: Mexico to
Guatemala. Length to 35 cm (14 in). Dorsal
scales strongly keeled. Biology poorly known.
● ***Diadophis*** Girard, 1853: **Ringneck
Snakes.** A genus containing a single species
with numerous subspecies. Some authorities
recognize up to three species.
D. punctatus (Linnaeus, 1766): **Ringneck
Snake.** Nova Scotia to Florida Keys, west to
the Pacific coast and south to central Mexico
in moist habitats. Length to 76 cm (30 in).
Uniformly olive, brown, or black above with
narrow (often broken but usually distinct)
yellow, cream, or orange neck ring.
Undersides bright yellow, orange, or red.
Nocturnal and secretive, hiding under flat
rocks or loose bark of dead trees. When
threatened, this species curls its tail and
elevates it to show the brightly colored
(usually reddish) underside. Feeds on
earthworms, slugs, salamanders, lizards, and
newborn snakes. Requires a humid, woodland
type terrarium. Oviparous, laying one to ten
elongate eggs.

Top Left: *Diadophis
punctatus regalis*.
Photo: L. Porras. Top
Right: *Diadophis
punctatus edwardsi*,
hatchling. Photo: J. K.
Langhammer. Center:
Diadophis punctatus.
Photo: R. A. Winstel.
Bottom: *Diadophis
punctatus punctatus*.
Photo: R. D. Bartlett.

- ***Diaphorolepis*** Jan, 1863: A genus containing a single species. Taxonomy uncertain, but included here under the Natricinae.
  D. wagneri Jan, 1863: Panama to Ecuador in tropical forest. Length to 70 cm (28 in). Head distinct from body. Large eyes. Dorsal scales keeled, the vertebral scales with double keels. Uniformly brown above. Terrestrial, feeding largely on frogs. Require a warm, moist terrarium.

- ***Gonyosoma*** Wagler, 1828: **Green Ratsnakes.** A genus containing three species. Taxonomy disputed (Colubrinae or Natricinae). Often considered a synonym of *Elaphe* (in Colubrinae!). Native to S.E. Asia in tropical rain and monsoon forests. Length 100-200 cm (40-80 in), slender but strongly built. Longish head, fairly distinct from body, which is slightly compressed laterally. Dorsal scales smooth to lightly keeled. Ventral scales angled to aid climbing. Adults are mostly uniformly green above, yellowish below; juveniles often have black bars. Diurnal and arboreal, feeding on frogs, lizards, and small

Top: *Diadophis punctatus regalis.* Photo: R. T. Zappalorti. Center: *Gonyosoma oxycephala.* Photo: R. D. Bartlett. Bottom: *Diadophis punctatus punctatus,* showing ventral pattern. Photo: J. Iverson.

Top: *Gonyosoma oxycephala*. Photo: B. Kahl. Center: *Gonyosoma oxycephala*. Photo: R. D. Bartlett. Bottom Left: *Helicops angulatus*. Photo: R. S. Simmons. Bottom Right: *Grayia smithi*. Photo: C. Banks.

mammals. Require a large, tall, planted terrarium with climbing facilities.

G. oxycephala (Boie, 1827): **Red-tailed Green Ratsnake.** Thailand and Kampuchea, over the Indonesian Archipelago to the Philippines. Usually occurs in lowland forest or bamboo and mangrove areas. Green with reddish brown tail.

G. prasina (Blyth, 1854): **Green Ratsnake.** N. India to Indo-China and Malayan Peninsula. Uniformly green.

● ***Grayia*** Guenther, 1858: **African Water Snakes.** A genus containing two species native to tropical Africa. Found in larger rivers and freshwater lakes. Length 120-250 cm (48-100 in). Head fairly distinct from body. Smooth dorsal scales. Dull olive-brown with indistinct darker rhomboidal or diagonal markings. Feed largely on fish and aquatic frogs. Require a large, heated aqua-terrarium.

G. smithi (Leach, 1818): Sudan to Tanzania and westward to Senegal, southward to Angola. Length to 250 cm (100 in), but usually smaller. Robust species.

G. tholloni Mocquard, 1906: Tanzania westward to Nigeria. Length to 120 cm (48 in). Slender species.

● ***Helicops*** Wagler, 1828: A genus containing at least 14 species native to South America from Colombia to Argentina. Length to 100 cm (39 in). Small, rounded head. Eyes and nostrils placed on top of head. Body covered

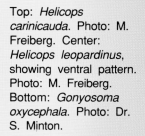

Top: *Helicops carinicauda.* Photo: M. Freiberg. Center: *Helicops leopardinus,* showing ventral pattern. Photo: M. Freiberg. Bottom: *Gonyosoma oxycephala.* Photo: Dr. S. Minton.

Top Left: *Helicops leopardinus*. Photo: M. Freiberg. Top Right: *Helicops carinicauda*, showing ventral pattern. Photo: M. Freiberg. Center and Bottom: *Macropisthodon rudis*. Photos: R. E. Kuntz.

with strongly keeled, overlapping scales. Much variation in color, from gray-blue to brown, uniform or with darker stripes or spots. Almost totally aquatic. Feed on fish and frogs. Require aqua-terrarium with large volume of water. Probably lays eggs in a late state of development (one species has apparently given birth to live young on occasion).

H. angulatus (Linnaeus, 1758): Colombia to Venezuela, Ecuador, Bolivia, and Peru.

H. carinicauda (Wied, 1825): S.E. Brazil to Uruguay and Argentina.

H. leopardinus (Schlegel, 1837): From the Guianas to Argentina. Spotted pattern.

H. polylepis Guenther, 1861: Amazon Basin.

and nostrils placed on top of head. Smooth dorsal scales. Brownish in color. Very aquatic, feeding mainly on fish. Require a heated aqua-terrarium with a large volume of water.
H. concolor Peters, 1859: Honduras and Costa Rica.

• ***Hydrops*** Wagler, 1830: A genus containing two species native to northern South America in heavily vegetated rivers and lakes. Length 50-120 cm (20-48 in). Smallish head indistinct from body. Small eyes and nostrils directed upward. Smooth dorsal scales. Brown to reddish brown with darker crossbands. Very aquatic, feeding largely on fish, frogs, and caecilians. Require a heated aqua-terrarium with large volume of water.
H. marti (Wagler, 1830): Upper Amazon region (Peru, Colombia, and N. Brazil). Female reaches twice length of male.
H. triangularis (Wagler, 1824): Eastern Peru to the Guianas and Trinidad.

• ***Limnophis*** Guenther, 1865: A genus containing a single species.
L. bicolor Guenther, 1865: **Bicolored Swamp Snake.** Angola to Zimbabwe in or near rivers and streams. Length to 60 cm (24 in). Head barely distinct from neck. Smooth dorsal scales. Light and dark brown longitudinal stripes. Undersides white to yellowish. Semi-aquatic, feeding on frogs and fish. Requires a medium sized aqua-terrarium. Oviparous, laying about four eggs.

• ***Macropisthodon*** Boulenger, 1893: A genus containing four species native to S.E. Asia. Very close to *Rhabdophis* and sometimes synonymized with that genus. Found mainly in montane forest to 2500 m (8000 ft). Length to 100 cm (39 in). Robustly built, with head distinct from body. Keeled dorsal scales. Enlarged rear fangs are present but the bite is not thought to be venomous to man. However, the species are aggressive so care must be taken to avoid bites. When threatened, they flatten the body and attempt to bite. Nocturnal and terrestrial, feeding on frogs and fish. Require a large, moderately heated and planted woodland terrarium with adequate hiding places. Oviparous, laying up to 25 eggs.
M. plumbicolor (Cantor, 1839): India and Sri Lanka in hills to 2500 m (8000 ft). Greenish with black and yellowish pattern.
M. rhodomelas (Boie, 1827): Malayan Peninsula and Indonesia to Sulawesi.
M. rudis Boulenger, 1906: S.E. China and Taiwan. Length to 90 cm (36 in). Light buff with pattern of dark brown triangles and diamonds.

• ***Macropophis*** Boulenger, 1893: A genus containing five species native to S.E. Asia. Closely related to preceding genus and requiring similar care. Some authorities feel that the proper name for this genus should be ***Tropidonophis*** Jan, 1863.
M. maculata (Edeling, 1864): Malaya, Sumatra, and Borneo.

Natrix maura. Photos: Top: B. Kahl; Bottom: Dr. D. Terver.

• ***Hydromorphus*** Peters, 1859: A genus containing three species found between Costa Rica and Panama in rivers and lakes of the lowland forest. Length to 100 cm (39 in). Head fairly distinct from body. Small eyes

M. hypomelas (Guenther, 1877): New Guinea.

● *Natriciteres* Loveridge, 1953: **Marsh Snakes.** A genus containing three species native to tropical Africa in and around rivers, lakes, and marshes. Length 40-60 cm (16-24 in). Smooth, overlapping dorsal scales. Amphibious, feeding mainly on frogs. Require medium sized, heated aqua-terrium.

N. olivacea (Peters, 1854): Sudan, west to Ghana and south to South Africa. Length to 60 cm (24 in). Olive to dark brown, usually with a darker vertebral stripe. Underside yellowish to orange.

● *Natrix* Laurenti, 1768: **Eurasian Water Snakes.** A genus containing three species native to Europe, W. Asia, and N. Africa. Length 80 to 150 cm (32-60 in). Head distinct from body. Large eyes. Dorsal scales heavily keeled. Color and pattern very variable, even among individuals of one species. Diurnal amphibious snakes feeding on fish and amphibians. Require a large aqua-terrarium with dry basking and resting places. Oviparous, laying up to 35 eggs. Rarely attempt to bite, but newly captured specimens discharge evil-smelling contents of cloaca. Some may feign death. Tame quickly and, given the right conditions, will make long-lived terrarium subjects. Period of hibernation recommended.

N. maura (Linnaeus, 1758): **Viperine Snake.** W. and S.W. Europe, N. Africa.

Natrix maura. Melanistic adult in center. Photos: B. Kahl.

Top: *Natrix natrix helvetica*. Photo: B. Kahl. Bottom: *Natrix natrix*. Photo: Dr. D. Terver.

Stocky. Olive green to brown with dark viper-like pattern. Fairly aquatic, feeding on fish and frogs.

N. natrix (Linnaeus, 1758): **European Grass Snake.** Europe, N.W. Africa, and W. Asia. Found in damper areas usually not too far from water, but not quite so dependent on water as the other species in the genus. Olive-brown to green with pattern of black spots. Most have conspicuous yellow neck collar, but this is absent in some subspecies. Feeds mainly on frogs. Eight subspecies.

N. tessellata (Laurenti, 1768): **Dice Snake.** Central and S. Europe, eastward to central Asia. Gray-green with black spots and blotches. Fairly aquatic, feeding on fish and amphibians.

● *Nerodia* Baird, 1853: **American Water Snakes.** A genus containing some eight species native to N. America east of the

Top: *Natrix natrix.*
Photo: Dr. D. Terver.
Bottom: *Natrix maura.*
Photo: B. Kahl.

Top: *Natrix tessellata.*
Photo: H. Hansen.
Bottom: *Natrix natrix helvetica.* Photo: B. Kahl.

Top: *Nerodia cyclopion floridana*. Photo: R. T. Zappalorti. Center: *Nerodia clarki compressicauda*, red phase. Photo: W. B. Allen, Jr. Bottom Left: *Nerodia clarki clarki*. Photo: R. D. Bartlett. Bottom Right: *Natrix tessellata*, female with eggs. Photo: K. H. Switak.

Top: *Nerodia erythrogaster*. Photo: J. Gee. Bottom: *Nerodia cyclopion floridana*. Photo: R. T. Zappalorti.

Rockies and south into N.W. Mexico. Similar in morphology and biology to *Natrix* (to which genus they were formerly assigned) but ovoviviparous, producing 7-60 (but sometimes record numbers of over 100) live young. Require a large aqua-terrarium with facilities for dry basking and resting.

The exact relationships to *Thamnophis* are unsettled. Several species are difficult to assign to either genus, which has led to some authorities considering *Nerodia* to be a subgenus of *Thamnophis*. **Clonophis** Cope, 1888, with one species, *C. kirtlandii*, is very closely related but usually considered distinct.

N. cyclopion (Dumeril & Bibron, 1854): **Green Water Snake.** South Carolina to Florida, west to Louisiana and Texas and along the Mississippi valley. In wooded swamps to weed-choked marshes. Length to 188 cm (74 in). Heavy-bodied. Olive-green to brownish or even reddish brown, with indistinct black bars on back and sides. Undersides cream to brown, with or without lighter spots. Primarily diurnal, often basking on branches overhanging water. Feeds mainly on fish.

N. erythrogaster (Forster, 1771): **Red-bellied Water Snake.** S.E. USA with the exception of the southern half of Florida. In

Top Left: *Nerodia erythrogaster erythrogaster*. Photo: W. B. Allen, Jr. Top Right: *Nerodia fasciata pictiventris*. Photo: R. T. Zappalorti. Center: *Nerodia fasciata fasciata*. Photo: W. B. Allen, Jr. Bottom: *Nerodia erythrogaster erythrogaster*. Photo: R. . T. Zappalorti.

and around rivers, streams and swamps. Length to 150 cm (60 in). Reddish brown to brown, gray, or greenish. Belly plain red, orange, or yellow. Crepuscular, often seen crossing roads on warm, rainy nights. Feeds on fish, frogs, and tadpoles.

N. rhombifera (Hallowell, 1852): **Diamondback Water Snake.** Central USA to N. Mexico in margins of rivers, streams, lakes, and marshes. Length to 160 cm (64 in). Heavy-bodied. Greenish brown to brown with a pattern of large, dark, rhomboidal spots on the back and bars along the flanks. Underside yellow with dark spots along sides. Diurnal to nocturnal (on warmer nights). Basks frequently on logs or vegetation at the water's edge.

N. sipedon (Linnaeus, 1758): **Northern Water Snake.** Central and eastern USA from S. Canada and the Great Lakes to the Gulf coast, but absent from most of the S.E. states.

Top Left: *Nerodia fasciata*. Photo: R. Anderson. Top Right: *Nerodia rhombifera*. Photo: R. Anderson. Center: *Nerodia fasciata pictiventris*, juvenile. Photo: R. T. Zappalorti. Bottom: *Nerodia fasciata fasciata*. Photo: K. T. Nemuras.

Top: *Nerodia harteri harteri*. Photo: Dr. S. Minton. Bottom: *Nerodia sipedon sipedon*. Photo: R. T. Zappalorti.

Top Left: *Nerodia sipedon sipedon*. Photo: J. Dommers. Top Right: *Nerodia taxispilota*. Photo: R. D. Bartlett. Bottom: *Nerodia rhombifera rhombifera*. Photo: R. D. Bartlett.

Found in or around lakes, ponds, rivers, streams, and swamps. Length to 130 cm (52 in). Reddish brown to gray or brownish black, with dark blotches on back and sides. Underside whitish to yellowish or gray with darker markings. Active day or night, often seen basking on rocks or tree stumps close to water. Feeds largely on fish, but also takes salamanders, small turtles, and crustaceans. Good terrarium subject.

Other species in the genus include *N. fasciata*, Southern Water Snake; *N. harteri*, Harter's Water Snake; and *N. taxispilota*, Brown Water Snake.

● *Oxyrhabdium* Boulenger, 1893: A genus containing two species native to the Philippines in tropical and montane rain forest to 2000 m (6500 ft). Length 60-80 cm (24-32 in). Head indistinct from body. Pointed snout. Semi-burrowing, living in ground litter. Feed on a variety of invertebrates and frogs. Require a warm humid terrarium with facilities to bathe.

O. modestum (Dumeril & Bibron, 1854) and *O. leporinum* (Guenther, 1858) are the species.

● *Paraptychophis* Lema, 1967: A genus containing a single species. A synonym of *Ptychophis* according to some workers.

P. meyeri Lema, 1967: Brazil, in the state of Rio Grande do Sul. Found in still and slow-flowing waters. Length to 60 cm. Head distinct from body. Keeled dorsal scales. Rear-fanged; venomous. Very aquatic, feeding on fish and frogs. Requires heated aqua-terrarium.

● *Pararhabdophis* Bourret, 1934: A genus containing a single species.

P. chapaensis Bourret, 1934: Indo-China. Similar to closely related *Rhabdophis* and *Pseudoxenodon*. Length to 90 cm (36 in).

● *Pliocercus* Cope, 1860: A genus containing seven species (several doubtful) found from tropical Mexico to the Amazon Basin. Inhabit lowland tropical forest. Length 30-80 cm (12-32 in). Head indistinct from body. Short-

Top: *Clonophis kirtlandii*, showing ventral pattern. Photo: Dr. S. Minton. Bottom: *Regina grahami*. Photo: J. Iverson.

• ***Pseudoeryx*** Fitzinger, 1826: A genus containing a single species.
P. plicatilis (Linnaeus, 1758): S. America, from Colombia to the Guianas and south to Argentina. In still and slow-moving waters of the tropical rain forest. Length to 145 cm (58 in) (female); 80 cm (32 in) (male). Small head indistinct from body. Small eyes and nostrils oriented upward. Dorsal scales large and smooth. Uniformly brown or with darker stripes. Very aquatic and nocturnal, feeding

Top: *Pliocercus elapoides*. Photo: L. Porras. Bottom: *Regina rigida*. Photo: Dr. S. Minton.

snouted. Banded with white, red, and black. Coral snake mimics. Terrestrial and active day or night near or in water. Feed on frogs and fish. Require an aqua-terrarium. Oviparous. Recently the species of *Pliocercus* have been combined with the species of the *Rhadinaea lateristriga* group as a distinctive genus, **Urotheca** Dumeril. This action combines coral snake mimics (*Pliocercus*) with brown-striped species. *Pliocercus* and *Rhadinaea* also often have been placed in different subfamilies, again pointing out the problems of generic and subfamily groups in the Colubridae.
   P. elapoides Cope, 1860: Mexico to Guatemala and Honduras.
   P. euryzonus Cope, 1862: Guatemala to Brazil and Colombia.

largely on fish. Requires an aqua-terrarium with a large, deep, heated water area.
• ***Pseudoxenodon*** Boulenger, 1890: A genus containing nine species native to Indo-China, eastward to S.E. China and southward to Indonesia. Most species are found in S.E. China. Inhabit monsoon, tropical, or montane rain forest to over 2000 m (6500 ft). Length 50-120 cm (20-48 in). Head distinct from body. Large eyes. Dorsal scales keeled. Rear-fanged and presumably venomous, though the action of the venom on humans (if any) is unknown; handle with care. Color and pattern very variable, the juvenile and adult markings often very different. Terrestrial and nocturnal, feeding on frogs, toads, and lizards. Require a large, heated, rain-forest terrarium with

facilities to bathe. Oviparous.

P. inornatus (Boie, 1827): Java.

P. jacobsoni (van Lidth de Jeude, 1922): Sumatra.

P. karlschmidti Pope, 1928: China (Fukien, Kwangsi, and Kwangtung).

P. macrops (Blyth, 1854): Nepal and eastward through Indo-China to S. China; also Malayan Peninsula.

● ***Ptychophis*** Gomes, 1915: A genus containing a single species.

P. flavovirgatus Gomes, 1915: States of Parana and Santa Catarina in Brazil. In still and slow-moving waters in rain forest. Length

to 60 cm (24 in). Head distinct from body. Dorsal scales strongly keeled. Rear-fanged, venomous. Very aquatic, feeding on fish and frogs. Requires a heated aqua-terrarium with a large body of water.

● ***Regina*** Baird, 1853: A genus containing four species native to the central and eastern USA. In and around rivers, lakes, and swamps. Length 35-80 cm (14-32 in). Dorsal scales smooth to strongly keeled. Feed on frogs and crustaceans. Require an aqua-terrarium with clean, filtered water.

R. alleni (Garman, 1874): **Striped Crayfish Snake.** S. Georgia and peninsular Florida.

Top: *Regina rigida rigida.* Photo: R. T. Zappalorti. Bottom: *Regina septemvittata.* Photo: R. T. Zappalorti.

Top: *Rhabdophis subminiatus*. Photo: R. D. Bartlett. Bottom: *Regina septemvittata*. Photo: Dr. S. Minton.

Length to 65 cm (26 in). Iridescent brown with wide yellow or orange stripe on flanks; three indistinct dark stripes along back. Underside yellow to orange-brown, marked with dark spots or blotches. Highly aquatic, often found among water hyacinths. Feeds mainly on crayfish. Ovo-viviparous, producing 6-36 young. Often placed in the genus *Liodytes* Cope, 1885.
R. grahami (Baird & Girard, 1853): **Graham's Crayfish Snake.** Central USA from Iowa and Illinois south to Louisiana and E. Texas. Length to 120 cm (48

in). Plain brown with a broad yellow stripe along flanks. Narrow black, irregular stripe along lower edge of yellow stripe. Sometimes a dark-bordered pale vertebral stripe. Belly dull yellow, usually marked with a median row of black spots. Secretive, often found under debris or in crayfish burrows. Feeds largely on crayfish but also frogs and snails. Ovoviviparous, producing 10-40 young.
R. rigida (Say, 1825): **Glossy Crayfish Snake.** Gulf coastal plain, from N.E. North Carolina to N. Florida and west to E. Texas. Length to 80 cm (32 in). Small headed, robust species. Shiny brown to olive with two faint dark stripes on back and two more stronger stripes on flanks. Underside yellow to cream with dark spots. Very secretive, concealing itself in mats of aquatic vegetation. Feeds on crayfish, salamanders, fish, frogs, and dragonfly nymphs. Ovoviviparous, producing 7-14 young.
R. septemvittata (Say, 1825): **Queen Snake.** From S. Great Lakes region almost to Gulf Coast. Light brown to olive or chocolate brown with yellow stripe on lower flanks. Sometimes three indistinct stripes along back. Belly yellow with brown stripes. Active day and night. Highly aquatic, feeding almost entirely on crayfish. Ovoviviparous, producing 5-25 young.
● ***Rhabdophis*** Fitzinger, 1843: A genus

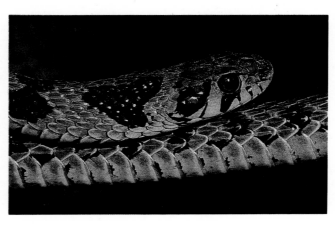

Top: *Rhabdophis subminiatus*. Photo: Dr. S. Minton. Center: *Rhabdophis swinhonis*. Photo: R. E. Kuntz. Bottom Left: *Rhabdophis swinhonis*. Photo: R. E. Kuntz. Bottom Right: *Rhabdophis tigrinus lateralis*. Photo: S. Kochetov.

Top Left: *Rhabdophis tigrinus lateralis.* Photo: S. Kochetov. Top Right: *Rhabdophis tigrinus,* juvenile. Photo: S. Kochetov. Bottom: *Seminatrix pygaea.* Photo: R. T. Zappalorti.

containing 12 species with a wide distribution in southern, eastern, and S.E. Asia. Length to 140 cm (56 in). Dorsal scales smooth to strongly keeled. Opisthoglyphic (rear-fanged) and venomous. Can be considered dangerous, as fatal bites to humans have been recorded from *R. tigrinus.* Color and pattern very variable among the species. Diurnal and amphibious, feeding on frogs and fish. Oviparous, producing up to 25 eggs. Require a heated aqua-terrarium.

R. chrysargus (Schlegel, 1837): Indo-China to Indonesia in tropical rain forest to 500 m (1600 ft). Feeds largely on toads.

R. subminiatus (Schlegel, 1837): **Red-necked Keelback.** Indo-China to S. China and Indonesia. Length to 105 cm (42 in). Greenish to olive above, sometimes with black and yellow pattern between scales. Neck marked with red between scales. Undersides yellow to whitish, sometimes with black spots.

R. tigrinus (Boie, 1827): **Yamakagashi, Tiger Keelback.** Far eastern USSR, Korea, Japan, Taiwan, and S. China. Very attractive coloration. Head steel-blue to dark gray or greenish with white labials. Wide chevrons of reddish brown along back, divided by narrower marks of steel-gray to greenish black.

● *Seminatrix* Cope, 1895: A genus containing

Top: *Seminatrix pygaea*. Photo: R. T. Zappalorti. Bottom: *Sinonatrix annularis*. Photo: Dr. S. Minton.

a single species.

S. pygaea (Cope, 1871): **Swamp Snake.** S.E. USA from coastal North Carolina to peninsular Florida and west to extreme S.E. Alabama. In cypress swamps, canals, ponds, and ditches. Length to 45 cm (18 in). Smooth dorsal scales. Glossy black with red underside. Largely aquatic, often found among mats of water plants. Feeds on a variety of invertebrates, small fish, and amphibians (will take earthworms in captivity). Requires an aqua-terrarium with a relatively large volume of water.

Ovoviviparous, producing 2-15 young.

● **Sinonatrix** Rossman & Eberle, 1977: A genus containing five species native to S.E. Asia. Closely related to and similar to the European *Natrix* species and requiring similar care but slightly warmer temperatures. Semi-aquatic, feeding on fish and amphibians.

S. aequifasciata (Barbour, 1908): S. China.

S. annularis (Hallowell, 1856): S. China.

S. percarinata (Boulenger, 1899): C. and S. China.

S. trianguligera (Boie, 1827): Malaysian Archipelago.

• ***Storeria*** Girard, 1853: **Brown Snakes.** A genus containing two species native to eastern USA and one species in Mexico. Found in various moist woodland habitats. Length 20-50 cm (8-20 in). Head distinct from body. Dorsal scales keeled.

S. dekayi (Holbrook, 1842): **Common Brown Snake.** Eastern half of N. America from S. Canada to Texas and into eastern Mexico. Found from moist uplands to lowland freshwater and saltwater marshes. Often common in residential areas. Length to 50 cm (20 in). Gray to brown or reddish brown. Indistinct dorsal stripe bordered by rows of darker spots. Underside pale yellow to tan or pinkish white with small black spots along edges. Diurnal, feeding on a variety of invertebrates (including earthworms, slugs, and snails). Requires a moist woodland terrarium. Ovoviviparous, producing 5-35 young.

S. occipitomaculata (Storer, 1839): **Red-bellied Snake.** Eastern half of N. America from S. Canada to E. Texas. In lowland to upland bogs and marshes. Plain brown, gray, or black with a single lighter stripe or four faint narrow dark stripes along back. Belly red, orange, or yellow.

Top: *Storeria dekayi dekayi*. Photo: R. T. Zappalorti. Bottom: *Storeria dekayi victa*. Photo: J. Iverson.

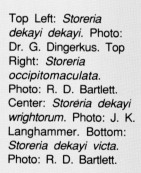

Top Left: *Storeria dekayi dekayi*. Photo: Dr. G. Dingerkus. Top Right: *Storeria occipitomaculata*. Photo: R. D. Bartlett. Center: *Storeria dekayi wrightorum*. Photo: J. K. Langhammer. Bottom: *Storeria dekayi victa*. Photo: R. D. Bartlett.

Top: *Storeria occipitomaculata*, showing typical reddish venter. Photo: Dr. S. Minton. Bottom: *Storeria occipitomaculata*, dark individual. Photo: J. Iverson.

Top: *Thamnophis brachystoma*. Photo: Dr. S. Minton. Bottom: *Thamnophis butleri*, albino. Photo: J. Gee.

Yellowish marks on nape of neck sometimes extend to form collar. Feeds on various invertebrates, especially slugs and earthworms, also small salamanders. Requires moist terrarium with facilities to bathe. Ovoviviparous, producing 1-21 young.

● ***Thamnophis*** Fitzinger, 1843: **Garter Snakes.** A genus containing about 22 species native to North and Central America. Very close to *Nerodia*, which sometimes is considered a subgenus. Found in a variety of habitats, including agricultural and residential areas. In view of their abundance, docile temperament, and ease of care, they are popular terrarium subjects ideally suited for beginners to snake-keeping. Length 30-130 cm (12-52 in). Head more or less distinct from body. Dorsal scales keeled. Most species striped and barred in various colors. Ovoviviparous. Require a moist terrarium with bathing facilities. Feed on earthworms and small fish. In captivity can be trained to take strips of raw meat or fish, but if this diet is the staple one, vitamin/mineral supplements must be included.

T. couchi (Kennicott, 1859): **Western Aquatic Garter Snake.** Coastal strip from S.W. Oregon to N. Baja California. In various aquatic habitats from brackish coastal marshes to ponds, lakes, rivers, and streams. Length to 130 cm (52 in). Color and pattern variable, usually three stripes or rows of spots and blotches in browns, yellows, and grays. Primarily diurnal, feeding on amphibians, fish, and invertebrates. Produces 10-25 young.

T. elegans (Baird & Girard, 1853): **Western**

Top Left: *Thamnophis elegans elegans*. Photo: R. Holland. Top and Center Right: *Thamnophis cyrtopsis*. Photos: Top: R. Holland; Center: K. H. Switak. Bottom: *Thamnophis butleri*. Photo: Dr. S. Minton.

Terrestrial Garter Snake. Western central N. America, from S. British Columbia and Manitoba southward into Mexico. In moist situations near ponds, lakes, streams, and rivers from sea level to 3200 m (10,500 ft). Length to 105 cm (42 in). Variable colors and markings, with stripes or rows of blotches or spots in grays, browns, or blacks. Diurnal and semi-terrestrial, but often takes to water if disturbed. Feeds on invertebrates, amphibians, fish, mice, and small birds. Produces 5-20 young.

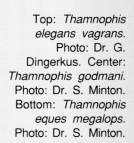

Top: *Thamnophis elegans vagrans.* Photo: Dr. G. Dingerkus. Center: *Thamnophis godmani.* Photo: Dr. S. Minton. Bottom: *Thamnophis eques megalops.* Photo: Dr. S. Minton.

Top Left: *Thamnophis hammondi*. Photo: R. D. Bartlett. Center Left: *Thamnophis marcianus*. Photo: R. Everhart. Top Right: *Thamnophis godmani*. Photo: R. D. Bartlett. Bottom: *Thamnophis marcianus*. Photo: K. Lucas, Steinhart.

Top Left: *Thamnophis marcianus*, albino juvenile. Photo: R. D. Bartlett. Top Right: *Thamnophis proximus rubrilineatus*. Photo: Dr. S. Minton. Bottom Left: *Thamnophis proximus proximus*. Photo: W. B. Allen, Jr. Bottom Right: *Thamnophis proximus*. Photo: J. K. Langhammer.

T. marcianus (Baird & Girard, 1853): **Checkered Garter Snake.** S.W. USA to N. Costa Rica. In arid areas but usually near permanent water. Length to 105 cm (42 in). Brown, olive, or tan with checkered pattern of black blotches. Yellow dorsal stripe. Mainly diurnal, feeding on amphibians, fish, and crayfish. Produces 6-18 young.

T. proximus (Say, 1823): **Western Ribbon Snake.** Central USA south to Costa Rica. Found at weedy margins of lakes, ponds, rivers, and streams from sea level to 2400 m (7800 ft). Length to 120 cm (48 in). Slender-bodied. Dark back and flanks with three well-defined longitudinal light brown, yellow, or reddish stripes. Mainly diurnal, feeding on frogs, tadpoles, and small fish. Produces 5-28 young.

T. sauritus (Linnaeus, 1766): **Eastern Ribbon Snake.** Eastern N. America from S. Canada to Florida and S.E. Louisiana. In moist, vegetated habitats near water. Length to 100 cm (39 in). Slender-bodied, similar to *T. proximus*. Dark back and flanks with three sharply defined bright yellow, whitish, or bluish longitudinal stripes. Mainly diurnal and semi-aquatic, feeding on amphibians and fish. Produces 3-25 young.

T. sirtalis (Linnaeus, 1766): **Common Garter Snake.** Most widely distributed snake in N. America. S. Canada and USA from Atlantic to Pacific coast, except desert regions of S.W. Always near water or in damp situations from sea level to 2400 m (7800 ft). Length to 130 cm (52 in). Highly variable coloration, but usually with well-defined

Top: *Thamnophis proximus*. Photo: B. Kahl. Bottom: *Thamnophis radix*. Photo: J. Iverson.

Top: *Thamnophis sauritus sackeni*. Photo: J. Iverson. Center: *Thamnophis scalaris*. Photo: Dr. S. Minton. Bottom Left: *Thamnophis hammondi*. Photo: K. H. Switak. Bottom Right: *Thamnophis sauritus*. Photo: Dr. G. Dingerkus.

Top Left: *Thamnophis sirtalis*. Photo: B. Kahl. Top Right: *Thamnophis sirtalis sirtalis*. Photo: R. T. Zappalorti. Bottom: *Thamnophis sirtalis sirtalis*, aberrant red phase. Photo: R. T. Zappalorti.

yellowish back and side stripes. Mainly diurnal, feeding on earthworms, amphibians, and fish. Produces 7-85 young. Probably the most commonly kept snake. Irritable when first captured, it will bite or expel musk, but it soon settles down, becoming docile and tame.

Other species in the genus that require similar care include **T. brachystoma**, Short-headed Garter Snake; **T. butleri**, Butler's Garter Snake; **T. cyrtopsis**, Black-necked Garter Snake; **T. eques**, Mexican Garter Snake; **T. ordinoides**, Northwestern Garter Snake; **T. radix**, Plains Garter Snake; and **T. rufipunctatus**, Narrow-headed Garter Snake.

Top: *Thamnophis sirtalis sirtalis*, melanistic. Photo: R. A. Winstel. Center: *Thamnophis sirtalis parietalis*. Photo: W. B. Allen, Jr. Bottom: *Thamnophis sirtalis sirtalis*. Photo: J. Iverson.

Thamnophis sirtalis parietalis. Photos: Top: J. Iverson; Bottom: R. Everhart.

Top: *Thamnophis sirtalis sirtalis*, aberrant stripeless individual. Photo: R. T. Zappalorti.
Bottom: *Thamnophis sirtalis similis*. Photo: J. Iverson.

Thamnophis sirtalis parietalis. Photo: B. Kahl.

Top: *Thamnophis sirtalis sirtalis*. Bottom: *Thamnophis sirtalis sirtalis*, albino. Photo: K. Lucas, Steinhart.

Top: *Thamnophis sirtalis tetrataenia*. Photo: W. B. Allen, Jr. Center: *Thamnophis sirtalis tetrataenia*. Photo: C. Banks. Bottom: *Thamnophis sirtalis infernalis*. Photo: K. Lucas, Steinhart.

T. pliolepis Cope, 1894: Costa Rica.
- *Tropidoclonion* Cope, 1860: A genus containing a single species.

T. lineatum (Hallowell, 1856): Central USA from South Dakota to Texas. Isolated populations in other states. Similar to *Thamnophis* in appearance but less aquatic. Found on open prairie, woodland margins, and suburban residential areas. Length to 50 cm (20 in). Light to dark olive-gray to brown with three distinct light longitudinal stripes. Crepuscular and nocturnal, hiding during the day under ground debris. Feeds largely on earthworms. Requires a warm woodland terrarium. Ovoviviparous, producing 2-12 young.

- *Virginia* Girard, 1853: **Earth Snakes.** A genus containing two species native to eastern USA. Found in various moist habitats. Length 20-35 cm (8-14 in). Secretive, hiding under litter and feeding on invertebrates and small amphibians. Require a semi-humid woodland terrarium with adequate dry hiding places.

V. striatula (Linnaeus, 1766): **Rough Earth Snake.** E. Virginia to N. Florida, west to S. Missouri and E. Texas. Length to 32.5 cm (13 in). Keeled dorsal scales. Pointed snout. Plain

Top: *Thamnophis sirtalis tetrataenia.* Photo: K. Lucas, Steinhart. Bottom: *Tropidoclonion lineatum.* Photo: Dr. S. Minton.

- *Trimetopon* Cope, 1885: A genus containing ten species native to Central America in tropical rain forest. Length 30-40 cm (12-16 in). Terrestrial snakes. Biology poorly known.
T. gracile (Guenther, 1872): Costa Rica.

Tropidoclonion lineatum. Top: Texas; Bottom: Kansas. Photos: J. Iverson.

Virginia valeriae valeriae. Photos: J. Iverson.

Top: *Xenochrophis cerasogaster*. Bottom: *Virginia valeriae elegans*. Photos: Dr. S. Minton.

Top: *Xenochrophis cerasogaster*, showing ventral pattern. Photo: Dr. S. Minton. Bottom: *Xenochrophis piscator*. Photo: R. E. Kuntz.

brown to gray above, whitish or yellowish below. Ovoviviparous, producing 3-12 young.
V. valeriae (Baird & Girard, 1853): **Smooth Earth Snake.** New Jersey to N. Florida and west to Kansas, Oklahoma, and Texas. Length to 35 cm (14 in). Similar to preceding species, but with smooth dorsal scales. Produces 2-14 young.

● ***Xenelaphis*** Guenther, 1864: A genus containing two species native to Indo-China and Malaysian Archipelago. Found near bodies of water. Length to 200 cm (80 in). Smooth, hexagonal dorsal scales. Light and dark brown markings. Amphibious, feeding largely on frogs. Require a large aqua-terrarium with heated and filtered water.
X. ellipsifer Boulenger, 1900: Borneo.
X. hexagonotus (Cantor, 1847): Thailand and Vietnam to Borneo and Java.

● ***Xenochrophis*** Guenther, 1864: A genus containing five species native to S.E. Asia found in and around bodies of water. Length to 130 cm (52 in). Head indistinct from body, with an extended and pointed rostral shield. Eyes relatively small. Brown with varying patterns of lighter or darker shades. Semi-aquatic to almost wholly aquatic. Feed largely on fish. Require a large aqua-terrarium with

heated water. Oviparous, laying about 20 eggs.

X. cerasogaster (Cantor, 1839): Pakistan and N. India. Length to 75 cm (30 in). Very aquatic.

X. piscator (Schneider, 1799): **Asiatic Water Snake.** Pakistan to S. China, south to Indo-Australian Archipelago.

X. vittata (Linnaeus, 1758): Sumatra, Java, Celebes. Light brown with dark brown stripes.

Top and Center: *Enhydris chinensis.* Photos: R. E. Kuntz. Bottom Left: *Xenochrophis piscator.* Photo: H. Hansen. Upper Bottom Right: *Xenochrophis piscator.* Photo: R. E. Kuntz. Lower Bottom Right: *Xenochrophis flavipunctatus.* Photo: M. J. Cox.

SUBFAMILY HOMALOPSINAE

A subfamily containing 11 genera and about 35 species ranging from India through Indo-China and the Indo-Australian archipelago to N. Australia. Very aquatic snakes found in fresh to brackish water; some species are even seen far out to sea and have populated estuaries and mangrove swamps on many islands. All are opisthoglyphic, with well-formed, grooved venom fangs in the rear of the upper jaw. Although the venom is not regarded as dangerous to humans, these species should be treated with the respect any venomous snake

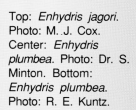

Top: *Enhydris jagori.* Photo: M. J. Cox. Center: *Enhydris plumbea.* Photo: Dr. S. Minton. Bottom: *Enhydris plumbea.* Photo: R. E. Kuntz.

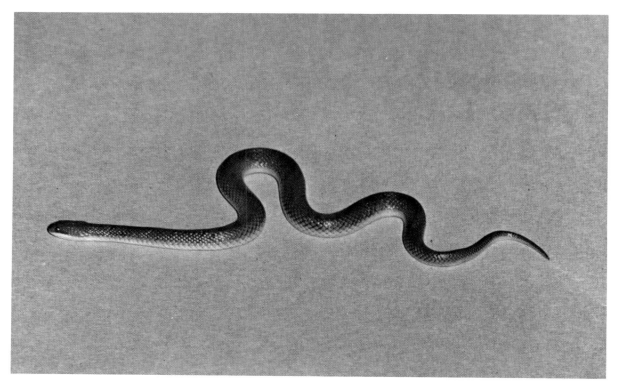

deserves. Eyes and valved nostrils are directed upward, a typical characteristic of aquatic animals.

- ***Bitia*** Gray, 1842: A genus containing a single species.

    B. hydroides Gray, 1842: From S. Burma through the Malayan Peninsula to Sumatra. Usually found in estuaries. Length to 50 cm (20 in). Small head indistinct from robust body. Small head shields. Smooth, overlapping dorsal scales. Broad belly scales keeled at edges. Tail laterally flattened. Grayish to brownish with darker crossbands. Requires a heated brackish water aquarium. Feeds on fish.

- ***Cerberus*** Cuvier, 1829: A genus containing two species ranging, in coastal areas, from India through the whole of S.E. Asia to N. Australia. Often common in brackish waters of estuaries but occasionally seen far out at sea. Length to 100 cm (39 in) (female); 75 cm (30 in) (male). Head distinct from body. Relatively large eyes. Dorsal scales keeled. Brownish to grayish, with or without darker markings. Undersides whitish. Dark stripe through eye and neck region. Feed largely on fish and crustaceans. Require a heated brackish aquarium.

    C. rhynchops (Schneider, 1799): **Bockadam.** Coastal areas of S.E. Asia to N. Australia.

- ***Enhydris*** Latreille, 1801: A genus containing about 16 species found from India through the whole of S.E. Asia to N. Australia. More likely to be encountered on land or in fresh water than other genera in the subfamily, though some species are found largely in brackish water. Common in and near paddy fields in some areas. Length 50-150 cm (20-60 in). Robust and short-tailed. Head more or less distinct from body. Dorsal scales smooth. Color and pattern variable from plain browns and olives to complex markings. Mainly diurnal, feeding on frogs and fish. Require a large heated aqua-terrarium. Usually remain vicious and bad-tempered, biting readily if handled. Ovoviviparous, producing 10-30 young.

    E. bocourti (Jan, 1865): Thailand, Kampuchea, and Malaysia. Length to 150 cm (60 in), males relatively shorter. Attractive dark and light color pattern.

    E. chinensis (Gray, 1842): **Chinese Water Snake.** N. Vietnam to S. China and Taiwan. Length to 75 cm (30 in). Brown to gray with small black blotches. Yellow, orange, or pinkish stripe along flanks.

    E. enhydris (Schneider, 1799): N. India to Malaysia. Common in cultivated areas (paddy fields).

    E. plumbea (Boie, 1827): **Rice Paddy Snake.** Burma to S. China and Taiwan, south through Indo-Australian Archipelago. Length to 60 cm (24 in). Drab olive above, yellowish below.

E. polylepis (Fischer, 1866): **Macleay's Water Snake.** New Guinea and N. Australia. Olive-brown to black above; lower flanks spotted with black and cream.

- ***Erpeton*** Lacepede, 1800: A genus containing a single species.

    E. tentaculatum Lacepede, 1800: **Tentacle Snake.** Indo-China and S. China. Almost totally aquatic, found in slow-moving and stagnant waters. Length to 70-90 cm (28-36 in). Head distinct from body. Two characteristic soft, scale-covered tentacles about 12 mm long protrude forward from just in front of nostrils. The function of these tentacles is not fully understood, but it seems they play some part in detecting or attracting prey. Keeled dorsal scales. Prehensile tail used to anchor itself to aquatic plants, etc. Brown with two dark dorso-lateral stripes; a further black stripe divided by white along the flanks. Undersides yellowish brown with dark spots. Feeds on small fish. Requires a heated, planted aquarium with slightly acid water (pH 6.0–6.5). Ovoviviparous, producing 9-15 young.

Top: *Enhydris plumbea.* Photo: R. E. Kuntz. Bottom: *Erpeton tentaculatum.* Photo: K. H. Switak.

Homalopsis buccata.
Photo: M. J. Cox.

● *Fordonia* Gray, 1842: A genus containing a single species.
F. leucobalia (Schlegel, 1837): From Bangladesh and along the coasts of South East Asia and the Indo-Australian Archipelago to N. Australia. Found in brackish or salt water in estuaries and mangrove swamps. Sometimes seen far out at sea. Length to 100 cm (39 in) (female); 75 cm (30 in) (male). Smallish head indistinct from robust body. Smooth dorsal scales and relatively short tail. Dorsal surface brown to reddish, yellowish, or blackish, often with lighter spots and blotches; underside yellowish white. Feeds on small fish and crabs, which it quickly overpowers with its venom (rear-fanged). Requires an aqua-terrarium with salt water.
● *Homalopsis* Kuhl & van Hasselt, 1822: A genus containing a single species.
H. buccata (Linnaeus, 1758): Southern Burma and through the Indo-Australian Archipelago, but not to New Guinea or Australia. May be found in fresh (often in paddy fields) or brackish water and often on adjacent land. Length to 130 cm (52 in). Large head distinct from body. Keeled dorsal

scales. Dark brown with or without lighter bands, contrasting with the yellowish white underside. Feeds mainly on fish. Requires a large, heated, planted aqua-terrarium with a dry land area. Ovoviviparous, producing 10-20 young.
● *Hurria* Daudin, 1803: A genus containing a single species. There are nomenclatural problems with this name as well as biological ones, and it probably will be changed eventually.
H. microlepis (Boulenger, 1896): A rare species from coastal areas of the Philippines. Similar to the closely related *Cerberus*. Biology poorly known.
● *Myron* Gray, 1849: A genus containing a single species.
M. richardsoni Gray, 1849: Coastal areas of New Guinea, adjacent islands, and N. Australia in mangrove swamps. Length to 60 cm (24 in). Gray, brown, or olive-brown above with darker head and irregular crossbands along body that extend into the yellowish underside. Feeds on crabs and fish. Requires a brackish water aqua-terrarium.

SUBFAMILY BOIGINAE

This subfamily contains about 73 genera and some 330 species, the majority of which are native to Africa and tropical America. A few genera are found in N. America, Europe, and Asia, while Australia has just a single genus. All are opisthoglyphic with grooved venom fangs at the rear of the upper jaw, these varying in size depending on the species. The toxicity of the venom to humans is varied, but fatal bites have been recorded from the genera *Dispholidus*, *Thelotornis*, and *Boiga*. All species in the subfamily should be treated with respect, remembering that the reaction to venom varies from person to person and that antivenin is available only for the highly dangerous Boomslang (*Dispholidus typus*). The species have colonized varying habitats, so details of their captive care will depend on the climatic zones and microclimates to which they are native. With a few isolated exceptions, all species in the subfamily are oviparous.

Like the other subfamilies of colubrid snakes, there is considerable controversy about whether or not this is a natural group. Many authorities consider the Boiginae to be an artificial grouping representing varied lineages of otherwise unrelated snakes that have independently developed the rear-fang condition. Such authorities doubt that Old and New World rear-fangs are related, but instead represent parallel evolution from unrelated

ancestors. The Boignae (like the other subfamilies) should be considered a convenient group but not necessarily a "real" subfamily.

- ● *Ahaetulla* Link, 1807: A genus containing eight species native to S.E. Asia in tropical rain and monsoon forests; some are in montane rain forest to 1800 m (5800 ft).

Top: *Erpeton tentaculatum*. Photo: J. K. Langhammer. Bottom: *Ahaetulla nasuta*. Photo: K. T. Nemuras.

Top Left: *Ahaetulla nasuta*. Photo: C. Banks. Top Right: *Ahaetulla prasina*. Photo: M. J. Cox. Bottom Left: *Ahaetulla prasina*. Photo: R. D. Bartlett. Bottom Right: *Ahaetulla prasina*. Photo: B. Kahl.

Length 60-200 cm (24-80 in). Extremely slender and elongated, with a long narrow head distinct from the body. The snout runs to a fine point or wedge. The large eyes have horizontal pupils shaped like a figure-8 lying on its side. A groove runs from the front of the eye along the snout, giving this genus the possibility of binocular vision, a phenomenon highly unusual among snakes. The dorsal scales are smooth and overlapping and the body is laterally compressed. Totally arboreal snakes that have difficulty moving over flat ground. Feed largely on lizards (especially geckos) and can recognize immobile prey by sight. In captivity, the snakes often can be persuaded to take small fish (guppies, for example) from a very shallow dish of water. Mainly diurnal. Require a tall, planted, humid terrarium with adequate climbing facilities. Oviparous, but the young may hatch during oviposition or shortly after.

Ahaetulla formerly was called **Dryophis,** a synonym and invalid name that should not be used.

A. mycterizans (Linnaeus, 1758): Malaya and Java. Length to 120 cm (48 in). Green to gray-green with a white lateral stripe. Underside lighter green to yellow.
A. nasuta (Lacepede, 1789): **Long-nosed Tree Snake.** Sri Lanka and India to Thailand. Length to 200 cm (80 in) (female), 130 cm (52 in) (male). Green to gray or pinkish gray.
A. prasina (Boie, 1827): Eastern Himalayas through Indo-China to Malaysian Archipelago. Snout somewhat shorter than in other species of the genus.
• *Alluaudina* Mocquard, 1894: A genus containing two species native to Madagascar in tropical rain forest. Length 30-50 cm (12-20 in). Large head distinct from body. Keeled

Top: *Amplorhinus multimaculatus.* Photo: J. Visser. Center: *Boiga cyanea.* Photo: M. J. Cox. Bottom: *Boiga cynodon.* Photo: J. Kellnhauser.

dorsal scales. Brown to olive with rows of darker spots. Biology poorly known; probably nocturnal and terrestrial, feeding on frogs and lizards.

A. bellyi Mocquard, 1894: Northern Madagascar.

A. mocquardi Angel, 1939: N.E. Madagascar.

- ***Amplorhinus*** A. Smith, 1847: A genus containing a single species.

A. multimaculatus A. Smith, 1847: **Cape Reed Snake.** Southern Africa, in damp marshlands, reed beds, etc. Length to 70 cm (28 in). Head indistinct from body. Lightly keeled dorsal scales. Green to olive-green or brown above, more or less uniform or with longitudinal series of dark brown to black spots. Undersides dull green to sooty bluish gray. Feeds largely on frogs. Requires a heated, planted aqua-terrarium with dry resting sites. Very aggressive. Ovoviviparous, producing four or five young.

- ***Apostolepis*** Cope, 1862: A genus containing 14 species native to South America, from the Guianas to Peru and south to Argentina. In dryer areas of the tropical forest. Length 25-65 cm (10-26 in). Head indistinct from body; relatively small eyes. Color and markings variable, but usually with a pattern of stripes. Terrestrial and semi-burrowing, feeding on earthworms, insects, and small reptiles. Require a terrarium with deep, loose substrate. Oviparous.

A. assimilis (Reinhardt, 1861): Central to S.W. Brazil and Argentina.

A. flavotorquata (Dumeril, Bibron & Dumeril, 1854): Central Brazil.

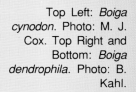

Top Left: *Boiga cynodon*. Photo: M. J. Cox. Top Right and Bottom: *Boiga dendrophila*. Photo: B. Kahl.

● ***Boiga*** Fitzinger, 1826: A genus containing about 25 species found mainly in Africa and Asia, but one species reaches Australia. Found in a variety of habitats from dry brushland to mangrove swamp, depending on the species. Length 80-250 cm (32-100 in). Head usually distinct from laterally compressed body. Large eyes. Variety of colors and patterns. All are nocturnal and, with one exception (*B. trigonota*), all species in the genus are arboreal. They feed on frogs, reptiles, birds, and small

Top: *Boiga fusca.*
Photo: Dr. S. Minton.
Bottom Left: *Boiga irregularis.* Photo: C.
Banks. Bottom Right:
Boiga dendrophila.
Photo: B. Kahl.

mammals. Require a tall, humid, planted terrarium with adequate climbing facilities. Most species are aggressive and the venom can be dangerous, so treat them with respect. Oviparous.

B. blandingi (Hallowell, 1844): **Blanding's Tree Snake.** Forests of tropical central Africa. Length to 240 cm (96 in). Adults almost uniformly black, juveniles brown with dark crossbands.

B. ceylonensis (Guenther, 1858): Sri Lanka.

Top and Center: *Boiga irregularis*, red phase. Photos: J. Kellnhauser. Bottom: *Boiga jaspidea*. Photo: S. Patramangor.

Length to 130 cm (52 in).

B. cyanea (Dumeril & Bibron, 1854): **Green Cat Snake.** N. India, over Indo-China to S. China. Length to 190 cm (76 in). Green above and lighter green below. Feeds mainly on other snakes.

B. cynodon (Boie, 1827): **Dog-toothed Cat Snake.** From Burma through Malaya to the Indonesian Archipelago. Length to 170 cm (68 in). Buff to brownish or grayish above with series of darker brown or black bars along body. Undersides yellowish or grayish with small black or gray spots. Feeds mainly on birds.

B. dendrophila (Boie, 1827): **Mangrove Snake.** Thailand through Malaysia and Indonesia to the Philippines. Length to 250 cm (100 in). Attractively marked with narrow bright yellow irregular bands on glossy black. Popular terrarium subject, but beware of possible envenomation.

B. irregularis (Merrem, 1802): **Brown Tree Snake.** From Indonesia to New Guinea and N. and E. Australia. Length to 200 cm (80 in). Color very variable, from brown to bright reddish brown or cream with numerous irregular darker or lighter crossbands. Undersides cream to pinkish.

B. multimaculata (Boie, 1827): **Many-spotted Cat Snake.** Indo-China, S. China, and Indonesian Archipelago. Length to 100

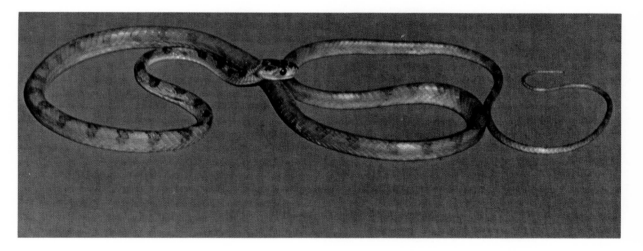

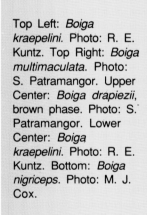

Top Left: *Boiga kraepelini*. Photo: R. E. Kuntz. Top Right: *Boiga multimaculata*. Photo: S. Patramangor. Upper Center: *Boiga drapiezii*, brown phase. Photo: S. Patramangor. Lower Center: *Boiga kraepelini*. Photo: R. E. Kuntz. Bottom: *Boiga nigriceps*. Photo: M. J. Cox.

Chrysopelea ornata. Photos: Top: K. T. Nemuras; Bottom: B. Kahl.

cm (39 in). Gray to grayish brown above, with series of round dark brown spots. Undersides whitish with brown spots. Feeds mainly on lizards, especially geckos.

B. pulverulenta (Fischer, 1856): Central African forests. Length to 110 cm (44 in). Brown with darker crossbands.

B. trigonata (Schneider, 1802): Soviet Central Asia south to central India. Length to 95 cm (38 in). The subspecies *B. t. melanocephala* is particularly attractive, having a black head, reddish brown body, and a dorsal row of dark-bordered whitish diamonds. Unlike other members of the genus, this species is terrestrial and requires a dry terrarium heated to 28°C during the day and cooled to 15°C or less at night. A winter temperature reduction is also recommended.

• ***Chamaetortus*** Guenther, 1864: A genus containing a single species. Possibly a synonym of *Dipsadoboa*.

C. aulicus Guenther, 1864: **Cross-barred Snake.** Eastern, central, and southern Africa in moist habitats. Length to 70 cm (28 in). Head distinct from body. Large eyes with vertical pupils. Smooth dorsal scales. Brown with small white spots or dark-edged bands. Nocturnal and semi-arboreal, feeding largely on frogs. Requires a heated woodland terrarium.

• ***Choristocalamus*** Witte & Laurent, 1947: A genus containing a single species. Considered by some workers to be a synonym or subgenus of *Amblyodipsas*, here treated as an aparallactine mole viper. Conflicts such as this show the highly subjective nature of most colubrid subfamilies.

C. concolor (A. Smith, 1849): Natal and N. Transvaal (South Africa). Length to 35 cm (14 in). Uniformly dark brown. Semi-burrowing, feeding on subterranean invertebrates and small vertebrates. Requires a terrarium with a deep, loose substrate.

• ***Chrysopelea*** Boie, 1826: **Flying Snakes.** A genus containing five species native to India and S.E. Asia. Found in the canopies of tropical and monsoon rain forests. Length 90-150 cm (36-60 in). Longish head set off distinctly from slender body. Square snout, large eyes, and long tail. Dorsal scales smooth. Diurnal and sun-loving. Extremely fast and agile, feeding mainly on lizards. Common name comes from ability to hang-glide by launching the body into air and a forming concave undersurface. Can glide a considerable distance to lower landing place when pursuing or being pursued. Oviparous. Require a roomy, tall, humid but well-ventilated terrarium, preferably planted and with adequate climbing facilities.

C. ornata (Shaw, 1802): **Golden Flying Snake.** India and Sri Lanka to Indo-China, S. China, and Malayan Peninsula. Green to yellow with black spots or bars.

C. paradisi Boie, 1827: **Paradise Flying**

Top: *Boiga trigonata*. Photo: J. Kellnhauser. Bottom: *Chrysopelea ornata*. Photo: K. T. Nemuras.

Top Left: *Chrysopelea ornata*. Photo: B. Kahl. Top Right: *Clelia rustica*. Photo: M. Freiberg. Bottom: *Clelia clelia*, juvenile pattern. Photo: Dr. S. Minton.

Snake. Indo-China, Malaysia, Sumatra, Java, and Borneo. Yellowish to reddish brown with black reticulations.

C. pelias (Linnaeus, 1758): **Banded Flying Snake.** Malaysia and Sumatra. Greenish to yellowish with broken blackish bands.

C. rhodopleuron (Boie, 1827): Moluccas and adjacent islands.

C. taprobanica M. Smith, 1943: S. India and Sri Lanka.

Top: *Clelia occipitolutea*. Photo: F. Achaval. Center: *Clelia clelia clelia*, adult. Photo: M. Freiberg. Bottom: *Clelia rustica*. Photo: H. Piacentini.

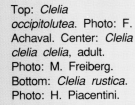

● *Clelia* Fitzinger, 1826: **Mussuranas.** A genus containing six species native to Central and South America east of the Andes in forest margins and riverine woodland. Length to 250 cm (100 in). Head more or less distinct from robust body. Nocturnal to partially diurnal. Terrestrial, feeding on lizards and snakes, especially venomous ones (e.g., *Bothrops*). They bite into the neck of prey and constrict powerfully. *Clelia* seem to be immune to crotalid venom. Oviparous, laying up to 40 eggs. Require a large, heated, dry to semi-humid woodland terrarium with facilities to hide, climb, and bathe.

C. clelia (Daudin, 1803): **Mussurana.** Belize and Guatemala south to Argentina. Juveniles are reddish brown with a black head and a yellow collar followed by a black band. As the reptile matures the head colors fade until the snake becomes uniformly blue-black. A popular and docile terrarium subject that rarely attempts to bite humans but should nevertheless be handled with care.

Top: *Coniophanes imperialis*. Bottom: *Coniophanes piceivittis*. Photos: Dr. S. Minton.

- *Coniophanes* Hallowell, 1860: A genus containing 12 species found from Texas through Central America to Ecuador and Peru in varied habitats from moist forest margins to semi-arid brushland. Length 50-75 cm (20-30 in). Head indistinct from body. Terrestrial, feeding on frogs, lizards, and small mammals. Require a heated, dry to slightly humid terrarium with adequate hiding places.
C. imperialis (Baird, 1859): **Black-striped Snake.** Texas to S. Central America in semi-arid coastal plain. Length to 50 cm (20 in). Light brown with three dark brown to blackish stripes, a thin one along midback and a broader one along either side. Undersides pink, red, or orange. Crepuscular and nocturnal, hiding under ground litter during the day. Oviparous, laying two to ten eggs.
C. fissidens (Guenther, 1858): Mexico to Ecuador.
- *Crotaphopeltis* Fitzinger, 1843: A genus containing two species native to tropical and southern Africa. In dry to moist habitats. Length to 100 cm (39 in). Short, flat, broad head. Cylindrical body with smooth dorsal scales and a long tail. Oviparous, laying up to 12 eggs.
C. degeni (Boulenger, 1898): Central E. Africa. Amphibious, feeding mainly on frogs.

Requires a heated aqua-terrarium.

C. hotamboeia (Laurenti, 1768): **Herald, Red-lipped, or White-lipped Snake.** E. to S. Africa. Length to 100 cm (39 in). Gray to olive-brown or blackish above, uniform or with pale, elongate specks. Upper lip red, yellow, or white. Underside white to creamy white. Feeds largely on frogs and toads. Requires a dry, heated terrarium but with facilities to bathe.

- ***Dipsadoboa*** Guenther, 1858: A genus containing four species native to tropical Africa in rain and riverine forests. Length 90-110 cm (36-44 in). Slender, with laterally compressed body. Head distinct from body. Very large eyes with vertical pupils. Arboreal and nocturnal, feeding largely on frogs. Require a tall, planted, rain-forest terrarium with adequate climbing facilities. Oviparous, laying up to six eggs.

D. unicolor Guenther, 1858: Guinea east to Uganda. Uniform grass-green to olive-brown above, darker between scales. Underside greenish to yellow. Underside of tail bluish black.

D. duchesni (Boulenger, 1901): Guinea to Ghana. Light brown to greenish brown.

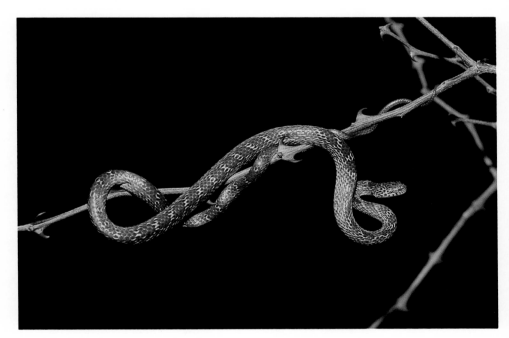

- ***Dispholidus*** Duvernoy, 1832: **Boomslang.** A genus containing a single species.

D. typus (A. Smith, 1829): **Boomslang.** Africa, from Senegal and Eritrea south to the Cape in savannah and brushland. Length to 170 cm (68 in). Short head distinct from body. Large eyes. Dorsal scales keeled. Uniformly green to brown or blackish above; scales may be darker edged. Underside yellowish to gray-green. Chin whitish. Diurnal, arboreal snakes that seldom descend to ground level. Feed on lizards, frogs, birds, and small mammals; also other snakes. Require a tall, dry, heated terrarium with facilities to climb. Oviparous, laying 8-24 eggs in the substrate.

Warning: This is probably the most dangerous of the opisthoglyphs, having caused many human fatalities. Even professional herpetologists have fallen victim. The long, grooved venom fangs are set relatively far forward below the eyes. When annoyed, the snake spreads the neck region vertically and strikes aggressively. A South African antivenin is available, and any would-be keeper of this species is advised to have stocks of the serum at hand.

Top: *Crotaphopeltis hotamboeia.* Photo: K. H. Switak.
Center: *Chamaetortus aulicus* (= *Dipsadoboa aulica*).
Photo: K. H. Switak.
Bottom: *Dispholidus typus.* Photo: J. Visser.

Dispholidus typus.
Photos: Top: Dr. G.
Dingerkus; Bottom: R.
T. Zappalorti.

● *Drepanoides* Dunn, 1928: A genus
containing a single species.
D. anomalus (Jan, 1863): S. Colombia to
central Bolivia. Length to 35 cm (14 in). Head
indistinct from body. Uniformly reddish
brown, with tip of the snout black and also a
black collar. Terrestrial, semi-burrowing snake
feeding on invertebrates and small
vertebrates. Requires a terrarium with deep,
loose substrate.
● *Dromophis* Peters, 1869: A genus containing
two species native to tropical Africa in marsh
and riverine areas. Length to 100 cm (39 in).
Morphologically similar to *Psammophis*, but
amphibious, feeding largely on frogs. Require
a planted aqua-terrarium.
D. lineatus (Dumeril & Bibron,

1854): **Striped Swamp Snake.** Sudan to
Guinea-Bissau and Zimbabwe and South
Africa. Olive-brown to greenish with dark-
edged scales and three well-defined greenish
yellow longitudinal stripes. Underside pale
green to greenish yellow. Oviparous.
● *Dryophiops* Boulenger, 1896: A genus
containing a single species. Sometimes treated
as a subgenus of *Chrysopelea*.
D. rubescens (Gray, 1834): Malaysia and
Indonesia. In rain forest. Length to 80 cm (32
in). Longish head set off from body by narrow
neck. Slender, laterally compressed body;
very long tail. Eyes with horizontal pupils
(similar to those of *Ahaetulla*). Smooth dorsal
scales. Reddish brown above with small black
spots. Arboreal, feeding mainly on lizards.
Requires a tall rain-forest terrarium.
● *Elapomojus* Jan, 1862: A doubtful genus
containing a single species. Often treated as a
synonym of *Apostolepis*, but considered by
some to be a synonym of *Elapomorphus*.
E. dimidiatus Jan, 1862: Brazil. Biology and
husbandry poorly documented.
● *Elapomorphus* Wiegmann, 1843: A genus
containing eight species found from N.E.
Brazil to Argentina in tropical rain forest.

Length 20-30 cm (8-12 in). Head indistinct from body. Small eyes. Smooth dorsal scales. Terrestrial burrowing snakes feeding on insects, worms, and small reptiles. Require a terrarium with deep, loose substrate.

E. bilineatus Dumeril, Bibron & Dumeril, 1854: S. Brazil, Uruguay, Paraguay, and Argentina. Dark head with a light collar; light brownish body with two dark stripes.

E. quinquelineatus (Raddi, 1820): Eastern and Central Brazil. Five dark longitudinal stripes on lighter ground.

● ***Enulius*** Cope, 1871: A genus containing three species found from S.W. Mexico to Colombia in tropical forest. Length 30-40 cm (12-16 in). Head indistinct from body. Shovel-shaped rostral overhanging mouth. Burrowing snakes. Biology poorly known.

E. flavitorques (Cope, 1869): S. Mexico to Colombia.

● ***Erythrolamprus*** Boie, 1826: **False Coral Snakes.** A genus containing six species native

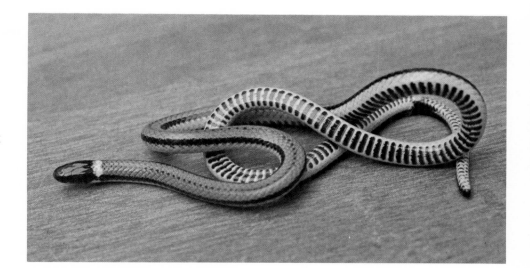

Top: *Elapomorphus bilineatus*. Photo: M. Freiberg.
Center: *Enulius flavitorques*, juvenile. Photo: P. Freed.
Bottom: *Erythrolamprus aesculapii*, male. Photo: K. H. Switak.

Top: *Erythrolamprus aesculapii*. Photo: A. I. Grasso. Bottom: *Erythrolamprus bizonus*. Photo: J. Iverson.

particularly snakes, including venomous species. Require a heated, semi-humid, forest terrarium with adequate hiding places.

E. aesculapii (Linnaeus, 1766): Amazon region to Tobago.

E. mimus (Cope, 1868): Honduras and Nicaragua to Peru.

● ***Ficimia*** Gray, 1849: **Hook-nosed Snakes.** A genus containing five species found from S.W. USA through Mexico to Honduras in dryer habitats. Closely related to *Gyalopion*. Length 30-45 cm (12-18 in). Head indistinct from body. Snout upturned into a hook-like point. Burrowing snakes feeding on spiders and centipedes. Require a terrarium with deep, loose substrate for burrowing.

F. olivacea Gray, 1849: **Mexican Hook-nosed Snake.** S.W. Texas to Veracruz (Mexico) in thorn forest to montane forest from sea level to 1500 m (4900 ft). Length to 50 cm (20 in). Light brown to buff with dark bars along body. Underside whitish.

F. publia Cope, 1866: Mexico to Honduras.

● ***Geodipsas*** Boulenger, 1896: A genus containing six species native to central Africa and Madagascar. In rain forest to dryer brushland. Length 35-80 cm (14-32 in). Head distinct from body. Large eyes with round

to Central and South America, from Nicaragua to S. Brazil in tropical forest. Length 60-100 cm (24-40 in). Head more or less distinct from body. Coral snake mimics in black, red, and yellow or white bands. Nocturnal and terrestrial, feeding on reptiles,

Top: *Erythrolamprus mimus*. Photo: J. Kellnhauser. Center: *Erythrolamprus aesculapii*. Photo: S. Kochetov. Bottom: *Ficimia streckeri*. Photos: P. Freed.

pupils. Nocturnal and terrestrial, feeding mainly on frogs. Require a heated, semi-humid terrarium.

G. boulengeri (Peracca, 1892): Madagascar. Brown with light flecks along flanks.

G. depressiceps (Werner, 1897): Cameroons to Uganda. Light head, darker body.

G. infralineata (Guenther, 1882): E. Madagascar. Brownish with darker longitudinal stripes.

● ***Gomesophis*** Hoge & Mertens, 1959: A genus containing a single species.

G. brasiliensis (Gomes, 1918): Eastern Brazil in tropical forest. Length to 70 cm. Head indistinct from body. Semi-burrowing, requiring a terrarium with a deep, loose substrate. Biology poorly known.

Top: *Gyalopion quadrangularis.* Photo: K. Lucas, Steinhart.
Bottom: *Hemirhagerrhis nototaenia.* Photo: J. Visser.

● *Gyalopion* Cope, 1860: A genus containing three species found from S.W. USA to Mexico. Length 30-40 cm (12-16 in). Closely related to *Ficimia* (and often synonymized with it), with an upturned, pointed snout. Burrowing snakes feeding on spiders, centipedes, and scorpions. Require a terrarium with a deep, loose substrate for burrowing.

G. canum Cope, 1860: **Western Hook-nosed Snake.** W. Texas to S.E. Arizona and S. to central Mexico in arid brushlands. Length to 35 cm (14 in). Pale brown, marked with dark-edged brown crossbands. Oviparous.

● *Hemirhagerrhis* Boettger, 1896: **Bark Snakes.** A genus containing two species native to E. and S. Africa. Very close to *Amplorhinus.* In savannah and mountains to 1800 m (5850 ft). Length to 40 cm (16 in). Narrow head more or less distinct from slender body. Smooth dorsal scales. Usually brownish with darker bands or zig-zag markings. Feed largely on lizards. Require a heated, dry terrarium. Oviparous, laying two to four eggs.

H. nototaenia (Guenther, 1864): **Bark Snake.** Central and S. Africa. Length to 40 cm (16 in). Ash-gray to grayish brown above with a double series of dark spots forming an indistinct but attractive zig-zag pattern. Underside paler, with dark spots. Often found under the loose bark of trees where it hunts lizards and skinks. Loose bark or hollow branches are useful for terrarium decoration for this species. Very docile, rarely attempting to bite, even when freshly captured. However, as always, all potentially venomous snakes should be handled with care.

● *Hologerrhum* Guenther, 1858: A genus containing a single species.

Top: *Hydrodynastes bicinctus*. Photo: J. Kellnhauser. Bottom: *Hypsiglena torquata nuchalata*. Photo: K. Lucas, Steinhart.

H. philippinum Guenther, 1858: Philippines. Length to 30 cm (12 in). Biology of this small burrowing species is poorly documented.

● *Hydrodynastes* Fitzinger, 1843: A genus containing a single species. Considered by many workers to be closely related to *Cyclagras* and even considered a senior synonym of that genus.

H. bicinctus (Herrmann, 1804): The

Guianas to the Amazon Basin in tropical lowland forest. Length to 200 cm (80 in). Head more or less distinct from body. Smooth dorsal scales. Reddish brown, marked with yellow-edged dark bands. Terrestrial and semi-aquatic, feeding mainly on frogs. Requires a large, heated aqua-terrarium.

● *Hypoptophis* Boulenger, 1908: A genus containing a single species (sometimes assigned to the Aparallactinae).

H. wilsoni Boulenger, 1908: Congo Basin (C. Africa) to Zambia in rain forest. Length to 35 cm (14 in). Triangular head distinct from relatively thick body and short tail give this species a viperine appearance. Terrestrial. Biology poorly known.

● *Hypsiglena* Cope, 1860: **Night Snakes.** A genus containing three species found from W. USA to Central America in varying dry habitats. Length to 60 cm (24 in). Head distinct from body. Pupils vertical. Nocturnal, feeding on frogs and lizards. Require a heated, dry terrarium with temperature reduction at night.

Top: *Eridiphas slevini slevini*. Photo: K. H. Switak.
Bottom: *Hypsiglena torquata texana*. Photo: K. Lucas, Steinhart.

Top: *Imantodes
cenchoa.* Photo: J.
Kellnhauser. Bottom
Left: *Hypsiglena
torquata ochrorhyncha.*
Photo: R. Holland.
Bottom Right:
Imantodes cenchoa.
Photo: K. T. Nemuras.

Eridiphas Leviton & Tanner, 1960, now contains the former *Hypsiglena slevini* Tanner.

H. torquata (Guenther, 1860): **Night Snake.** S.W. USA to Costa Rica. Length to 65 cm (26 in). Beige, yellowish, or gray, patterned with numerous dark brown or gray blotches along back and flanks. Broad dark collar. Oviparous, laying four to six eggs.

● *Imantodes* Dumeril, 1853: A genus containing five species found from Mexico to Argentina in the canopies of tropical and montane rain forests. Length to 120 cm (48 in). Large head distinct from extremely slender body by narrow neck. Very large eyes. Tail long and thin. Light brown to olive with dark bands. Arboreal, feeding on lizards or

Top: *Imantodes cenchoa*. Photo: R. S. Simmons. Bottom Left: *Leptodeira annulata*. Photo: M. Freiberg. Bottom Right: *Leptodeira annulata rhombifera*. Photo: J. Kellnhauser.

frogs. Require a tall, heated (cooler at night), planted, rain-forest terrarium. Oviparous, laying two to four elongate eggs.

I. cenchoa (Linnaeus, 1758): Tropical Mexico south to Bolivia and Paraguay. Feeds largely on lizards.

I. lentiferus (Cope, 1894): Amazon Basin. Feeds largely on frogs.

● *Ithycyphus* Guenther, 1873: A genus containing two species native to Madagascar in dry forest or rain forest. Length to 110 cm (44 in). Head distinct from body. Large eyes. Rear fangs relatively large; effect of venom on humans unknown. Nocturnal and terrestrial, feeding on lizards and frogs. Require a semi-humid woodland terrarium.

I. goudoti (Schlegel, 1854): Length to 90 cm

(36 in). Brown to grayish brown with dark chevron markings.

I. miniatus (Schlegel, 1837): Length to 110 cm (44 in). Uniform brown to gray.

● *Langaha* (Bonnaterre, 1790): **Leaf-nosed Snakes.** A genus containing two species native to Madagascar in tropical forest. Length to 100 cm (39 in). Snakes in this genus possess a remarkable 2-3 cm (1 in) long leaf-like extension to the snout, the function of which is not clearly understood. The scaled extension on the snout of the male is cone-shaped and pointed, while that of the female spreads at its tip somewhat like a flattened pineapple rosette. The eyes are relatively large, with vertical pupils. The color is brown to gray with darker crossbands. Nocturnal and

crepuscular terrestrial snakes feeding on frogs, lizards, and birds. Require a heated planted terrarium with facilities to climb.

The correct author and date of this generic name are controversial. It was described (or at least the name was used) by Bruguiere in 1784 and Lacepede in 1789, but many believe these names are unacceptable for technical reasons, leaving Bonnaterre, 1790, as the first valid use of the name. It also has had its spelling modified (unacceptably) at least five times, some purists believing *Langaia*, *Langaya*, or *Langhaha* to be better formed than *Langaha*, based on a native name.

L. alluaudi Mocquard, 1901: S. Madagascar. In this species the female possesses a pair of horn-like extensions above the eye as well as the extended snout.

L. nasuta (Shaw, 1790): N. Madagascar. Horns on female absent.

● **Leptodeira** Fitzinger, 1843: **Cat-eyed Snakes.** A genus containing nine species

Top: *Leptodeira annulata pulchriceps*. Photo: G. Scrocchi. Bottom Left: *Leptodeira septentrionalis*. Photo: K. T. Nemuras. Bottom Right: *Leptodeira nigrofasciata*. Photo: P. Freed.

Top: *Leptodeira septentrionalis septentrionalis.* Photo: Dr. S. Minton. Bottom: *Macroprotodon cucullatus brevis.* Photo: K. H. Switak.

found from S. Texas (USA) south through Central America to N. Argentina and Paraguay. In woodland of various types. Length 75-110 cm (30-44 in). Head distinct from slender, laterally compressed body, the neck narrow. Relatively long tail. Large eyes with vertical pupils. Smooth dorsal scales. Markings consist largely of a dark rhomboidal pattern on a lighter ground. Nocturnal and semi-arboreal, they also swim well, hunting mainly frogs. Require a well-heated tropical woodland terrarium with facilities to climb and bathe.

L. annulata (Linnaeus, 1758): Mexico to Argentina.

L. septentrionalis (Kennicott, 1859): **Cat-eyed Snake.** S. Texas to Peru. Northern subspecies pale yellow to yellowish tan, marked with dark brown or black saddle-shaped blotches that extend onto the flanks.

● ***Lycodryas*** Guenther, 1879: A genus containing eight species native to Madagascar and the Comoros islands in dry or moist woodland. Length 40-110 cm (16-44 in). Short, broad head set off very distinctly from narrow, laterally compressed body. Eyes large, with vertical pupils. Nocturnal and arboreal, feeding on frogs and lizards. Require a tall, heated, woodland terrarium with facilities to climb and bathe.

L. arctifasciatus (Dumeril & Bibron, 1854): N. and C. Madagascar, island of Nossi-Be.

L. gaimardi (Schlegel, 1837): Madagascar and Comoros.

L. variabilis (Boulenger, 1896): Madagascar. Largest species in genus, attaining a length of 110 cm (44 in).

● ***Macroprotodon*** Dumeril & Bibron, 1850: A genus containing a single species.

M. cucullatus (Geoffroy, 1827): **False Smooth Snake.** Southern Iberia and N. Africa from Morocco to Egypt and Israel. Usually in stony or rocky areas including dry stone walls and ruins. Length to 65 cm (26 in). Flattened head distinct from body. Small eyes with oval pupils. Smooth dorsal scales. Grayish to brownish above with small dark flecks or indistinct bars. Black collar extending to top of head. Underside yellowish or pinkish with darker markings. Mainly nocturnal, hiding under rocks, etc., during the day. Feeds mainly on small lizards (largely lacertids and geckos). Requires a dry terrarium with rocky hiding places.

● ***Madagascarophis*** Mertens, 1952: A genus containing a single species.

M. colubrina (Schlegel, 1837): Madagascar in dry to moist forest. Length to 100 cm (39 in). Blunt-snouted head distinct from body. Large eyes. Brownish with three or four rows of dark spots. Dark streak from eye to corner of jaw. Feeds on frogs, lizards, and small mammals. Requires a semi-humid, heated terrarium with facilities to climb and hide.

● ***Malpolon*** Fitzinger, 1826: A genus containing two species native to S. Europe, N. Africa, and Asia Minor in dry but vegetated habitats. Length to 170 cm (68 in).

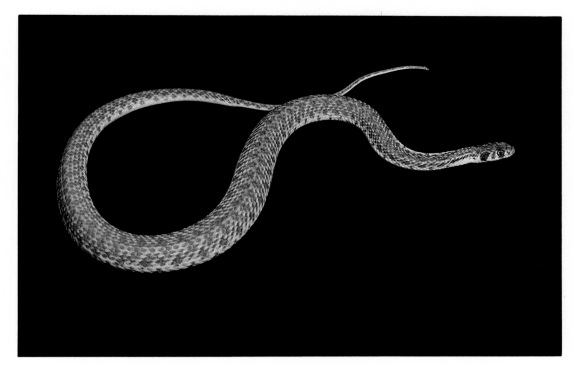

Top: *Madagascarophis colubrinus*. Photo: P. Freed. Center: *Malpolon* cf. *moilensis*. Photo: J. Kellnhauser. Bottom: *Malpolon moilensis*. Photo: J. Visser.

Top: *Malpolon monspessulanus.* Photo: Dr. D. Terver. Bottom Left: *Malpolon monspessulanus.* Photo: S. Kochetov. Bottom Right: *Mimophis mahafalensis.* Photo: P. Freed.

Head indistinct from robust body. Ridged brows and large eyes give it a fierce, penetrating expression. Dorsal scales smooth. Uniformly gray to reddish brown, olive, greenish, or blackish. Undersides yellowish with darker markings. Diurnal, feeding on lizards, snakes, small mammals, and birds. Require a dry terrarium with facilities to climb. Nighttime reduction in temperature recommended. Oviparous, laying up to 20 eggs.

M. monspessulanus (Hermann, 1804): **Montpellier Snake.** Iberia, Mediterranian coast of France, Italy, S. Balkans, N. Africa, and Asia Minor.

M. moilensis (Reuss, 1834): S. Morocco to Egypt.

- **Manolepis** Cope, 1885: A genus containing a single species.

M. putnami (Jan, 1863): Pacific coastal highlands of Mexico. In varying dry habitats to 2800 m (9000 ft). Length to 60 cm (24 in). Head distinct from body. Eyes with vertical pupils. Nocturnal and terrestrial, feeding mainly on lizards. Require a heated, dry terrarium with a temperature reduction at night.

- **Mimophis** Guenther, 1868: A genus containing a single species.

M. mahafalensis (Grandidier,

Top: *Mimophis mahafalensis madagascariensis.* Photo: P. Freed. Center: *Oxybelis aeneus.* Photo: K. T. Nemuras. Bottom: *Oxybelis argenteus.* Photo: B. Kahl.

1867): Madagascar in dryer areas. Length to 100 cm (39 in). Long, narrow head distinct from body. Large eyes protected by overhanging supraocular scales. Light brownish with dark brown vertebral stripe. Diurnal and terrestrial, feeding mainly on lizards. Requires a dry, planted terrarium with facilities to hide.

● *Opisthoplus* Peters, 1882: A genus containing a single species.

O. degener Peters, 1882: The state of Rio Grande do Sul in Brazil. Length to 65 cm (26 in). Closely related to *Tomodon* and often considered a synonym. Biology poorly documented.

● *Oxybelis* Wagler, 1830: **Vine Snakes.** A genus containing four or five species found from extreme S.W. USA to Brazil in tropical rain forest to secondary forest and thick brushland. Length to 130 cm (52 in). Long head with pointed snout on a long, slender body and tail (superficially resembling *Ahaetulla*). Brown to greenish with or without a longitudinal stripe or stripes. Diurnal and arboreal, feeding largely on lizards. Require a well-planted woodland terrarium. Oviparous, laying two to five eggs.

O. aeneus (Wagler, 1824): **Mexican Vine Snake.** S. Arizona, through Mexico to Brazil. Brownish gray to gray, becoming tan or yellowish brown on anterior part of body. A narrow dark brown streak runs through the eye to side of neck. May descend to the ground to hunt.

O. fulgidus (Daudin, 1803): Mexico to northern South America.

● *Oxyrhopus* Wagler, 1830: A genus containing 11 species found from S. Mexico to Brazil, Argentina, and Peru in tropical lowland forest. Length 80-100 cm (32-40 in). Large opisthoglyphic fangs below eye region.

Top: *Oxybelis argenteus*. Photo: B. Kahl. Bottom: *Oxybelis brevirostris*. Photo: R. S. Simmons.

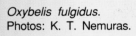

Oxybelis fulgidus.
Photos: K. T. Nemuras.

Head distinct from body. Most species banded with red, black, and white (coral snake mimics). Diurnal or nocturnal, feeding mainly on lizards. Require a heated rain-forest terrarium. Oviparous, laying up to 18 eggs.

O. petolarius (Linnaeus, 1758): **Forest Flame Snake.** Mexico to Amazon Basin.

O. rhombifer Dumeril, Bibron & Dumeril, 1854: Amazon Basin to Argentina.

O. trigeminus Dumeril, Bibron & Dumeril, 1854: Amazon Basin and Mato Grosso (Brazil).

- ***Parapostolepis*** Amaral, 1930: A genus containing a single species.

  P. polylepis (Amaral, 1921): The state of Piaui in Brazil. Similar to *Apostolepis* in many respects and usually considered a synonym.

- ***Phimophis*** Cope, 1860: A genus containing four species found from Panama to Argentina in grassland and pampas to semi-desert. Length 60-100 cm (24-40 in). Head distinct from body. Rostral shield overhangs lower jaw. Eyes with vertical pupils. Smooth dorsal scales. Uniform in color or with dark longitudinal stripes. Nocturnal and terrestrial, feeding mainly on lizards. Require a heated, dry terrarium with a temperature reduction at night.

  P. guerini (Dumeril, Bibron & Dumeril, 1854): S.E. Brazil to Argentina.

- ***Procinura*** Cope, 1879: A doubtful genus containing a single species. Usually considered a synonym of *Sonora*.

  P. aemula Cope, 1879: The state of Chihuahua and vicinity in Mexico (Sierra Madre) in cactus desert and similar dry habitats to 2800 m (9000 ft). Length to 40 cm (16 in). Head indistinct from body. Dorsal scales of anal region and tail heavily keeled,

Top: *Oxybelis fulgidus* (green) and *Oxybelis aeneus* (brown). Photo: G. Marcuse. Center: *Phimophis* cf. *guerini*. Photo: R. S. Simmons. Bottom: *Oxyrhopus petolarius*. Photo: R. S. Simmons.

Top: *Oxyrhopus petolarius*. Photo: Dr. S. Minton. Center Right: *Oxyrhopus rhombifer*. Photo: M. Freiberg. Bottom Left: *Phimophis* cf. *guerini*. Photo: R. S. Simmons. Bottom Right: *Oxyrhopus trigeminus*. Photo: M. Freiberg.

Top: *Procinura aemula.*
Photo: K. H. Switak.
Center: *Procinura aemula.* Photo: K.
Lucas, Steinhart.
Bottom:
Psammodynastes pulverulentus. Photo: R.
E. Kuntz.

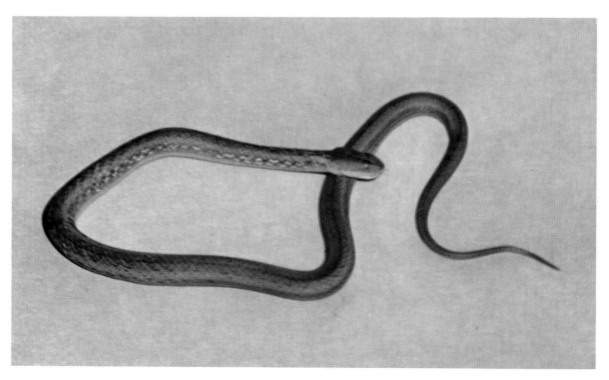

otherwise smooth. Yellowish or tan with a tremendously varied pattern of bands—no two individuals are alike. Nocturnal and burrowing, feeding on subterranean invertebrates and small vertebrates. Requires a dry terrarium with deep, loose substrate. Temperature reduction at night.

- *Psammodynastes* Guenther, 1858: A genus containing two species native to S.E. Asia from the eastern Himalayas through Indo-China to the Indo-Australian Archipelago and the Philippines. Found in lowland and montane rain forest. Length 50-65 cm (20-26 in). Head distinct from slender body. Large eyes. Smooth dorsal scales. Semi-arboreal, feeding on frogs and lizards. Requires a humid woodland terrarium with facilities for climbing. Ovoviviparous, producing three to ten young.

P. pulverulentus (Boie, 1827): **Mock Viper.** Whole range as described above. Color variable, from brown to grayish above with black spots or vague reticulations. Undersides brown or gray with darker spots.

P. pictus Guenther, 1858: Malaya, Sumatra, and adjacent islands.

- *Psammophis* Boie, 1826: **Sand Racers.** A genus containing 16 species found from Africa to central Asia in dry habitats from thorn-

Top: *Psammodynastes pulverulentus*. Photo: R. E. Kuntz. Center: *Psammophis condanarus indochinensis*. Photo: M. J. Cox. Bottom: *Psammophis condanarus*. Photo: Dr. S. Minton.

bush scrub to semi-desert. Length 70-170 cm (28-68 in). Long, narrow head indistinct from neck. Large eyes with round pupils. Smooth dorsal scales. Most species striped in various shades of browns and yellows. Diurnal and terrestrial; fast-moving and agile. Move with head raised to increase field of vision. Require a large, heated, dry terrarium with facilities to bask. Reduced temperatures at night. Feed mainly on lizards in the wild but will take mice.

P. crucifer (Daudin, 1803): **Cross-marked Grass Snake.** S. Africa. Length to 70 cm (28 in). Silvery gray to pale olive or olive-brown above, with three longitudinal black-bordered dark brown stripes. Dark crossbars on nape.

P. lineolatum (Brandt, 1838): Soviet Central Asia to N.W. China, south to Iran. Pale silvery gray to buff with darker uneven stripes.

P. schokari (Forskal, 1775): Afro-Asian Sand Snake. N. Africa through Arabia to Turkmenistan. Silvery gray to buff with a dark brown stripe along each upper flank; lighter stripes along back.

Top: *Psammophis jallae*. Photo: P. Freed. Center: *Psammophis leightoni namibensis*. Photo: P. Freed. Bottom: *Psammophis leithi*. Photo: Dr. S. Minton.

Top: *Psammophis leightoni trinasalis.* Photo: K. H. Switak. Center Left: *Psammophis phillipsii.* Photo: B. Kahl. Center Right: *Psammophis lineolatum.* Photo: S. Kochetov. Bottom Left: *Psammophis lineolatum.* Photo: S. Kochetov. Bottom Right: *Psammophis notostictus.* Photo: P. Freed.

P. sibilans (Linnaeus, 1758): **Sand Snakes.** Most of Africa, except rain forest. Length to 170 cm (68 in). ***P. s. sibilans***, Olive Sand Snake, has uniform coloration; other subspecies have stripes.

Top: *Psammophis schokari*. Photo: Dr. S. Minton. Bottom: *Psammophis subtaeniatus subtaeniatus*. Photos: Left: P. Freed; Right: C. Banks.

● *Psammophylax* Fitzinger, 1843: **Skaapstekers.** A genus containing two species native to southern Africa. Mainly found in savannah. Length 80-110 cm (32-44 in). Similar in form and habit to *Psammophis*. Feed on frogs, lizards, and small mammals. Require a dry terrarium with facilities for basking, cooler at night. Oviparous, laying up to 30 eggs.

P. rhombeatus (Linnaeus, 1754): **Skaapsteker.** South Africa, from Cape Province to Transvaal. Length to 110 cm (44 in). Gray to olive-brown above, with three rows of longitudinally arranged large squarish,

Top Left: *Psammophylax tritaeniatus*. Photo: B. Kahl.
Top Right: *Psammophylax rhombeatus*. Photo: K. H.
Switak. Bottom: Portrait of *Psammophylax
tritaeniatus*. Photo: B. Kahl.

dark brown blotches that sometimes merge to form a zig-zag pattern along the back. Underside creamy white to yellow with gray to black marbling.

P. tritaeniatus (Guenther, 1868): **Striped Skaapsteker.** Southern Tanzania and Angola to Zimbabwe and Mozambique, plus northern and central South Africa. Length to 90 cm (36 in). Gray to brown above with three well-defined black-bordered dark brown stripes running the length of body and tail. Vertebral stripe often split by narrow yellow stripe. Underside white to yellow.

- ***Pseudablabes*** Boulenger, 1896: A genus containing a single species.

P. agassizi (Jan, 1863): S. Brazil, Uruguay, N. Argentina. Length to 40 cm (16 in). Small head indistinct from body. Nocturnal burrowing snake. Biology poorly known.

Top Left: *Psammophylax tritaeniatus.* Photo: B. Kahl. Top Right: *Psammophylax tritaeniatus.* Photo: J. Coborn. Center: *Psammophylax tritaeniatus.* Photo: P. Freed. Bottom: *Pseudoboa neuwiedii.* Photo: R. D. Bartlett.

● ***Pseudoboa*** Schneider, 1801: A genus containing four species found from Panama to South America on both sides of the Andes. In grassland and riverine forest usually near water. Length to 100 cm (39 in). Terrestrial, feeding on lizards and small mammals. Require a heated terrarium with facilities to bathe. Oviparous, laying four to six eggs.

P. coronata Schneider, 1801: Amazon Basin and the Guianas to Peru. Reddish brown with blackish head.

● ***Pseudoleptodeira*** Taylor, 1938: A genus containing two species native to Mexico in dry highlands between Michoacan and Oaxaca. Length 40-60 cm (16-24 in). Head distinct from body. Vertical pupils. Smooth dorsal scales. Nocturnal and terrestrial, feeding mainly on lizards. Require a dry terrarium with adequate hiding places. Reduction in temperature at night.

P. discolor (Guenther, 1860): Brown with pale-bordered dark crossbands. Often placed in the monotypic genus ***Tantalophis*** Duellman, 1958.

P. latifasciata (Guenther, 1894): Brown with whitish crossbars.

Top: *Pseudoboa neuwiedii*. Photo: H. Bleher. Upper Center: *Pseudoboa neuwiedii*. Photo: R. S. Simmons. Lower Center: *Pseudotomodon trigonatus*. Photo: H. Piacentini. Bottom: *Rhamphiophis oxyrhynchus rostratus*. Photo: C. Banks.

Top: *Pythonodipsas carinata*. Photo: P. Freed. Center: *Rhamphiophis (Dipsina) multimaculatus*. Photo: P. Freed. Bottom: *Rhamphiophis oxyrhynchus rostratus*. Photo: K. H. Switak.

● *Pseudotomodon* Koslowsky, 1896: A genus containing a single species.

P. trigonatus Koslowsky, 1896: South America. Taxonomy disputed. Closely related to and similar to *Tomodon*. Possibly identical to *T. ocellatus*.

● *Pythonodipsas* Guenther, 1868: A genus containing a single species.

P. carinata Guenther, 1868: **Keeled Snake.** S.W. Africa in dry, rocky habitats. Length to 60 cm (24 in). Longish, flattened head distinct from body. Vertical pupils. Pale buff to sandy gray above with a series of darker-edged brown or grayish brown squarish blotches along each side of the body. Underside whitish. Nocturnal and terrestrial, feeding mainly on lizards. Requires a dry

terrarium with adequate hiding places
(preferably rocks).

● *Rhachidelus* Boulenger, 1908: A genus
containing a single species.

R. brazili Boulenger, 1908: S. Brazil, N.E.
Argentina. Uniformly blackish brown.
Diurnal and terrestrial. Feeds on a variety of
small vertebrates. Oviparous. Biology
otherwise poorly known.

● *Rhamphiophis* Peters, 1854: **Beak-nosed
Snakes.** A genus containing five species

native to central and southern Africa and
generally in dryer habitats. Length 50-240 cm
(20-96 in). Large head distinct from body.
Beak-like, extended rostral shield. Smooth

Top Left: *Rhamphiophis
oxyrhynchus rostratus.*
Photo: J. Visser. Top
Right: *Rhamphiophis
(Dipsina)
multimaculatus.* Photo:
K. H. Switak. Bottom:
Rhinobothryum bovalli.
Photo: B. Kahl.

dorsal scales. Diurnal and terrestrial, feeding on a variety of vertebrates (frogs, reptiles, birds, mammals). Require a large, dry, well-ventilated terrarium with facilities to bask. Oviparous, laying 10-20 eggs.

R. multimaculatus (A. Smith, 1847): **Western Beaked Snake.** Length to 50 cm (20 in). Brown to gray or slate above, with three to five longitudinal rows of dark spots. Underside white to yellowish. Often placed in the genus or subgenus *Dipsadina*.

R. oxyrhynchus (Boulenger, 1843): **Rufous Beaked Snake.** Central to S.E. Africa. Length to 130 cm (52 in). Uniformly sandy brown above, yellowish below.

R. rubropuncatus (Fischer, 1884): **Red Beaked Snake.** East Africa. Length to 240 cm (96 in). Largest species in the genus. Reddish brown above, yellowish below.

● *Rhinobothryum* Wagler, 1830: A genus containing two species ranging from Panama to Paraguay. In tropical lowland forest. Length to 160 cm (64 in). Head distinct from neck. Broad rostral shield. Vertical pupils. Body compressed laterally. Keeled dorsal scales. Nocturnal and arboreal, feeding on frogs and lizards. Require a tall, heated, humid rain-forest terrarium.

R. bovalli Anderson, 1916: From Costa Rica south to N.W. Colombia, Ecuador, and Venezuela. Red, yellow, and black bands (coral snake mimic).

R. lentiginosum (Scopoli, 1785): Amazon Basin to Rio Paraguay. Red and black bands on pale tan.

● *Scolecophis* Fitzinger, 1843: A genus containing a single species.

Sonora episcopa. Photos: Top: R. Holland; Bottom: J. Iverson. This is a species showing tremendous diversity in patterns.

Top: *Sonora episcopa*, ringed phase. Photo: J. Iverson. Bottom: *Sonora michoacanensis*. Photo: Dr. S. Minton.

Nocturnal and arboreal, feeding largely on frogs and lizards.

S. cervinus (Laurenti, 1768): Panama to C. Bolivia and north to Trinidad.

S. longicaudatus (Andersson, 1907): Brazil, Espirito Santo to Rio Grande do Sul.

S. pulcher (Raddi, 1820): Brazil (Guanabara and Minas Gerais to Rio Grande do Sul).

● ***Sonora*** Girard, 1853: A genus containing up to seven species (taxonomy disputed) native to S.W. USA and Mexico in desert and semi-desert to 3000 m (10000 ft). Length to 50 cm (20 in). Head indistinct from cylindrical body. Colors range from uniformly brown to striped or banded with red and black, even within a single population. Nocturnal and semi-burrowing, feeding mainly on invertebrates (millipedes, spiders, scorpions, crickets, etc.). Require a dry desert terrarium with temperature reductions at night. Oviparous, laying up to six eggs.

S. episcopa (Kennicott, 1859): S.W. USA and N.E. Mexico.

S. semiannulata Baird & Girard, 1853: W. USA and N.W. Mexico. Usually considered a synonym of *S. episcopa*.

● ***Stenorrhina*** Dumeril, 1853: A genus containing two species found from S. Mexico to Colombia, Venezuala, and Ecuador in tropical rain forest. Length to 75 cm (30 in). Small head indistinct from body. Small eyes. Colors vary from gray to brown, with or without darker longitudinal stripes. Nocturnal

S. atrocinctus (Schlegel, 1837): El Salvador to Costa Rica in tropical rain forest. Length to 40 cm (16 in). Head more or less distinct from body. Black-banded. Nocturnal and terrestrial. Biology poorly known.

● ***Siphlophis*** Fitzinger, 1843: A genus containing five species found from Panama to Brazil and Bolivia in tropical rain forest. Length 70-100 cm (28-40 in). Head distinct from slender body. Olive-green to brownish with rows of darker spots along flanks.

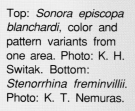

Top: *Sonora episcopa blanchardi*, color and pattern variants from one area. Photo: K. H. Switak. Bottom: *Stenorrhina freminvillii*. Photo: K. T. Nemuras.

Stenorrhina freminvillii.
Photos: Top: K. T.
Nemuras; Bottom: J.
Coborn.

and terrestrial. Biology poorly known.
S. freminvillii Dumeril, Bibron & Dumeril,
1854: Mexico to Panama.
S. degenhardti (Berthold, 1846): Mexico to
Ecuador.
● **Symphimus** Cope, 1870: A genus containing
a single species.
S. leucostomus Cope, 1870: Mexico
(Isthmus of Tehuantepec) in dry habitats.
Length to 80 cm (32 in). Nocturnal and
burrowing, feeding on lizards. Biology
otherwise poorly known.
● **Sympholis** Cope, 1861: A genus containing a
single species.
S. lippiens Cope, 1861: W. Mexico (Jalisco
to Nayarit). Length to 60 cm (24 in). Head
indistinct. Small, smooth dorsal scales.
Yellowish with black rings. Burrowing snakes.
Biology otherwise poorly known.
● **Tachymenis** Wiegmann, 1834: A genus
containing six species native to South America
along Pacific coastal areas of Chile and Peru
and also from Bolivia to the Guianas. Some
authorities consider this genus to be so close
to *Thamnodynastes* that it should be treated as
a synonym. Found mainly in dryer habitats,
from forest margins to semi-desert and to
altitudes of 3500 m (11000 ft). Length 50-70
cm (20-28 in). Head indistinct from slender
body. Most species have dark longitudinal
stripes along the dorsal surface. Nocturnal
and terrestrial, feeding mainly on lizards.
Require a dry terrarium with adequate hiding
places (reduced temperature at night for
desert and montane species). Ovoviviparous.

T. peruviana Wiegmann, 1834: Chile and
Peru.
● **Tantilla** Girard, 1853: A genus containing
about 50 species found from S. USA to
Argentina in dryer habitats from forest
margins to scree slopes and semi-desert.
Length 25-40 cm (10–16 in). Head indistinct
from body in most species. Smooth dorsal
scales. Patterns range from uniform to
longitudinally striped. Nocturnal and
burrowing, feeding on various invertebrates.
Require a dry terrarium with deep, loose
substrate.
T. coronata Baird & Girard,
1853: **Southeastern Crowned Snake.** S.E.
USA, from Virginia to Louisiana. Tan to
reddish brown above, underside whitish.

Top: *Tantilla bocourti.*
Bottom: *Tantilla coronata.* Photos: Dr. S. Minton.

Distinct black cap extending to corner of mouth. White and black collar bands on neck. Oviparous, laying one to three eggs.

T. gracilis Baird & Girard, 1853: **Flat-headed Snake.** Central USA into Mexico. Light brown to reddish brown with slightly darker head. Underside pinkish. Lays one to four eggs.

T. melanocephala (Linnaeus, 1758): **Black-headed Snake.** Mexico to Argentina.

Other United States species in the genus include ***T. atriceps*,** **Mexican Black-headed Snake;** ***T. nigriceps*,** **Plains Black-headed Snake;** ***T. oolitica*,** **Rim Rock Crowned Snake;** ***T. planiceps*,** **Western Black-headed Snake;** ***T. relicta*,** **Florida Crowned Snake;** ***T. rubra*,** **Big Bend Black-headed Snake;** ***T. wilcoxi*,** **Chihuahuan Black-headed Snake;** and ***T. yaquia*,** **Yaqui Black-headed Snake.**

● ***Tantillita*** Smith, 1941: A genus containing a single species.

T. lintoni (Smith, 1940): Guatemala. Closely related and similar to *Tantilla*.

● ***Telescopus*** Wagler, 1830: **Cat Snakes.** A genus containing 11 species native to S.E. Europe, S.W. Asia, and Africa. In dry habitats from semi-desert to savannah.

Length 80-130 cm (32-52 in). Head distinct from body. Large eyes with vertical pupils. Body slightly compressed laterally. Smooth dorsal scales. Most species brownish with darker bands or spots. Nocturnal and terrestrial, feeding on lizards and small mammals, sometimes birds and their eggs. Require a heated, dry terrarium with a moderate temperature reduction at night.

T. fallax (Fleischmann,

Top: *Tantilla nigriceps.* Photo: A. Kerstitch. Center: *Telescopus beetzii.* Photo: K. H. Switak. Bottom: *Tantilla rubra cucullata.* Photo: P. Freed.

Top: *Telescopus dhara*.
Photo: J. Visser.
Bottom: *Telescopus fallax*. Photo: Dr. S. Minton.

Telescopus semiannulatus. Photos: H. Nicolay.

1831): **Mediterranean Cat Snake.** E. Adriatic coast and islands, S. Balkans, Greek Islands, and Malta, Caucasus, and S.W. Asia. Length to 100 cm (39 in). Gray, beige, or brownish with a series of transverse bars or blotches on the back. Underside pale yellow, whitish, or pinkish, with or without darker markings. Oviparous, laying seven to eight eggs.

T. semiannulatus A. Smith, 1849: **Tiger Cat Snake.** Central and southern Africa. Length to 100 cm (39 in). Pinkish buff, yellowish, to reddish brown above with a series of dark brown to black transverse rhomboidal spots, crossbars, or bands.

Underside yellowish, often tinged with salmon pink to orange. Oviparous, laying six to ten eggs.

- ***Thamnodynastes*** Wagler, 1830: A genus containing five species found from Caribbean coastal areas of South America to Argentina. Mostly in lowland forest margins and secondary forest. Common in plantations. Length to 80 cm (32 in). Head distinct from body. Large eyes with vertical pupils. Usually brownish with darker stripes. Nocturnal and terrestrial to semi-arboreal, feeding mainly on lizards and small mammals. Require a heated, semi-humid terrarium with facilities to climb and bathe.

T. strigatus (Guenther, 1858): S.E. Brazil, Paraguay, and N.E. Argentina. Smooth dorsal scales.

T. strigilis (Thunberg, 1787): Brazil. Keeled dorsal scales.

T. pallidus (Linnaeus, 1758): Amazon Basin. Smooth dorsal scales.

- ***Thelotornis*** A. Smith, 1849: A genus containing a single species.

T. kirtlandi (Hallowell, 1844): **Bird or Twig Snake.** Central to southern Africa. Length to 130 cm (52 in). Long, narrow head and large eyes with horizontal figure-8 pupils

similar to *Ahaetulla*. Large opisthoglyph fangs. Bites have caused fatal envenomation in humans, so the greatest care in handling is advised. To date, no antivenin is available for this species. Body slightly compressed laterally. Light grayish to greenish with dark-bordered lighter crossbands. Arboreal, feeding mainly on lizards, also possibly frogs and other snakes. Requires a tall planted terrarium with facilities to climb. Oviparous, laying six to ten eggs.

Top: *Thelotornis kirtlandi capensis.* Photos: Left: J. Visser; Right: Dr. G. Dingerkus. Center: *Trimorphodon biscutatus vilkinsoni.* Photo: K. H. Switak. Bottom: *Toluca lineata.* Photo: Dr. S. Minton.

Top: *Toluca lineata.* Photo: R. D. Bartlett. Center: *Tomodon dorsatus.* Photo: M. Freiberg. Bottom Left: *Trimorphodon biscutatus vandenburghi.* Photo: K. H. Switak. Bottom Right: *Tomodon ocellatus.* Photo: M. Freiberg.

• ***Toluca*** Kennicott, 1859: A genus containing three species native to central and S. Mexico. Length to 50 cm (20 in). Terrestrial. Biology poorly known.

T. lineata Kennicott, 1859.

• ***Tomodon*** Dumeril, 1853: A genus containing two species found from the Mato Grosso in Brazil to central Argentina in dry forested areas and in pampas. Length 50-75 cm (20-30 in). Head distinct from cylindrical body. Smooth dorsal scales. Brownish with rows of dark spots. Nocturnal and terrestrial, feeding mainly on lizards. Require a well-heated dry terrarium with temperature reduction at night.

T. dorsatus Dumeril, Bibron & Dumeril, 1854: C. Brazil to Argentina.

T. ocellatus Dumeril, Bibron & Dumeril, 1854: S. Brazil, Paraguay, Uruguay, and Argentina.

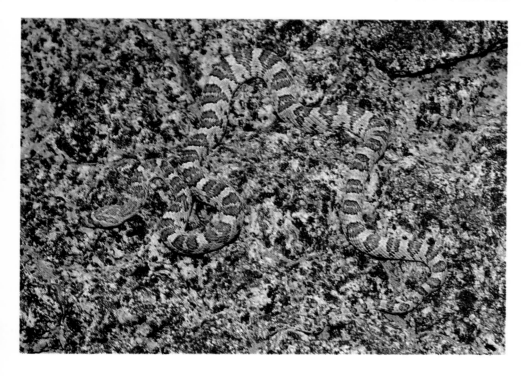

Top: *Trimorphodon biscutatus lambda*. Photo: K. Lucas, Steinhart. Bottom: *Trimorphodon biscutatus biscutatus*. Photo: Dr. S. Minton.

Top: *Trimorphodon tau.*
Photo: Dr. S. Minton.
Bottom: *Xenocalamus*
mechovi inornatus.
Photo: J. Visser.

● *Trimorphodon* Cope, 1861: **Lyre Snakes.** A genus containing 11 species (many doubtfully distinct) found from S.W. USA to Costa Rica in pine forests to rocky and desert areas to an altitude of 3500 m (11000 ft). Length to 100 cm (39 in). Head distinct from body. Large eyes with vertical pupils. Nocturnal and terrestrial, feeding mainly on lizards and small mammals. Require a dry terrarium with adequate hiding and climbing facilities.

T. lambda Cope, 1886: **Sonoran Lyre Snake.** California south to Mexico. Lyre-shaped mark on head. Light brown to gray with darker brown or gray saddle-shaped blotches with light centers on back. Smaller blotches along sides. Oviparous, laying about ten eggs. Usually considered a subspecies of *T. biscutatus.*

T. biscutatus (Dumeril & Bibron, 1854): **Coastal Lyre Snake.** Mexico to Guatemala and Costa Rica.

● *Tripanurgos* Fitzinger, 1843: A genus containing a single species.

T. compressus (Daudin, 1803): Panama to South America (Guianas, Trinidad, and the Amazon Basin) in tropical rain forest. Length to 75 cm (30 in). Head distinct from very slender body. Very thin neck and long thin tail. Dark brown head, separated from light brown body by yellow collar. Body marked with darker crossbands. Nocturnal and arboreal, feeding on lizards and frogs. Requires heated rain-forest terrarium with adequate climbing facilities.

● *Xenocalamus* Guenther, 1868: **Slender Quill-nosed Snake.** A genus containing four species found from tropical West Africa to central South Africa mainly in dryer habitats. Length 40-60 cm (16-24 in). Head indistinct from body. Rostral shield extended over lower jaw to form a point. Burrowing snakes feeding on other snakes, lizards, and amphisbaenians.

Top: *Dipsas* sp. Photo: A. Kerstitch. Bottom Left: *Xenocalamus mechovi inornatus.* Photo: J. Visser. Bottom Right: *Dipsas catesbyi.* Photo: P. Freed.

Require a terrarium with deep, loose substrate. Oviparous.

X. bicolor Guenther, 1868: S.E. and S. Africa. Length to 75 cm (30 in). Color very variable, from plain black or yellow to various reticulated or banded forms. Underside ranges from black to off-white.

X. mechovi Nieden, 1913: Zaire, Angola, and South Africa. Length to 75 cm (30 in). Color varies almost as much as in *X. bicolor.*

SUBFAMILY DIPSADINAE— AMERICAN SNAIL-EATING SNAKES

This subfamily contains three genera and about 48 species native to Central and South America in rain forest and montane forest. Lengths range from 25-90 cm (10-36 in). Highly specialized, some species feed exclusively on snails that are extracted from their shells by the long teeth at the front of the lower jaw. They require a heated rain-forest terrarium. Local garden snails usually will be accepted as food.

● ***Dipsas*** Laurenti, 1768: A genus containing 33 species found from Mexico to Paraguay in tropical or montane rain forest. Length to 90 cm. Short, broad head distinct from body. Most species are dark brown to olive with lighter reddish to yellowish rhomboidal or banded patterns. Nocturnal and semi-arboreal, feeding exclusively on snails. Require a humid, heated, heavily planted rain-forest terrarium.

D. bicolor (Guenther, 1895): S. Nicaragua to Costa Rica in montane rain forest.

D. indica Laurenti, 1768: South America from the Guianas to Paraguay in lowland rain forest.

D. oreas (Cope, 1868): Ecuador, in montane

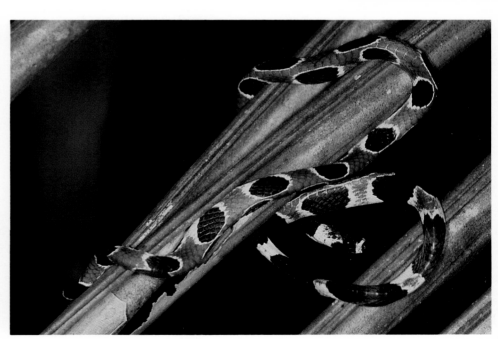

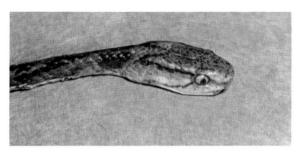

rain forest of the western Andes.

D. pratti (Boulenger, 1897): Rain forest of the central Colombian cordilleras.

- **Sibon** Fitzinger, 1826: A genus containing nine species found from Mexico to N. South America. Similar to *Dipsas* in form, habit, and care. Probably feed on frogs and lizards as well as snails.

S. annulata (Guenther, 1872): Eastern side of Panama to Costa Rica in montane rain forest. Banded.

S. nebulata (Linnaeus, 1758): S.E. Mexico to N.W. Ecuador. Brownish with faint darker markings.

- **Sibynomorphus** Fitzinger, 1843: A genus containing six species native to South America south of the equator. Length to 85 cm (34 in). More terrestrial than other species in subfamily.

S. mikani (Schlegel, 1837): Brazil, in lowland rain forest and dryer areas.

S. turgidus (Cope, 1862): S. Bolivia to N. Paraguay in rain forest.

SUBFAMILY PAREINAE—ASIAN SNAIL-EATING SNAKES

This subfamily contains two genera with about 15 species native to S.E. Asia, in monsoon, rain, or montane rain forest. Similar in many respects to Dipsadinae (parallel evolution). Length to 90 cm (36 in). Head distinct from laterally compressed body. Large eyes with vertical pupils. Long anterior teeth in lower jaw. Feed almost exclusively on snails. Care similar to that described for Dipsadinae.

- **Aplopeltura** Dumeril, 1853: A genus containing a single species. Often spelled *Haplopeltura*, an unallowable correction of the

original spelling.

A. boa (Boie, 1827): S. Thailand through Malayan Peninsula to Indo-Australian Archipelago and Philippines in rain forest. Short head distinct from body. Brown with darker markings. Oviparous, laying two to five eggs.

● ***Pareas*** Wagler, 1830: A genus containing about 14 species native to southern Asia from the southern Himalayas to Indo-China and the Indo-Australian Archipelago in tropical rain forest. Mostly brownish with a darker pattern; some species have an X-shaped mark on dorsal surface of neck. Oviparous, laying two to ten eggs.

P. carinatus Wagler, 1830: Thailand to Indonesia in lowland rain forest.

P. margaritophorus (Jan, 1866): S. China and Hainan through Indo-China to Malayan Peninsula. In rain forest and montane rain forest to 1500 m (5000 ft).

P. monticola (Cantor, 1839): Montane rain forest of the eastern Himalayas.

SUBFAMILY ELACHISTODONTINAE—INDIAN EGG-EATING SNAKES

A subfamily containing only a single genus and a single species.

● ***Elachistodon*** Reinhardt, 1863: A genus containing a single species.

E. westermanni Reinhardt, 1863: **Indian Egg-eating Snake.** N. Bengal. Similar in many respects to *Dasypeltis* but head less

distinct from body and dorsal scales smooth. Like *Dasypeltis*, possesses extended hypophyses of the cervical vertebrae adapted to cutting into eggshells. Olive-brown to blackish above with yellowish to whitish spots; underside whitish with brown flecks. A rare species, only a few specimens known. Biology poorly understood.

SUBFAMILY APARALLACTINAE— MOLE VIPERS

This subfamily contains ten genera and about 45 species native to Africa and the Middle East. Taxonomy of this group is highly uncertain. Some genera have previously have been placed in the subfamily Boiginae or even in the families Elapidae and Viperidae. Recent revision places all genera in the Aparallactinae, with the possible exception of *Atractaspis*, which may

Top: *Aparallactus capensis*. Photo: J. Visser. Bottom: *Calamelaps ventrimaculatus*. Photo: J. Visser.

Top: *Atractaspis bibroni*. Photo: Dr. S. Minton. Bottom: *Aparallactus capensis*. Photo: K. H. Switak.

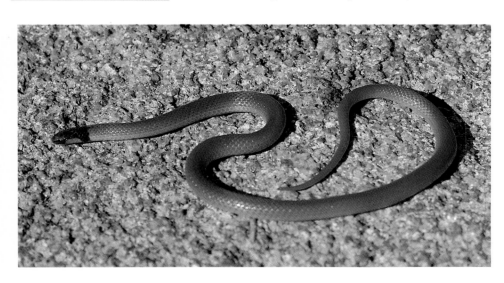

warrant its own subfamily (Atractaspinae). Many species in the subfamily have relatively long opisthoglyph or solenoglyph fangs set forward in the jaw and supplied with large venom glands. Like those of viperids, the fangs of some species are hinged and lie against the jaw until ready to be erected as necessary. Although the effects of the venom on man are not fully researched, all species in the group should be regarded as venomous and dangerous. Bites from *Atractaspis*, for example, can cause intense pain and swelling. Most species in the subfamily are burrowers and should be kept in a terrarium with a deep, loose substrate.

- *Amblyodipsas* Peters, 1857: A genus containing a single species.

  A. microphthalma (Bianconi,

1850): **Purple Glossed Snake.** Mozambique and eastern South Africa. Length to 45 cm (18 in). Head indistinct from body. Smooth dorsal scales. Brown with purplish sheen above, whitish below. Burrowing, feeding largely on amphisbaenians and burrowing lizards.

- *Aparallactus* A. Smith, 1849: A genus containing ten species native to central and southern Africa, mainly in dryer savannah regions. Length 25-50 cm (10-20 in). Small head set off indistinctly from neck; very short but tapered tail. Smooth dorsal scales. Small eyes. One or two short opisthoglyphic fangs set below the eye. Most species plain brown to blackish. Burrowing, feeding on centipedes, snails, and termites. Require a terrarium with deep, loose substrate.

  A. capensis (A. Smith, 1849): **Centipede Eater.** Zaire to South Africa. Reddish, yellowish, or grayish brown with darker head.

  A. lineatus (Peters, 1870): Guinea to Ghana. Longitudinal dark stripes on a brownish background.

- *Atractaspis* Smith, 1849: **Mole Vipers.** A genus containing 16 species native to tropical and southern Africa and the Middle East. In various habitats from forest to semi-desert. Length to 65 cm (26 in). Head has a shovel-like snout and is indistinct from body. Large solenoglyphic fangs at front of upper jaw. Fatal bites to humans are recorded from some of these species. Burrowing snakes that feed on lizards, snakes, and small mammals.

Require a terrarium with a deep substrate for burrowing. Temperature reduction at night desirable for semi-desert species. Oviparous.

A. bibroni Smith, 1849: **Mole Viper.** Southern half of Africa in varied habitats. Length to 60 cm (24 in). Uniformly dark purplish brown to black above, creamy white to yellowish beneath, sometimes spotted.

A. engaddensis Haas, 1950: Egypt to Israel in semi-desert.

A. microlepidota Guenther, 1866: Mauritania and Nigeria eastward to Kenya, Ethiopia, and Arabian Peninsula in savannah and grassland.

● **Calamelaps** Guenther, 1866: A genus containing four species native to central and southern Africa. Length to 100 cm (39 in). Head indistinct from body. Short tail. Extended rostral shield forming flattish, shovel-shaped snout. Small eyes. Smooth dorsal scales. Mostly uniformly brownish with purplish sheen above. Underside yellowish to brownish. Burrowing snakes feeding on snakes, lizards, and amphisbaenians. Require a terrarium with deep, loose substrate. Recently some authorities have suggested that *Calamelaps* is a synonym of *Amblyodipsas*.

C. unicolor Guenther, 1888: Eastern and

Top: *Chilorhinophis gerardi*. Photo: J. Visser. Center: *Homoroselaps lacteus*. Photo: J. Visser. Bottom: *Acanthophis antarcticus*. Photo: C. Banks.

Acanthophis antarcticus. Photos: Top: C. Banks; Bottom: K. Lucas, Steinhart.

habitats. Formerly classified as an *Elaps* in the Elapidae. Name commonly spelled *Homorelaps*. Length to 50 cm (20 in). Head indistinct from body. Nocturnal burrowing snakes often found in termite mounds. Feed mainly on small lizards and snakes. Require a dry terrarium with deep, loose substrate. Temperature reduction at night.

H. dorsalis (A. Smith, 1849): **Striped Dwarf Garter Snake.** South Africa from the Transvaal to Natal and Orange Free State. Length to 35 cm (14 in). A yellow vertebral stripe against a blackish background.

H. lacteus (Linnaeus, 1758): **Spotted Dwarf Garter Snake.** Length to 50 cm (20 in). Juveniles similar in color to *H. dorsalis.* Adults take on a banded phase, becoming yellowish brown to whitish with black bands running around the and tail, plus a reddish brown vertebral stripe.

- ***Macrelaps*** Boulenger, 1896: A genus containing a single species.

  M. microlepidotus (Guenther, 1860): **Natal Black Snake.** S.E. Africa in moist habitats. Length to 100 cm (39 in). Head indistinct from body. Very small eyes. Uniformly ashy to jet black above and below, sometimes a little lighter on the underside. Burrowing snakes that sometimes enter water and swim well. Feeds mainly on frogs. Requires a humid but not waterlogged terrarium with facilities to burrow. Rear-fanged and venomous; severe reactions in humans have been recorded.

- ***Micrelaps*** Boettger, 1879-80: A genus containing two species native to East Africa in thorny brushland and savannah. Length to 40 cm (16 in). Head distinct from body. Smooth dorsal scales. Nocturnal and terrestrial. Biology poorly known.

  M. boettgeri (Boulenger, 1901): Kenya and Sudan.

  M. vaillanti (Mocquard, 1888): Somalia.

- ***Miodon*** Dumeril, 1859: A genus containing three species native to tropical Africa in various woodland habitats to 2000 m (6500 ft). Length to 85 cm (34 in). Small head with rounded snout indistinct from body. Smooth dorsal scales. Mostly uniformly brown. Nocturnal and terrestrial, feeding mainly on other snakes. Require a humid rain forest terrarium with adequate hiding places. Sometimes considered a synonym of *Polemon.*

  M. collaris (Peters, 1881): Central Africa from Nigeria to Uganda. Blackish brown with a narrow yellowish collar.

- ***Polemon*** Jan, 1858: A genus containing three species native to tropical West Africa in rain forest. Very similar to *Miodon.* Length 30-100 cm (125-39 in). Nocturnal and terrestrial, feeding mainly on other snakes. Care as for *Miodon.*

  P. barthi Jan, 1858: Ivory Coast to Cameroons. Length to 100 cm (39 in).

  P. neuwiedi (**Jan, 1858**): Ghana to Benin. Length to 30 cm (12 in).

southern Africa. Uniformly brown to black above, lighter below.

C. ventrimaculatus Roux, 1907: Southeastern Africa. Length to 45 cm (18 in). Dark gray to purplish brown above with lighter scale edges. Underside yellowish to brownish.

- ***Chilorhinophis*** Werner, 1907: A genus containing three species native to tropical Africa. Length to 40 cm (16 in). Head indistinct from body. Short tail. Opisthoglyphic venom fangs near front of upper jaw. Brownish to black above with rows of yellow spots or stripes. Burrowing snakes feeding largely on invertebrates and also small lizards and amphisbaenians. Oviparous.

  C. gerardi (Boulenger, 1913): Zaire and Zimbabwe to South Africa.

- ***Homoroselaps*** Jan, 1858: **Dwarf Garter Snakes.** A genus containing two species native to southern Africa in semi-desert

Family Elapidae—Cobras, Mambas, Kraits, Coral Snakes, etc.

A family containing about 50 genera and some 200 species of venomous snakes distributed throughout the tropics and subtropics and only absent from most of the temperate zones and the colder parts of the Northern Hemisphere. The family has its headquarters in Australia, where elapids are the ruling group of snakes. Thus Australia has the distinction of being the only country where venomous snake species outnumber nonvenomous ones. It has been suggested recently that the majority of Australian elapids should be assigned to the family Hydrophiidae; however, in the present work they will be left in Elapidae. Lengths of most species are in the range of 30-100 cm (12-40 in); notable exceptions are the King Cobra, *Ophiophagus hannah*, with a record length of 5.6 m (18.2 ft), and the Taipan, *Oxyuranus scutellatus*, with a record length of 4 m (13 ft). Most of the species are slender and colubrid-like in form, but there are a few exceptions (for example, *Acanthophis*). Upper side of the head is covered with large scales. All species possess a pair of fixed proteroglyph fangs at the front of the upper jaw. These are relatively short when compared with the fangs of the Viperidae and Crotalidae. The venom of almost all elapids is mainly neurotoxic, with only a minimal hemotoxic effect in most cases. Some species are highly dangerous to humans, and all species in the group must be handled with the greatest of care. They are not recommended to the home terrarium-keeper and are best left to the attentions of the zoo-keeper or professional herpetologist.

Elapids have found their way into a variety of habitats. There are those that are primarily terrestrial (including burrowing types), those that are primarily arboreal, and a few that are semi-aquatic. They may be oviparous or ovoviviparous.

● *Acanthophis* Daudin, 1803: **Death Adders.** A genus containing two species native to Australia in dryer brushland to desert or semi-desert. Length to 100 cm (39 in). Viper-like in appearance. Broad triangular head distinct from short, stout body by narrow neck. Small eyes with vertical pupils. Short, thin tail (which is wriggled and used as a lure to attract prey). Dorsal scales slightly keeled. Nocturnal and secretive, hiding during the day under ground litter. Rely on cryptic coloration for protection, but are aggressive and dangerous when disturbed. Feed on small mammals, birds, and reptiles. Require a dry, brushland terrarium with a loose substrate.

A. antarcticus (Shaw, 1794): **Common Death Adder.** Australia except central and western desert areas and wetter parts of New South Wales and Victoria. Length to 100 cm (39 in), though averages about 50 cm (20 in). Color variable from reddish brown to gray, usually with lighter or darker irregular crossbands. Underside gray to cream with numerous darker spots. Oviparous, producing up to 20 young.

A. pyrrhus Boulenger, 1898: **Desert Death Adder.** Desert regions of central and Western Australia. Similar to *A. antarcticus* apart from having more strongly keeled scales. Usually bright reddish brown (including underside) with lighter crossbands often bordered with black at their rear edges. Biology probably similar to preceding species but largely unknown.

Acanthophis pyrrhus.
Photos: C. Banks.

● ***Aspidelaps*** Fitzinger, 1843: **Shield-nosed Cobras.** A genus containing two species native to southern Africa in dry savannah to semi-desert. Length to 80 cm (32 in). Head indistinct from neck. Broad rostral shield used in burrowing. Like cobras, they rear the front part of the body and spread the neck when confronted, showing black and white coloration on the throat. Nocturnal and terrestrial, feeding on lizards, snakes, small mammals, and birds. Require a dry terrarium with deep, loose substrate. Reduce temperature at night.

A. scutatus (A. Smith, 1849): **Shield-nosed Cobra.** Central and southern Africa. Yellowish to brownish with variable amount of dark blotching or crossbanding.
A. lubricus (Laurenti, 1768): **Cape Coral Snake.** Cape Province, South Africa.

Top Left: *Aspidelaps lubricus*. Photo: K. H. Switak. Top Right: *Aspidelaps scutatus*. Photo: P. Freed. Bottom: *Aspidelaps scutatus*. Photo: K. H. Switak.

Conspicuously banded in black and orange to coral-red.

- **Aspidomorphus** Fitzinger, 1843: A genus containing three species native to New Guinea and adjacent islands, New Britain and New Ireland. In tropical rain forest. Length to 65 cm (26 in). Short, rounded head indistinct from body and short tail. Small eyes. Nocturnal and semi-burrowing. Biology poorly known but probably similar to *Micrurus*.

A. lineaticollis (Werner, 1903): Papua New Guinea and adjacent islands.
A. muelleri (Schlegel, 1837): New Guinea, New Britain, Duke of York Island and New Ireland. Four subspecies.
A. schlegeli (Guenther, 1872): New Guinea and adjacent islands.
- **Austrelaps** Worrell, 1963: **Australian Copperhead.** A genus containing a single species.
A. superbus (Guenther, 1858): S.E Australia

Austrelaps superbus.
Photos: Top: Dr. S. Minton; Bottom: R. Everhart.

and Tasmania in moist areas of the highlands. Length to 170 cm (68 in). Narrow head only slightly distinct from neck. Large eyes with round pupils. Variable in color from reddish brown to chocolate-brown or black above, cream to yellow or red along the flanks, and yellowish to grayish below. Active both day and night, feeding principally on frogs and lizards. Requires a humid terrarium with seasonal temperature changes as indicated by the range. Ovoviviparous, producing up to 20 young. Venom considered dangerous to humans.

● ***Boulengerina*** Dollo, 1885: **Water Cobras.** A genus containing two species native to central Africa. Found in rivers and lakes. Length to 120 cm (48 in). Head indistinct from neck and robust body. Brown with black rings. Very aquatic, feeding almost exclusively on fish. Requires a large aqua-terrarium with a dry basking area. Not very aggressive, but venom is known to be potent.
B. annulata (Buchholtz & Peters, 1877): Gabon, Cameroon, Zaire, Tanzania, and Malawi.
B. christyi Boulenger, 1904: W. Congo.

● ***Bungarus*** Daudin, 1803: **Kraits.** A genus containing 12 species native to India and S.E. Asia. Found in varied habitats from dry grasslands to tropical rain forest. Length to 200 cm (80 in). Head more or less distinct from body, which is triangular in cross-section. Most species carry a banded pattern, but a few are uniform in color. Nocturnal and terrestrial, feeding almost exclusively on other snakes. In the absence of snakes as food, force-feeding is often necessary in captive specimens, though some will learn to take lizards or small mammals. Require a large dry or humid terrarium depending on origin of species. Venom is considered highly dangerous, but the snakes rarely attempt to bite during the day. However, after dark they

Top: *Austrelaps superbus.* Photo: C. Banks. Center: *Boulengerina annulata.* Photo: A. Norman. Bottom: *Bungarus caeruleus.* Photo: Dr. S. Minton.

Top: *Bungarus candidus*. Photo: R. D. Bartlett. Center Left: *Bungarus fasciatus*. Photo: G. Marcuse. Center Right: *Bungarus caeruleus sindanus*. Photo: R. D. Bartlett. Bottom: *Bungarus fasciatus*. Photo: R. T. Zappalorti.

Top: *Bungarus flaviceps.* Photo: M. J. Cox. Center: *Cacophis squamulosus.* Photo: K. H. Switak. Bottom: *Bungarus multicinctus.* Photo: R. E. Kuntz.

are highly irascible. They should be treated with respect at all times.

B. bungaroides (Cantor, 1839): India (Assam, Kachar, and Sikkim) and Burma.

B. caeruleus (Schneider, 1801): **Indian Krait.** India, Sri Lanka, and Bangladesh.

B. candidus (Linnaeus, 1758): Indo-China through Malaysia to Indonesia.

B. ceylonicus Guenther, 1864: **Sri Lankan Krait.** Sri Lanka.

B. fasciatus (Schneider, 1801): **Banded Krait.** India through Burma to Indo-China, Malaysia, and Indonesia. Ochre yellow with black bands.

B. flaviceps (Reinhardt, 1843): **Red-headed Krait.** Indo-China through Malaysia to Indonesia. Uniformly brown to blackish with a yellowish or reddish head.

B. javanicus Kopstein, 1932: **Javan Krait.** Java.

B. lividus Cantor, 1839: India (Assam, Bengal, and Sikkim). Uniformly blackish brown.

B. magnimaculatus Wall & Evans, 1901: Burma.

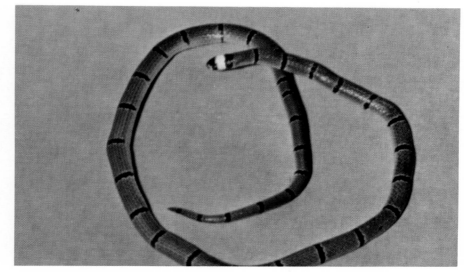

Top: *Calliophis macclellandi*. Photos: R. E. Kuntz.
Center: *Bungarus multicinctus*. Photo: R. E. Kuntz.
Bottom: *Bungarus multicinctus*. Photo: Dr. S. Minton.

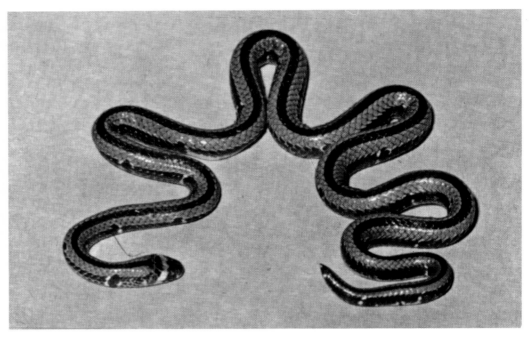

Top: *Calliophis sauteri.*
Photos: R. E. Kuntz.
Bottom: *Calliophis maculiceps.* Photo: M. J. Cox.

B. multicinctus Blyth, 1861: S.E. China and Taiwan. Glossy black with narrow white bands.

B. niger Wall, 1908: India (Assam & Sikkim). Uniformly black.

B. walli Wall, 1907: India (Bihar, West Bengal and Uttar Pradesh).

• ***Cacophis*** (Guenther, 1863): A genus containing three to six species (taxonomy disputed) native to Australia in dry to moist brushland. Length 25-100 cm (10-39 in). Rounded head indistinct from body. Brownish to grayish with a light collar or crown. Nocturnal and terrestrial, hiding under ground litter during the day. Feed on invertebrates and small vertebrates. Require a dry to semi-humid (seasonal) brushland terrarium. Ovoviviparous, producing three to ten young.

C. harriettae Krefft 1869: **White-crowned Snake.** Eastern Queensland. Length to 40 cm (16 in). Brown to gray with white to yellow crown or collar.

C. kreffti Guenther, 1863: **Dwarf Crowned Snake.** Extreme eastern New South Wales and Queensland. Black with narrow white collar.

C. squamulosus (Dumeril, Bibron & Dumeril, 1854): **Golden-crowned Snake.** Eastern New South Wales and Queensland. Dark brown to gray with yellow crown or collar.

• ***Calliophis*** Gray, 1835: A genus containing about 13 species native to S.E. Asia from India and Sri Lanka to Indo-China, Malaysia, Indonesia, and the Philippines. In tropical lowland to montane rain forest. Length to 50 cm (20 in). Many species colorfully banded like coral snakes. Nocturnal and terrestrial secretive snakes feeding on small snakes and lizards. Require a tropical terrarium with deep, loose substrate.

C. bibroni (Jan, 1858): India (Western Ghats).

C. calligaster (Wiegmann, 1834): Philippines.

C. gracilis Gray, 1835: Malaysia and Indonesia.

C. japonicus Guenther, 1868: Ryukyu Islands, Taiwan.

C. kellogi (Pope, 1928): S. China.

C. macclellandi (Reinhardt, 1844): Nepal to S. China and Ryukyu Islands.

C. maculiceps (Guenther, 1858): India to Indo-China.

C. melanurus (Shaw, 1802): Thailand and Laos.

C. nigrescens Guenther, 1862: S. and W. India.

● *Cryptophis* Worrell, 1961: A genus containing two species native to E. and N. Australia. Very close to *Denisonia* and *Rhinoplocephalus*. In dry to moist woodland. Length to 100 cm (39 in). Head distinct from body. Small eyes. Nocturnal and secretive, hiding under ground litter during the day. Feed on lizards and frogs. Require a dry to humid woodland terrarium.

C. nigrescens (Guenther, 1862): **Eastern Small-eyed Snake.** Coastal strip and ranges from Victoria to Cape York Peninsula. Uniformly black above, cream to pinkish below, often with blackish flecks and blotches. Ovoviviparous, producing two to five young.

C. pallidiceps (Guenther, 1858): **Northern Small-eyed Snake.** Northern parts of Northern Territory. Black with paler head. Habits poorly known.

● *Demansia* Gray, 1842: A genus containing four species native to New Guinea and Australia, mainly in dryer habitats. Length 50-100 cm (20-39 in). Slender and whip-like, with narrow head more or less distinct from body. Very large eyes. Diurnal and terrestrial but climb well. Feed mainly on small vertebrates, especially lizards. Require a dry terrarium with facilities to climb and bathe. Oviparous.

D. atra Macleay, 1884: **Black Whip Snake.** Northern Australia. Light to dark olive-brown or black above, lighter laterally. Scales edged with darker color to give a fine

Cryptophis nigrescens.
Photos: Top: C. Banks;
Bottom: Dr. S. Minton.

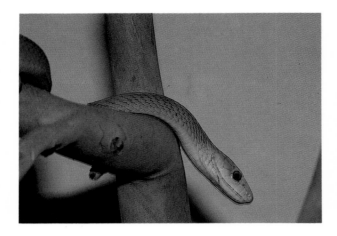

reticulate pattern. Belly yellowish to greenish. **D. olivacea** (Gray, 1842): **Olive Whip Snake.** N.W. Australia and New Guinea. Gray-brown above, usually flushed with rich brown or russet. Underside white to cream. **D. psammophis** (Schlegel, 1837): **Yellow-faced Whip Snake.** Most of continental Australia except the far central north. Color variable, ranging from gray to greenish with dark-edged scales forming fine reticulate pattern.

D. torquata (Guenther, 1862): **Collared Whip Snake.** Northeastern Australia. Gray-brown above, darker on head. Neck with variable series of black and yellow crossbands.

• *Dendroaspis* Schlegel, 1848: **Mambas.** A genus containing four species native to central and southern Africa (excepting the Cape). In tropical forest to open woodland and brushland. Length 250-400 cm (100-160 in). Long, narrow head more or less distinct from long, slender, but robust body. Unlike most other elapids, mambas are able to erect their venom fangs in a similar manner to the viperids by rotation of the maxilla. Fast-moving, highly venomous, and dangerous to humans. Arboreal and mainly diurnal but may also be active at night. Feed on a variety of vertebrates. Require a secure, large, tall terrarium with sturdy branches for climbing and facilities to bathe. Oviparous, laying 10-25 eggs.

D. angusticeps (A. Smith, 1849): **Eastern Green Mamba.** Kenya to Natal. Length to 200 cm (80 in). Juveniles bluish green, changing to bright leaf-green as they mature. Underside usually yellow. Almost exclusively arboreal.

D. jamesoni (Traill, 1843): **Jameson's Mamba.** Western and central Africa. Green with black edges to scales.

D. polylepis Guenther, 1864: **Black Mamba.** Eastern Africa from Somalia to Natal and west to Angola. Length to 400 cm (160 in) or more. After the King Cobra, *Ophiophagus hannah*, this is the longest venomous snake. Much feared in Africa on account of its size, aggressiveness, speed, and potency of venom, though encounters are often exaggerated. In spite of common name it is rarely black but instead is uniformly dark olive to brown or steel-gray above and grayish white below. Less arboreal than other mambas but equally at home on the ground or in the trees.

D. viridis (Hallowell, 1844): **Western Green Mamba.** Tropical West Africa. Green with darker edges to scales.

● ***Denisonia*** Krefft, 1869: A genus containing four species native to Australia in grassland to brushland. Length to 50 cm (20 in). Head indistinct from body. Smooth dorsal scales. Nocturnal and secretive terrestrial species hiding under ground litter during the day. Feed principally on lizards. Require a dry terrarium with loose substrate. Biology poorly known.

D. devisii Waite & Longman, 1920: **De Vis's Banded Snake.** Queensland and New South Wales in Great Dividing Range. Light brown above with a series of dark brown bands. Belly white or cream.

D. fasciata Rosen, 1905: **Rosen's Snake.** Western Australia. Head and body light brown with numerous darker bands closer together than those of preceding species.

D. maculata (Steindachner, 1867): **Ornamental Snake.** Central eastern Queensland. Brown, gray-brown, to black above, lighter on flanks; often with darker streaks or flecks. Underside white to cream. Ovoviviparous, producing about eight young.

D. punctata Boulenger, 1896: **Little Spotted Snake.** Northern Australia from W. Australia coast to far western Queensland. Reddish brown with a few dark blotches on head and neck.

● ***Drysdalia*** Worrell, 1961: A genus containing three species native to southern Australia in arid brushland to semi-desert. Very close to *Notechis* and *Elapognathus*. Length to 40 cm (16 in). Head more or less distinct from body. Smooth dorsal scales. Nocturnal, terrestrial, and secretive, hiding under ground litter during the day. Feed on invertebrates, lizards, and frogs. Require a dry terrarium with temperature reduction at night. Period of winter hibernation recommended. Ovoviviparous.

D. coronata Schlegel, 1837: **Crowned Snake.** Extreme southwestern Australia. Pale brown to olive-brown or dark brown. Head darker than body, with blackish crown.

D. coronoides (Guenther, 1858): **White-lipped Snake.** S.E. Australia and Tasmania. Color variable from light gray through various

Top: *Drysdalia coronoides*. Photo: C. Banks. Center: *Drysdalia mastersi*. Photo: C. Banks. Bottom: *Elapsoidea sundevalli boulengeri*. Photo: P. Freed.

shades of brown to almost black above. White stripe along upper lip. Underside cream to yellowish or pinkish.

D. mastersi (Krefft, 1886): **Masters's Snake.** Nullarbor Plain to Victoria and New South Wales. Reddish to grayish brown, sometimes with faint lighter longitudinal stripes. Head darker, with a light yellow, orange, or brown collar. Underside yellow with darker spots.

• *Echiopsis* Fitzinger, 1843: A genus containing a single species.

E. curta (Schlegel, 1837): **Bardick.** Southern Australia in dry sandy areas. Length to 60 cm (24 in). Head indistinct from robust body. Smooth dorsal scales. Uniformly brown to olive or gray, with a few lighter spots on sides of head and neck. Nocturnal and terrestrial, usually found under logs and other ground litter during the day. Feeds on invertebrates, lizards, and frogs. Requires a dry terrarium with loose, sandy substrate and adequate hiding places. Temperature reduction at night and period of hibernation recommended. Ovoviviparous, producing eight to ten young.

• *Elapognathus* Boulenger, 1896: A genus containing a single species.

E. minor (Guenther, 1863): **Little Brown Snake.** Extreme southwestern Australia in dry semi-desert. Length to 40 cm (16 in). Uniformly brown above. Faint light collar in juveniles and some adults. Throat yellow, fading to light yellow or cream on belly with black bars. Biology poorly known. Requires a

desert terrarium with temperature reduction at night. Probably feeds largely on lizards.

• *Elapsoidea* Bocage, 1866: A genus containing a single species.

E. sundevalli (A. Smith, 1848): **African Garter Snake.** Central and southern Africa. Small head indistinct from cylindrical body. Color variable, from uniformly yellowish brown to banded dark and light. Nocturnal and terrestrial, often living in termite mounds. Feeds largely on lizards and their eggs. Requires a heated terrarium with adequate hiding places. Eleven subspecies, some of which are given specific status by some herpetologists.

• *Furina* Dumeril, 1853: A genus containing a single species.

F. diadema (Schlegel, 1837): **Red-naped Snake.** Continental Australia except for far south. Length to 40 cm (16 in). Longish head more or less distinct from body. Smooth dorsal scales. Rich reddish brown above merging to yellowish along the flanks. Scales edged with dark brown or black, giving a reticulate effect. Head and neck glossy black with a red band across nape. Underside white or cream. Nocturnal and terrestrial, hiding under rocks, logs, or ground litter during the day. Often found in ant and termite colonies. Feeds on invertebrates and small lizards. Requires a dry, heated terrarium with temperature reduction at night. Oviparous, laying eight to ten eggs.

• *Glyphodon* Guenther, 1858: A genus

Furina diadema. Photo: Dr. S. Minton.

containing three species native to Australia
and New Guinea in tropical woodland. Very
close to *Furina*. Length to 100 cm (39 in).
Head distinct from slender body. Nocturnal,
hiding under ground litter during the day.
Require a humid rain-forest terrarium with
adequate hiding places. Biology poorly
known.

G. barnardi Kinghorn, 1939: **Yellow-naped
Snake.** Coast and interior of N.E.
Queensland. Length to 50 cm (20 in). Dark
brown to black above; scales light-edged,
giving reticulate appearance. Yellow or light
brown collar, darker head. Underside white
to cream.

G. dunmalli Worrell, 1955: **Dunmall's
Snake.** Inland ranges of S.E. Queensland.
Length to 70 cm (28 in). Uniformly dark
brown above; whitish below. Biology poorly
known.

G. tristis Guenther, 1858: **Brown-headed
Snake.** Eastern Cape York Peninsula, Torres
Strait Islands, and New Guinea. Shiny
blackish brown with lighter brown head and
yellowish collar. Underside white or cream.

● *Hemachatus* Fleming, 1822: A genus
containing a single species.

H. haemachatus (Lacepede,
1790): **Ringhals or Ring-necked Spitting
Cobra.** S. and S.E. Africa in range of dryer
habitats. Length to 120 cm (48 in). Differ
from the closely related *Naja* in having keeled
dorsal scales and being ovoviviparous. Spreads

*Hemachatus
haemachatus.* Photos:
Top Left: C. Banks; Top
Right: Banded phase,
K. H. Switak; Center:
S.Kochetov;
Bottom: K. H. Switak.

hood when aroused and can squirt venom from fangs in direction of opponent's eyes (it is advisable to wear goggles when dealing with these snakes). Uniformly light brown to dark brown or blackish above, sometimes spotted with black to light brown to form irregular bars or crossbands. Underside dark brown to black with two or three white crossbands on neck. Feeds on small mammals, snakes, lizards, and toads. Requires a secure, heated, dry terrarium with facilities to bathe. Ovoviviparous, producing 20 to (in exceptional cases) 60 young.

- *Hemiaspis* Fitzinger, 1861: A genus containing two species native to eastern Australia in various brushland to swampy habitats. (*H. damelli* sometimes is placed in a distinct genus, ***Drepanodontis*** Worrell.) Length to 50 cm (20 in). Head indistinct from neck. Smooth dorsal scales. Diurnal or crepuscular to nocturnal (especially in warmer weather). Require a heated terrarium with adequate hiding places and facilities to bathe. Feed on lizards and frogs. Oviparous, producing up to 20 young.

H. damelli (Guenther, 1876): **Gray Snake.** Central inland New South Wales to Queensland coast around Rockhampton. Uniformly gray to olive-gray above. Scales along flanks may be tipped with black. Head black in juveniles, becoming only black neckband in adults, though black may disappear altogether.

H. signata Jan, 1859: **Black-bellied Swamp Snake.** Coastal and near coastal areas of eastern Australia from S. New South Wales to N. Queensland. Brown to olive-brown above with darker head. Underside dark gray to black.

- *Hoplocephalus* Wagler, 1830: A genus containing three species native to eastern Australia in grassland to rocky brushland. Length to 60 cm (24 in). Head distinct from body. Smooth dorsal scales, keeled ventrals. Nocturnal and terrestrial to partially arboreal, feeding largely on lizards and frogs. Require a tall terrarium with facilities to climb (rocks or tree branches). Ovoviviparous.

H. bitorquatus (Jan, 1859): **Pale-headed Snake.** Ranges of eastern Australia from central New South Wales to northern Queensland. Length to 50 cm (20 in). Uniformly light brown to gray above, with a broad dark-bordered white or cream band on the nape. Underside grayish, sometimes with darker flecks.

H. bungaroides (Schlegel, 1826): **Broad-headed Snake.** Central coastal New South Wales. Length to 60 cm (24 in). Black with irregular narrow yellow crossbands. Underside gray to gray-black, sometimes with yellowish blotches.

H. stephensi Krefft, 1869: **Stephen's Banded Snake.** Central N.S.W. to southern Queensland in coastal ranges. Length to 45 cm (18 in). Brown to yellowish brown with darker irregular crossbands. Head black.

● ***Leptomicrurus*** Schmidt, 1937: **Slender Coral Snakes.** A genus containing three species native to northern South America in tropical rain forest. Length to 60 cm (24 in). Unlike most *Micrurus*, the colored bands do not extend right round the body. Biology probably similar to *Micrurus*. Most authorities now consider this genus to be a synonym of *Micrurus*.

L. collaris (Schlegel, 1837): S.E. Venezuela, the Guianas, and Para, Brazil.

L. narducci (Jan, 1863): E. Peru, Ecuador, Bolivia, Colombia, and Acre, Brazil.

L. schmidti Hoge & Romano, 1966: Tapurucuara and Amazonas, Brazil.

● ***Maticora*** Gray, 1835: A genus containing two species native to S.E. Asia from Indo-China through Malaya to Indonesia and the Philippines In tropical and montane rain forest. Length 60-150 cm (24-60 in). Head indistinct from body. Characteristic enormously developed venom glands that extend through the front third of the body. Variable in color and pattern; usually a dark ground color with faint to obvious longitudinal stripes. When threatened the tail is raised, showing the red underside. Nocturnal and terrestrial, feeding mainly on reptiles, including other snakes. Require a heated rain-forest terrarium with adequate hiding places.

M. bivirgata (Boie, 1827): Thailand, Kampuchea, Malaysia, and Indonesia.

M. intestinalis (Laurenti, 1768): Malaysia through Indonesia to Philippines.

● ***Micruroides*** Schmidt, 1928: **Arizona Coral Snake.** A genus containing a single species.

M. euryxanthus (Kennicott, 1860): **Arizona Coral Snake.** S.W. USA and Mexico in dry prairie. Length to 55 cm (22 in). Short head with blunt snout indistinct from body. Glossy, with alternating wide black, wide red, and relatively narrow yellow or white bands. Head uniformly black to angle of jaw. Nocturnal and terrestrial, hiding below ground during the day. Feeds on invertebrates, lizards, and

possibly small mammals. Requires a secure desert terrarium with a deep, loose substrate. Oviparous, laying two or three eggs.

● ***Micrurus*** Wagler, 1824: **Coral Snakes.** A genus containing about 48 species found from S. USA to Argentina in varied habitats from moist to semi-dry brushland and rain forest.

Top: *Micruroides euryxanthus*. Photo: J. K. Langhammer. Center: *Micrurus corallinus corallinus*. Photo: M. Freiberg. Bottom: *Micruroides euryxanthus*. Photo: Dr. S. Minton.

Top: *Micrurus dumerili.*
Photo: R. S. Simmons.
Center Left: *Micrurus frontalis frontalis.*
Photo: M. Freiberg.
Center Right: *Micrurus frontalis pyrrhocryptus.*
Photo: M. Freiberg.
Bottom: *Micrurus fulvius fulvius.* Photo: J. Iverson.

Length 40-150 cm (16-60 in). Head indistinct from body. Almost all species show a pattern that is considered the characteristic coral snake warning coloration: wide black and red bands separated by narrower white or yellow ones. All coral snakes are highly venomous and must be treated with the greatest of care. When threatened, coral snakes flatten their short tail and curl it upward from the ground while hiding the head in the ground or among the coils of the body. Nocturnal and terrestrial, feeding on a wide range of invertebrates, frogs, lizards, other snakes, juvenile birds, and small mammals. Require a heated, humid, rain-forest terrarium with a microclimate to match the natural biotope of the species. Adequate hiding places (moss, bark, etc.) should be provided.

M. albocinctus Amaral, 1926: Mato Grosso (Brazil).

M. annellatus Peters, 1871: Peru, Ecuador, and Bolivia.

M. bernardi (Cope, 1887): Mexico (western Hidalgo and northern Puebla).

M. bocourti (Jan, 1872): Ecuador and Colombia.

M. browni Schmidt & Smith, 1943: Mexico to Guatemala.

M. corallinus Merrem, 1820: Eastern Brazil and northern Argentina. Highly dangerous!

M. decoratus (Jan,1858): Brazil (Rio de Janeiro to Santa Catalina).

M. diastema (Dumeril, Bibron & Dumeril, 1854): Mexico, Honduras, Guatemala, and Belize.

M. dissoleucus (Cope, 1859): Panama to Colombia and Venezuela.

Top: *Micrurus lemniscatus carvalhoi.* Photo: M. Freiberg. Center and Bottom: *Micrurus fulvius tenere.* Photos: R. T. Zappalorti.

Top: *Micrurus nigrocinctus nigrocinctus.* Photo: Dr. S. Minton. Bottom Left: *Naja melanoleuca.* Photo: L. Edmonds. Bottom Right: *Naja haje.* Photo: Dr. G. Dingerkus.

M. distans (Kennicott, 1860): Mexico.
M. dumerili (Jan, 1858): Ecuador, Colombia and Venezuela.
M. elegans (Jan, 1858): Mexico.
M. ephippipher (Cope, 1886): Mexico (Oaxaca).
M. filiformis (Guenther, 1859): Brazil, Colombia.
M. fitzingeri (Jan, 1858): Mexico (Distrito Federal and Morelos).
M. frontalis (Dumeril, Bibron & Dumeril, 1854): S.W. Brazil, Uruguay, Paraguay, N. Argentina. Southernmost species. Highly dangerous!
M. fulvius (Linnaeus, 1766): S.E. USA and N. Mexico. Northermost species.
M. hemprichi (Jan, 1858): Peru and Colombia.
M. hippocrepis (Peters, 1862): Eastern Belize and northern Guatemala.
M. ibiboboca (Merrem, 1820): N.W. Brazil.
M. laticollaris (Peters, 1869): Mexico.
M. lemniscatus (Linnaeus, 1758): Brazil, the Guianas, and Trinidad.
M. mertensi Schmidt, 1936: Peru and S.E. Ecuador.
M. mipartitus (Dumeril, Bibron & Dumeril, 1854): Nicaragua to Colombia, Ecuador, and Venezuela.

M. nigrocinctus (Girard, 1854): Mexico to northern Colombia.

M. psyches (Daudin, 1803): Colombia, Venezuela, the Guianas, and Trinidad.

M. spixi Wagler, 1824: Amazon Basin.

M. steindachneri (Werner, 1901): Ecuador.

M. stewarti Barbour & Amaral, 1928: Panama (Sierra de la Bruja).

M. stuarti Roze, 1967: Guatemala (San Marcos and Suchitepequez).

M. surinamensis (Cuvier, 1817): Ecuador,

Colombia, Bolivia, Venezuela, the Guianas, and Brazil.

M. tschudii (Jan, 1858): Peru, Ecuador.

● *Naja* Laurenti, 1768: **Cobras.**

A genus containing six species found from Africa to southern and S.E. Asia. Found in margins of forests to dry savannah. Length 140-250 cm (56-100 in). Characteristic of the genus is the rearing of the front third of the body and the spreading of a hood in the neck region. This is accomplished by spreading the elongated ribs

Singapore snake charmer with *Naja naja*.
Photo: K. H. Switak.

Top Left: *Naja melanoleuca*. Photo: C. Banks. Top Right: *Naja mossambica*. Photo: L. Edmonds. Center Right: *Naja mossambica pallida*. Photo: S. Kochetov. Bottom: *Naja naja*, golden phase. Photo: M. J. Cox.

Top Left: *Naja naja kaouthia*. Photo: M. J. Cox. Top Right: *Naja naja*. Photo: K. T. Nemuras. Center: *Naja naja*, black phase. Photo: M. J. Cox. Bottom: *Naja naja philippinensis*. Photo: Dr. S. Minton.

Top Left: *Naja naja*, abnormal pattern. Photo: M. J. Cox. Top Right: *Naja nigricollis*. Photo: S. Kochetov. Bottom Left: *Naja naja kaouthia*, albino. Photo: M. J. Cox. Bottom Right: *Naja naja*. Photo: R. Everhart.

that are hinged with the vertebrae in the neck region. The front or back of the hood may be decorated with various warning patterns. Venomous and highly dangerous, cobras should be kept only by qualified or experienced herpetologists. Nocturnal or diurnal, feeding on a variety of vertebrates. Some species are more or less specialized to certain prey items (for example, *N. melanoleuca* and *N. oxiana* feed primarily on bufonid toads). Require a large, heated, roomy terrarium with a water bath. Oviparous, laying 8-25 eggs that hatch in a relatively short time (14-21 days).

N. haje (Linnaeus, 1758): **Egyptian Cobra.** Africa except the Cape; Arabian Peninsula. Length to 250 cm (100 in). Typically uniformly brown but may have lighter bands along back. Underpart yellowish brown with darker band across throat.

N. melanoleuca Hallowell, 1858: **Black and White Cobra.** Africa south of 15th parallel. Length to 220 cm (88 in). Head and neck brown, remainder of dorsal surface glossy black. Underside white with black patches at intervals.

N. mossambica Peters, 1854: **Mozambique Spitting Cobra.** S. Egypt through eastern

Africa to Natal, westward to Mali, Nigeria, Ghana, Angola, and S.W. Africa. Length to 150 cm (60 in). Tawny brown to olive or slate above with black edges to scales. Underside salmon-pink to yellowish with black speckles and black bars across throat. Can spit venom; handle with care!

N. naja (Linnaeus, 1758): **Indian Cobra.** India to Indo-China, Indonesia, and the Philippines. Length to 200 cm (80 in). Mostly gray to brown or buff above, lighter beneath with variable darker crossbanding.

Top: *Naja haje*. Photo: K. Lucas, Steinhart. Center: *Naja naja*. Photo: R. E. Kuntz. Bottom: *Naja nivea*. Photo: K. H. Switak.

Top: *Naja nivea*. Photo: C. Banks. Center: *Naja nivea*. Photo: Dr. G. Dingerkus. Bottom: *Naja oxiana*, juvenile at left. Photos: S. Kochetov.

The best-known subspecies are the Spectacled Cobra, *N. n. naja* (with spectacle marking on rear of hood), and the Monocled Cobra, *N. n. kaouthia* (with monocle marking).

N. nigricollis Reinhardt, 1843: **Black-necked Spitting Cobra.** Africa south of 25th parallel. Length to 200 cm (80 in). Dark olive-brown, slate-gray, or black above; yellow to

reddish below with broad dark band on throat. Like *Hemachatus*, this species is capable of spitting venom in the direction of an adversary's eyes. Goggles should therefore be worn when dealing with this species.

N. nivea (Linnaeus, 1758): **Cape Cobra.** South Africa and Namibia. Length to 150 cm (60 in). Enormous color variation from yellow to dark brown, reddish, or black above and below.

N. oxiana (Eichwald, 1831): **Central Asian Cobra.** Soviet Central Asia to Kazachstan. Length to 160 cm (64 in). Formerly classed as a subspecies of *Naja naja*. Uniformly brown above, lighter beneath. Northernmost species in the genus. Northern populations hibernate for two to three months.

● *Neelaps* Guenther, 1863: A genus containing two species native to S.W. Australia in scrubland. Closely allied to *Simoselaps* and like it probably a subgenus of *Vermicella*. Length 25-40 cm (10-16 in). Burrowing snakes, the biology of which is poorly known.

N. bimaculatus (Dumeril, Bibron & Dumeril, 1854): **Western Black-naped Snake.** S.W. Western Australia and east to western half of South Australia. Light reddish brown to orange or pinkish above with each scale edged in dark reddish brown. Head blackish. Belly white to cream.

N. calonotus (Dumeril, Bibron & Dumeril, 1854): **Western Black-striped Snake.** Narrow coastal strip of S.W. Western Australia from Lancelin to Rockinham. Dorsal scales creamish, edged with pink to reddish orange. Narrow vertebral stripe of black-edged, light-centered scales. Underside white or cream.

● *Notechis* Boulenger, 1896: **Tiger Snakes.** A genus containing two species native to S.E and S.W. Australia, the southern islands, and

Tasmania. In a wide range of habitats, from rocky areas to dunes and marshland and from rain forest to dry, open sclerophyll woodland. Length 120-150 cm (48-60 in). Short, cobra-like head indistinct from robust body. Variable color and pattern. Mainly diurnal and crepuscular, but nocturnal in warm weather. Terrestrial snakes feeding mainly on frogs, but also reptiles and small mammals. Island populations are specialized to feeding (in season) on juvenile mutton birds (*Puffinus*, a type of petrel); out of season they tend to be cannibalistic! Require a large, secure terrarium with seasonal temperature variance. Highly dangerous and should be handled with the greatest of care.

N. ater (Krefft, 1866): **Black Tiger Snake.** S.W and isolated parts of S. Australia, offshore islands, and Tasmania. Length to 150 cm (60 in). Smooth scales. Head and body black to very dark brown with faint darker or lighter crossbands (especially in juveniles). Underside light to dark gray.

N. scutatus (Peters, 1862): **Eastern or Mainland Tiger Snake.** S.E. South Australia through Victoria and New South Wales to S.E. Queensland. Length to 120 cm (48 in). Light gray to brown, reddish, or almost black, with or without a series of narrow crossbands formed by lighter yellow-edged scales. Underside cream, yellow, olive-green, or gray. Ovoviviparous, producing

Top: *Notechis ater niger*. Photo: C. Banks. Bottom: *Notechis scutatus*. Photo: Dr. S. Minton.

about 30 young (but record number of 109 recorded).

● **Ogmodon** Peters, 1864: A genus containing a single species.

O. vitianus Peters, 1864: Confined to the islands of Fiji. Length to 40 cm (16 in). Small

Top: *Notechis scutatus.*
Photo: C. Banks.
Bottom: *Ophiophagus
hannah.* Photo: K. H.
Switak.

head with pointed snout and small eyes; short tail. Brownish, lighter along flanks. Juveniles with dark pattern. Burrowing snakes that probably feed largely on invertebrates. Biology poorly known. Care probably similar to that required by *Micrurus*.

● *Ophiophagus* Guenther, 1864: **King Cobras.** A genus containing a single species. *O. hannah* (Cantor, 1836): **King Cobra or Hamadryad.** India to Indo-China and S. China, plus the Indo-Australian Archipelago to Bali and the Philippines. In tropical and montane woodland, especially near water (good swimmers). Length to 400 cm (156 in) (record lengths of 553 cm [18 ft] have been recorded). The largest venomous snake. Closely related to *Naja*. Adults are medium to dark brown with faint lighter crossbands. Juveniles blackish with lighter bands. Like cobras, King Cobras can rear and spread a hood (which is relatively somewhat narrower than that of *Naja* species). Large specimens can rear as much as 120 cm (48 in) of the body off the ground and, unlike *Naja* species, can move forward while in this striking position. Highly dangerous and, in view of their size and strength, very difficult to handle (two people required with large specimens). Feeds almost exclusively on other snakes, especially *Naja* and *Bungarus*. Captive specimens usually have to be force-fed in the absence of snake prey. Require a very large terrarium with large water bath and a system of box traps. Oviparous, laying up to 40 eggs. Females build a nest by pushing ground litter (leaves, etc.) into a pile, laying the eggs beneath. Both sexes guard the nest site and become extremely aggressive if disturbed.

● *Oxyuranus* Kinghorn, 1923: **Taipans.** A genus containing a single species. *O. scutellatus* (Peters, 1868): **Taipan.** N. and N.E. Australia and New Guinea, from scrubland to tropical forest. Length to 400 cm (156 in). Long, narrow head distinct from body. Uniformly light to dark brown above, paling to creamy brown on flanks. Head often lighter, especially in juveniles. Underside cream to yellow. A large, highly venomous snake. Diurnal and crepuscular, sometimes nocturnal. Terrestrial, feeding mainly on small mammals. Requires a large, secure, heated terrarium. Handle with care! Australian subspecies, *O. s. scutellatus*, to 300 cm (120 in); New Guinea subspecies, *O. s. canni*, to 400 cm (156 in).

- ***Parademansia*** Kinghorn, 1955: A genus containing a single species. Some authorities unite this genus with *Oxyuranus*.

  P. microlepidota (McCoy, 1879): **Fierce Snake or Inland Taipan.** W. and S.W Queensland, N.W. South Australia, and W. New South Wales to Victoria border. Length to 250 cm (100 in). Closely related to *Oxyuranus*. Scales brown with darker edges. Recent research has shown the venom of *Parademansia* to be probably the most potent of all snake venoms. A rare snake, unlikely (fortunately) to come into the hands of the private collector. Diurnal. Habits probably similar to *Oxyuranus*.

- *Paranaja* Loveridge, 1944: A genus containing a single species.

  P. multifasciata (Werner, 1902): Tropical West Africa. Similar to *Pseudohaje*. Length to 150 cm (60 in). Brown with darker bands. Terrestrial to semi-arboreal. Biology poorly known.

- ***Parapistocalamus*** Roux, 1934: A genus containing a single species.

Top: *Ophiophagus hannah.* Photo: C. Banks. Bottom: *Oxyuranus scutellatus.* Photo: Dr. S. Minton.

- ***P. hedigeri*** Roux, 1934: Island of Bougainville (Solomons) and Papua New Guinea in tropical forest. Length to 60 cm (24 in). Short, blunt snout and small eyes. Dark brown and iridescent above; flanks and underside whitish. Nocturnal and burrowing, believed to feed almost exclusively on the eggs of large land snails. Otherwise biology poorly known.

Top and Center:
Oxyuranus scutellatus.
Photos: C. Banks.
Bottom: *Pseudechis australis*. Photo: Dr. S. Minton.

● ***Pseudechis*** Wagler, 1830: A genus containing five species native to Australia and New Guinea in a variety of habitats, from dry scrubland and semi-desert to rain forest and swampy areas. Length 150-200 cm (60-80 in). Short head distinct from robust body. Smooth dorsal scales. Diurnal to nocturnal, feeding on a variety of vertebrates from frogs and reptiles to birds and small mammals. Require a large terrarium with conditions compatible with origin of inmates. Ovoviviparous, producing up to 40 young. Highly dangerous and must be handled with the greatest of care!

P. australis (Gray, 1842): **Mulga or King Brown Snake.** Australia except the far south and S.E., also southern New Guinea. Length to 200 cm (80 in). Reddish to coppery or dark brown above, with darker edges to scales. Underside cream to pinkish, often with orange blotches.

P. colleti Boulenger, 1902: **Collet's Snake.** Central Queensland. Length to 150 cm (60 in). Dark brown to black above with numerous pink to orange crossbands. Underside cream to orange.

P. guttatus De Vis 1905: **Spotted Black Snake.** S.E. Queensland and N.W. New South Wales. Length to 150 cm (60 in). Color

Top: *Pseudechis guttatus.* Bottom: *Pseudechis porphyriacus.* Photos: Dr. S. Minton.

Top: *Pseudonaja textilis*. Photo: Dr. S. Minton. Center: *Pseudonaja textilis*, hatchling. Photo: C. Banks. Bottom: *Pseudonaja nuchalis*. Photo: C. Banks.

variable, uniformly black or with varied amounts of cream or white spots. Underside gray to bluish gray.

P. papuensis Peters & Doria, 1868: Eastern Papua New Guinea. Biology poorly known.

P. porphyriacus (Shaw, 1794): **Red-bellied Black Snake.** Southeastern and eastern Australia from extreme E. South Australia to S. Cape York Peninsula. Length to 150 cm (60 in). Glossy black above, bright red to pink below.

● *Pseudohaje* Guenther, 1858: A genus containing two species native to central Africa in forest and montane forest. Length 200-270 cm (80-108 in). Large eyes. Reduced hood compared to true cobras. Darkly colored. Nocturnal and arboreal, feeding largely on frogs. Biology otherwise poorly known. Require a large terrarium with facilities to climb and bathe.

P. goldii (Boulenger, 1895): **Gold's Forest Cobra.** Tropical West Africa to Uganda and Zambia.

P. nigra Guenther, 1858: **Hoodless Cobra.** Tropical West Africa. Black above, yellowish beneath.

● *Pseudonaja* Guenther, 1858: A genus containing six species native to Australia and New Guinea in dryer desert, semi-desert, brushland, and forest. Taxonomy disputed and in process of revision. Length 50-150 cm (20-60 in). Narrow-headed and slender-bodied. Agile diurnal to crepuscular snakes feeding largely on lizards. Require a secure, heated, dry terrarium. Oviparous, laying up to 35 eggs.

P. affinis Guenther, 1872: **Dugite.** S.W. Australia. Length to 150 cm (60 in). Gray to olive or brown above, the head usually lighter in color, often with inverted dark V or W marking on nape. Underside yellowish with darker flecks and orange blotches.

P. guttata (Parker, 1926): **Spotted Brown Snake.** Central Queensland into eastern

Northern Territory. Fawn to orange-brown above, spotted or banded with black. Underside orange-yellow with orange blotches.

P. ingrami (Boulenger, 1908): **Ingram's Brown Snake.** Barkly Tableland of Queensland and Northern Territory. Length to 120 cm (48 in). Dark brown to grayish above with darker head. Underside white to cream with orange blotching.

P. modesta (Guenther, 1872): **Ringed Brown Snake.** Central and western Australia. Length to 50 cm (20 in). Light to dark brown with darker head and widely spaced blackish bands along body. Underside cream to yellowish with orange patches.

P. nuchalis Guenther, 1858: **Western Brown Snake or Gwardar.** Whole of continental Australia except eastern ranges and extreme S.W. Length to 150 cm (60 in). Light to reddish brown or blackish above, with or without darker bands, spots, or patches. Underside whitish to yellowish or grayish, often with orange and dark gray patches.

P. textilis (Dumeril, Bibron & Dumeril, 1854): **Eastern Brown Snake.** Eastern Australia and possibly isolated populations in central Australia; also eastern New Guinea. Length to 150 cm (60 in). Uniformly brown to orange or blackish. Underside cream to yellowish, often with orange blotches.

- ***Rhinoplocephalus*** Mueller, 1885: A genus containing a single species.

R. bicolor Mueller, 1885: Extreme S.W. Western Australia in dry scrubland. Length to 40 cm (16 in). Uniformly olive-gray to dark gray above, darker along flanks. Underside creamy white. Biology poorly known.

- ***Salomonelaps*** McDowell, 1970: A genus containing a single species.

S. par (Boulenger, 1894): Solomon Islands, in woodlands. Length to 75 cm (30 in). Reddish to dark brown above with faint darker banding. Head lighter. Underside whitish. Feeds on frogs and lizards, otherwise biology poorly known.

- ***Simoselaps*** Jan, 1859: A genus containing six species native to Australia. Considered by some to be a subgenus of *Vermicella*. Found in desert to semi-desert, brushland, and forest. Length to 50 cm (20 in). Head indistinct from body. Variety of colors (some bright) and patterns. Terrestrial and semi-burrowing, feeding on lizards and blindsnakes. Otherwise biology poorly known. Require a terrarium with deep, loose substrate and temperatures compatible with their native habitat.

S. australis (Krefft, 1864): **Australian Coral Snake.** Central New South Wales to S.E. Queensland. Length to 50 cm (20 in). Salmon pink to bright red above, with numerous irregular dark-bordered creamish crossbands. Light-bordered black bar across neck and another narrower one across head, taking in the eyes.

Suta suta. Photo: C. Banks.

S. bertholdi (Jan, 1859): **Desert Banded Snake.** Western half of Australia except northern third and extreme S.W. Length to 30 cm (12 in). Boldly marked with equal-sized cream to reddish and black bands that extend onto belly.

S. fasciolatus (Guenther, 1872): **Narrow-banded Snake.** Southwestern Australia through to extreme S.W. Queensland and N.W. New South Wales. Length to 40 cm (16 in). Cream to pinkish with numerous irregular narrow black bands interspersed with reddish spots. Top of head black; a wide black band across neck. Underside creamy white.

S. incinctus (Storr, 1967): Central Australia to N.W. Queensland. Length to 30 cm (12 in). Pale brown to pinkish, uniform or with faint darker edges to scales. Black band across head and another wider band across neck. Underside creamy white.

S. semifasciatus (Guenther, 1863): **Half-girdled Snake.** Western half of Australia except extreme S.W.; also N.E. Queensland (split populations). Length to 40 cm (16 in). Enormous variation could indicate separate subspecific or even specific status. Gray, brown, fawn, or reddish, banded with dark brown to dark gray or black. Underside whitish.

S. warro (De Vis, 1884): N.E. Queensland. Length to 40 cm (16 in). Bright orange to orange-brown above, the scales darker edged to form a fine reticulate pattern. Head dark brown with large black patch on neck. Underside creamy white.

- ***Suta*** Worrell, 1961: A genus containing a single species. Very close to *Denisonia* and *Cryptophis*.

S. suta (Peters, 1864): **Myall or Curl Snake.** Central, northern, and eastern Australia except coastal ranges. In dry woodland to sandy scrub. Length to 60 cm (24 in). Narrow head distinct from body. Pale fawn to reddish brown above, paler on the

Top: *Vermicella annulata.* Photo: C. Banks. Center: *Unechis nigrostriatus.* Photo: K. H. Switak. Bottom: *Vermicella annulata.* Photo: Dr. S. Minton.

flanks. Head and neck distinctly darker than body. Underside creamy white. Nocturnal and terrestrial, hiding during the day under ground litter or in burrows of animals. Feeds largely on geckos. Requires a dry terrarium with adequate hiding places.

● ***Toxicocalamus*** Boulenger, 1896: A genus containing nine species native to New Guinea and adjoining islands in tropical to montane rain forest. Length 35-100 cm (14-39 in). Short, rounded head indistinct from body. Eyes very small. Short tail ending in spine. Most species uniformly brown to blackish above, some with lighter neck collar or longitudinal stripes. Nocturnal and terrestrial, biology otherwise poorly known. Care probably similar to that described for *Micrurus.* ***Ultrocalamus*** Sternfeld is considered a full genus or subgenus for *preussi* and allies.

T. buergersi (Sternfeld, 1913): Papua New Guinea (Toricelli and Prince Alexander Ranges).

T. grandis (Boulenger, 1914): Western New Guinea (West Irian).

T. holopelturus McDowell, 1969: Papua New Guinea (Mount Rossel).

T. longissimus Boulenger, 1896: Papua New Guinea (Woodlark and Fergusson Islands).

T. loriae (Boulenger, 1898): Irian Jaya and Papua New Guinea.

T. misimae McDowell, 1969: Papua New Guinea (Misima Island).

T. preussi (Sternfeld, 1913): Northern New Guinea.

T. spilolepidotus McDowell, 1969: Papua New Guinea (Purosa, near Okapa, Eastern Highlands).

T. stanleyanus Boulenger, 1903: Southern New Guinea.

● ***Tropidechis*** Guenther, 1863: A genus containing a single species.

T. carinata (Krefft, 1863): **Rough-scaled Snake.** Eastern coastal Australia, probably in split populations. In rain or wet sclerophyll forest. Length to 75 cm (30 in). Head more or less distinct from body. Spreads neck when angered. Body scales strongly keeled. Olive-brown to dark brown above, usually with irregular narrow, darker crossbands. Underside cream to yellowish or greenish, usually with darker blotches. Normally nocturnal, but occasionally basks and feeds during the day. Terrestrial, feeding on small mammals, lizards, and frogs. Requires a secure, humid woodland terrarium with adequate hiding places.

● ***Unechis*** Worrell 1961: A genus containing six species native to southern and eastern Australia in varied habitats from dry semi-desert to rain forest and wet sclerophyll woodland. Possibly a synonym of *Rhinoplocephalus*. Length to 50 cm (20 in). Long, narrow head more or less distinct from slender body. Nocturnal and terrestrial, hiding under rocks and logs, etc., during the day. Feed almost exclusively on lizards. Require a terrarium with climatic factors compatible with wild habitat.

U. brevicaudus (Brongersma & Knapp Van Meeuwen, 1964): Southern South Australia and N.W. Victoria. Brown with black vertebral stripe.

U. carpentariae (Macleay, 1887): **Carpentaria Whip Snake.** Central to northern Queensland, mostly west of Great Divide. Length to 45 cm (18 in). Uniformly

Top: *Unechis gouldi*. Photo: Dr. S. Minton. Bottom: *Unechis brevicaudus*. Photo: C. Banks.

Walterinnesia aegyptia.
Photos: Top: Dr. S.
Minton; Bottom: R. T.
Zappalorti.

light tan to dark brown above. Underside creamy white.

U. flagellum (McCoy, 1978): **Little Whip Snake.** Extreme S.W. South Australia through Victoria to S.E. New South Wales. Length to 40 cm (16 in). Light to dark brown above with dark and light edges to scales,

producing a reticulate pattern. Top of head and nape black except for light band in front of eyes. Underside creamy white to brown.

U. gouldi (Gray, 1841): **Black-headed Snake.** Southern Australia from western to eastern coasts. Length to 40 cm (16 in). Light tan to dark brown above with dark edges to

Walterinnesia aegyptia.
Photos: Top: R. T.
Zappalorti; Bottom: C.
Banks.

scales producing reticulate pattern. Head and
nape black except for lighter snout. Underside
creamy white.

U. monachus (Storr, 1964): **Hooded
Snake.** Central Western Australia from coast
eastward to Northern Territory and South
Australia. Length to 40 cm (16 in). Similar to
U. gouldi in color but lacks lighter snout.

U. nigrostriatus (Krefft, 1864): **Black-
striped Snake.** Eastern Queensland ranges to
coast. Length to 40 cm (16 in). Reddish to
dark brown with dark brown to black
vertebral stripe. Top of head dark brown to
black. Underside creamy white.

● ***Vermicella*** Gray, 1858: A genus containing
two species native to Australia in varied dryer
habitats. Length to 50 cm (20 in). Head
indistinct from body. Short tail. Nocturnal
and burrowing, feeding largely on blind
snakes (family Typhlopidae). Oviparous.

V. annulata (Gray, 1841): **Bandy-
Bandy.** Continental Australia except S.W.,
N.W., and extreme S.E. Distinctively marked
with glossy black and white bands.

V. multifasciata (Longman,
1915): **Northern Bandy-Bandy.** N.E.
Western Australia to N.W. Northern
Territory. Similar in color and pattern to
preceding species.

● ***Walterinnesia*** Lataste, 1887: A genus
containing a single species.

W. aegyptia Lataste, 1887: **Desert
Cobra.** Egypt through Asia Minor to
Lebanon and Iran. Length to 150 cm (60 in).
Uniformly dark brown to black. Less likely to
rear and spread neck than true cobras and has
reduced facility to do so. Nocturnal and
terrestrial, feeding largely on toads and
lizards. Requires a large desert terrarium with
hiding places. Temperature reduction at night.

Family Hydrophiidae—
Sea Snakes

A family containing two subfamilies, 16 genera, and some 56 species of sea snakes native to the Pacific and Indian Oceans and adjacent tropical and subtropical seas, occasionally venturing accidentally into temperate waters. One or two species possibly have become endemic to freshwater lakes. Length to 275 cm (110 in). Most are strongly adapted to a marine existence, with laterally compressed bodies and rudder-like tails to aid in swimming. Most have a tendency to reduce or lose the strap-like ventral scales, these being mostly replaced by scales of a size comparable to the dorsals. As with most aquatic snakes, the eyes are relatively small. The nostrils are valved and kept closed when the reptiles are submerged. Sea snakes possess in the floor of the mouth surrounding the tongue sheath a gland that is adapted to removing excessive salt from the bloodstream, the salt being expelled when the tongue is extended. The tooth structure is similar to that of the Elapidae: short proteroglyphic venom fangs at the front of the upper jaw followed by varying numbers of smaller, backwardly directed teeth on the maxillas and dentaries and usually on the palatines and pterygoids. Sea snakes feed largely on fish, especially eels. With a single exception (*Laticauda*) all genera are ovoviviparous, giving birth to live young in the water, and thus have no need to come onto land to nest. Some live near the shore and make excursions out to sea. *Laticauda* must come onto land in order to lay its eggs.

Hydrophiidae is considered a doubtful family by many herpetologists. *Laticauda* is very similar to *Bungarus* and allies (Elapidae), and probably most workers now would remove it from the true sea snakes. The Hydrophiinae proper could be treated as a full family (Hydrophiidae) or a subfamily of an expanded Elapidae. One school of thought, not generally accepted currently, combines the Australian elapids with the hydrophiids to produce a greatly enlarged Hydrophiidae and a very small and uniform family Elapidae. The systematics of these groups is sure to change in the future.

Sea snakes have rarely been kept in captivity, thus their husbandry is poorly researched, though in recent times some public aquaria have exhibited them in huge seawater tanks and marine biologists are making progress in understanding their husbandry. In the wild many species migrate considerable distances, and it can be assumed that they require a large amount of space in order to behave normally. In addition, they require the relatively complicated conditions demanded in aquaria for marine fish. Most sea snakes do not transport well. Once removed from their watery environment they are subject to internal injuries caused by collapse of the body, and they also cannot respire adequately. The venom of most species is highly toxic to humans, although most species seem reluctant to bite once out of the water. Once the aforementioned problems can be overcome, there is no need to doubt that aquaria containing sea snakes will take their place alongside the terraria of their terrestrial cousins. The herpetologist who also has an interest in marine aquaria has an almost unlimited opportunity to discover new and exciting factors concerning the biology of sea snakes.

SUBFAMILY LATICAUDINAE

This subfamily contains only a single genus. Many authorities now consider this to be a genus of Elapidae, not a true sea snake.

● *Laticauda* Laurenti, 1768: **Flat-tailed Sea Snakes; Sea Kraits.** A genus containing five species found in coastal areas of the Indian Ocean, eastward to S. China and S. Japan and southward to Australia and the Pacific islands. Length 80-100 cm (32-39 in). Short, cobra-like head indistinct from oval body. Venom fangs at the front of the upper jaw. Tail laterally compressed. Relatively large ventral scales. Ground color varies among the species from yellowish to bluish or off-white, but all show numerous black crossbands (in some

Laticauda colubrina. Photos: Top: Dr. B. Carlson; Bottom: R. E. Kuntz.

species these may fade with age). Mainly active at night. More amphibious than most sea snakes, spending a large amount of time on land, where the eggs are laid. Feed mainly on eels, but will take other fish. Require a large marine aqua-terrarium with facilities to bask out of the water.

L. colubrina (Schneider, 1799): **Yellow-lipped Sea Krait.** Found in whole area as described for genus.

L. crockeri Slevin, 1934: Solomon Islands.

L. laticaudata (Linnaeus, 1754): Found in whole area as described for genus.

L. semifasciata (Reinhardt, 1837): China, Taiwan, Japan, Philippines, and Indonesia.

L. schistorhynchus (Guenther, 1874): New Guinea and W. Pacific islands.

SUBFAMILY HYDROPHIINAE

This subfamily contains 15 genera and some 51 species found mainly in coastal areas and estuaries (as described for family), but some may be found far out to sea. One genus (*Hydrophis*) may be found in freshwater lakes. Unlike Laticaudinae, which have normal nostrils, the nostrils of Hydrophiinae are set

Top: *Laticauda colubrina*. Photo: Dr. S. Minton. Lower Left: *Laticauda colubrina*. Photo: R. E. Kuntz. Lower Right: *Laticauda semifasciata*. Photo: R. E. Kuntz.

high back on the snout to increase the efficiency of respiration. The short venom fangs are back in the upper jaw on the shortened maxilla and may be preceded by short palatine teeth. All show the tendency to lose the broad ventral scales, these being replaced by scales more or less similar to the dorsals. The musculature of the body is greatly reduced, and most species find it difficult or impossible to move or respire on land. All are ovoviviparous, giving birth to two to six large, well developed young in the water.

● *Acalyptophis* Boulenger, 1896: A genus containing a single species.
   A. peroni (Dumeril, 1853): Seas between northern Australia and southern New Guinea. Length to 100 cm (40 in). Head indistinct

from body. Projecting spines on supraocular and postocular scales. Dorsal scales keeled. Cream, gray, to pale brown above with a series of dark brown crossbands tapering into the flanks. Feed on a variety of fishes. Produce up to ten young.

● *Aipysurus* Lacepede, 1804: A genus containing seven species found in the Indo-Pacific area from Indo-China to Australia and New Caledonia. Length 50-200 cm (20-80 in). Relatively large ventral scales. Colors and patterns vary among the species from uniform light to dark or purplish brown with or without paler spots, flecks, or patches. Largely inhabit coral reef areas, feeding on a variety of fish.
   A. apraefrontalis Smith, 1926: **Sahul Reef Snake.** Timor Sea.
   A. duboisi Bavay, 1869: New Guinea, Australia, Melanesia.
   A. eydouxi (Gray, 1849): Malaysia, Gulf of Thailand, and Indonesia to New Guinea and Australia.
   A. foliosquama Smith, 1926: Timor Sea.
   A. fuscus (Tschudi, 1837): **Timor Reef Snake.** Indonesia to New Guinea and N.W. Australia.
   A. laevis Lacepede, 1804: New Guinea, Australia, and Melanesia.
   A. tenuis Lonnberg & Andersson, 1913: Near Broome on the N.W. coast of Australia and the Arafura Sea.

● *Disteira* Lacepede, 1804: A genus containing three species found from the Persian Gulf to the waters of the Indo-Australian region. Length to 150 cm (60 in). Similar to the closely related *Hydrophis*.
   D. kingi (Boulenger, 1896): Off northern Australia. Length to 150 cm (60 in). Black head. Body gray above with series of darker gray patches. underside cream to pale brown.
   D. major (Shaw, 1802): Seas between N. Australia and New Guinea. Length to 130 cm

Top: *Aipysurus apraefrontalis.* Bottom: *Disteira stokesi,* juvenile. Photos: Dr. S. Minton.

Top: *Aipysurus fuscus.*
Bottom: *Enhydrina schistosa.* Photos: Dr. S. Minton.

(52 in). Brown head. Body grayish above with darker crossbars or blotches. underside cream to yellowish.

D. stokesi (Gray, 1846): **Stokes' Sea Snake.** Persian Gulf to Australia. Length to 120 cm (48 in). Body massive. Uniformly creamy white to leaden-gray or almost black, sometimes with paler reticulate pattern on flanks. Usually placed in its own genus, *Astrotia* Fischer.

● **Emydocephalus** Krefft, 1869: A genus containing two species occurring from South China Sea to N. Australia. Length to 75 cm (30 in). Projecting rostral shield makes head of mature male resemble that of a sea turtle. Colors variable, uniform or banded. Apparently feed exclusively on fish eggs, which are foraged from the sea floor.

E. annulatus Krefft, 1869: **Egg-eating Sea Snake.** Indonesia, Melanesia, N. Australia.

E. ijimae Stejneger, 1898: S. China Sea.

● **Enhydrina** Gray, 1849: A genus containing a single species.

E. schistosa (Daudin, 1803): **Beaked Sea Snake.** From Persian Gulf and Madagascar to New Guinea and Australia. Length to 160 cm (64 in). Loose folded skin (more apparent when removed from water) somewhat reminiscent of *Acrochordus.* Keeled body scales. Juveniles light gray, banded with darker bars that join along the vertebral region. Adults become more uniformly gray. Often found in estuaries and sometimes far upstream in fresh water.

● **Ephalophis** Smith, 1931: A genus containing a single species.

E. greyi Smith, 1931: Off N.W. coast of Australia. Small head indistinct from slender neck and massive body that is heavier in the rear half. Gray-green to gray-blue with darker bands. Biology poorly known.

● **Hydrelaps** Boulenger, 1896: A genus

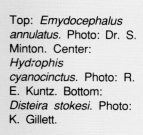

Top: *Emydocephalus annulatus*. Photo: Dr. S. Minton. Center: *Hydrophis cyanocinctus*. Photo: R. E. Kuntz. Bottom: *Disteira stokesi*. Photo: K. Gillett.

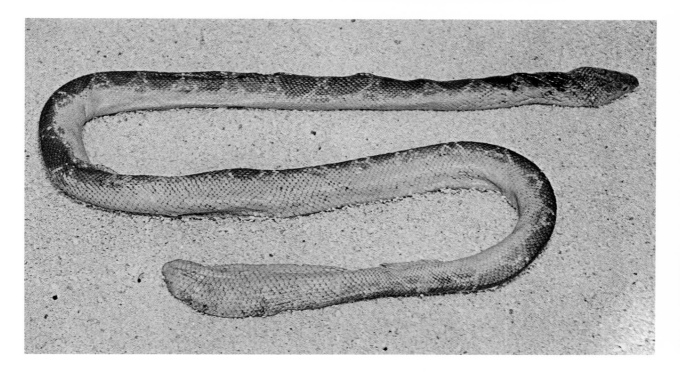

Top: *Hydrophis cyanocinctus.* Photo: Dr. S. Minton. Lower Left: *Hydrophis cyanocinctus.* Photo: R. E. Kuntz. Lower Right: *Hydrophis* cf. *klossi.* Photo: Dr. G. Dingerkus.

containing a single species.

H. darwiniensis Boulenger, 1896: Seas between N. Australia and New Guinea but especially in coastal mangrove forests. Length to 50 cm. Broad ventral scales. Yellowish with dark banding. Biology poorly known.

● ***Hydrophis*** Latreille, 1801: The largest genus of sea snakes, with 25 species found from coastal waters of India to China and Japan and southward to Australia in coral reefs and mangroves to brackish or even fresh water. Length 50-275 cm (20-110 in). Small head indistinct from massive body, which is heaviest in the rear half. Rudder-like tail. Most species are dark-banded on a lighter background.

H. belcheri (Gray, 1849): New Guinea to Philippines and Melanesia.

H. brooki Guenther, 1872: South China Sea.

H. cyanocinctus Daudin, 1803: **Annulated Sea Snake:** From Persian Gulf to Philippines and Japan. Blue-banded.

H. fasciatus (Schneider, 1799): India to Indonesia and Australia.

H. gracilis (Shaw, 1802): Persian Gulf to Taiwan, Philippines, and Australia. Very small head. Dark crossbands on lighter body.

H. melanocephalus Gray, 1849: Japan, Taiwan, and China to N. Australia. Black head. Body with light brown bands on darker brown.

H. ornatus (Gray, 1842): Persian Gulf to New Guinea and Australia. Blue-gray with numerous broad transverse bars or blotches. underside cream to white.

H. semperi Garman, 1881: **Lake Taal Snake:** Lake Taal, Luzon, Philippines. Freshwater species reaching only 50 cm (20 in) total length.

H. spiralis (Shaw, 1802): Persian Gulf to Philippines. Length to 275 cm (110 in), making it the longest sea snake.

H. stricticollis Guenther, 1864: Eastern India, Sri Lanka, and Burma.

H. torquatus Guenther, 1864: Malaysia and Gulf of Thailand.

● **Kerilia** Gray, 1849: A genus containing a single species.
K. jerdoni Gray, 1849: East India to Gulf of Thailand and Indonesia. Short head distinct from laterally compressed body. Dark blotches on lighter background. Biology poorly known.

● **Kolpophis** Smith, 1926: A genus containing a single species. Considered by some to be a synonym of *Lapemis*.
K. annandalei (Laidlaw, 1901): South China Sea. Prefers mangrove swamps and may venture far upstream into freshwater. Length to 100 cm (39 in). Head indistinct from body.

Top: *Hydrophis semperi*. Bottom: *Hydrophis inornatus*. Photos: Dr. S. Minton.

Pelamis platurus.
Photo: R. E. Kuntz.

Olive-green with darker banding; underside whitish.
- ***Lapemis*** Gray, 1835: A genus containing two species found from the Persian Gulf to Japan and southward to the N. Australian coast. Length to 100 cm (39 in). Large head indistinct from robust body. Uniformly brownish above, whitish below. Adult males have tubercles (absent in females) on the scales along the flanks, making the skin very rough. Little is known about their feeding and reproductive behavior.
L. curtus (Shaw, 1802): Persian Gulf and western India.
L. hardwicki Gray, 1835: **Hardwicke's Sea Snake.** Eastern India to Japan and N. Australia.
- ***Parahydrophis*** Burger & Natsuno, 1974: A genus containing a single species.
P. mertoni (Roux, 1910): Between Australia and New Guinea, especially in Gulf of Carpentaria. Closely related to *Ephalophis*. Length to 50 cm (20 in). Head distinct from body. Blue-gray to gray-brown above with numerous irregular blackish rings or crossbands, often joined along the vertebral line; underside brown at the front, paling toward the rear.

- ***Pelamis*** Daudin, 1803: A genus containing a single species.
P. platurus (Linnaeus, 1766): **Pelagic Sea Snake.** Most widely distributed of sea snakes, perhaps of all snake species. Occurs from eastern coast of Africa to western coast of tropical America and swims far out to sea. Although the species has been observed in the Panama Canal, to date no sightings have been made in the Atlantic. Length to 100 cm (39 in). Long, narrow head and large gape. Scales do not overlap. Black above, sharply divided from the yellow underside. Flat tail patterned in black and yellow. Feeds on various fish. Has been kept with some success in a few large public aquaria.
- ***Thalassophis*** Schmidt, 1852: A genus containing two species found from the Persian Gulf to southern China. Mainly inhabit coastal mangrove swamps. Length to 100 cm (40 in). Short, blunt head indistinct from body. Scales carry thorn-like keels, giving the skin a rough texture. Bluish green with dark crossbanding.
T. anomalus Schmidt, 1852: Gulf of Thailand to Indonesia.
T. viperinus Schmidt, 1852: Persian Gulf to S. China and Indonesia.

Lapemis hardwicki. Photo: Dr. S. Minton.

Pelamis platurus.
Photos: Top: Dr. S.
Minton; Center: P.
Freed; Bottom: R. E.
Kuntz.

Family Viperidae— Typical or Old World Vipers

A family containing three subfamilies, 11 genera, and 49 species native to Europe, Asia, and Africa in tropical to temperate climates. Most authorities include the pit vipers here as a subfamily Crotalinae. One species (*Vipera berus*) reaches within the Arctic Circle in Europe. Many species are adapted to desert conditions, but others are found in savannah to tropical rain forest. Many species are active at night but may spend much of the day basking. They possess a pair of relatively long solenoglyphic venom fangs that rest along the roof of the mouth and are brought forward by rotation of the maxilla as the reptile strikes at prey or in defense. In most cases prey is released after envenomation. The prey animal dies in a few minutes and the snake then follows its scent trail and devours it. All species in the family are highly venomous and dangerous to man, mostly producing hemotoxic/cytotoxic venom, and strict safety precautions are required when such species are kept in captivity.

SUBFAMILY AZEMIOPHINAE—FEA VIPERS

This subfamily contains a single genus.
● *Azemiops* Boulenger, 1888: **Fea Vipers.** A genus containing a single species.
A. fea Boulenger, 1888: **Fea Viper.** N. Burma, S.E. Tibet, N. Vietnam, and S. China in humid montane forest in the tropical Himalayan foothills. Length to 80 cm (32 in).

The most primitive viperid, superficially resembling a colubrid, with large symmetrical plates covering the head. Smooth dorsal scales. Relatively short venom fangs. Dark brown to blackish with widely spaced narrow whitish crossbands. A rare terrestrial species feeding largely on lizards. Otherwise biology poorly known. Requires a medium-sized, planted, humid terrarium with adequate hiding places.

SUBFAMILY VIPERINAE—TRUE VIPERS

This subfamily contains nine genera and some 46 species found in Europe, Africa, and Asia. Length 30-200 cm (12-80 in). Characterized in most cases by a broad, triangular head distinct from robust body by relatively narrow neck. Head covered generally with small scales instead of large plates. Dorsal scales partially to strongly keeled. Many have a characteristic zig-zag pattern, others are uniformly colored, and some have an amazing multicolored pattern. Most species are more or less ovoviviparous.
● *Adenorhinos* Marx & Raab, 1965: A genus containing a single species.
A. barbouri (Loveridge, 1930): East Africa (Tanzania) in tropical montane forest. Length to 40 cm (16 in). Arboreal; habits probably similar to *Atheris*. Otherwise biology poorly known.
● *Atheris* Cope, 1862: **Bush Vipers.** A genus containing eight species native to tropical Africa in forest and brushland. Length to 75 cm (30 in). Overlapping scales strongly keeled and in some cases stand out from the body,

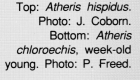

Top: *Atheris hispidus.* Photo: J. Coborn. Bottom: *Atheris chloroechis*, week-old young. Photo: P. Freed.

giving an almost hairy appearance. Colors range from uniformly yellowish brown to green, with or without darker patterns. Arboreal, with a prehensile tail. Feed on lizards, frogs, and possibly small mammals and birds. Require a tall, semi-humid, planted terrarium with adequate facilities to climb. Ovoviviparous, producing up to 20 young.

A. chloroechis (Schlegel, 1855): Western and central Africa in lowland forested areas. Leaf-green.

A. ceratophorus Werner, 1895: Tanzania (Usambara Range).

A. desaixi Ashe, 1968: Kenya (near Chuka).

A. hindii (Boulenger, 1910): Kenya (Kinangop and Aberdare Ranges).

A. hispidus Laurent, 1955: **Hairy Bush Viper.** Zaire to Uganda and Kenya. Erect scales. Light olive-green with faint darker markings.

Top: *Atheris nitschei*, juvenile. Photo: P. Freed. Center: *Atheris squamiger*. Photo: K. H. Switak. Bottom: *Atheris squamiger*. Photo: J. Visser.

A. katangensis De Witte, 1953: Zaire (Katanga).

A. nitschei Tornier, 1902: East Africa.

A. squamiger (Hallowell, 1854): **Rough-scaled Bush Viper.** Western and central Africa. Green with darker markings.

A. superciliaris (Peters, 1854): Southern Tanzania, Malawi, and Mozambique.

● *Bitis* Gray, 1842: **Puff Adders.** A genus containing 11 species native to tropical and southern Africa in a variety of habitats from dry sandy desert to humid tropical rain forest. Length 30-200 cm (12-80 in). Large triangular head distinct from robust body. Short tail. In some species certain head scales have developed into horns over the eyes or above

Top: *Atheris squamiger*. Photo: S. Kochetov. Center: *Atheris superciliaris*. Photo: K. H. Switak. Bottom: *Bitis arietans*. Photo: R. T. Zappalorti.

Top and Center: *Bitis arietans*, striped phase, compared with normal in center photo. Photos: K. H. Switak. Bottom: *Bitis atropos*. Photo: K. H. Switak.

the snout. Variable colors and markings. Most species are nocturnal, feeding on lizards, frogs, mammals, and birds. Terrarium requirements are varied depending on the size and natural habitat of the individual species.

B. arietans (Merrem, 1820): **Puff Adder.** N. Africa and Arabia to South Africa in semi-desert to dry savannah. Length to 150 cm (60 in). Color variable from yellowish to olive-brown or almost black, with a series of creamy white chevrons along the dorsal surface. Requires a dry terrarium with facilities to bathe. Highly irritable and dangerous and should be handled with the greatest of care. Record number of young in captivity 157.

B. atropos (Linnaeus, 1758): **Mountain Adder.** Zimbabwe and South Africa in mountainous country. Length to 60 cm (24 in). Head relatively longer than in other species in the genus. Dark brown to greenish above with series of triangular to semi-circular light-edged black markings along either side and bordered with a white to yellowish stripe. Below the stripe is another series of smaller circular markings; underside uniformly yellowish to blackish. Requires a dry terrarium with temperature reduction at night. Ovoviviparous, producing 8-15 young.

B. caudalis (Smith, 1839): **Cape Horned Adder.** Zimbabwe, Angola, and South Africa in sandy areas. Length to 50 cm (20 in). Single horn above each eye. Attractive color pattern in various shades of brown, blue, and whitish. Requires a dry terrarium with a deep, sandy substrate. Temperature reduction at night. Ovoviviparous, producing 12-18 young.

B. cornuta (Daudin, 1803): **Many-horned Adder or Hornsman.** Desert areas of the Cape. Length to 35 cm (14 in). Group of two to seven horns above each eye. Grayish to reddish brown above with two or three rows of pale-edged dark brown to black spots along body; underside uniformly white to brownish or with darker blotches. Requires a dry terrarium with a deep, sandy substrate.

B. gabonica (Dumeril, Bibron & Dumeril, 1854): **Gaboon Viper.** Central and eastern Africa in forested areas. Length to 200 cm (80 in). Largest species in the genus. Small to medium-sized horns above nostrils. Massive body. Remarkably patterned in range of colors for good camouflage. Requires a large, humid terrarium with facilities to bathe. Ovoviviparous. Venom highly toxic, although the species normally is quite docile. However,

Top Left: *Bitis gabonica*. Photo: S. Kochetov. Top Right: *Bitis cornuta*. Photo: J. Visser. Bottom: *Bitis caudalis*. Photo: R. Everhart.

Top Left: *Bitis gabonica rhinoceros*. Photo: K. T. Nemuras. Top Right: *Bitis peringueyi*. Photo: K. H. Switak. Bottom: *Bitis gabonica rhinoceros*. Photo: R. T. Zappalorti.

it should be treated with the greatest of respect.

B. heraldica (Bocage, 1889): Central Angola.

B. inornata (Smith, 1849): **Hornless Adder.** Southeastern Cape Province. Length

to 40 cm (16 in). Similar in many respects to *B. cornuta* but lacks raised horns, these being replaced by raised ridges.

B. nasicornis (Shaw, 1802): **Rhinoceros Viper or River Jack.** Central Africa from

Top: *Bitis inornata*. Photo: K. H. Switak. Center: *Bitis nasicornis*. Photo: K. Lucas, Steinhart. Bottom Left: *Bitis nasicornis*. Photo: W. B. Allen, Jr. Bottom Right: *Bitis gabonica rhinoceros*. Photo: R. T. Zappalorti.

west to east in tropical forest, especially in the vicinity of rivers. Length to 130 cm (52 in). Characteristic horns above nostrils. Remarkably patterned in a range of colors and perhaps even more spectacular than *B. gabonica*. Requires a humid terrarium with facilities to bathe.

B. peringueyi (Boulenger, 1888): **Dwarf Puff Adder or Side-winding Adder.** Namib Desert area, S.W. Africa. Length to 30 cm (12 in), often smaller. Sandy gray to pale buff above with three rows of brown to blackish spots along body. Underparts off-white with brown blotches. Moves by sidewinding. Requires a dry desert terrarium with a deep sandy substrate. Feeds mainly on lizards, using its black-tipped tail as a lure.

B. schneideri (Boettger, 1886): **Namaqua Dwarf Adder.** Coastal areas of Little Namaqualand. Length to 30 cm (12 in). Gray to grayish brown above with three longitudinal rows of dark brown to black light-centered spots. Underside grayish to yellowish white. Similar in habits to *B. peringueyi*.

B. worthingtoni Parker, 1932: Kenya. Length to 40 cm (16 in).

B. xeropaga Haacke, 1975: South Africa (Dreikammberg, north of Orange River).

● ***Cerastes*** Laurenti, 1768: A genus containing two species native to N. Africa, Asia Minor, and Arabia in dry desert to semi-desert. Length to 75 cm (30 in). Broad, triangular head distinct from relatively slender body. The flanks are adorned with saw-edged scales that produce a warning sound as the snake rubs its coils together (similar to *Echis*). Sandy yellow to brown with darker blotches. Move by sidewinding and are able to quickly bury

Top: *Bitis nasicornis.* Photo: J. K. Langhammer. Bottom: *Bitis peringueyi.* Photo: Dr. D. Terver.

Top: *Bitis xeropaga*. Photo: J. Visser. Left Center: *Cerastes cerastes*. Photo: C. Banks. Right Center: *Bitis worthingtoni*. Photo: J. Coborn. Bottom: *Bitis schneideri*. Photo: K. H. Switak.

Top: *Cerastes vipera.*
Photo: Dr. S. Minton.
Bottom: *Cerastes cerastes.* Photo: R. T. Zappalorti.

themselves in loose sand, leaving just the eyes exposed. Feed largely on lizards. Require a desert terrarium with a deep, sandy substrate. Should have access to a moist area. Oviparous, laying 8-24 eggs that hatch in four to seven weeks.

C. cerastes (Linnaeus, 1758): **Desert Horned Viper.** Morocco to Arabia. Horn above each eye, though these may be absent in some individuals.

C. vipera (Linnaeus, 1758): **Sahara Sand Viper or Avicenna Viper.** Sandy areas of Sahara. Lacks facial horns.

● **Daboia** Gray, 1842: A genus containing six species formerly included in the genus *Vipera*. Considered by some authorities to be better treated as a subgenus of *Vipera* than a full genus. Found from N. Africa to Asia Minor and in the Middle to Far East in a variety of habitats. Length 80-200 cm (32-80 in). Long, triangular head distinct from body. Color and pattern highly varied, even within a single species. Highly venomous; *D. russelli* is responsible for many human fatalities. Require a dry to semi-humid terrarium depending on the natural habitat of the individual species. Ovoviviparous, with the exception of most subspecies of *D. lebetina*, which lay eggs.

D. lebetina (Linnaeus, 1758): **Levantine Viper.** Greek Islands (Milos), Cyprus, and Asia Minor to the Caucasus and Central Asia. Requires a dry terrarium with a temperature

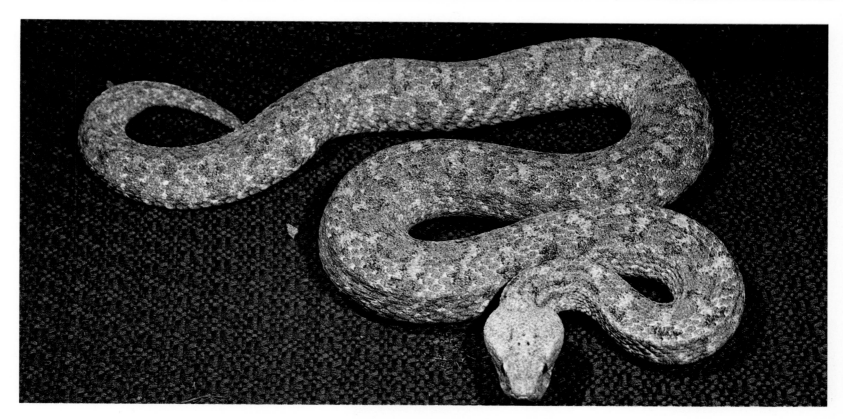

Top: *Daboia lebetina* cf. *schweizeri*. Photo: S. Kochetov. Bottom: *Cerastes vipera*. Photo: R. Everhart.

Top: *Daboia lebetina*. Photo: B. Kahl. Center and Bottom: *Daboia lebetina turanica*. Photos: S. Kochetov.

reduction at night. Period of hibernation recommended.

D. mauretanica (Gray, 1849): N.W. Africa to Libya. Care as for preceding species.

D. palaestinae Werner, 1938: **Palestine Viper.** Syria, Jordan, and Israel.

D. raddei (Boettger, 1890): **Caucasus Viper.** Armenian SSR, Turkey, N.W. Iran, Lebanon, Israel, and Jordan.

D. russelli (Shaw, 1802): **Russell's Viper or Daboia.** Pakistan to China and Indonesia. Colorful, with reddish oval markings bordered in black and whitish, on a brown-buff background. Highly venomous.

D. xanthina (Gray, 1849): Turkey.

● ***Echis*** Merrem, 1820: A genus containing six species native to northern Africa and the Near and Middle East, east to India and Sri Lanka. In a variety of dry habitats, from desert to rocky slopes, savannah, and forest margins. Length 70-90 cm (28-36 in). Large eyes with vertical pupils. About five rows of scales along the flanks are arranged at a 45° angle to the other scales and are furnished with serrated keels. These are rubbed together when the snake is threatened, producing a loud rustling sound. Color and pattern variable, various shades of brown, reddish, grayish, yellowish, or whitish and black with angular to circular markings or bars. Nocturnal, feeding on a range of vertebrates. Juveniles probably also feed on invertebrates. May move by sidewinding. Require a dry terrarium with a deep, sandy substrate and a temperature reduction at night. Ovoviviparous, producing 8-16 young. Highly venomous and irascible.

E. carinatus (Schneider, 1801): **Saw-scaled or Carpet Viper.** East Africa to Egypt and Middle East to India and Sri Lanka.

E. coloratus Guenther, 1878: **Palestine Saw-scaled Viper.** Egypt, Israel, and Arabia.

Top Left: *Daboia lebetina obtusa*. Photo: S. Kochetov. Top Right: *Daboia raddei*. Photo: Dr. O. Klee. Bottom: *Daboia palaestinae*. Photo: R. Everhart.

Top: *Daboia russelli*.
Photo: R. Everhart.
Bottom: *Daboia raddei*.
Photo: R. T. Zappalorti.

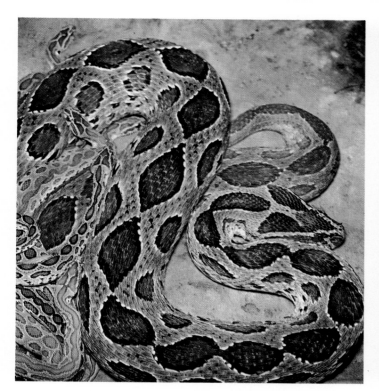

Top Left: *Daboia russelli*. Photo: H. Hansen. Top Right: *Daboia russelli*, mating pair. Photo: S. Kochetov. Bottom: *Daboia xanthina*. Photo: B. Kahl.

Top Left: *Echis coloratus*. Photo: J. Kellnhauser. Top Right: *Echis coloratus*. Photo: C. Banks. Center: *Pseudocerastes fieldi*. Photo: K. H. Switak. Bottom Left: *Echis carinatus*. Photo: J. Kellnhauser. Bottom Right: *Daboia xanthina*. Photo: B. Kahl.

Largest species in the genus.
E. multisquamatus Cherlin, 1981: Soviet Central Asia, Iran.

- ***Eristicophis*** Alcock, 1896: A genus containing a single species.
E. macmahoni Alcock & Finn, 1897: **McMahon's Desert Viper.** High altitude border regions of Afghanistan and Pakistan in stony desert. Length to 60 cm (24 in). Characteristic of this species is the pair of flap-like scales on either side of the broad rostral. Sandy brown above with light-bordered dark eye-spots along the flanks. Nocturnal, feeding on lizards and small mammals. Requires a dry terrarium with a deep, sandy substrate and a temperature reduction at night. A winter hibernation period of three to four months is recommended. Highly venomous.

- ***Pseudocerastes*** Boulenger, 1896: A genus containing three species native to the Middle East in desert to semi-desert. Often considered a subgenus of *Vipera*. Length to 100 cm (39 in). Horn-like scale over eye. Keeled dorsal scales. Moves by sidewinding. Sandy brown with darker crossbars. Nocturnal, feeding on lizards and small mammals. Requires a dry desert terrarium with a deep, sandy substrate and reduced temperature at night. Ovoviviparous,

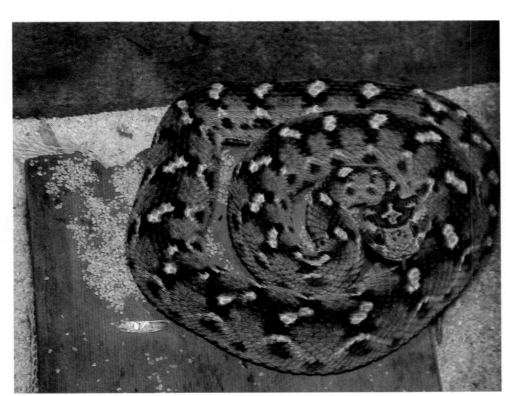

Top Left: *Eristicophis macmahoni*. Photo: S. Kochetov. Top Right: *Echis coloratus*. Photo: S. Kochetov. Bottom: *Eristicophis macmahoni*. Photo: B. Kahl.

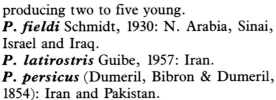

Top: *Vipera ammodytes.* Photo: R. T. Zappalorti. Bottom: *Pseudocerastes persicus.* Photo: J. Coborn.

producing two to five young.

P. fieldi Schmidt, 1930: N. Arabia, Sinai, Israel and Iraq.

P. latirostris Guibe, 1957: Iran.

P. persicus (Dumeril, Bibron & Dumeril, 1854): Iran and Pakistan.

● ***Vipera*** Laurenti, 1768: A genus containing six species native to Europe, Western Asia, and N. Africa in a variety of habitats, from semi-desert to montane meadows, heathland, and even semi-tundra. One species (*V. berus*) reaches just into the Arctic Circle, making it the most northerly-ranging of all snakes. The taxonomy of this genus is very complex, and most species have several subspecies. Some, such as *V. berus bornmuelleri* and *V. b. seoanei*, are considered full species by many workers. The genera *Daboia* and *Pseudocerastes* are very similar.

Length 50-100 cm (20-39 in). Often divided into two subgenera: *Vipera* (*V. berus, V. kaznakovi, V. ursinii*) with large head shields, and *Rhinaspis* (*V. ammodytes, V. aspis, V. latastii*) with the head covered with small scales. (Technical research has shown the name *Rhinaspis* Bonaparte to be both a nomen nudum and preoccupied by a beetle, so another name will have to be used for this subgenus.) Pattern usually consists of a dark zig-zag vertebral band on a paler background color. Require a terrarium compatible with natural habitat. Northern and montane specimens are suited to outdoor enclosures. Ovoviviparous, producing 8-25 young.

V. ammodytes (Linnaeus, 1758): **Nose-horned Viper.** S.E. Europe and S.W Asia. In dry areas, often on sparsely vegetated rocky slopes. Length to 100 cm (39 in), but usually shorter. Distinct horn on snout. Males usually light gray, females grayish, brownish, or reddish brown, with a clearly defined dark-edged vertebral stripe forming a zig-zag or joined lozenge pattern, underside grayish to

Vipera ammodytes.
Photo: B. Kahl.

Top: *Vipera aspis*.
Photo: Dr. D. Terver.
Center: *Vipera berus*.
Photos: Left: Dr. D.
Terver; Right: B. Kahl.
Bottom: *Vipera aspis*.
Photo: B. Kahl.

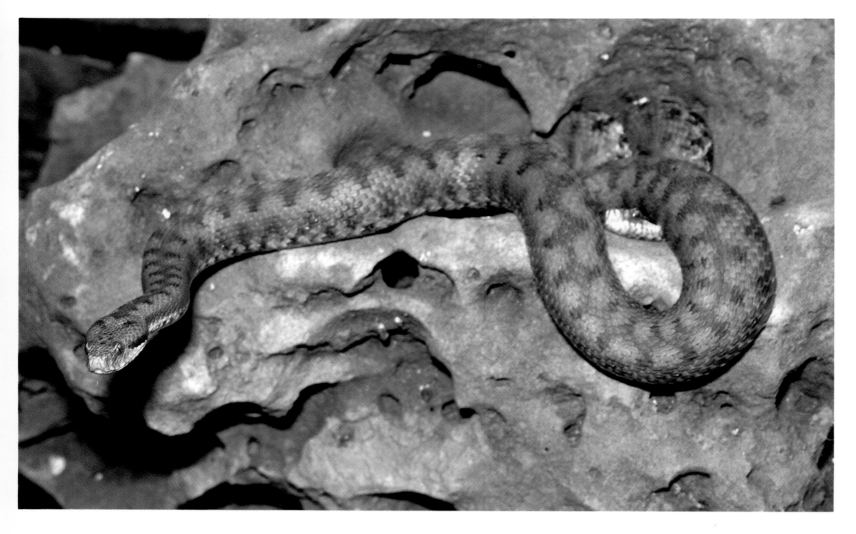

Top: *Vipera berus*, melanistic. Photo: B. Kahl. Bottom: *Vipera aspis*, melanistic. Photo: Dr. D. Terver.

Top: *Vipera berus* giving birth. Photos: S. Kochetov. Center: *Vipera berus bornmuelleri*. Photo: Dr. S. Minton. Bottom Left: *Vipera berus*. Bottom Right: *Vipera aspis*. Photos: Dr. D. Terver.

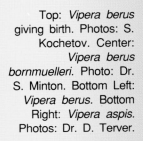

Top: *Vipera kaznakovi.*
Photo: Dr. S. Minton.
Center: *Vipera ursini.*
Photo: Dr. D. Terver.
Bottom: *Vipera kaznakovi*, young at left, adult at right.
Photos: S. Kochetov.

pinkish with darker mottling. Feeds on a variety of vertebrates. Highly venomous.
V. aspis (Linnaeus, 1758): **Asp Viper.** W. and central Europe from N.E. Spain through France to S.W. Germany, Switzerland, and Italy to Sicily. On dry hillsides to damp montane meadows to 3000 m (9750 ft). Length to 70 cm (28 in). Upturned snout. Color and pattern variable, usually with a dark zig-zag vertebral stripe on lighter ground. Melanistic (all black) specimens not uncommon. Feeds mainly on small mammals.

Top: *Vipera latifi*. Photo:
Dr. S. Minton. Bottom:
Vipera ursini. Photos:
Left: Dr. D. Terver;
Right: S. Kochetov.

V. berus (Linnaeus, 1758): **Adder or
Northern Viper.** Almost the whole of
Europe except the south; also across USSR to
Pacific coast. Northern populations adapted to
quite extreme cold-weather conditions, being
active only four to five months in the year.
Length to 90 cm (36 in), usually shorter.
Blunt-snouted. Female usually light brown
with a dark brown zig-zag stripe, the male
light gray with a black zig-zag stripe along the
back. Melanistic and uniformly brown
specimens not uncommon. Underside gray to
gray brown or black, with or without
mottling. Feeds largely on lizards (especially
Lacerta vivipara in northern part of range).

V. kaznakovi Nikolsky, 1909: **Caucasus
Viper.** Western Caucasus to N.W. Anatolia.
Orange-brown above with narrow dark gray
zig-zag line along back, gray to black along
flanks and underside.
V. latastii Bosca, 1878: **Lataste's
Viper.** Iberian Peninsula (except extreme
north) and N.W. Africa, mainly in dry, rocky
areas or open woodland. Feed mainly on small
mammals, sometimes fledgling birds or
lizards. Length to 75 cm (30 in). Usually has
a small horn on snout. Ground color grayish
to brownish or reddish with a wavy or zig-zag
dorsal stripe with a darker edge.
V. ursini (Bonaparte, 1835): **Orsini's or**

Meadow Viper. Isolated populations in central Europe, extending eastward to central Asia. Found in dry to moist montane meadows and grasslands. Length to 50 cm (20 in). Small and narrow head with a thickish body. Grayish to pale brown or yellowish with a black-edged dark zig-zag dorsal stripe. Underside whitish to grayish, with or without darker spots.

SUBFAMILY CAUSINAE—NIGHT ADDERS

This subfamily contains only a single genus.

● ***Causus*** Wagler, 1830: **Night Adders.** A genus containing four species native to Africa south of the Sahara in dry to semi-humid localities, but usually near water. Length 40-80 cm (16-32 in). Narrowish head covered with large symmetrical shields and indistinct from neck and moderately robust body. Relatively large venom glands that reach into front third of body; however, the venom is considered to be relatively innocuous to humans (but treat with respect!). Color and pattern highly variable. When threatened, they spread the neck cobra-like, though they do not rear. Nocturnal and terrestrial, feeding largely on frogs and toads. Require a heated, dry terrarium with a large water container and adequate hiding places. Oviparous, laying 8-25 eggs.

C. defilippii (Jan, 1862): **Snouted Night Adder.** East Africa, including island of Zanzibar. Yellowish brown with pale-bordered dark rhomboidal markings. Prefers dryer conditions than other species in genus.

C. resimus (Peters, 1862): **Green Night Adder.** East Africa, Uniformly green or with darker blotches. More dependent on water than preceding species.

C. rhombeatus (Lichtenstein, 1823): **Rhombic Night Adder.** Africa south of Sahara, except Eritrea, tropical West Africa, and S.W. South Africa. Varying

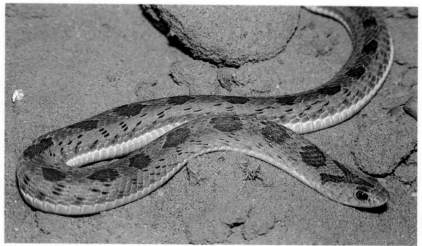

shades of gray to olive or light brown above, with a row of usually pale-bordered dark rhomboidal markings along back. V-shaped marking on back of head with apex reaching between eyes. Underside dirty white to yellowish or gray, uniform or with dark-edged ventrals.

Top: *Causus defilippii.* Photo: J. Visser. Center: *Causus maculatus.* Photo: C. Banks. Bottom: *Causus rhombeatus.* Photo: J. Visser.

Family Crotalidae—Pit Vipers

This family contains at least seven genera and some 130 species native mainly to the Americas, but with some representatives in S. and S.E. Asia. Some authorities include this family as the subfamily Crotalinae within the Viperidae. It is found in a range of climates from cool to warm temperate, subtropical, and tropical. Length 60-350 cm (24-140 in). Large, often triangular head distinct from robust body by relatively narrow neck. The more primitive types (*Agkistrodon, Sistrurus*) possess large, symmetrical head shields, while the majority have a head covered with small scales. The main characteristic of the family is the pit, a thermoreceptor organ situated on each side of the head between the eye and the nostril and similar in function but more efficient than the pit on the boid lip. This contains an infra-red heat sensitive diaphragm that enables the reptile to seek prey and orient in the dark. There are large solenoglyphic fangs in the front of the upper jaw. Most of the species are highly venomous, and all require very secure housing. Other factors pertaining to housing are dependent on the natural habitat of the individual species. Most are ovoviviparous, but there are exceptions.

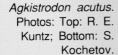

Agkistrodon acutus.
Photos: Top: R. E. Kuntz; Bottom: S. Kochetov.

● *Agkistrodon* Beavois, 1799: A genus containing 13 species native to Asia and N. America. Length 70-160 cm (28-64 in). Recent taxonomic research has suggested that only the American species should remain in the genus *Agkistrodon*, while the Asian species may be divided into two or three separate genera (*Deinagkistrodon, Calloselasma,* and *Gloydius*). In the present work the genus will be left intact. (But see *Hypnale,* treated as a full genus.) The various species occur in a variety of habitats and climates, from swamps and marshes to mountain slopes and from temperate woodland to tropical rain forest. The triangular head has a more or less pointed snout and is distinct from the body. May be a variety of colors and patterns, but usually a cryptic combination of browns, yellows, and black. Mostly nocturnal, feeding on a variety of vertebrates; juvenile specimens of many species take invertebrates. Tip of tail may be vibrated to attract prey. Require a secure terrarium with adequate, controllable hiding places and environmental conditions compatible with the natural range of the individual species. Period of hibernation

recommended for more northerly species. Highly venomous and lightning fast in striking. Should be treated with the greatest respect.

A. (Deinagkistrodon) acutus (Guenther, 1888): **Chinese Moccasin.** S. China and N. Vietnam. Length to 150 cm (60 in). Spine-like snout projection.

A. bilineatus Guenther, 1863: **Mexican Moccasin or Cantil.** S. Mexico to Nicaragua.

A. (Gloydius) blomhoffi (Boie, 1826): **Mamushi.** Japan, Taiwan, Korea, E. China, and E. USSR. Yellowish brown with

Top: *Agkistrodon acutus.* Photo: R. Everhart. Center Left: *Agkistrodon blomhoffi.* Photo: S. Kochetov. Bottom Left: *Agkistrodon bilineatus gloydi.* Photo: R. D. Bartlett. Bottom Right: *Agkistrodon bilineatus.* Photo: B. Kahl.

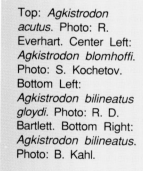

Top: *Agkistrodon blomhoffi blomhoffi.* Photo: Dr. S. Minton. Bottom: *Agkistrodon caliginosus.* Photo: Dr. S. Minton.

Agkistrodon bilineatus. Photos: R. Everhart.

Top Left: *Agkistrodon contortrix contortrix.* Photo: R. T. Zappalorti. Top Right: *Agkistrodon blomhoffi brevicaudis.* Photo: J. Kellnhauser. Center: *Agkistrodon contortrix pictigaster.* Photo: K. H. Switak. Bottom Left: *Agkistrodon bilineatus taylori,* juvenile. Photo: R. T. Zappalorti. Bottom Right: *Agkistrodon contortrix mokasen.* Photo: R. T. Zappalorti.

dark crossbanding; yellow with dark spots beneath.

A. contortrix (Linnaeus, 1776): **American Copperhead.** E. and S.E. USA. Length to 135 cm (54 in). Light copper to orange-brown with bold, broad, reddish brown to chestnut saddle markings along back. Usually occurs near water. Ovoviviparous, producing 1-14 young.

A. (Gloydius) halys (Pallas, 1776): **Haly's Pit Viper.** Siberia and Eastern Asia. Light gray to light brown with dark crossbanding.

A. (Gloydius) himalayanus (Guenther, 1864): Western Himalayas between altitudes of 2000 and 5000 m (6500-16000 ft).

Top: *Agkistrodon contortrix laticinctus.*
Photo: R. Everhart.
Bottom: *Agkistrodon contortrix mokasen.*
Photo: R. T. Zappalorti.

Top: *Agkistrodon intermedius caucasicus.* Photo: Dr. S. Minton. Center and Bottom Left: *Agkistrodon piscivorus.* Photos: S. Kochetov. Bottom Right: *Agkistrodon contortrix mokasen.* Photo: R. T. Zappalorti.

Top and Center: *Agkistrodon piscivorus piscivorus*. Photos: R. T. Zappalorti. Bottom: *Agkistrodon piscivorus*, juveniles. Photo: W. B. Allen, Jr.

Top Left: *Agkistrodon piscivorus leucostoma*, juvenile. Top Right: *Agkistrodon saxatilis*. Photos: S. Kochetov. Bottom: *Agkistrodon rhodostoma*. Photo: Dr. S. Minton.

A. *piscivorus* (Guenther, 1864): **Cottonmouth or Water Moccasin.** S.E. USA. Length to 190 cm (76 in). Heavy-bodied. Uniformly dark brown or olive to black above or with faint lighter crossbands. Semi-aquatic, living in and around swamps, lakes, rivers, canals, ditches, and streams. Feeds on fish, amphibians, snakes, and birds. Requires a large aqua-terrarium.

A. *(Calloselasma) rhodostoma* (Boie, 1827): **Malayan Pit Viper.** Indo-China

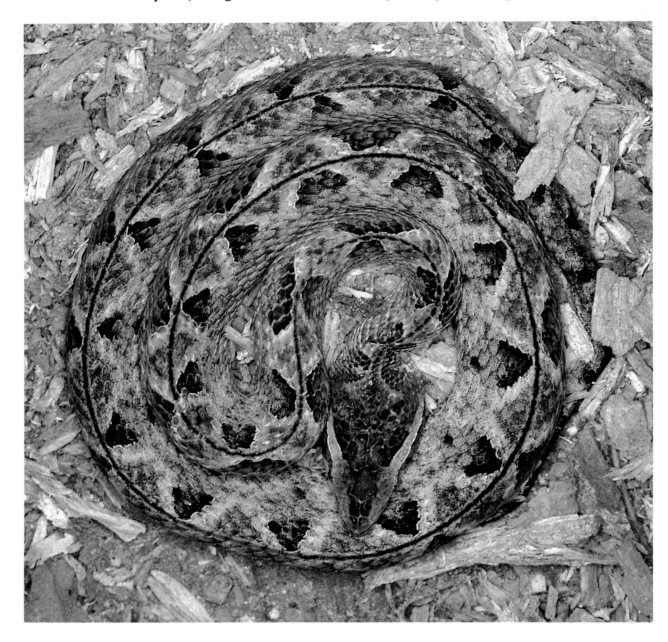

Top: *Agkistrodon piscivorus leucostoma.* Photo: R. Everhart. Center: *Bothrops alternatus.* Photo: M. Freiberg. Bottom: *Agkistrodon rhodostoma.* Photo: C. Banks.

through Malaya to Sumatra and Java in rain forest. Length to 100 cm (39 in). Attractive cryptic color pattern in browns, yellows, and black. Feeds on a variety of vertebrates. Requires a humid rain-forest terrarium. Oviparous, laying up to 20 eggs. Shows parental care to eggs by coiling around them until they hatch.

● ***Bothrops*** Wagler, 1824: A genus containing about 50 species native to Central and South America. Show parallel evolutionary characteristics to the S.E. Asian genus *Trimeresurus* and exhibit a range of morphological characteristics, habits, and habitats. Length 60-240 cm (24-96 in). All species in the genus are ovoviviparous, producing 10-60 young. All species are highly venomous, some extremely dangerous to man. Recently *Bothrops* has been broken into some five subgenera or genera, some of which are

Top Left: *Bothrops alternatus*. Photo: M. Freiberg. Top Right: *Bothrops atrox*. Photo: R. T. Zappalorti. Center: *Bothrops ammodytoides*. Photo: M. Freiberg. Bottom Left: *Bothrops andianus*. Photo: J. Coborn. Bottom Right: *Bothrops aurifer*, one day old. Photo: P. Freed.

recognizable for distinctive species groups. These names are not used here, but for future reference they are: *Bothriechis* Peters (palm vipers, *schlegeli, lateralis,* etc.); *Bothrops* Wagler (fer-de-lances, urutus, *atrox, alternatus, jararaca,* etc.); *Porthidium* Cope (hognosed pit vipers, *nasutus, nummifer, ophryomegas,* etc.); *Ophryacus* Cope *(undulatus); Bothriopsis* Peters *(castelnaudi).*

B. alternatus Dumeril, Bibron & Dumeril,

Top: *Bothrops insularis*. Photo: Dr. S. Minton. Center: *Bothrops atrox*. Photo: M. Freiberg. Bottom Left: *Bothrops godmani*. Photo: J. Kellnhauser. Bottom Right: *Bothrops brazili*. Photo: P. Freed.

Top: *Bothrops jararaca*.
Photo: M. Freiberg.
Center and Bottom:
Bothrops jararacussu.
Photos: Center: S.
Kochetov; Bottom: M.
Freiberg.

Top Left: *Bothrops lanceolatus*. Photo: C. Banks. Top Right: *Bothrops jararaca*. Photo: S. Kochetov. Center and Bottom: *Bothrops lateralis*. Photos: Center: J. Iverson; Bottom: J. Kellnhauser.

Top Left: *Bothrops moojeni*. Photo: M. Freiberg. Top Right: *Bothrops neuwiedii*. Photo: S. Kochetov. Center: *Bothrops neuwiedii pubescens*. Photo: F. Achaval. Bottom: *Bothrops nasutus*. Photo: Dr. S. Minton.

Top: *Bothrops nigroviridis.* Photo: Dr. S. Minton. Center: *Bothrops nummifer.* Photo: K. H. Switak. Bottom: *Bothrops neuwiedii diporus.* Photos: Left: S. Kochetov; Right: L. M. Lozzia.

Top: *Bothrops nummifer*. Photos: Left: S. Kochetov; Right: J. Kellnhauser. Bottom: *Bothrops ophryomegas*. Photo: Dr. S. Minton.

1854: **Urutu.** Southern Brazil and northern Argentina in tropical dry to wet forest and margins. Length to 200 cm (80 in). Highly dangerous. Brownish with lighter and darker pattern. Nocturnal and terrestrial, feeding on a variety of vertebrates, especially small mammals. Requires a large, semi-humid terrarium with facilities to bathe.

Top Left: *Bothrops pirajai*, young. Photo: M. Freiberg.
Top Right: *Bothrops schlegeli*, yellow phase. Photo: J.
Kellnhauser. Bottom: *Bothrops schlegeli*. Photo: B.
Kahl.

Top Left: *Bothrops rowleyi*, female. Photo: P. Freed.
Top Right and Bottom: *Bothrops schlegeli*, yellow
phase. Photos: Top: A. Kerstitch; Bottom: B. Kahl.

Bothrops schlegeli.
Photos: Top: J. Iverson;
Bottom: R. T.
Zappalorti.

B. ammodytoides Leybold, 1873: **Yararanata.** S. Brazil and Argentina in pampas to semi-desert. Terrestrial, feeding on lizards and small mammals. Requires a dry terrarium with adequate hiding places. Other species in the genus requiring similar conditions include *B. lansbergi*, *B. melanurus*, and *B. roedingeri*.

B. andianus Amaral, 1923: Peru in montane rain forest to meadows and scree slopes. Requires a cool, humid terrarium with facilities for dry basking. Other species in the genus requiring similar conditions are *B. barbouri*, *B. bicolor*, *B. venezuelae* and *B. xanthogrammus*.

B. atrox (Linnaeus, 1758): **Caicaca, Barba Amarilla, or Fer-de-Lance.** Mexico to tropical South America, also Trinidad and Tobago, St. Lucia, and Martinique. In tropical dry to humid forested regions.

Length to 240 cm (96 in), though usually shorter. Brown to blackish with a pale diamond pattern. Nocturnal and terrestrial, feeding on small mammals and birds. Requires a large, semi-humid to dry terrarium with facilities to bathe. Highly dangerous.

B. bilineatus (Wied, 1825): **Green Jararaca.** Amazon Basin and tributaries in tropical rain forest. Uniformly green. Arboreal, with prehensile tail. Feeds largely on lizards and frogs. Requires a tall, humid, planted terrarium with a relatively constant temperature.

B. insularis (Amaral, 1921): **Golden Lancehead.** Island of Queimada Grande (Sao Paulo, Brazil). This species is remarkable in having a genetic defect that constantly produces sterile, hermaphroditic offspring that, it is supposed, will eventually lead to its extinction. Terrestrial.

B. jararaca (Wied, 1824): **Jararaca.** Most abundant member of the genus in Brazil and N. Argentina. Found in a variety of habitats. Terrestrial.

B. lateralis (Peters, 1863): **Coffee Palm Viper.** Costa Rica. Uniformly green. Requires care similar to that described for *B. bilineatus*.

B. nasutus Bocourt, 1868: **Hognosed Pit Viper.** Mexico to Colombia and Ecuador in moister and montane forests. Horn on snout.

B. neuwiedii Wagler, 1824: **Jararaca Pintada.** From Bolivia through Brazil to N. Argentina in a variety of habitats. Enormous range of colors and patterns. Terrestrial.

B. schlegeli (Berthold, 1846): **Speckled Palm Viper** or **Eyelash Viper.** S. Mexico to Venezuela and Ecuador. Range of colors and patterns. Arboreal, feeding mainly on lizards and frogs. Care as for *B. bilineatus.* Many specimens have a series of small horns over the eyes.

• *Crotalus* Linnaeus, 1758: **Rattlesnakes.**
A genus containing about 27 species native to
North and Central America and northern
South America. Found in a variety of dryer
habitats, from prairie to desert and semi-
desert. Characteristic of the genus (except for
one species, *C. catalinensis*) is the warning
rattle at the tip of the tail that is composed of
a series of keratinous, loosely interlocked,
dumb-bell shaped hollow shells. Each time
the snake molts a new section to the rattle is
formed, but the older sections at the tip
constantly wear away and fall off. Most
rattlers rarely have more than six to ten
sections to the rattle at any one time, but as
many as 30 have been recorded. Length 60-
250 cm (24-100 in). Head covered with small
scales. Dorsal scales keeled. Colors and
patterns vary, but usually shades of brown to
buff with black and white markings. Mostly
crepuscular and nocturnal terrestrial snakes
that feed on a variety of vertebrates, the large
species on mammals and birds, the smaller
ones mainly on lizards. Require a secure,
large, dry terrarium with controllable hiding
places. Highly venomous and dangerous.
Treat with the utmost care. Ovoviviparous.

C. adamanteus Beavois, 1799: **Eastern
Diamondback Rattlesnake.** S.E. USA in
warm, dry to humid lowland areas. Length to
250 cm (100 in); largest species in the genus.
Massive. Grayish with a pattern of white and
black diamonds down back. Regarded as
North America's most dangerous snake.

C. atrox Baird & Girard, 1853: **Western
Diamondback Rattlesnake.** S.E California
eastward to central Arkansas and southward
to Mexico in arid to semi-arid areas from sea
level to 2100 m (7000 ft). Length to 210 cm
(84 in). Marked similarly to preceding species
but duller, except for broad, conspicuous
black and white rings encircling the tail
anterior to the rattle. Highly dangerous and
irritable.

C. basiliscus (Cope, 1864): **Basilisk
Rattlesnake.** Mexico, in dry western
woodlands. Highly venomous.

C. catalinensis Cliff, 1954: **Santa Catalina
Rattlesnake.** Island of Santa Catalina in Gulf
of California. The only species consistently
without a rattle on its tail.

C. cerastes Hallowell,
1854: **Sidewinder.** S.W. USA into N.W.
Mexico in arid desert flatland to 1500 m (5000
ft). Length to 80 cm (32 in). Prominent
triangular horn over each eye. Pale sandy buff
with alternate darker and lighter patches along
back. Typical sidewinding locomotion. Feeds
on desert rodents and lizards.

C. durissus Linnaeus, 1758: **Cascabel
Rattlesnake.** S. Mexico to Brazil and N.
Argentina in dryer areas. Length to 180 cm
(72 in). Light brown ground color with light
and dark rhomboidal pattern. Most potent
venom in the genus; highly dangerous.

C. enyo (Cope, 1861): Central Mexico and

Top: *Crotalus adamanteus*, "snowflake" albino. Photo: K. H. Switak. Center: *Crotalus adamanteus*, female with young. Photo: R. T. Zappalorti. Bottom: *Crotalus atrox*, juvenile. Photo: R. Everhart.

Top: *Crotalus adamanteus*. Bottom: *Crotalus atrox*, albino. Photos: R. Everhart.

Baja California.

C. exsul Garman, 1893: Cedros Island, west coast of Baja California.

C. horridus Linnaeus, 1758: **Timber Rattlesnake or Canebrake Rattlesnake.** Eastern USA from extreme S.W. Maine to N. Florida and west into S.E. Minnesota and central Texas. In woodlands. Length to 190 cm (76 in). Color variable, from yellow to brown, gray, or blackish with dark blotches along back and sides, becoming bands toward rear end of the body and tail. Dangerous.

C. intermedius Troschel, 1865: Central and S.W. Mexico.

C. lannomi Tanner, 1966: Near Jalisco, Mexico.

C. lepidus (Kennicott, 1861): **Rock Rattlesnake.** S.W. USA to central Mexico. Mainly in rocky areas between 500-2900 m

Top: *Crotalus basiliscus*. Photo: K. H. Switak. Bottom: *Crotalus atrox*. Photo: R. Everhart.

(1500-9600 ft). Length to 85 cm (34 in). Small-headed, slender species. Greenish to bluish gray or pinkish tan with widely spaced light-bordered narrow black or brown crossbands. Amount of spotting varies between mottled and banded subspecies.

C. mitchelli (Cope, 1861): **Speckled Rattlesnake.** S.W. USA and Baja California in rugged, rocky terrain. Length to 130 cm (52 in). Color and pattern highly variable, but generally has a sandy, speckled appearance.

C. molossus Baird & Girard, 1853: **Black-tailed Rattlesnake.** S.W. USA to central Mexico, mainly in rocky, mountainous areas to 2750 m (9000 ft). Length to 125 cm (50 in).

Crotalus cerastes. Photos: Top: S. Kochetov; Bottom: R. Everhart.

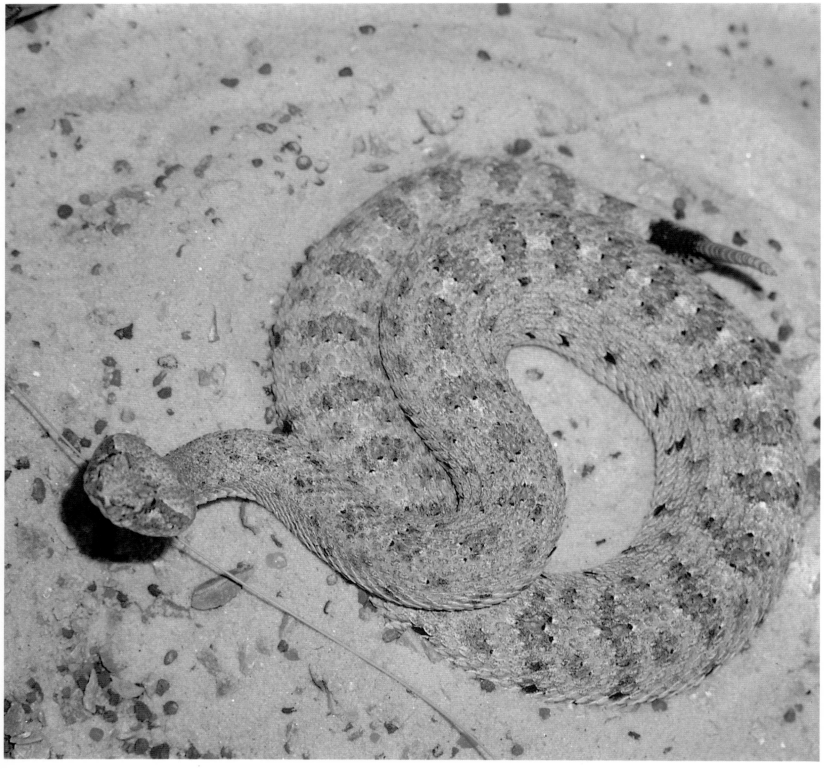

Light gray to greenish with light-bordered and light-centered darker crossbands. Tail sharply contrasting black.

C. polystictus (Cope, 1865): Mexico (southern Zacatecas to central Vera Cruz).

C. pricei Van Denburgh, 1895: **Twin-spotted Rattlesnake.** S.E. Arizona into Mexico in arid, rocky areas at 2-3000 m (6-10000 ft). Length to 65 cm (26 in). Light yellowish with a double row of dark spots along back.

C. pusillus Klauber, 1952: Mexico (Michoacan and Jalisco).

C. ruber Cope, 1892: **Red Diamond Rattlesnake.** S.W. California through Baja California in dry, dense chaparral. Length to 160 cm (64 in). Tan to brick red with dark brown and white diamond-shaped markings.

Top: *Crotalus durissus*. Photo: R. Everhart. Bottom: *Crotalus cerastes*. Photo: C. Banks.

Top Left: *Crotalus enyo enyo*. Photo: K. H. Switak. Top Right: *Crotalus durissus totonacus*. Photo: K. H. Switak. Bottom: *Crotalus horridus atricaudatus*. Photo: J. Iverson.

Top Left: *Crotalus basiliscus*, juvenile. Photo: R. Everhart. Top Right: *Crotalus enyo cerralvensis*. Photo: K. H. Switak. Center: *Crotalus horridus atricaudatus*. Photo: R. T. Zappalorti. Bottom: *Crotalus exsul*. Photo: K. H. Switak.

Top: *Crotalus horridus*,
color variants. Photo:
W. B. Allen, Jr. Bottom:
Crotalus basiliscus.
Photo: R. Everhart.

Top: *Crotalus horridus horridus*. Photo: R. Everhart. Bottom: *Crotalus catalinensis*. Photo: K. H. Switak.

Crotalus horridus horridus, newborn at top. Photos: R. T. Zappalorti.

Top Left: *Crotalus lepidus lepidus*. Photo: J. K. Langhammer. Center Left: *Crotalus lepidus klauberi*. Photo: R. T. Zappalorti. Top Right: *Crotalus horridus horridus*. Photo: R. T. Zappalorti. Bottom: *Crotalus lepidus klauberi*. Photo: S. Kochetov.

Top: *Crotalus mitchelli pyrrhus*. Bottom: *Crotalus mitchelli stephensi*. Photos: R. Everhart.

Top: *Crotalus molossus*. Bottom: *Crotalus polystictus*. Photos: R. Everhart.

Top Left: *Crotalus pricei*. Photo: R. T. Zappalorti. Top Right: *Crotalus molossus*. Photo: J. K. Langhammer. Bottom: *Crotalus pricei*. Photo: R. Everhart.

Top: *Crotalus ruber*. Photo: R. Everhart. Bottom Left: *Crotalus scutulatus*. Photo: F. J. Dodd, Jr. Bottom Right: *Crotalus pricei miquihuanus*. Photo: J. Wines.

Top: *Crotalus ruber*, dark phase. Bottom: *Crotalus tigris*. Photos: R. Everhart.

Top: *Crotalus vegrandis*. Bottom: *Crotalus triseriatus*. Photos: R. Everhart.

C. scutulatus (Kennicott, 1861): **Mojave Rattlesnake.** S.W. USA to central Mexico in upland desert and sparsely vegetated lowlands. Greenish to olive or yellowish with light-centered, black diamonds along back. Black and white rings encircling tail.

C. stejnegeri Dunn, 1919: Mexico (Sinaloa and Durango).

C. tigris Kennicott, 1859: **Tiger Rattlesnake.** C. Arizona to southern Sonora, Mexico, in arid rocky foothills and canyons. Length to 90 cm (36 in). Pale gray to buff, lavender, or pinkish gray, marked with gray or brown crossbands.

C. tortugensis Van Denburgh & Slevin, 1921: Mexico (Tortuga Island, Gulf of California).

C. transversus Taylor, 1944: Mexico

Top Left: *Crotalus viridis lutosus*. Photo: R. Everhart. Top Right: *Crotalus viridis viridis*. Photo: F. J. Dodd, Jr. Bottom: *Crotalus viridis oreganus*, female. Photo: R. Everhart.

Top Left: *Crotalus willardi obscurus.* Photo: R. T. Zappalorti.
Top Right: *Crotalus willardi willardi.* Photo: R. T. Zappalorti.
Bottom: *Crotalus virdis oreganus,* female with young. Photo: R. Everhart.

(Distrito Federal and Morelos).
C. triseriatus (Wagler, 1830): Central and S.W. Mexico.
C. unicolor Van Lidth de Jeude, 1887: Surinam (Aruba Island).
C. vegrandis Klauber, 1941: Venezuela (Monagas and Anzoateguy).
C. viridis (Rafinesque, 1818): **Prairie or Western Rattlesnake.** S. Canada to N.W. Mexico in a variety of habitats. Length to 160 cm (64 in). Great variation in color and pattern.
C. willardi Meek, 1905: **Ridge-nosed Rattlesnake.** S.E. USA (Arizona and New Mexico) to Durango and Zacatecas, Mexico. Length to 60 cm (24 in). Prominent ridge along edge of snout. Light brown to reddish or gray above, marked with narrow, dark-bordered white crossbands.

● *Hypnale* Fitzinger, 1843: A genus containing

Top: *Crotalus viridis viridis*. Photo: R. Everhart. Bottom: *Crotalus viridis nuntius*. Photo: F. J. Dodd, Jr.

Top: *Hypnale hypnale*, juvenile. Photo: R. T. Zappalorti. Center: *Hypnale hypnale*. Photo: Dr. S. Minton. Bottom Left: *Hypnale hypnale*. Photo: C. Banks. Bottom Right: *Lachesis muta*. Photo: R. S. Simmons.

three species native to S. India and Sri Lanka in tropical and montane rain forest. Length to 50 cm (20 in). Similar to *Agkistrodon*. Tip of snout turned up. Brownish with darker markings. Terrestrial to semi-arboreal, feeding on frogs, lizards, and small mammals. Require a humid tropical woodland terrarium with dry basking and resting areas. Ovoviviparous, producing four to ten young.

H. hypnale (Merrem, 1820): **Hump-nosed Moccasin.** India south of 16° N. and Sri Lanka.

H. nepa (Laurenti, 1768): Sri Lanka.

H. walli Gloyd, 1977: Sri Lanka.

• ***Lachesis*** Daudin, 1803: A genus containing a single species.

L. muta (Linnaeus, 1766): **Bushmaster or Sururucu.** Nicaragua to northern South America and Trinidad in tropical and montane rain forest. Length to 375 cm (150 in), making it the third largest venomous snake after *Ophiophagus* and *Oxyuranus*. Top of head covered with small scales. Tail tipped with a spine that is vibrated when snake is disturbed. Brownish with light-bordered dark

Top and Center: *Lachesis muta*. Photos: Top: H. Schultz; Center Left: R. S. Simmons; Center Right: S. Kochetov. Bottom: *Sistrurus catenatus*. Photo: W. B. Allen, Jr.

Top and Bottom Left:
Sistrurus catenatus.
Photos: Top: R.
Everhart; Bottom: R. T.
Zappalorti. Bottom
Right: *Sistrurus miliaris
barbouri.* Photo: F. J.
Dodd, Jr.

diamond-shaped markings. An uncommon nocturnal snake that feeds largely on small mammals. Requires a humid tropical rain-forest terrarium with constant but not too high temperature (20-24°C). Dry basking and resting places are important. Highly dangerous.

● *Sistrurus* Garman, 1884: Pigmy Rattlesnakes A genus containing three species native to USA and Mexico in varied habitats, depending on the species. Length 50-100 cm (20-39 in). Head covered with large plates; relatively small rattle on tail. Nocturnal, feeding on a variety of invertebrates and small vertebrates. Require a small to medium terrarium with conditions compatible with the native habitat of the the individual species. Ovoviviparous, producing four to ten young.

S. catenatus (Rafinesque, 1818): **Massasauga.** Great Lakes to S.E. Arizona and S.E. Texas into extreme N. Mexico in bogs and marshland to dryer woodlands in the east, prairie and desert grassland in the west. Length to 100 cm (39 in). Color varies; usually various shades of light brown to buff or sandy colored with dark-bordered blotches along back. Feeds largely on frogs and lizards.

S. miliaris (Linnaeus, 1766): **Pigmy Rattlesnake.** S.E. USA from E. North Carolina to Florida Keys and west to E. Oklahoma and E. Texas. Although never far

Top: *Sistrurus miliaris miliaris*. Photo: J. K. Langhammer. Bottom: *Sistrurus catenatus*. Photo: R. Everhart.

Top: *Sistrurus miliaris miliaris.* Photo: R. T. Zappalorti. Center and Bottom: *Sistrurus miliaris streckeri.* Photos: Center: F. J. Dodd, Jr.; Bottom: R. Everhart.

from water, this species prefers dryer areas. Length to 80 cm (32 in). Gray to reddish with black or brown blotches along center of back and one to three rows of spots along the flanks. Feeds on invertebrates, lizards, small snakes, and nestling mammals.

S. ravus (Cope, 1865): **Mexican Massasauga.** Mexico in dryer areas. Length to 100 cm (39 in).

● **Trimeresurus** Lacepede, 1804: A genus containing about 32 species native to S.E. Asia. Similar to American *Bothrops* (parallel evolution). Variety of habits and habitats, with terrestrial and arboreal species. Recent taxonomic revision suggests further division of the genus into three genera (*Ovophis*, *Trimeresurus*, and *Tropidolaemus*), but in the present work all species will be regarded as *Trimeresurus*. Length 70-160 cm (28-64 in). All possess the typical broad, triangular viperine head, distinct from the more or less robust body by a narrow neck.

Most species feed on lizards and frogs, but many will learn to take mice in the terrarium. Terrarium requirements must be compatible with the natural habits and habitat of the individual species. There are arboreal (with prehensile tail) and terrestrial forms. All are ovoviviparous, producing 6-35 young, with the exception of *T. kaulbacki*, *T. monticola*, and *T. mucrosquamatus*. The first two of these exhibit parental care of the egg clutch (similar to *Agkistrodon rhodostoma*).

T. albolabris Gray, 1842: N. India and Nepal to S. China. Uniformly green. Arboreal.

T. cantori (Blyth, 1846): Andaman and Nicobar Islands.

T. (Ovophis) chaseni Smith, 1931: North

Sistrurus ravus. Photos:
R. Everhart.

Borneo (Mount Kinabalu).

T. (Ovophis) convictus Stolicza, 1870: Malayan Peninsula (south of Isthmus of Kra).

T. cornutus Smith, 1930: North Vietnam.

T. elegans (Gray, 1849): Ryukyu Islands.

T. erythrurus (Cantor, 1839): India (West Bengal and Assam), Burma, and Bangladesh.

T. flavomaculatus (Gray, 1842): Philippines. Uniformly green.

T. flavoviridis (Hallowell, 1860): **Habu.** Ryukyu Islands. Length to 150 cm (60 in). Variety of colors and patterns, usually brown to olive with rhomboidal markings or stripes. Terrestrial. This is the type species of the genus or subgenus *Protobothrops* Hoge and Romano-Hoge.

T. gracilis Oshima, 1920: Taiwan.

T. gramineus (Shawe, 1802): **Common Bamboo Viper.** Pakistan through India to Indo-China. Uniformly green.

T. hageni (Van Lidth de Jeude, 1886): Sumatra and adjacent islands.

Top and Center Left: *Trimeresurus elegans.* Bottom Left: *Trimeresurus flavoviridis.* Center and Bottom Right: *Trimeresurus gramineus.* Photos: S. Kochetov.

Top Left: *Trimeresurus flavomaculatus*, yellow phase. Photo: M. J. Cox. Top Right: *Trimeresurus mcgregori*. Photo: R. D. Bartlett. Center: *Trimeresurus mucrosquamatus*. Photo: R. E. Kuntz. Bottom: *Trimeresurus okinavensis*. Photos: Left: J. Kellnhauser: Right: S. Kochetov.

Top: *Trimeresurus popeorum*. Photo: R. T. Zappalorti. Bottom Left: *Trimeresurus puniceus*. Photo: M. J. Cox. Bottom Right: *Trimeresurus mucrosquamatus*. Photo: R. E. Kuntz.

T. huttoni Smith, 1949: India (Madras).

T. jerdoni Guenther, 1875: India (Assam) to Vietnam and China (Yunnan, Szechuan, and Hupeh).

T. kanburiensis Smith, 1943: Thailand (near Kanburi).

T. kaulbacki Smith, 1940: Northern Burma.

T. labialis Steindachner, 1867: Andaman and Nicobar Islands.

T. macrolepis Beddome, 1862: Southern India. Large head shields and other morphological characteristics suggest this species should be included in the monotypic genus *Peltopelor* Guenther, 1864. Semi-arboreal, montane species.

T. malabaricus (Jerdon, 1854): Southern and western India.

T. (Ovophis) monticola Guenther, 1864: India (Assam and Sikkim) through Burma and Indo-China to China (Yunnan, Szechuan, Chekiang, and Fukien) and Taiwan.

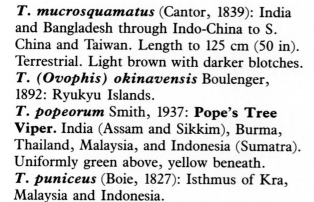

T. mucrosquamatus (Cantor, 1839): India and Bangladesh through Indo-China to S. China and Taiwan. Length to 125 cm (50 in). Terrestrial. Light brown with darker blotches.
T. (Ovophis) okinavensis Boulenger, 1892: Ryukyu Islands.
T. popeorum Smith, 1937: **Pope's Tree Viper.** India (Assam and Sikkim), Burma, Thailand, Malaysia, and Indonesia (Sumatra). Uniformly green above, yellow beneath.
T. puniceus (Boie, 1827): Isthmus of Kra, Malaysia and Indonesia.
T. purpureomaculatus (Gray, 1830): India (West Bengal and Assam) through Burma and

Top: *Trimeresurus purpureomaculatus*. Photos: Left: R. T. Zappalorti; Right: C. Banks. Center: *Trimeresurus sumatranus*. Photo: J. Kellnhauser. Bottom Left: *Trimeresurus stejnegeri*. Photo: S. Kochetov. Bottom Right: *Trimeresurus wagleri*. Photo: B. Kahl.

Malaya to Sumatra; also Andaman and
Nicobar Islands. Length to 160 cm (64 in),
making it the largest species in the genus.
T. schultzei Griffin, 1909: Philippines
(Balabac and Palawan).
T. stejnegeri Schmidt, 1925: India (Assam
and Sikkim), Nepal, and Burma to China and
Taiwan. Uniformly green above, yellow
beneath. Arboreal.

Top: *Trimeresurus
tokarensis.* Photo: J.
Kellnhauser. Center:
Trimeresurus wagleri.
Photo: S Kochetov.
Bottom Left:
*Trimeresurus
trigonocephalus.* Photo:
S. Kochetov. Bottom
Right: *Trimeresurus
stejnegeri.* Photo: R. E.
Kuntz.

T. strigatus (Gray, 1842): Southern India.
T. sumatranus (Raffles, 1822): Sumatra and Borneo.
T. tokarensis Nagai, 1928: Ryukyu Islands.
T. (Ovophis) tonkinensis Bourret, 1934: Vietnam.
T. trigonocephalus (Sonnini & Latreille, 1801): Sri Lanka.
T. (Tropidolaemus) wagleri (Boie, 1827): Thailand, Malaysia, and Indonesia to Philippines. Very colorful species. Dark green to black with yellow and white diamond markings. Unfortunately this species is a difficult captive that often requires force-feeding. Arboreal.

Top: *Trimeresurus* sp. ("wiroti"). Photo: S. Patramangor. Center: *Trimeresurus wagleri.* Photo: H. Bielfeld. Bottom: *Trimeresurus stejnegeri.* Photo: R. E. Kuntz.

APPENDIX 1
Snake Venoms, Antivenins, and Treatment of Snakebite

SNAKE VENOMS

The venoms of poisonous snakes are highly complicated and variable in composition, and only the venoms of closely related species are similar. When released from the venom glands, snake venom is a viscous, yellowish, greenish, amber, straw-colored, or almost clear fluid. In this state it is composed of 50-70% water, the remainder being composed of a complicated mixture of toxic and non-toxic protein enzymes plus very small quantities of amino acids, peptides, nucleotides, carbohydrates, lipids, and compounds of metals such as calcium, sodium, potassium, manganese, and zinc. The effect of envenomation on prey animals varies considerably, depending on the composition of the venom. However, snake venoms can be broadly divided into two categories: neurotoxic, causing damage to the nervous system (predominating mainly in the elapid and hydrophiid snakes); and hemotoxic/cytotoxic, causing destruction of red blood cells and damage to the tissues (predominating in the viperid and crotalid species). There are exceptions to the rule. For example, the Taipan, *Oxyuranus scutellatus* of Australia/New Guinea, is an elapid that produces a considerable proportion of cytotoxin in its venom, while the Cascabel Rattlesnake, *Crotalus durissus* of South America, is a crotalid that produces a high proportion of neurotoxin.

Though snake venom is produced primarily for subduing prey, its effect on humans has been the subject of considerable research. In predominantly neurotoxic poisoning there are often few apparent symptoms at the site of the bite other than fang marks and minor pain. However, the patient soon feels sleepy, intoxicated, and weak and there is a gradual development of paralysis resulting in drooping eyelids, speech difficulty, staggering gait, and eventual complete paralysis of the voluntary muscles. Death is finally brought about by respiratory failure and/or cardiac arrest.

In hemotoxic/cytotoxic poisoning local symptoms are prominent at the site of the bite, fang marks will be clearly visible, intensive swelling will occur, and there will be a blood and mucous discharge from the wound. An intense burning pain is severe and persistent. General symptoms are initially characterized by subcutaneous hemorrhages and blistering of the skin, followed by bleeding from the mucous membranes and bloody urine and feces. There is no paralysis, but massive internal hemorrhaging gives rise to severe abdominal pain and vomiting. The condition of the patient will rapidly deteriorate and result in unconsciousness. Death is finally brought about by heart and/or renal failure.

Should the patient survive the envenomation, there is still likely to be severe tissue damage at and near the site of the bite. This may include extensive local suppuration and sloughing, followed by malignant edema and gangrene, including bone damage if the bite has occurred

Top: *Daboia russelli.* Bottom: *Echis carinatus.* Photos: R. T. Zappalorti.

Top: *Bitis gabonica*. Photo: K. Lucas, Steinhart. Bottom: *Crotalus durissus terrificus*. Photo: M. Freiberg.

at an extremity. Intravascular injection of hemotoxins may result in rapid onset of convulsions followed by death.

In some snake venoms there may be a mixture of neurotoxins and hemotoxins, while in others not all of the above described symptoms may appear. There are many factors that affect the severity of envenomation. These include the species of snake and the composition of its venom. Even among single species there may be a relatively large variation of venom composition between geographical populations; this, for example, has been demonstrated in the European Adder, *Vipera berus berus*. The amount of venom injected at the time (there is evidence to suggest that many venomous snakes use less venom in defense than they would for subduing prey) and the age or size of the snake (juvenile venomous snakes would normally release a relatively smaller amount of venom) are also important factors. The site of the bite, the depth of the injection, and whether the venom

is released into a vein, an artery, or into fat tissue will also affect the degree of poisoning. In general, intravenous envenomation is the most dangerous to the life of the victim; the degree of venom absorption in fat is much less rapid. The size and health of the victim will affect the severity of envenomation; a small anemic child, for example, is more likely to succumb than a large healthy adult. The psychological condition of the victim will also play a part; extreme fear will increase the rate of blood circulation and therefore the rapidity of venom absorption. In addition, shock may further weaken the patient's resistance.

ANTIVENINS

(The word antivenom is now being widely used and may eventually replace the word antivenin, which has long been in general use.) Snake antivenin is an antidote introduced into the body to combat the debilitating effects of envenomation from snakebite. Although antitoxins for various diseases had already been produced by the middle of the 19th century, the first antivenom for the treatment of snakebite (cobra) was not produced until 1895 at the Pasteur Institute in Paris. Since that time various establishments for research into snakebite and production of antivenin have been formed in many parts of the world, particularly in those countries where there is a real danger of envenomation.

The basic procedure for producing antivenom was, and still is, as follows. Snake venom (from the species for which the antivenom is being prepared) is injected in very small quantities (initially ⅟₁₀₀ to ⅟₁₀ lethal dose, usually progressively) into the bloodstream of horses. Over a period of time (usually about 90 days) the horse develops an immunity to the venom by producing antibodies that neutralize the venom so the horse becomes able to withstand several times the lethal dose without any serious effects. After immunization, the horse is bled and the antibody-containing serum is separated out. Known as horse serum, this is the basis of most antivenins. The serum is usually dried out into a crystalline form to give greater stability and shelf life, and it is reconstituted with sterile water before use.

Separate antivenins may be necessary for different species of snakes. An antivenom for a single species is known as a *monovalent* serum, while that prepared as an antidote to the bites of a number of species is known as a *polyvalent* serum. Some monovalent antivenins are effective against the venom of more than one species of snake, but, in general, a polyvalent antivenin is more useful in those parts of the world where a number of dangerous species occur. Should a bite occur from a snake that cannot be identified (i.e., it makes its escape before it can be killed or captured), then there is a good chance that treatment with a polyvalent antivenom from that particular area will be successful.

VENOM EXTRACTION

Venomous snakes may be kept in snake farms or laboratories so that a ready and regular supply of venom is available for research and/or the production of antivenins. Methods of venom extraction (or milking, as it is commonly termed) vary depending on the size and species of the snake and the relative risk of snakebite to the operator(s). A relatively safe procedure is as follows. Please understand that this procedure is given for information only. It should NEVER be attempted by an amateur. In fact, amateurs probably should not keep venomous snakes in the first place.

1. With a pair of padded forceps or tongs (depending on the size of the snake) in the left hand, secure the body of the snake about 5 cm (2 in) behind the head.

2. With a second pair of padded forceps or tongs, restrain the snake's head across its broadest point.

3. Releasing the first pair of forceps (or tongs), grip the snake's neck with the left hand as closely as possible behind the mandibles.

4. Release the second pair of forceps and use the right hand to restrain the snake's body in the area of the vent. With a large or very active snake, an assistant may have to restrain the middle of the snake's body at this stage, though from a safety angle it is preferable that the whole procedure is carried out by a single operator.

5. The head of the snake is then brought to the venom receptacle, which is placed on a firm, level surface and preferably anchored with a clamp. For rear-fanged snakes, elapids, hydrophiids, and small viperids, a petri dish may be used as a venom receptacle; for larger viperids and crotalids, a 100 mm (4 in) beaker may be used. A thin plastic film, through which the snake will bite, is tightly stretched over the top of the venom receptacle.

6. The snake usually bites eagerly, inserting its fangs through the film, but sometimes the snake's mouth may have to be opened with a spatula.

7. As soon as the snake bites, its snout is anchored into position on the rim of the venom receptacle using the right forefinger, while simultaneously the thumb and forefinger of the left hand are brought forward to compress the venom glands behind the eyes.

8. As soon as venom has been discharged into the receptacle, the left thumb and forefinger are moved to behind the head and the snake's mouth is disengaged from the venom receptacle.

9. With the right hand, forceps are again used to restrain the snake's head and the reptile is returned to its container, releasing and removing the forceps at the last moment before the door is closed.

FIRST AID FOR SNAKEBITE

Herpetologists, laboratory animal technicians, and others dealing with venomous snakes are in a relatively high-risk category of potential snakebite casualties, though stringent safety

Extracting venom from *Crotalus horridus*.
Photo: P. Vargas.

procedures should minimize or preferably prevent accidents. Any case of snakebite should receive medical attention as quickly as possible and, where appropriate, antivenin should be administered with all haste, preferably by a medical practitioner. However, there are certain immediate first aid procedures that should be carried out.

1. Do not panic; carry out the following procedures calmly and rationally!

2. Firmly apply a broad bandage over and around the bitten area (unless this is on the head or neck). On a limb, the bandage should extend as far above and below the site of the bite as possible. A crepe bandage is ideal, but in an

emergency any flexible material can be used (torn up strips of clothing or towels, for example). Do not wash the bitten area. Do not incise or excise at the area of the bite; this can cause more damage than the venom itself and there is little evidence that this will remove any appreciable amount of venom. Do not give alcohol to the patient, as it will increase the rate of circulation.

3. Keep the patient as still as possible. If the bite is on a limb, apply a splint; any rigid object (broom handle, piece of timber) will suffice to immobilize. Do not apply a tourniquet to the limb; it is now considered that the constrictive action of a tourniquet is more dangerous than the snakebite.

4. Wherever possible, bring transport to the victim rather than mobilize the patient. Get the patient to a hospital as soon as possible. Leave bandages and splint in position until under medical care. Continually reassure the patient throughout the whole procedure.

Many different types of first aid and treatment for snakebite have been suggested, and all have their adherents and detractors. The author and publisher should not be thought of as dispensing or approving any particular method. If you feel that you are at risk of suffering snakebite, consult with your doctor and local emergency medical staff to determine the first aid and treatment procedures they recommend. Again, amateurs should not keep venomous snakes without considering the risks and problems in their care.

TREATMENT OF SNAKEBITE

Administration of antivenom should preferably take place in a hospital where expert medical attention is available. The following notes are not to be regarded as instructions for the layman to apply treatment.

Efficient treatment for envenomation is greatly facilitated if the species of snake responsible has been identified. If a species has not been positively identified by an expert or if the species is unknown, an appropriate polyvalent antivenom for the area should be used. Fortunately, in the case of captive specimens the identity of the species responsible usually is known and a more efficient monovalent serum may be available.

The doctor will remove the splint and bandages, after ensuring that the appropriate drugs and antivenin are at hand. Antivenin is usually slowly infused intravenously in a quantity advised by the manufacturer's instructions. The objective is to neutralize as quickly as possible all of the venom injected by the snake. When signs of envenomation develop further or persist, further doses of antivenin are given. In some cases, a blood transfusion may be recommended.

Some patients show allergic reactions to horse serum, and this must be taken into account by the doctor when administering antivenins. Sometimes an allergic reaction test may be necessary before administration begins. In allergic cases, the antivenin may be given more slowly in diluted form. The use of additional drugs (antihistamines, adrenaline) and resuscitation equipment may be necessary in severe cases of allergic reaction.

SAFETY PROCEDURES IN THE CARE OF VENOMOUS SNAKES

The keeping of venomous snakes in captivity should only be carried out by responsible and experienced individuals or institutions. It is essential that all local and regional laws be followed to the letter, including posting of bonds where required. Venomous snakes are outlawed or tightly regulated in many cities and counties, with stiff fines assessed for violations. The following basic rules should apply in all establishments keeping venomous snakes in order to prevent the danger of snakebite to the keeper, staff, family, or general public.

1. Venomous snakes should be kept in strongly built terraria with access doors secured with two padlocks that should be kept locked at all times except when access is required.

2. Terraria should be kept on a solid, stable surface where there is no danger of them falling and breaking open.

3. Terraria should ideally be kept in a locked room or shed that has been thoroughly checked for potential escape routes should a snake manage to get out of its cage. The floor should be kept free of cluttered material so an escaped snake can be easily recaptured.

4. Adequate snake-handling equipment, including snake sticks, grabs, trapping boxes, and thick leather gloves, should be kept close at hand.

5. When handling venomous snakes always ensure that another responsible person is within earshot.

6. Never handle venomous snakes after imbibing alcohol or other stimulants or medications that may inhibit normal reactions.

7. Never perform rash familiarities with venomous snakes.

8. An obvious and permanent notice should be placed on the door of the snake room warning of its contents.

9. A card on which is recorded the name of the species, the location of the appropriate antivenin, and the procedure to be taken in the event of an emergency should be attached in a secure position on each cage. The card should accompany a patient to hospital.

10. Ensure that the correct antivenin for the species in question is available and kept up to date (antivenins have a limited life). They should be stored to the manufacturer's instructions (usually in a refrigerator). It is prudent to come to some arrangement with a local medical practitioner or hospital that the antivenin is stored there, ready for immediate professional administration in case of emergency.

11. Children and inexperienced persons

should not have unsupervised access to the snake room.

12. All persons living or working in an establishment in which venomous snakes are kept should be aware of the above rules and first aid procedures. Copies of rules and procedures should be pinned up in several prominent positions.

Top: Drop of venom coming from fang of milked *Agkistrodon.* Photo: S. Kochetov. Bottom: *Crotalus vegrandis.* Photo: R. Everhart.

Bibliography

It would be impractical to list the many books and papers available for those interested in snakes. The following is merely a selection of the literature that will be of interest to the snake enthusiast. The field guides, in particular, will be useful in the correct identification of species.

Amaral, A. do. 1976. *Brazilian Snakes: a Color Iconography*. Ed. Melhoramentos, Inst. Nac. Livro, Sao Paulo, Brazil.

Arnold, E.N. and Burton, J.A. 1978. *A Field Guide to the Reptiles and Amphibians of Europe*. Collins, London, UK.

Ashton, R.E., Jr. and P.S. Ashton. 1981. *Handbook of Reptiles and Amphibians of Florida. Part One: The Snakes*. Windward Publ., Miami, Florida, USA. (Excellent modern coverage.)

Banks, C. 1980. *Keeping Reptiles and Amphibians as Pets*. Thomas Nelson, Melbourne, Australia.

Bannikov, A.G., Darevsky, I.S., Istschenko, V.G., Rustamov, A.K. and Scerbak, N.N. 1977. *Guide to the Amphibians and Reptiles of the Soviet Union*. Moscow (in Russian).

Behler, J.L. and King, F.W. 1979. *The Audubon Society Field Guide to North American Reptiles and Amphibians*. Alfred A. Knopf, New York, USA.

Basoglu, M. and Baran, I. 1980. *Turkiye Surungenleri Kisim II. Yilanlar (The Reptiles of Turkey, Part II. The Snakes)*. Ege Universitesi Matbaasi, Bornova-Izmir, Turkey.

Bellairs, A. 1969. *The Life of Reptiles* (Vols. 1 & 2). Weidenfield and Nicholson, London, UK.

Boulenger, G.A. 1893. *Catalogue of Snakes in the British Museum*. Br. Mus. (N.H.), London. (Reprinted.)

Breen, J.F. 1974. *Encyclopedia of Reptiles and Amphibians*. TFH Publications, New Jersey, USA.

Broadley, D.G. and Cock, E.V. 1975. *Snakes of Rhodesia*. Longman Rhodesia, Salisbury (Zimbabwe).

Bruno. S. 1977. *Rettili d'Italia*. Giunti-Martello, Firenze (Florence), Italy.

Buckland, F.T. 1857. *Curiosities of Natural History*. Macmillan and Co., Ltd., London and New York.

Cann, J. 1986. *Snakes Alive - Snake Experts and Antidote Sellers in Australia*. Kangaroo Press, Kenthurst, Australia.

Cansdale, G.S. 1961. *West African Snakes*. Longman Group Ltd., London, UK.

Carr, A. 1963. *The Reptiles*. Life Nature Library, Time Inc., New York, USA.

Cedhagen, T. and Nilson, G. 1978. *Grod- och kraeldjur i Norden (Scandinavian Amphibians and Reptiles)*. Faeltbiologerna, Sollentuna, Sweden.

Coborn, J. 1985. *Beginner's Guide to Snakes*. Paradise Press, Queensland, Australia.

Coborn, J. and Lawrence, K. 1987. *Snakes and Lizards*, in *UFAW Handbook on the Care & Management of Laboratory Animals*. Longman Scientific and Technical, Harlow, Essex, UK.

Cogger, H.G. 1979. *A Field Guide to the Reptiles & Amphibians of Australia*. A.H. & A.W. Reed, Sydney, Australia.

Colbert, E.H. 1980. *Evolution of the Vertebrates*. Third Edition. John Wiley and Sons, Inc., New York, USA.

Conant, R. 1975. *A Field Guide to the Reptiles & Amphibians of Eastern North America*. Houghton Mifflin, Boston, USA.

Cooper, J.E. and Jackson, O.F. 1981. *Diseases of the Reptilia* (Vols. 1 & 2), Academic Press, London, UK.

Ditmars, R.L. 1951. *Snakes of the World*. Macmillan, New York, USA.

Dixon, J.R. and P. Soini. 1986. *The Reptiles of the Upper Amazon Basin, Iquitos Region, Peru*. Milwaukee Publ. Mus., Milwaukee, Wisc., USA.

Dobie, J.F. 1965. *Rattlesnakes*. Hammond and Hammond, London, UK and Little, Brown & Co. Canada.

Dunson, W.A. (Ed.), 1975. *The Biology of Sea Snakes*. University Park Press, Baltimore and London.

Engelmann, W.E. and Obst, F.J. 1981. *Snakes - Biology, Behaviour and Relationship to Man*. Edition Leipzig, Leipzig, German Democratic Republic.

Ferner, J.W. 1979. *A Review of the Marking Techniques for Amphibians and Reptiles*. Herp. Circular No. 9, SSAR. Athens, Ohio, USA.

Fitch, H.S. 1960. "Autecology of the Copperhead" *Univ. Kansas Pub. Mus. Nat. Hist.*, 13 (4): 85-288.

Fitch, H.S. 1970. *Reproductive Cycles in Lizards & Snakes*. Museum of Natural History, University of Kansas.

Fitzsimmons, V.F.M. 1962. *Snakes of Southern Africa*. Macdonald, London, UK.

Frazer, D. 1983, Reptiles and Amphibians in England. William Collins, Sons and Co., Glasgow, UK.

Freiberg, M. 1982. *Snakes of South America*. TFH Publ., Neptune, NJ, USA.

Fretey, J. 1975. *Guide des Reptiles et Batraciens*

de France. Hatier, Paris, France.

Frye, F.L. 1973. *Husbandry, Medicine and Surgery in Captive Reptiles.* V.M. Publishing, Kansas, USA.

Frye, F.L. 1991. *Reptile Care: An Atlas of Diseases and Treatments.* T.F.H. Publ., Neptune, NJ, USA. Published also by Krieger Publ., Malabar, Florida, as second edition of *Biomedical and Surgical Aspects of Captive Reptile Husbandry.*

Gadow, H. 1901 (reprint 1968): *Amphibia and Reptiles.* Macmillan, London, UK (Reprint: Wheldon & Wesley, Codicote, UK).

Geus, A. 1960 (reprint 1983). *Schlangen.* Albrecht Philler Verlag GmbH, Minden, German Federal Republic.

Goin, C.J. and Goin, O.B. 1971. *Introduction to Herpetology.* W.H. Freeman, New York, USA.

Guenther, A.C.L.G. 1885–1902. *Biologia Centrali-Americana. Reptilia and Batrachia.* R.H. Porter, London. (Reprinted in 1987 by SSAR.)

Harding, K.A. and Welch, R.G. 1980. *Venomous Snakes of the World - A Checklist.* Pergamon Press, Oxford, UK.

Heatwole, H. 1976. *Reptile Ecology.* University of Queensland Press. Australia.

Henderson, R.W. and A. Schwartz. 1984. *A Guide to the Identification of the Amphibians and Reptiles of Hispaniola.* Milwaukee Publ. Mus., Milwaukee, Wisc., USA.

Hodge, R. P. 1976. *Amphibians and Reptiles in Alaska, The Yukon & Northwest Territories.* Alaska Northwest Publishing Company, Anchorage, Alaska, USA.

Honegger, R. 1979. "Marking Reptiles and Amphibians for Future Recognition," *International Zoo Yearbook,* Vol 19: 14-22. Zoological Society of London, UK.

Huff, T.A. 1977. "Caging and Feeding Techniques Employed at the Reptile Breeding Foundation," *Proceedings of the Second Annual Symposium on Captive Propagation and Husbandry,* pp 15-20. Thurmont, Md. USA.

Jackson, O.F. 1976. "Reptiles," *Manual of the Care and Treatment Children's and Exotic Pets.* BSAVA Publications, London UK.

Kauffeld, C. 1957. *Snakes & Snake Hunting.* Hanover House, Garden City, New York, USA.

Kauffeld, C. 1969. *Snakes: The Keeper and the Kept.* Doubleday, New York, USA.

Klauber, L.M. 1956. *Rattlesnakes* (Vols. 1 & 2). University of California Press, Berkely, California, USA.

Klingelhoffer, W. and Scherpner, C.H.R. 1955-59. *Terrarienkunde* (Vols. 1-4). Alfred Kernon Verlag, Stuttgart, German Federal Republic.

Kuntz, R.E. 1977. *Snakes of Taiwan* (Reprint). US Naval Medical Research Unit No. 2, San Francisco, USA.

Lane, M. 1963. *Life With Ionides.* Hamish Hamilton Ltd., London, UK.

Leutscher, A. and Dekeyne, H. 1952. *Vivarium Life.* Cleaver Hume Press, London, UK.

Loveridge, A. 1945. *Reptiles of the Pacific World.* Macmillan, New York, USA.

Markel, R. 1989. *Kingsnakes and Milk Snakes.* TFH Publ.,Neptune, NJ, USA.

Mattison, C. 1982. *The Care of Reptiles & Amphibians in Captivity.* Blandford Press, Poole, Dorset, UK.

Mattison, C. 1986. *Snakes of the World.* Blandford Press, Poole, Dorset, UK.

McCoy, M. 1980. *Reptiles of the Solomon Islands.* Wau Institute Handbook No. 7, Papua New Guinea.

McDowell, S.B. 1974–. "A catalogue of the snakes of New Guinea and the Solomons." *J. Herpetology,* 8:1–57; 9:1–80, 13:1–92, continuing.

Mertens, R. and Wermuth, H. 1960. *Die Amphibien und Reptilien Europas.* Kramer, Frankfurt am Main, German Federal Republic.

Minton, S.A. and Minton, M.R. 1971. *Venomous Reptiles.* George Allen & Unwin, London, UK.

Morris, D. and Morris R. 1965. *Men and Snakes.* McGraw-Hill, New York, USA.

Murphy, J.B. and Collins, J.T. (Ed.). 1980. *Reproductive Biology and Diseases of Captive Reptiles.* Society for the Study of Amphibians and Reptiles (SSAR), USA.

Naulleau, G. 1984. "Les serpents de France," *Rev. Franc. d'Aquar.,* 11(3/4):1–56. (Nancy, France.)

Nietzke, G. 1969-72. *Die Terrarientiere* (Vols. 1 & 2). Eugen Ulmer Verlag, Stuttgart, German Federal Republic.

Obst, F.J., Richter, K. and Jacob, U. 1984. *Lexicon der Terraristik.* Edition Leipzig, Leipzig, German Democratic Republic. (Translated as *Atlas of Reptiles and Amphibians,* 1988, TFH Publ., Neptune, NJ, USA.)

Oliver, J.A. 1958. *Snakes in Fact and Fiction.* The Macmillan Company, New York, USA.

Parker, H.W. and Grandison, A.C.G. 1977. *Snakes - A Natural History.* British Museum (Natural History) and Cornell University Press, London and Ithaca.

Peters, J.A. and Orejas-Miranda, B. 1970. *Catalogue of the Neotropical Squamata. Part I: Snakes. U.S. Nat. Mus. Bull. 297.* Washington, USA. (Recently reprinted with a supplement.)

Phelps, T. 1981. *Poisonous Snakes.* Blandford Press, Poole, Dorset, UK.

Pienaar, U.V., et al. 1982. *The Reptiles of the Kruger National Park.* Natl. Parks Board South Africa.

Pitman, C.R.S. 1974. *A Guide to the Snakes of Uganda.* Wheldon & Wesley, Codicote, UK.

Pope, C.H., 1961. *The Giant Snakes.* Alfred A. Knopf, New York, USA.

Reichenbach-Klinke, H. and Elkan, E. 1965. *Principal Diseases of the Lower Vertebrates - III Reptiles.* Academic Press (London) and TFH Publications, Inc., New Jersey, USA.

Reitinger, F.F. 1978. *Common Snakes of South East Asia and Hong Kong.* Heinemann Educational Books (Asia), Hong Kong.

Riches, R.J. 1976. *Breeding Snakes in Captivity.* Palmetto Publishing, Florida, USA.

Rose, W. 1955. *Snakes - Mainly South African.* Maskew Miller, Cape Town, South Africa.

Roze, J.A. 1966. *La Taxonomia y Zoogeografia de los Ofidios de Venezuela.* Central University of Venezuela Press, Caracas.

Schwartz, A. and R.W. Henderson. 1985. *A Guide to the Identification of the Amphibians and Reptiles of the West Indies.* Milwaukee Publ. Mus., Milwaukee, Wisc., USA.

Smith, H.M. and E.H. Taylor. 1945. "An annotated checklist and key to the snakes of Mexico," *Bull. USNM,* 187. (Reprinted, 1966.)

Smith, H.M., R.B. Smith, and H.L. Sawin. 1977. "A summary of snake classification," *J. Herpetology,* 11(2): 115–121. (Essential to understand the problems of snake classification.)

Smith, M. 1943. *The Fauna of British India, Ceylon and Burma, Including the Whole of the Indo-Chinese Sub-Region. Reptilia and Amphibia. Vol 3. Serpentes.* Taylor and Francis, London, UK.

Stafford, P.J. 1986. *Pythons and Boas.* TFH Publ., Neptune, NJ, USA. (Excellent modern coverage.)

Stebbins, R.C. 1966. *A Field Guide to Western Reptiles and Amphibians.* Houghton Mifflin, New York, USA.

Stettler, P.H. 1978. *Handbuch der Terrarienkunde.* Fraenck'sche Verlagshandlung, W. Keller & Co., Stuttgart, German Federal Republic.

Sutherland, S.K. 1983. *Australian Animal Toxins.* Oxford University Press, Melbourne, Australia.

Swaroop, S. and Grab, B. 1954. "Snakebite Mortality in the World," *Bulletin of the World Health Organization,* 10:35-37.

Tinoco, R.A. 1978. *Las Serpientes de Colombia.* Ediciones Editorial Mejoras, Universidad del Atlantico, Colombia.

Townson, S. et al. (Eds.). 1980. *The Care and Breeding of Captive Reptiles.* British Herpetological Society, Zoological Society of London, UK.

U.S. Navy Bureau of Medicine and Surgery. 1968. *Poisonous Snakes of the World* (revised edition). U.S. Government Printing Office, Washington, USA.

Visser, J. and Chapman, D.S. 1978. *Snakes and Snakebite.* Purnell and Sons (SA) (Pty) Ltd., Cape Town, South Africa.

Wall, F. 1921. *Ophidia Tabrobanika, or the Snakes of Ceylon.* H.R. Cottle, Colombo, Ceylon.

Webb, J.E., Wallwork, J.A., and Elgood, J.H. 1978. *Guide to Living Reptiles.* Macmillan, London and Basingstoke, UK.

Welch, K. 1982. *Herpetology of Africa.* Krieger Publ., Malabar, Florida.

Welch, K. 1983. *Herpetology of Europe and southwest Asia.* Krieger Publ., Malabar, Florida.

Welch, K. 1988. *Snakes of the Orient.* Krieger Publ., Malabar, Florida.

Williams, K.L. and V. Wallach. 1989. *Snakes of the World. I. Synopsis of Snake Generic Names.* Krieger Publ., Malabar, FL.

Wilson, L.D. and J.R. Meyer. 1985. *The Snakes of Honduras.* Milwaukee Publ, Mus., Milwaukee, Wisc, USA.

Witte, G.-F. 1962. "Genera des serpents du Congo et du Ruanda–Urundi," *Ann. Mus. Roy. Afr. Cent.,* 8(104):1-203. (Belgium.)

Wright, A.H. and A.A. Wright. 1957. *Handbook of Snakes of the United States and Canada.* Cornell Univ. Press, NY, USA.

Wykes, A. 1960. *Snake Man - The Story of C.J.P. Ionides.* Hamish Hamilton, London, UK.

Herpetological Journals and Proceedings

There are a number of notable herpetological journals and proceedings of herpetological symposia that are useful reading for keeping up with current trends in all aspects of herpetology. As the addresses of many herpetological societies are subject to change, most are not given here. Information regarding contacts may be obtained from museums, libraries, universities, or zoological gardens. The following are some of the better known publications:

ASRA Journal and *Rephiberary*, published by the Association for the Study of Reptiles and Amphibians, c/o Cotswold Wild Life Park, Burford, Oxon., UK.

British Journal of Herpetology, published by the British Herpetological Society, London, UK.

Copeia, published quarterly by the American Society of Ichthyologists and Herpetologists.

Herpetofauna, published jointly by the Australian and New Zealand Herpetological Societies.

Herpetologica, published by the Herpetologists' League (USA).

The Herptile, published by the International Herpetological Society (UK).

International Zoo Yearbook, Zoological Society of London, Regents Park, London, UK (many papers on reptile care and husbandry).

Journal of Herpetology and *Herpetological Review*, published by the Society for the Study of Amphibians and Reptiles (SSAR) (USA).

Proceedings of the Annual Reptile Symposium on Captive Propagation and Husbandry, Cacoctin Mtn. Zoological Park, Thurmont, Md., USA.

Proceedings of Melbourne Herpetological Symposium (1981), The Royal Melbourne Zoological Gardens, Melbourne, Australia.

The Vivarium, published by the American Federation of Herpetoculturists, Box 1131, Lakeside, California. Excellent general herpetology magazine with good color-illustrated articles.

Glossary

The following glossary includes scientific and herpetological terms included in the text and, in addition, other terms that will be useful to the herpetologist.

Acrodont: With teeth fused to the summit of the jawbones.

Adaptive radiation: Evolutionary divergence of animals from a single ancestral stock to fill many ecological niches, thus forming new species, genera, and families.

Aglyphic: Pertaining to snakes that do not possess venom fangs.

Albumen: The clear gelatinous proteinaceous part of an egg (the egg white).

Allanto-chorion: An embryonic membrane.

Allantois: A sac in the developing egg that functions primarily as a vessel for waste products.

Allopatry: Biogeographical term denoting the separation of certain species into different areas or ranges (see Sympatry). Also refers to two or more species with non-overlapping ranges.

Amnion: The membrane enclosing the amniotic cavity.

Amniotic cavity: An enclosed fluid-filled sac protecting the embryo in reptiles, birds, and mammals.

Anal gland: A paired gland situated at the base of the tail in many snakes and evacuating into the vent. It produces a foul-smelling fluid used in defense when the reptile is attacked.

Anapsid: An absence of temporal openings in the roof of the skull.

Anterior: Pertaining to the front part of the body.

Antivenin: Serum produced to combat the effects of (snake) venom. Also spelled antivenom.

Aorta: The primary artery carrying blood away from the heart.

Aposematic: Being marked with gaudy, contrasting colors as a warning to aggressors that the potential victim is venomous or noxious.

Arboreal: Predominantly tree-dwelling and modified for a tree-dwelling existence.

Arcade: Parts of the skull roof separating the orbits and the temporal openings.

Atlas vertebra: The first neck vertebra, articulating with the occipital region of the skull.

Autotomy: The voluntary shedding of parts of the body in animals, usually as a means of defense. Autotomy of the tail is common in many lizard genera, but it does not occur in snakes (with a very few possible exceptions).

Axis vertebra: The second neck vertebra, which articulates with the atlas.

Behavior: In snakes, the study of the processes by which they respond both internally and externally to changes in their environment. Can be approached both psychologically and physiologically.

Binomial: The system of double naming in scientific nomenclature using generic and specific names to indicate species.

Brille: The transparent immovable spectacle, formed from part of the epidermis, that covers and protects the eye in snakes and some lizards.

Broad-spectrum: In this work, used in relation to terrarium lighting apparatus that emits light of a quality as near as possible to that of natural daylight.

Buccal cavity: The cavity of the mouth.

Cerebellum: The large, paired lobe of the hind brain.

Cerebrum: The lobes of the forebrain.

Cervical vertebrae: The bones of the neck.

Chorion: The outer membrane enclosing the embryo in higher vertebrates.

Classification: The cataloging of living things into systematic groups.

Cleidoic: Pertaining to an egg that is protected from the atmosphere by a relatively impervious shell.

Cloaca: The chamber in many vertebrates into which the contents of the alimentary, urinary, and reproductive systems discharge.

Condyle: The rounded part of a bone fitting into the socket of another to form a joint.

Constriction: The method used by some snakes to overpower prey by using the application of pressure from the coils to produce asphyxiation.

Convergence: Similarity in form of unrelated organisms due to evolutionary development in similar but often widely separated habitats.

Cranium: The bony part of the skull enclosing the brain.

Crepuscular: Being active mainly during the twilight hours (dawn and dusk).

Cryptic coloration: Type of pattern and color in snakes that causes them to be camouflaged in their environment.

Cutaneous: Pertaining to the skin.

Cytology: The study of cell structure and function.

Dentary: The anterior tooth-bearing bone of the lower jaw.

Dermis: The inner layer of skin.

Diapsid: The condition of a skull that possesses two temporal openings.

Display: A ritualized pattern of behavior directed at other animals for sexual, territorial, or defensive motives.

Diurnal: Being active mainly during the hours of daylight.

Dorsal: Referring to the upper side of the body.

Ecdysis: The periodic shedding (or molting) of the outer epidermal layer in lizards and snakes.

Ecology: The study of living organisms in relation to their environment. A knowledge of snake species ecology is important for successful keeping of many species in terraria.

Ecosystem: The complete environmental unit in which an animal lives, composed of living and non-living entities together with the elements.

Ectoparasite: A parasite that attaches itself to the exterior of the body in order to extract nourishment from its host (e.g., mites, ticks, etc.).

Ectothermic: A condition in which an animal's body warmth is derived from external sources such as solar radiation (also called poikilothermic or cold-blooded).

Endoparasite: A parasite which lives and gains nourishment inside the body of its host.

Endothermic: A condition in which an animal's body heat is maintained at a more or less constant temperature, as exhibited in birds and mammals (also called homoiothermic or warm-blooded).

Epidermis: The outer layer of skin, that which is shed by reptiles at regular intervals.

Epizootic: Epidemic among a population of animals (usually referring to a disease outbreak).

Esophagus: The part of the alimentary canal anterior to the stomach.

Estivation: The period of inactivity undergone by many species during the dry season or dry periods in tropical and subtropical climates.

Ethology: The study of animal (snake) behavior in their natural habitat.

Evolution: The gradual development of a complex organism from a simpler ancestral form over the course of geological time. Snake evolution is incompletely understood.

Fang: In snakes, a large specialized tooth adapted for the introduction of venom into prey.

Foramen magnum: The opening at the base of the skull that allows the spinal cord to connect to the brain.

Frontal scale: The scale situated anterior to the parietal scale.

Hemipenes: The paired sex organs of the male, typical of lizards and snakes (singular, hemipenis).

Herpetology: The study of amphibians and reptiles.

Herptiles: A name used to describe amphibians and reptiles collectively.

Hibernation: The act of spending the cold winter months in a state of torpor, as exhibited by snakes from temperate regions.

Hibernaculum: A winter retreat in which hibernation takes place.

Homodont: Possessing teeth of a single type. The opposite of heterodont.

Hybrid: The usually sterile offspring produced as a result of a cross-mating between two different species.

Hypervitaminosis: A nutritional disorder caused by an overabundance of a certain vitamin(s) in the diet.

Hypovitaminosis: A nutritional disorder caused by a deficiency of a certain vitamin(s) in the diet.

Intergrade: A population or individual that may show mixed characteristics of two subspecies at the borders of their respective ranges.

Internasal scale: The scale above the nasal scale.

Jacobson's organ: A paired organ situated in the anterior part of the palate, corresponding with and closely allied to the internal nares. Used to smell the contents of the mouth and in snakes used in conjunction with the forked tongue.

Labial: Pertaining to the lips.

Labial scales: The row of scales bordering the lips (upper and lower labials).

Larynx: The upper part of the trachea.

Ligament: Non-elastic, bone-connecting tissue.

Loreal scale: The scale(s) situated anterior to the preocular(s).

Mandible: The lower jaw.

Maxilla: The marginal tooth-bearing bone at the front of the upper jaw.

Medulla: The section of the brain linking the spinal cord with the higher centers.

Melanism: A condition in which an animal possesses an unusually abundant amount of dark pigment in the skin such as to make it appear black. Fairly common in certain snake species.

Mimicry: The condition in which some non-venomous snakes mimic the colors, patterns, or behavior of venomous snakes in order to become predator-resistant.

Mental scale: The scale situated at the point of the chin.

Montane: Pertaining to a mountain habitat.

Morphology: The study of form, especially in relation to appearance, anatomy, and development of animals.

Nasal scale: The scale surrounding or adjoining the nostril.

Neural canal: The canal in the vertebral column that contains the spinal cord.

Nocturnal: Active mainly during the hours of darkness.

Ocelli: Eye-spots. Markings resembling eyes occurring in the skin patterns of reptiles (ocellated: with eye-spots).

Ocular scale: The transparent scale covering the eye in worm snakes and similar forms.

Opistoglyphic: Pertaining to snakes with grooved poison fangs at the rear of the jaw (also called rear-fanged).

Orbit: The cavity in the skull containing the eye.

Osmosis: The passage of solvent molecules through a semi-permeable membrane from a less concentrated to a more concentrated solution.

Ossification: Being converted to bone.

Oviduct: The canal that carries the ova from the ovary to the exterior via the cloaca.

Oviposition: The act of laying or depositing eggs in specific sites.

Oviparous: Egg-laying.

Ovoviviparous: Describing an animal in which the eggs develop and hatch within the uterus of the female. Often today this term is simply replaced by viviparous, as it is a matter of degree as to whether a live birth is viviparous or ovoviviparous.

Palate: The roof of the mouth.

Palatine: The main bone plate in the palate.

Parietals: A pair of bones forming the main skull roof.

Parietal scales: The plates covering the top of the skull.

Pelagic: Pertaining to the open ocean (e.g., pelagic sea snake).

Pelvic girdle: The bony arch that supports the bones of the hind limbs in tetrapods. Occurs as a vestige in some snake genera but is absent in most.

Pharynx: The part of the alimentary canal anterior to the esophagus.

Phylogeny: The history of the evolution of species; used as a tool for taxonomy and classification.

Pleurodont: With teeth set in a cavity on the inner side of the jawbone.

Posterior: Pertaining to the rear end of the body.

Postocular scale: Scale(s) posterior to and adjacent to the eye.

Prehensile: Adapted for holding or grasping (e.g., the tail in many arboreal snakes).

Premaxilla: The tooth-bearing bone at the front of the upper jaw.

Preocular scale: Scale(s) anterior to and adjacent to the eye.

Proteroglyphic: Pertaining to snakes with canalized venom fangs at the front of the upper jaw and usually fixed (e.g., in the Elapidae and Hydrophiidae).

Pulmonary artery: The vessel supplying blood to the lung, coming directly from the heart.

Pulmonary vein: The vessel returning blood to the heart directly from the lung.

Quadrate: The part of the upper jaw that forms the point of articulation with the lower jaw.

Rami: The pair of structures forming the lower jaw or mandible (singular, ramus).

Rectilinear crawling: A method of locomotion in snakes in which the reptile moves forward by complex movements of the ribs, muscles, and belly scales in a system of waves.

Reticulated: Having a pattern of markings resembling a net.

Rostral scale or plate: The scale at the front of the snout.

Saliva: The mucal secretion of the salivary glands discharging into the buccal cavity. Contains enzymes and performs a lubricatory function. Venom glands in certain snakes are modifications of a pair of salivary glands.

Scrub: Area of land covered with one or more types of low vegetation. Ideal habitat for many snake species (also: brushland).

Sexual dimorphism: The condition in which male and female of a species show obvious differences in color or structure.

Sidewinding: A mode of locomation used by certain snake species in desert areas with shifting substrate.

Solenoglyphic: Pertaining to snakes with movable (hinged) canalized venom fangs at the front of the upper jaw (e.g., in the Viperidae and Crotalidae).

Spinal cord: The main nerve of the body running from the brain to the tail via the neural canal.

Stress: A condition in animals in which psychological effects reduce resistance to disease. Applies particularly to newly captured wild specimens.

Subcaudal scales: Scales below the tail.

Supraocular scale: Scale(s) above and adjacent to the eye.

Sympatry: Biogeographical term referring to the occurrence of different species together within a given area.

Symphysis: The joining of two bones with interlocking parts.

Taxonomy: The study of the theory, rules, and procedure of classification.

Temporal: The area of the skull posterior to the orbits.

Terrestrial: Mainly ground-dwelling.

Thecodont: Having teeth inserted in sockets.

Thermoreceptor: A heat-detecting organ (e.g., the pit in pit vipers).

Thermoregulation: The process used by ectotherms to maintain their preferred body temperature by moving in and out of areas of environmental warmth.

Trachea: The canal that allows passage of air to the lungs (also: wind-pipe).

Uric acid: A white, almost insoluble crystalline acid to which nitrogenous waste is converted by snakes (and other animals) as an aid against fluid loss.

Vena cava: A principal vein carrying blood to the heart from the posterior part of the body.

Vent: The orifice of the cloaca.

Ventral: Pertaining to the underside of the body.

Ventrals: The broad belly scales of snakes.

Vestige: The remains of an anatomical structure that has degenerated through evolution.

Warning coloration: Brilliant or striking patterns and colors occurring in some snakes making them predator resistant (see mimicry).

INDEX

Page numbers in **bold** indicate photographs.